Pearl River Delta

The Urban Connection

SEEDS

The Urban Connection
An actor-relational approach to urban planning

Luuk Boelens

010 Publishers, 2009

Preface

An internet saying runs as follows: *It's not them, it's just a whole lot of us.* As I see it, this also applies to the spatial layout of our country. It's not *them* that determine the layout, but *us*.

In this book, Luuk Boelens researches the relationship between the various actors in spatial development. So just who are *we*, and what do *we* do? In regional development, governmental authorities co-operate with the market on the policy of doing things 'decentrally wherever possible'. With the New Law on Spatial Development, the mutual relationships between governmental authorities have become clearer and other involved parties have gained a firmer foothold. At the same time, the notion of 'doing things centrally where necessary' must be legally established in policy.

The state is investing in co-operation with other governing bodies, market parties and residents. I wish to expand this collaboration further. In this context, scientific study is important to ensure good foundations. Accordingly, the publication of this book is a welcome addition to the body of knowledge of this subject.

For sustainable development, it is essential to involve the inhabitants of a region in the planning schedules. The future user should actually be invited to join the planners at the discussion table right from the outset. The district of Roombeek in Enschede is an excellent example of this. The residents had a loud voice in the planning process. The state contributed by providing the funding. Residents, companies and the municipality examined the wishes for the new neighbourhood and worked together from the plan-forming to the implementation stages. The result is a sustainable housing estate that is interesting in architectonic terms, with much private clientship, and with social housing, various facilities, activities and culture.

Research provides invaluable information. Trial projects lead to an efficient working method which, in turn, leads to a good result. Science helps advance real-life practice. This book supplies insight into such processes, and is the consequence of a five-year study by professor Dr. Ir. Luuk Boelens at the VROM Chair of 'Scientific Applications in Spatial Planning' at the University of Utrecht.

I expect this book to supply even more inspiration for the co-operation between the many parties involved in regional planning.

Jacqueline Cramer
Minister of the Environment and Spatial Planning

Introduction

In his valedictory speech given at the University of Amsterdam on 20 November 2008, professor Hans van der Cammen pointed out a so-called 'planning paradox' within current spatial planning of the Ministry Housing, Regional Development and the Environment (hereafter VROM). On the one hand, he noted that – as a result of increased complexities, more divergent interests, interactive planning, etc. – the time required for making spatial policy plans had become longer and longer. The actual Dutch National Policy Document on Spatial Planning needed about 8 years to be accepted. But on the other hand, the content of Dutch spatial planning had been very much the same, at least for the past 20 years. Just like 20 years ago, one still speaks about 'powerful cities in a nice transportation & distribution area', there is a preference for 'compact city planning', if necessary extensions will be realized at the near outskirts, 'buffer zones' will deliver nice green areas between cities, one will allow 'space for large rivers', the retention of water and robust nature areas connected with 'ecological corridors' will provide 'an adequate environmental system', etc. [Van der Cammen 2008] Here, he included the report of the Duijvenstein parliamentary working group which had already noted a high degree of sangfroid of the national land-use policy practice (and that of the provincial and municipal planning alike) as far back as 2000: 'put the Fourth Report on Spatial Planning of 1988 next to the Governmental Key Decision on Spatial Planning (PKB) VINEX of 1993 and that of VINAC in 1999 and many texts or policies are almost unchanged.' [Lower House of Parliament 2000] Moreover, in Van der Cammens and my view, even the now current Policy Document on Spatial Planning (delivered in 2006) can be added to that list. With the apparent exception of the management philosophy of that document ('Centralize what you must, decentralize whatever you can!') one seems to have made hardly any progress the last twenty years in terms of substance or content. While the *Fourth Report on Spatial Planning* (1988), like the former white papers, still represented a clear break with its predecessor – that is, the First with its focus on the Randstad (1960), the Second as the one offering the most comprehensive blueprint (1966) and the more procedural *Third Report on Spatial Planning* (1973-83) –, the actual *White Paper on National Spatial Planning* seems to have remarkable similarities with that Governmental Report of nearly 20 years ago. Although some planning concepts (such as the A, B, C-location policy,[1] for example) disappeared from the scene, key policies of the Fourth Report on Spatial Planning, such as that of the Mainports, Randstad, National Urban Nodes, the Hinterland Corridors, the Green Hart and Open Space Policy etc. are still proudly maintained in the current planning policy. At the same time, strict legislation, combined with (financial) incentives, public-private partnerships, voluntary agreements, the concession model or integrated area development etc. are still major planning instruments of the (national) government. In similar sense, the recent Randstad design explorations for 2040 [VROM, 2008b] resemble the design scenarios of the New Netherlands Project from 1987; [Van der Cammen eds. 1987] though the latter – instead of almost

---

1 In 1988 ABC planning policy as it is known, was introduced in Dutch location policy when the Fourth National Policy Report on Spatial Planning laid the basis for drawing up procedural plans for each region. Representatives of the central government, the provinces and the municipalities have to consult with representatives from businesses, industries, public transport operators and interest groups in order to reach agreement ↓

pure traditional architectural designs – were still based on extensive research and four distinct ideological political programme lines: a christian-democratic, social-democratic, liberal and a more relaxed, civic perspective.

Although Van der Cammen and the parliamentary working group Duijvenstein partly condone this conclusion by emphasizing plannings' momentum and importance in the long run, it also raises uncomfortable questions about the prestige and the accountability of that spatial policy. After all, the social dynamics in the last twenty years have been enormous. Since the 1980s, the number and proportion of TransNational Corporations (TNCs hereafter) have increased dramatically, doubling the amount of world trade and increasing foreign direct investment from less than 500 to now more than 10,000 billion dollars a year. [Dicken 2003] In the mid-eighties there were about 30,000 active computers connected worldwide, at the end of 2008 there are approximately 1.5 billion internet users, almost 500 million hosts and, according to different estimates, between 15 and 30 billion webpages. [Yahoo 2005, Google 2008] At the same time mobility has doubled to about 40 billion passenger-kilometres a year, not only in the Western countries, but also in and around South-East Asia in the last few decades. [Schäfer 2004] Partly as a result of this, the burden on the environment has grown by more than 40%, representing an equivalent from 0.9 to 1.3 planets, to provide the resources we use and to absorb our waste. [Global Footprint Network 2008] Also, the number of people with dual nationality grew enormously; in the Netherlands for example it tripled towards around 1 million people, almost 7% of the population. [CBS 2008] Moreover, again in the Netherlands, a number of former state businesses, such as post offices, railways, telecommunications, social housing, health care and the like, have been privatized or deregulated according to similar processes in neighbouring and other western countries, and in reaction on the final breakdown of the welfare state. That these major social changes would have no effect on the content of spatial planning is unlikely. At least, when one has kept in mind the definition of what spatial planning should actually be: 'The best possible reciprocal interaction between space and society, such in the sake of society'. [Van Veen Committee 1973]

During my planning career since the 1980s, I have always wondered why this was not actually the case. Why is there still – despite all the magnificent theories, sophisticated research instruments and increasing knowledge about society and policy itself – an enormous gap between what planners think, propose and do, and what is actually going on in everyday life? I came to the conclusion

---

on the classification of future urban locations and their infrastructure requirements. The classifications indicate the type of development and form the basis for setting priorities in development. This kind of large scale, long-term urban land-use planning has a major impact on extension plans in many Dutch cities, especially in Randstad which is going to strengthen its importance as the economic heart of the Netherlands. The ABC planning classification distinguishes in the following three categories:

- A localities are places with excellent public transport and poor car accessibility. These localities are typically suitable for offices with a large number of employees and many visitors. The sites have to be within 600 meters of a national or regional railway interchange or within 400 meters of a high-quality tram or bus stop; not more than 10 minutes ride from a national railway station and a good connection to park & ride facilities at the outskirts of the city has to be available. Within this category is a further distinction between AI and AII locations. An AI location has to be directly adjacent to a railway station whereas an AII location does not.
- B localities are places with a good public transport as well as good car accessibility. These locations are characteristically chosen for offices and institutions with a large number of employees which depend partly on car journeys for professional reasons. Such sites are

within 400 meters of a high-quality tram or bus stop and no more than 5 minutes ride from a regional railway station. In addition, they have to be within 400 meters of a main road connected to a national highway. BI, BII, and BIII localities have to be defined according to needs of organizations in the area (e.g. parking facilities are attuned to encourage minimum use of cars).
• C localities are places with poor public transport and excellent car accessibility. In particular, such sites are suitable for car-dependent companies like haulers, couriers or other industries. These sites are within 1000 meters of a direct connection to a highway. C locations are normally situated in the outskirts of metropolitan areas.

that it had something to do with the fact that planners' practices were government or public-sector-oriented, time and time again and, as such were focused inside-out rather than outside-in. They dealt nicely with themselves on an (inter)national, provincial and local governmental level, in communication with other experts, civic or business intermediaries and, of course, with the representative politicians, but were still mainly internally oriented in a warm, but increasingly alarming lock-in; at least in the Netherlands. Such thought resembled the ideas of my supervisor at the time, professor Ton Kreukels, who stressed as far back as the mid-eighties that planning was primarily associated with theorizing and rationalizing of spatial, governmental policies rather than with the stimulating and alternative ideas, discoveries, dedication, commitment, trends etc. advanced by involved civic and business actors in everyday life. [Kreukels 1985] Nevertheless this reversal, from an inside-out perspective towards an outside-in one, proved to be difficult to implement in planning practice, even in those cases where the general, long-term goals of spatial planning did correspond with the ideas of individual business and civic actors. So the development-oriented (instead of regulation-oriented) entrepreneurial style of planning which arose at the time, with a focus on urban regimes, on interactive, collaborative, and even recent relational planning options, has not brought us what we had originally expected from it. There are several identifiable causes, with which I shall deal later. But here I want to stress – referring to actual developments in society and geographical science – that we need a new embedded actor-oriented perspective, based on those experiences, to overcome the present lock-ins of spatial planning mentioned before.

In fact that is the main objective of this book. It reports on a five-year study that has been conducted within the faculty of Geosciences at the University of Utrecht, Department of Urban and Regional planning, in co-operation with the Dutch Ministry of VROM. It was conducted under the extraordinary VROM Chair at the university during one day a week in the period between 2004 and 2008. And it derived its main scientific argument from innovative scholars in the field of the relational approach in planning, economics, social geography and political sciences. But it assumes its own position in that debate too, reflecting on experiments with the Actor Network Theory towards a more proactive actor-relational approach to planning. This results in a handful of concrete planning proposals for ongoing projects, in the spatial-economical, social-cultural and political-institutional fields. These fields of research also refer to recent Dutch governmental white papers on international competitiveness (the *Peaks in de Delta* or *Pieken in de Delta* report 2006), multi-cultural integration and neighbourhood development (the *power districts* or *krachtwijken* 2007), and spatial planning (the *White Paper on National Spatial Planning* or *Nota Ruimte* 2006) respectively. The goal is to investigate those reports, referred to as 'fields of planning practice', from a more substantial relational perspective. The idea is that they would then better deal with recent developments in our networked society and especially relate to recent planning and scientific insights derived from that. Moreover, the expectation is that, from that stance, we could also make more engaged recommendations about improving the declining capacity and implementation of actual planning policies. Therefore in contrast to the usual retrospective case studies and scientific analyses, this study approaches that governmental (national) planning practice with a pro-active and operational attitude. In that sense, this book further refers to developments in the Netherlands, which were executed during the same period, more or less parallel to that investigation. These experiments and cases were implemented in close co-operation with Urban Unlimited, Telos, ZKA consultancy, Stratagem, Fabric, Urban Affairs and other Dutch consultancy firms, public or private clients with regard to economic, social and spatial planning. They try to bridge the widening gap between the scientific theories of urban planning on the one hand, and the more operational approaches within the daily affairs of planning on the other.

According to this broad engagement, the book is divided into three lines of argument.

The first line of argument deals with more or less scientific arguments, derived from recent economic-geographic, social, administrative and planning sciences. As mentioned before, it will give a kind of state-of-the-art overview of the current, more or less post-structural ideas with regard to economic, social and political progress and the way that engaged scientists are looking at it. In fact they are all relational in nature and will refer to the so-called 'relational turn in economic geography', the 'transnational turn in social migration studies' and the 'associative turn in democratic, political and administrative processes'. In addition, it will also lead towards an actor-relational approach, consisting of a dedicated, but embedded spatial planning focus of governmental planning from the outset. It will be organized in bottom-up fashion, based on the ambitions and goals of business and civic society itself.

The second line of argument will supplement these scientific deliberations, with practical solutions and possible practitioners' proposals. They refer to factors of success and failure with regard to real-life actor-relational-experiments in private or semi-private planning situations, specific case explorations, and historical analyses. They will be presented in eight extensive boxes included after the concerned chapters of the main, scientific text and will give insight in the possibilities and problems that occur if one wants to implement a more engaged, post-structural view of spatial planning; especially in such a highly developed, governmental planning world as the Netherlands. I will show that first preliminary ambitions to go beyond planning are promising, but still fragile and in a state of nascence, constantly trying to survive from the lock-ins and overwhelming forces of state-regulatory planning. We need additional research on instrumental renewal and institutional settings to cope with that problem.

Finally, a third line of argument will give referential cases. They will refer to three research journeys that were organized in December 2005, March 2007 and March 2008 to Denver and Dallas-Fort Worth, Pearl River Delta and Greater Metropolitan Area of Tokyo, and Buenos Aires and São Paulo respectively, that were closely related to the scientific and practitioners lines of argument. The results of these research trips are summarized in a separate photographic storyline at the end of this book. They will be introduced by a characterization of global metropoles from an Asian, European and American point of view, crossed with a Capital, Delta or Colonial metropolitan point of view. This will stress the central focus of this book – that although the urbanized world of today can be defined as a chain of metropolitan areas, connected by corridors of airports, railways, motorways and electronic highways, space is always relational, not only in this physical sense, but also in the sense that it is constantly co-structured by the reciprocal interaction between (leading) actors and their networks, e.g. strategies and (institutional) settings.

That said, I wish to stipulate in advance that this book has neither a beginning nor end. It is not a usual scientific work, sequentially written with a foreseeable problem definition, question mark, theoretical framing, empirical assessment and conclusions. Neither is it a common architectural or urban design read with only examples to fill the toolbox. It is neither modern, nor post-modern; it is rather trans-modern, meaning that society and planning are actually fragmented (and could only be looked at from a Lyotardian 'micrological' perspective). However, there are still some threads and connections in-between. Each of the above-described parts, boxes or storylines can therefore also be read in itself; you can even choose your own order. But in a sense, there is also a cross line – a speech bound to be discovered – which reflects the relational bond of the various themes and items described. Nevertheless, the considerations and examples given are still experimental and fragile and will continue to require more extensive proof in practice and theory. But that also leaves much that is open-ended and on that basis you can even draw your own actor-oriented line of approach. I hope that this book can inspire you to that end, and will give a new boost on reflection and the actor-engaged revitalization of spatial planning itself.

Word of thanks

Like many others, such a book would not be possible without the help and aid of many friends, colleagues and affiliated organizations. First of all, I want to thank the recent and present minister of the Dutch Ministry of VROM (Sybille Dekker and Jacqueline Cramer) and their prime civil servants (Ineke Bakker and Johan Osinga, respectively Chris Kuijpers, Henk Ovink, Elize de Kock, Hanna Lara Pálsdottír, Marijn van der Wagt) for making this research and book (financially) possible. Although this research was implemented under the extraordinary VROM chair, I advanced my criticism of a government-centred view of spatial planning right from the outset. Nevertheless, I have always received much support and backing in the expression of my often also unconventional ideas. I thank them for tolerating me. The same goes for the University of Utrecht, Faculty of Geosciences, Department of Human Geography and Spatial Planning. I am not only much indebted to the deans (first Pieter Hooimeijer, later on Bert van der Zwaan), but also and especially to Ton Kreukels, Tejo Spit, Oedzge Atzema and other erudite and well-read colleagues of the Department. I always started of from a practitioner's point of view and they backed me up with scientific discussions from the beginning. Furthermore, I wish to thank some 20 practitioners, 35 Master's degree students and 4 PhD students, who have or are acquiring their Master's thesis within this programme, but nevertheless have developed their own ideas about it. They (all mentioned by name at the rear of this book) have inspired me greatly and have given me new ideas to pursue. In addition, I want to thank Maurits Schaafsma, Michel van Wijk, Francisco Colombo and Roberto Rocco de Campos Pereira for their help, especially with regard to the third line (the referential part) of this book. Furthermore, I would like to thank the Schiphol Group (especially Gerlach Cerfontaine and Joop Krul), the Port of Rotterdam Authority (especially Henk de Bruijn), Movares (Klaas Strijbis), the housing associations HaagWonen (Annius Hoornstra), Com.Wonen (Nick Nieuwpoort), Het Oosten (Frank Blijdendijk) and the local governments of Amsterdam (Zef Hemel) and Rotterdam (Tom Boot) for making parts of this research possible, the last in particular because he took part in the curatorial board as the external advisor in the past five years. Finally I would like to thank Nigel Thrift, Susan Fainstein, Ed Taverne, Hans Mommaas and Ton Kreukels again, for their readings and reviews of the first preliminary manuscript of the book. I have learned a great deal from their comments and they have improved the argument profoundly. And last but not least, I am deeply indebted to my 'partner in crime' Wies Sanders. She co-authored Box 4.1 and edited the illustrations. Her support, wise comments, new ideas and endurance with my sometimes impatient character are unimaginable. Therefore I will not even try to put it into words, but thank her from the deepest vibes of my heart.

Luuk Boelens
Antwerp/Rotterdam, March 2009

Contents

[1] Dutch spatial planning in transition 18
A real planning paradise? 19
Paradoxical social developments – beyond the idées fixes 22
The conceptualization of space and time 27
Initial ideas about a new approach 30

[2] Main and brainport planning 2.0 36
Spatial and infrastructural determinism 37
Shifting economic-geographical foundations 39
Relational spatio-economic approaches 41
Main/Brainport polis revisited 52
Initial conclusions and recommendations 56
BOX [2.1] Rotterdam: from staple port to mainport and further 60
BOX [2.2] Schiphol: Airport planning in actor-network constellations 74
BOX [2.3] Brainport: economy versus spatial planning 85

[3] Transnational communities 98
Misconceptions 100
Migrant communities 105
Diasporic metropoles – introducing Buenos Aires and São Paulo 107
Back to the Netherlands 117
Initial conclusions and recommendations 123
BOX [3.1] The world of Delfshaven: towards transnational housing 126
BOX [3.2] Randstad Holland: the EURO, USA and ASIA Housing 132

[4] Institutional order via association 146
Resetting democracy 147
Associative democracy 151
The first rudimentary forms of *associative democracy* 154
Prospects for the future 163
BOX [4.1] Unmappables: connecting people to possible worlds 166

[5] Outlines for new planning futures 182
The growing gap between planning practice and spatial-scientific dynamics 183
Towards a behavioural actor-oriented view on planning 187
Actor Network Theory and beyond 189
New practical and theoretical impulses 193
Recommendations for a practical actor-relational course 197
BOX [5.1] Transit-Oriented Development in South-Holland 202
BOX [5.2] The case 'Hillside Delights' in South-Limburg 214

The referential argument

A relational tale of metropolises 228
Asian model – the paradox of strict regulation and local freedom 230
European model – the story of the public trading space 237
American model – liberal colonization by means of real estate 240
The Capital, Colonial and Delta metropolises 244

References as suggestion for further research 250
Denver and Dallas – the metropolises of regimes, TIFs, PIDs and special districts 250
The Pearl River- and EuroDelta – competing where possible, co-operating where necessary 257
Buenos Aires and São Paulo – trans-colonial communities in a Spanish and Portuguese variant 263
Conclusion in the form of an assignment 266

Annexes 276

Index of names 280

Index of places 282

Index of subjects and actors 284

References 290

[1]

Dutch spatial planning in transition
Going beyond the planning paradise

In February 1929, less than a lifetime ago, Joël Meijer De Casseres introduced the Dutch term *planologie*, equivalent to the English term *spatial planning*, for the first time. [De Casseres 1929] In fact, *plano-logics* or the study of spatial surfaces (*logicus planum*) was the logical outcome of the transition from a mercantile to an industrial society. All the side-effects of industrialization – growth, environmental overload, increasing traffic, a general assault on nature and the landscape – called for a new, adapted response. The concept of urban design as 'architecture on a large scale' – which had been introduced two decades earlier by Hendrik Pieter Berlage in the Netherlands [Berlage 1904] – was no longer enough. In its place, or at least alongside the aesthetic concept of designing cities, more attention needed to be paid to politics, land ownership, production methods, traffic, culture, sociology and geography. What De Casseres contended was that urban development should undergo a scientific extension in order to be transformed into urban planning. He was not alone in this. At around the same time, ideas on *Raumplanung* and *Raumordnung* were introduced in Germany by Gustav Langen. [Kegler 2000] In the UK, Raymond Unwin, Patrick Abercrombie and Patrick Geddes had already been talking for two decades about *town and country planning* as a research and sociologically based discipline. [Unwin 1994, Abercrombie 1933, Mackwell 1970] In America, too, the idea of a *planned society* was born with the City Beautiful movement in the early 20th century. [Schaffer 2003] It had even resulted in the marvellous and far-reaching *Plan of Chicago*, by then prepared by Burnham and Bennett under the direction of a commercial club of social entrepreneurs. [Burnham/Bennett 1993] Nevertheless, also in the USA, these neologisms anticipated a growing awareness on the part of governments of an ever-greater need for planned urban development. This was equally the case at this time in communist states such as the USSR, National-socialist or Fascist countries such as Germany and Italy, and parts of the Western world with more social-democratic or liberal inclinations, such as the USA (in particular after Roosevelt's New Deal), the UK and the Netherlands. In short, a wide-ranging, rationally based form of social planning was emerging, crossing states and borders. In an excellent book about the man's life and work, Koos Bosma shows that De Casseres, unlike many of his contemporaries, persisted in also organizing the artistic as well as the plan-related aspects of the profession. [Bosma 2003] In his view, urban planning was the profound profession of the pencil and the pen. He regarded graphical and cartographic presentation as not just a means of popularization, but also an essential element of scientific research. It was precisely this that filled the Utrecht geographer L. van Vuuren with major enthusiasm for urban planning. Through his intercession, De Casseres had been nominated for an appointment as extraordinary professor of Urban Planning at the University of Utrecht by 1931. However, for various reasons, the appointment ultimately fell through, and De Casseres settled for an appointment as private teacher in geography, with focus on spatial planning. It was made financially possible by his employer at that time: the Municipality of Eindhoven.

A real planning paradise?

Although mostly without De Casseres, but backed up by the upcoming Social Democrats Movement (SDAP) and The Netherlands Institute of Spatial Planning and Social Housing (NIROV), a government-driven spatial planning was rapidly put into practice from that time onward. After the Dutch municipalities had received the authority to develop land use, and after the structure plan in the Housing Bill of 1901, the legislative amendment of 1931 introduced the concept of a regional plan on a provincial level. Moreover, the Basic Planning Act of 1941 – which was prepared before World War II, but approved under German occupation – not only determined that all municipal provisions in conflict with that regional plan would be forfeited, it was actually also the official start of national spatial planning and announced the creation of an Office for the National Plan under the responsibility of the Secretary-General of the Ministry of Interior Affairs, mr. K.J. Frederiks, and under the direction of dr.ir. F. Bakker-Schut. Just prior to this, he had just published his thesis on *The National Plan*. [Bakker-Schut 1937] The ideal of a smooth, but vertical controlling triad of (inter)national, regional and local plans arrived on the planning horizon. In principle, it ought to be designed by a team of multidisciplinary experts, 'composed of a sociologist, a geographer, an agricultural and urban planner and a lawyer, all under the direction of an overall, synthetic-thinking planner, with aesthetic feeling and an open eye for the overall line'. [Kloos 1939] After the Second World War, this tripartite planning idea would be implemented reluctantly, in view of the still-strong Liberals and Dutch merchants. But later it came into force more convincingly. This was not only due to the inspiring leadership of the successive *National Plan* directors – Bakker-Schut, Van Oyen and Vink – but also due to the need for a strong top-down directive to rebuild the Netherlands from the ruins of the War; mainly until the Office of the National Plan was reorganized into the National Planning Office in 1965 and later the Ministry of Spatial Affairs and Environment in 1982. But even at that time the *National Plan* seemed to be successful, especially because of the effective linked interests with the regional and local governments on the one hand and national sectorial policies with regard to public housing, infrastructure and agricultural zoning on the other. That so-called 'polder-system of practical deliberations', which was developed over here and year after year adapted and improved by a growing number of Dutch planners, even received broad international approval during the next few decades. More recently, Alterman [1997] described the Netherlands as a country with 'one of the world's most successful systems of planning and land management'. Peter Hall [1997] even claimed that the Netherlands had the 'worldwide lead' in the co-ordination of spatial planning with traffic and transport planning. The Japanese Mori [1998], in turn, regarded the Netherlands as having a 'superbly efficient' system of spatial planning and building production compared with the United Kingdom and Japan. The American Bolan [1999] was 'impressed by the spatial planning achievements' of the Netherlands. And in Germany, reference was made to 'ein gut funktionierendes System der Baulandbereitstellung' and 'ein geschickt ausgestaltetes Enteignungsrecht'. [Schmidt-Eichstaedt 1999] But what was it that made Dutch planning so attractive for these foreign scholars? Apparently and according to Andreas Faludi and Arnold van der Valk [1994] it had something to do with highly successful spatial concepts and planning strategies – such as the Randstad or the Green Heart for instance – which were carefully constructed and maintained by the planners themselves. Moreover Dutch planners would have constructed a useful prescriptive institutional framework of national, provincial and local planning, which would sufficiently address the ways governments could pursue their policies in the face of mounting pressure from a more volatile and dynamic society. And finally, the system would have so much public support that it could effectively co-ordinate the various (investment) strategies of the Departments of Housing, Traffic, Agriculture, Economics, Environment, and the like.

Although Faludi and Van der Valk proudly proclaimed a true Dutch Planning Paradise in the mid-nineties, one had already been speaking of a fundamental crisis for many years within the more critical part of Dutch planning profession itself. As far back as the early eighties, reference was made to a widening gap between planning and its implementation. [Van der Cammen 1986] Comments were made about the remarkable proliferation of the planning institutions, coupled with declining planning success, [Wigmans 1982] about the superfluity of urban development and planning in the coordination of the Government's spatial policy [De Jong 1985] and about the double failure of its future perspective, either to promote a human environment or to achieve an overall vision coupled with a comprehensive social ideal. [Bolte/Meijer 1981] Partly in conjunction with the (post-)modern debate at that time, the reality of Dutch urban planning was described as 'an early modern practice through and through'. It fitted neatly into all Adorno and Horkheimer's basic features for characterizing the modern project: it was holistic, it was convinced of the malleability of society, it was based on truly emancipatory interest, and all these fine ideals had turned into their opposite. Following Jürgen Habermas's *Theory of Communicative Practice*, [1985] my call issued for a kind of new 'trans-modern spatial planning and urban design', to depart from the more realistic claims of post-modern theorists – from the micrologies[2] – but still dealing with structure and the modernist claim of a kind of emancipatory interrelation between those 'small spatial stories'. [Boelens 1990] Others stipulated that, due to the on-going individualization and network society, there would no longer be a universal centre of shared values, which would legitimate public action. Planning should become an interactive and interpretative process, drawing on the multidimensionality of life-worlds or the practical sense of different groups and categories of people, rather than on a single formalized dimension. [Healey 1997]

2 Due to the above-mentioned deliberations, Jean-Francois Lyotard's claim about the condition of post-modernity mainly focused on a counter-attack on the 'big social storylines' and a return to the small researches on specific items, themes and deliberations: the so-called 'micrologies'. [Lyotard 1979]

However, this type of appeal turned out to be not so easy to realize in planning practice. As far back as the seventies, planners had experimented with communicative, procedural and participatory plans, but eventually one had to conclude that this kind of spatial planning ultimately only dealt with processes, and not with content. [De Klerk/v.d. Cammen 2003] Since the mid-eighties, therefore, interactive planning was increasingly focused on specific public-private partnerships in a kind of entrepreneurial style of planning but, after a while, one concluded that the private parties were mostly restricted to project developers, that there occurred a kind of non-democratic decision-making in backrooms, and even a kind of hit & run mentality of private parties, leaving the public sector with the consequences and exploitation. [Logan/Molotch 1987, Sartori 1991, Imbroscio 1998] As a result – and after fine examples in Barcelona and Sienna [Bohigas 1991, Secchi 1984] – there was some experimentation with urban and regional design in order to render those things visible that could only be rendered visible by design, and to seduce other private, more placid entrepreneurs into spatial planning. [Taverne 1989, Boelens 1993] In addition, others dealt with a relational, place-bound planning in order to introduce more specific – as opposed to generic – elements into Dutch planning. [HNS 1998] And finally planners experimented with a socalled *stratified approach* or *lagen benadering* – addressing first of all the stake and shareholders of water management and environmental issues in a *longue durée*; second, those of infrastructure in a planning timespan of 20-40 years; and finally those of dwelling with often volatile and highly changing preferences – in order to cope with the contemporary, dynamic complexity and take advantage of the heterogeneous and enticing rather than the mostly single issue focus of planning. But after a few initial successes such as *Parkstad van Hof tot Haven 1988, Interprovinciale Verstedelijkingsvisie Randstad 1990, Plan Ooievaar 1991, Kop van Zuid Rotterdam 1993* and *Nadere Uitwerking Groene Hart 1994*, a reversion to the familiar regulatory planning generally occurred. In part, this was because the alternative approaches had not been sufficiently institutionalized. At the same time, profound neo-liberal changes occurred within public housing, infrastructural and (agricultural) zoning policies, which permanently undermined the traditional co-ordinating Dutch planning system based on linked interest between specific sectorial policies. [Spit 1995, Dieleman et al. 1999] The malaise was expressed in wider-ranging terms in the *Spatial Development Policy* or *Ruimtelijke ontwikkelingsplanologie* report from the Netherlands Scientific Council for Government Policy. [WRR 1999] Here the diminishing effectiveness of Dutch spatial planning was attributed not just to the decreasing relevance of linked interests, but also to the rise of the network society, the need for multi-level and multi-actor governance, the changing dynamic between spaces and flows and the need for a more proactive as opposed to regressive attitude in the Dutch planning system. It promoted the need for a more active, *development-oriented planning* or *ontwikkelingsplanologie* as opposed tot the traditional passive, permission-based attitude of spatial planning. And although these ideas received much consent within Dutch planning system and even became the leading ideology of the actual *White Paper on National Spatial Planning* or *Nota Ruimte* (2006), it also gave rise to revisionist calls – with justifiable commitment, yet opportunistically – for a return to the strong,

dirigiste government policy of earlier decades. [Geuze et al. 2003] Some still stress the direction-determining position of the planner through 'telling the right stories', [Hemel 2004] emphasize the importance – correct in itself, but not exclusively so – of strict rules and spatial legislation, [Needham 2005b] or even, and unabatedly, seek the 'restoration' of confidence in the possibility of a planned society that can be created by designers and planners. [Weeber et al. 2007] In short, the actual planning endeavour in the Netherlands seems to represent a chaos of simultaneous degradation, enforcement and reconstruction effort. Nevertheless at least three deliberations make most of these calls hopelessly anachronistic and outdated. They have to do with:
a key paradoxical developments within actual society,
b changing conceptualizations of space and time and
c initial ideas about a different, more multi-perspective urban planning approach which accompanies that.

Paradoxical social developments – beyond the *idées fixes*

In my view, the social and institutional contexts of spatial planning have drastically changed over the last few decades. It is not only the pace, range and dimensions which has changed so much; for instance, in the last 25 years the global population has not only grown from some 4.5 to almost 7 billion, the global car stock has also doubled from approximately 350 to 700 million vehicles and the use of internet boosted from 1000 hosts to approximately 2 billion users worldwide. But it has especially affected the economic, social and political interdependent performance too. Some have called this a 'neo-liberal society without an ideological history', [Fukuyama 1989] others 'a post-modern society', [Harvey 1989] 'post-capitalist society', [Drucker 1993] or a new kind 'network society' [Castells 1996] in 'an age of access'. [Rifkin 2000] But mostly one referred to general developments within (Western) societies, which were unlike previous ones, not only a little larger and more mobile, but also increasingly characterized by:
• economies which have become globally interdependent, introducing a new form of relationship between economy, state and society in a system of variable geometry, clusters and networks;
• socio-cultural developments, which are not only driving towards an ongoing process of individualization, demystification and the loss of traditional institutions, but also towards new collectives and new defensive reactions and
• political dimensions, which are not only facing new challenges with regard to global migration and the system of representational democracy, but also with new interactions between state and non- or transgovernmental organizations.

Plenty has already been written about this, and I do not intend to repeat it all. Moreover, more specific characteristics of my view on these ideas of network societies will also receive sufficient coverage in the argument I will present in this book. But what I would like to emphasize here is that I don't belong to the so-called hyperfluid camp, which argues that economic globalization is bringing about the death of distance through the establishment of transnational networks of production, trade, migration and culture. [Ohmae 1995; Cairncross 1997] Nor do I belong to the camp of the profound sceptics, who argue that nodes and networks still need a place and therefore geographic rules and regionalization still dominate society's worldwide development. [Thompson 1996; Kerski 2003] I would like to use the concept of the network society to look at the present situation of space and time in a more precise way. Our present-day interconnected, fragmented society has been made possible (though not initiated or driven) by age-old processes, whereby our means of transport have become faster and faster, the cost of transport measures has fallen drastically, and the size of technological tools has been minimized so that we can now communicate, do business, work, enjoy entertainment or take recreation even while on the move. Yet I also believe that precisely as a result of these developments, not only latent age-old developments have been taken a step further, but society has also been undergoing fundamental changes that blur the formerly clear distinction between internal and external (domestic and foreign) or macro and micro (global and local).

Two buzzwords repeatedly crop up here in varying quantity and intensity. The first is *globalization*, a term used to refer to the fact that we increasingly live in a world without boundaries, in which, supposedly, national and regional frontiers are less and less relevant and the time-space compression mentioned earlier has led to the 'death of distance', foot-loose settlement patterns, or even the 'end of geography'. [Held et al. 1999] The second is *fragmentation*, which refers to the fact that the new networks only open up access to specific places and population groups (and not others) and hence lead to an increasing fragmentation and cordoning-off of regions, in which some are physically fenced off from the world around them with video cameras and digital technology. [Graham/Marvin 1996] Quite apart from the fact that I have always found these two concepts far too coarse and generalized, I also believe that they fail even to cover half the problem because a process of *re-territorialization* is occurring alongside an increasing *de-territorialization*. Alongside the ongoing fragmentation, reclustering is taking place around new motivations for interacting, living and being together. [Boelens 2004] Even more markedly, the processes of re-territorialization and reclustering are far more important than those of globalization and fragmentation, because it is precisely through them that the new urbanism arises. And incidentally it is an urbanism, which – I would like to emphasize – diverges completely from what is traditionally understood by the term. This is equally true on the economic, socio-cultural and political fronts. And it is precisely this that will also need to be the focus of more detailed and targeted research of present-day urbanists and planners.

Economic Let us take the spatial economy for example. Under the influence of an ongoing and virtually cut-throat global competition, the economy has seen a trend of businesses going back to their core competencies, i.e., doing what they are good at and/or earn most money from, and outsourcing other activities to subsidiaries or specialist businesses. In the same vein, businesses are also splitting the remaining core activities into the smallest possible sub-units and relocating them where they will do best, for reasons of cost, product optimization, distribution or market access (in-sourcing). Finally, in order to spread the risks or to be able to afford enormous research and development costs, they are also initiating varying forms of collaboration, such as equity investments, joint ventures, mutual licensing or mergers in specific market sectors, sometimes even with (former) competitors. [Atzema, Boelens 2006] This latter strategy could also be described as co-sourcing.

In both physical and organizational terms, new economic clusters are arising all over the world comprising interdependent businesses and affiliated enterprises. These clusters are sometimes closely organized, but are also very flexible, because each participating business or enterprise is also tied to its own much larger organizational, financial and/or market-economical structures. The global economy is thus composed of intrinsically connected local or regional clusters of economic activity in varying forms of (inter)sectoral networks which are in principle without boundaries. Incidentally, these also differ greatly in terms of their geographical extent and degree of specialization. [Dicken 2003] Here clusters in specific business networks (instead of networks of clusters) pattern the current economic landscape. [Porter 1990; Bathelt, Glückner 2002] Leader firms are at the cutting edge in this. [De Langen/Nijdam 2006] These are businesses that deploy financial and strategic resources and hence have the will to invest in projects with positive outcomes for other businesses in a chain, network or cluster. Leader firms are not just focused on their own business, but realize that their success depends on the performance of the chains, networks and clusters to which they belong. They are capable of co-ordinating the various production networks across the various borders, to gain advantage from differing geographical production conditions and, where necessary or desirable, to relocate their own activities accordingly. This business trend has major consequences for the economic side of urban planning. It involves a noticeable paradigm shift from the traditional *object* approach to a new *actor* approach. Not that the time-honoured location factors are no longer relevant, but, they have been incorporated into a much broader, more dynamic perspective of regional or local embeddedness, in which it is precisely the individual and structural relations at the spatio-economic, social and organizational levels that matter. [Storper/Malais 1997] I shall return to this theme in chapter two.

Socio-cultural This kind of a more qualified actor-based approach, which is relational (rather than location or enterprise-oriented), has emerged on the socio-cultural front too. By the end of the last century, various researchers of different stripes were already stressing that, under the influence of growing mobility, globalization and the accompanying unilateral rise in Western prosperity, growing individualization and immigration were occurring. They did not mean that society was becoming infinitely lawless and footloose, or that it was being progressively 'atomized' into purely antisocial, egotistical and self-centred individuals. [Schnabel et al. 2004] Rather, the developing network society and the associated up-scaling and freedom of choice implied a complex system of all kinds of new forms of collectivism in which individual autonomy and common involvement are balanced out through changing networks. Thus, what is disappearing in this case is not so much communal life itself, but rather a simple form of communal life, in a single location and in clear relationships. [see also Tilly 2002] In socio-geographical terms, what is disappearing is especially the situation where social settings – such as work, the local neighbourhood, conventions, leisure, care, culture, etc. – largely overlap one another in space. Instead, all these social settings are diverging more and more and are increasingly being practised in varying locations and changing contexts. [Brinkgreve in Schnabel 2004] Conversely, under the influence of increased mobility and new computer and telecommunication tools, it is also possible to specifically set one's own priorities. One can seek contact and identify with like-minded folk, over great distances if necessary, and completely ignore other people.

Just as in the spatio-economic sphere, varied clusters in networks are determining the socio-cultural landscape too. Moreover, just as in the economy, these clusters consist of independent lifestyles or subcultures, which, in turn, belong to larger networks. It fits with the 'split household' discerned as far back as 1986 by the sociologist Ulrich Beck, i.e., the 'household which has several bases from which it functions and several orientation points, which if necessary in a single day need to be connected to one another in a particular way'. [Beck 1986] It fits also with the growing body of sociological thought of Henk Flap and others, which distinguishes strong and weak ties within increasingly networked communities. [Flap in Völker 2005] Finally, it fits in with the new research focus of what scholars like Anderson, [1983] Appadurai [1991] or the political geographer Peter Taylor [2004] term a new type of 'global network cosmopolitanism'. They suggest that around the new means of satellite TV, GSM, internet and growing remittances, new 'imagined communities' are arising, with representatives and members in all kinds of cosmopolitan cities, e.g., a Jewish community in New York, Tel Aviv, Amsterdam, Antwerp and Brussels, a German community in various Eastern European cities, several Muslim communities in the capitals of the original host countries, etc. This trend should form the focus of more detailed residential typology research, particularly because such concepts also touch on the issue of multiculturalism or transnationalism and the need for an adapted democracy. [Hirst in Pierre 2000] I shall come back to that later on too.

Political All this now brings me to spatial policy, especially government policy, as the government has hitherto been the main patron and client of spatial planning. Policy, too, has witnessed an obvious fragmentation of state activities inwards, upwards and downwards (multi-level and multi-agencies structure), along with a simultaneous relocation of planning decision-making to bodies outside the government. Under this harsh spotlight, the time-honoured Westphalian state model, so-called after the *Treaty of Westphalia* of 1648,[3] seems to have had its day. [De Wit 1980, Cassese 1986] Real changes are afoot on the basis of more complex and dynamic multi-level approaches.

In a clearly written book entitled *New State Spaces: Urban Governance and the Rescaling of Statehood*, Neil Brenner describes the ongoing 'state rescaling' and simultaneous 'state rebordering' of past decades, depending on the changing state of the economy, socio-cultural circumstances, settlement patterns and political opportunity. [Brenner 2004] Since the 1960s, all kinds of regional public bodies have arisen that were supposed to coincide more closely with the emergent network reality of the urban economy, housing market, social life and transport market of large-scale metropolises. [Brenner 1999] However, all these public bodies were abolished in the early eighties as quickly as they had been set up. They had merely added an extra bureaucratic link to the decision-making process extending from local neighbourhood to region. They were no more effective than other governments at providing a response to the ever-changing network dynamic. Nevertheless, when the economy started to improve again in the mid-nineties, virtually all of them were replaced by other, apparently more flexible and entrepreneurial organizations, such as the Metropolitan City Agreement of Bologna (1994), the Stuttgart Regional Agency (1994), the Stadsregio Rotterdam, the urban regions of Amsterdam, The Hague, Utrecht and other network cities (1996), the Greater London Authority (2000), the Hannover Regional County (2001), Greater Copenhagen Authority (2001), the Metropolitan Region of Frankfurt/Rhein-Main (2001), etc. By this time, these regional organizations were also supplemented with others, which also operated at subsequent levels. Moreover, decision-making and legislation also functions at the European level as a hidden power. [Van Ravesteyn 2004] The still-expanding European Union has also acquired a growing number of continental counterparts, such as EFTA (1960), ASEAN (1967), CARICOM (1973), CCC (1981), ACC (1989), AMU (1989), ANCOM (1990), MERCOSUR (1991) and NAFTA (1994). And, as if all this were not enough, all kinds of bilateral international governmental organisations (IGOs) have also arisen around the oil-producing nations (such as OPEC), a defence structure (NATO), world trade (G8) or specific forms of collaboration between Europe and South-East Asia or around the Pacific (APEC) etc. The number of such IGOs worldwide is now around 260. [Held et al. 1999] Administrative density has gradually become so great that urban planning is increasingly seen as a game of chess played simultaneously at various levels. [Schrijnen in Dijkink et al. 2002]

3 Many scholars assert that the actual international system of states refer to the agreements made in 1648 at the Peace of Westphalia. At that time, national state sovereignty was based on two principles: territoriality and the exclusion of external influence in domestic authority structures. Until recently this model has been championed in international mores. But new transnational systems, like the EU, NATO etc., or military interventions in Yugoslavia, Afghanistan, Iraq and Sudan for instance, for the sake of the universal rights of mankind or global security, respectively the so-called 'universal war on terrorism', shake the fundamental principles of the Westphalia model profoundly.

Intricate and time-consuming though all this may be, much decision-making now also occurs outside these government bodies. In fact, it takes less and less notice of a government, or operates parallel to it. Here, I am referring primarily to the public itself, which, highly mobilized and using computers, internet and telecommunications, is also starting to organize itself around specific issues and concrete interests. Take, for instance, the intriguing study of Mark Zacher and Brent Sutton, [Governing global networks 1996] in which they convincingly show that international postal services, shippers, airlines and telecommunication industries have developed efficient and fruitful regimes on their own, and mostly beyond and through the borders of the separate governments. In addition, the number of international non-governmental organizations (INGOs), such as Greenpeace, Amnesty International, World Wildlife Fund etc., has increased over the past century from 175 to nearly 5,500. [Union of International Associations 1996] I am also referring to the fact that private stakeholders find the internal administrative processes as handled by the various layers and departments to be so vicious that they bring their own networks and strategic alliances to bear, cutting right across the various layers and boundaries. [Salet, Molenaar 2003] Thus they have put the concept of governance on the agenda by repositioning both formal and informal structures to create working relationships among key actors within the business, civic and public society, to bring about effective action. [Salet, Kreukels and Thornley 2003] Whatever one may think about that, it all requires a radical reorientation of spatial decision-making and planning, not only around what Brenner calls 'scalar multiplicity' and 'administrative customization', but also around a more relational 'market demand and alliance-oriented actor approach'. [Brenner 2004]

The conceptualization of space and time

Not only society's dynamics has changed drastically, but, partly in reference to that, the conceptualization of space and time has also been substantially elaborated in the past two or three decades. Compared with developments that have taken place within other sciences, it is even striking that architecture, urban design and spatial planning (those professions for which time and space are fundamental) remain overwhelmingly dominated by an outmoded Cartesian concept of space and time.[4] Although Torsten Hägerstrand introduced his ideas on individual time-space diffusions more than thirty years ago, [Hägerstrand 1973] and David Harvey, [1989] Doreen Massey, [1995] Nigel Thrift [1996] and others developed a more relational idea on time-space assemblages, and recently some preliminary ideas have been developed about a actor-relational and post-structural inspired planning methodology,[5] [Hillier 2007, 2008] urban planning practice still largely operates within the traditional, Cartesian, respected concept of space and time, each consisting of three general dimensions – length, width and height in the former case, and yesterday, today and tomorrow in the latter. As a result, the future of urban planning is still often presented as a logical continuation of

4 Evidently it is hard to convert Einstein's theory of relativity, Flusser's quantum mechanics or Deleuze's and Guattari's rhizomes into concrete, workable planning strategies. [Einstein 1919, Flusser 1992, Guattari/Deleuze 1988]

5 See chapter five.

the past, and urban planning ultimately talks about property rights or, at best, air rights, often for a single programme in places or zones deemed most suitable for that purpose. This presentation of matters precisely fails to do justice to the experiences of time and space in the context of the above-mentioned key social developments, because time and space have acquired new significance's for many people, precisely in combination with the rise of mobility over the past centuries.

The double-sided compression of space-time Several people have already analysed the importance of the development of the railway-network in this respect. [Thrift 1981, Urry 2000] Following the success of the first Stockton to Darlington Railway, this network began to boom from 1825 onwards. It stimulated the introduction of a new uniform time-keeping (the Greenwich Mean Time), which had hitherto been determined very much on a local basis from the position of the sun. Moreover, journeys that had previously taken several days were minimized to a few hours. As early as 1839, a commentator was enthusiastically hailing this enormous compression of time and space: 'Should the railways extend over the whole of England, the entire population will, in a manner of speaking, live two-thirds closer to one another and the whole country will in fact shrink down to a single mighty city'. [Schivelbush 1986] These same arguments are now being used again in connection with the development of the high-speed lines, container shipping, or even more in connection with the development of the aviation sector, especially after the deregulation measures of 1992. The whole world should come in reach with one another within one day flying, at least for an ever-growing number of people, against even fewer costs. [Burghouwt 2005] Nevertheless, be that as it may, here arises indeed a new, fascinating space of nodes and lines, hubs and spokes, in which specific elements of an urban world are or are not at all connected in an ever-shrinking time-space frame. [Castells 1996] The spatial field is no longer straightforward and determined by a single time-space reality. Above all, it has become a selective, somewhat distorted world, in which some (but not all) parts of some major cities are getting closer to parts in other cities in the world, while other are not. And this is assumed to invoke increasingly pronounced forms. Because in accordance with the already somewhat outdated spatio-economic conceptions of Don Janelle, [1968] the distance in time measured between already important centres is usually reduced more by infrastructural improvements than the distance between other places.

Multiple dwelling in space-time However theoretically, things seem different with the car. Whereas the railway and air travel force the traveller into a somewhat predefined trajectory; the car, provided it is not held up by road congestion, allows any kind of peregrination in principle and any kind of stopping place. When mass production techniques made the automobile available to a broader public at the start of the last century, it was precisely this aspect that was loudly acclaimed. 'The car,' stressed Paul Morand, 'has given us back the countryside, the roads, inns and adventure. (...) Delivered from points and rails, the horizon stretches out for the motorist, who becomes free and alone at the steering wheel, (...) the discoverer of a still virgin and unknown world'. [Morand 2000] Nevertheless, due to the enormous success of automobiles and the adjoining ongoing suburbanization, drive-in offices, shopping malls, leisure-entertainment centres etc. and also an ever greater number of traffic jams, this nature of *dwellingness* has changed: 'from dwelling-on-the-road to dwelling-within-the-car', according to John Urry. [2000] He is referring to the fact that cars are being increasingly filled with high-fidelity stereo, cruise control, navigation systems, mobile phone, fax, voice recognition computers, DVD and LCD TV and are actually turning into a home-from-home: a place where you do business, relax, make love, look after yourself, conduct family life and communicate, remotely or otherwise. Others, however, perceive that the local environment is already responding to this alertly. Petrol stations have already more or less developed from newsagents into mini shopping malls, all kinds of residential, care and leisure boulevards are being intensively integrated with the motorway, and hotels and roadside restaurants are no longer exclusively places where you stop for a brief break. This has hence also become an extremely fragmented time-space reality, in which the objective scheduled service of the railways has been replaced with the post-modern, almost personified temporalities of various car-related lifestyles and the public domain has been replaced by the atrium, the shopping mall, the wellness centre or the safety of privatopia.[6] [Fogelson 1993]

6 After Mike Davis [1990] and Evan McKenzie [1994], 'privatopia' refers to private protected or exploited public spaces mutual connected by similar protected or private corridors.

Cocooning in virtual interconnectivity It was originally anticipated that this subjective, post-modern reality would be further reinforced with the introduction and unexpectedly fast adoption of the PC and telecommunication technologies. Thus, in the early nineties, the computer giant Apple introduced its 'click on a building city map', thereby expressing its view that individual buildings or businesses were now all that mattered, and not the spaces in between. [Mitchell 1996] This was in line with several theorists who talked about the rise of a kind of 'capsular society', referring to the idea that humans, surrounded by the walkman, mobile phone, laptop and video glasses, will end up becoming turned in on themselves, cut off from the immediate environment, although, paradoxically enough, they simultaneously remain in online contact with the rest of the world. [Fassler et al. 1994, De Cauter 2001] Some went even as far as to state that this also meant the final death of urban planning: not because public spaces would no longer be planned, but above all because planning would not make any difference to them. [Koolhaas 1995] Nevertheless, this is merely a superficial account – half of the story at best, because the introduction of computer, internet and wireless telecommunication has not simply led to deterritorialization as such; in other words, to a situation in which one's precise place of residence does not particularly matter any more, as long as one is connected to the worldwide web. Nor has it led to a reduction of physical traffic, as originally anticipated. [Graham/Marvin 1996] On the contrary, more detailed research into teleworking and homeworking has in fact shown that people:

a are starting to live further from their workplace, precisely as a result of this trend, and hence need to cover greater distances on those days when they do need to be physically present,

b on the days when they are teleworking at home, make more smaller trips, which taken together equal or even exceed their original radius of action and

c the space freed up during the rush hour is quickly taken up again by other road and rail users for their mobility purposes. [Wheeler et al. 2001]

Telemobility thus does not imply decreasing physical mobility, as many have assumed, but rather a more far-reaching hypermobility. [Gillespie et al. 2000] In a comparable approach, Nigel Thrift [1996] also offers a new argument in favour of the need for mutual proximity, by claiming that worldwide telecommunications in certain service sectors also generate a need for instant information, which can still best be guaranteed in a face-to-face context. For Thrift, however, this does not mean a return to the familiar geography of the place. Rather, he calls for a relational approach, in which places and human activities are thought of not so much in direct relation to their environment, but above all in relation to other connected places and activities, even at a great distance if necessary. Again, it is in the age of telematics that the proximate starts to derive from the remote, accompanied by a corresponding displacement of the proximate. Instead of the nostalgic idea of the city or the urban region as a unit, this requires a rethinking of urbanism as a system of separate activities in open, meaningful global-local connectivities. [May/Thrift 2001]

Initial ideas about a new approach

Concluding, we are confronted with a picture of a layered (trans)urban reality, in which some districts are close to one another and others are not. Personified temporalities also occur, along with introverted activities in continual contact with the rest of the world. Dwelling on the road has developed into a kind of lifestyle, as well as dwelling in railway stations, airports and airplanes, or dwelling in specific landscapes or privatopias, etc. [Warhol 1976, Pascoe 2001] And although sometimes a place looks the same as fifty years ago, we do live in a world of a multiplicity of times, a multiplicity of different spatial realities, and move at different speeds in different directions. In other words, and put more formally, the clear and unambiguous Cartesian reality, which previously largely determined our understanding of spatial development and planning, has increasingly disintegrated into varying perceptions of time and space, related at times to the sort of nostalgic reality of medieval times, at times to the reality of nodes and lines and the daily dwelling-within-the-car, and at times to the worldwide internet. If you experience increasing uglification, continual inconstancy and growing complexity on your daily drive from work to home, this has less to do with the failure of planning to check unbridled urban growth against one big Cartesian time-space frame: rather, it is due to our inability to cope with this heterogeneous, but layered time-space reality. In my view, it is in line with the recent ideas of post-structuralist geographers, who stress that spaces are not containers for entities and processes, closed or fixed, but are fundamentally open and engaged with other spaces and/or the different time-space frames within, as previously described. [Doel 1999, Massumi 2002, Murdoch 2006] Therefore, in Massey's view, space is a product of interrelation within and between, made of differing spatial practices, identifications and forms of belonging. When these multiple and heterogeneous relations 'meet' in space, new relations are formed and new spatial identities come into being; temporarily or not. [Massey 1999, 2005] Planning theory therefore could never again be a theory *of* planning, as stated by Faludi, neither could planning again go for a kind of meta-level, to tell what is right or wrong, to forbid or approve from a rational-comprehensive, single minded Cartesian view on time and space.[7] [Faludi 1973, 1986] Rather spatial planning itself takes part in the ongoing struggle against those whose 'reading in space' could take priority, and could better be attached to new meaningful interrelations and therefore possible spatial identities. Planning therefore is neither a director, nor stage-manager, let alone an 'orchestra leader' of specific time-space frames; at its best it is only a(n) (f)actor of importance within specific heterogeneous processes of spatial 'becoming'. In other words, it is highly embedded and relational, instead of taking a general, moral stand on what is right and wrong.

7 I have explained this in more detail in my dissertation of 1990. Planning needs to be specific instead of holistic, embedded in concrete actor-networks constituting the specific content as the specific methods and processes alike.

This said, and with reference to the practitioners' experiences previously mentioned, it seems not to be easy to implement this idea in planning practice. Reading all those finely elaborated and perspicacious social, geographical and time-space views of the so-called *Key Thinkers on Space and Place*, [Hubbard et al. 2004] they still remain highly general, analytical and abstract in my opinion. They have to be reworked and translated profoundly to be useful in planning practice. Nevertheless, also referring to the failures of the planning experiments mentioned before, I shall assume a modest stand in this book. Instead of elaborating a proposal how to proceed on the basis of those 'key thinkers', I will first analyse how these initial ideas about a new kind of relational approach works out in different, main realms of planning. I will take the realms already mentioned before; that is, the economic-geographical, social-cultural and political-institutional developments of present-day society. In fact, they also refer to recent Dutch governmental white papers and policies on respectively international competitiveness (the report *Peaks in the Delta 2006*), social integration and neighbourhood development (the *Vogelaar neighbourhood policy 2007*) and the *New Law on Spatial Development* or *de Nieuwe Wet op de Ruimtelijke Ordening 2008*, already referred to in the preface. I will show how these white papers and policies still rest on mainly traditional ideas of time, space, planning and society, and how they could be reworked towards a more relational perspective.

To be more precise, in the next chapter I shall focus on the spatial-economic dimensions of planning, because these seem to be the most volatile, cross-border, shifting and hard-to-grasp for spatial planners, while at the same time 'the promotion of competitive regions in an increasing global world economy' has become the planners' principal focus in these neo-liberal or post-liberal times. Besides general examinations on these points, I would like to go specifically into the mainport, gateway and brainport strategies of Dutch planning. I will show that these strategies are still characterized by a kind of 'infrastructural determinism' and that therefore these planning strategies collide with final ecological, environmental and socio-referential limits: *Not in My Backyard*. A (re)new(ed) actor-oriented economic and spatial approach is needed in order to go beyond the dilemmas that accompany those limits.

In the third chapter I will go into the social-cultural dimensions of planning. The focus is specifically on the developments within community building, multi-culturalization and related urban renewal practices. Here the *power districts approach* or *krachtwijkenbenadering* of former Dutch Minister Vogelaar, recently Minister Van der Laan is the object of research. I will show that these planning strategies are still highly devoted to the traditional neighbourhood approaches, although many scholars have already shown that, instead of closed spatial circuits, communities rather develop along thematic lines. Moreover, especially in the problem neighbourhoods concerned, new insights evolve around the latent or potential transnational character of those communities. To make the strong-neighbourhood approach a success, a reorientation is needed from a specific neighbourhood approach towards an inter-relational approach in which transnational actors also play a specific role.

In the fourth chapter, I will go into the institutional realm of spatial planning. Here I will focus the investigation specifically on the issue and intended planning ambition of 'Centralize what you must, decentralize whatever you can!', also with regard to the manifest dualism of representational versus associative democracy. I will show that these planning ambitions, motivations and deliberations are still highly motivated from the inside out; that is, mainly related to internal deliberations and power shifts within governments, with hardly any real reference to or significance of their external world. Moreover, I will show that a more interrelated outside-in approach of planning will not only produce better results, but also that it will make the ongoing and in fact permanent 'governmental state-rescaling and state-rebordering' superfluous according to the actor-network-approach.

Finally I will return from these insights to planning itself. I will show that if we wish to take these insights seriously, spatial planning has to shift its focus from a primarily inside-out towards an outside-in approach, based on the following three structuring ideas:

a a broad relational orientation to the planning of time and space, in a kind of adapted actor-network-approach;
b an elaboration of that alternative within the triangle of interrelational (f)actors of importance, networking/institutional setting(s) and spatial strategies;
c a necessary overturn of the exclusive governmental focus towards a focus on areas beyond that government.

From here I will first develop initial ideas about an actor-relational approach of spatial planning, focusing on a seven-step methodology, which should be able to force conventional planning schemes in a more engaged and embedded transmodern way.

As mentioned previously, each of these chapters will be flanked by several boxes in which specific actor-oriented cases will be discussed, either historically or in present-day terms. It underlines the fact that a stronger interrelation between planning-theory and planning-practice is necessary. In fact, it is not only the main subject, but also the main goal of this book: bridging practice and its practitioners to theory and theorists, and vice versa.

[2]

Main and brainport planning 2.0
Spatial-economics beyond infrastructural determinism

The increasing globalization of the world economy due to ongoing development, the falling costs of mobility and the rise of ICT have by now been abundantly described. [Toffler 1981, Gordon 1988, Sassen 1991, Taylor et al. 1995, Castells 1996-1998, Harvey 2001, Friedman 2005] Peter Dicken has even reported the occurrence of a quadratic multiplication in the past few decades. [Dicken 2003a] He himself stressed that 'without doubt, one of the most significant economic-geographic developments of the (last decades of the) twentieth century was the growth and spread of international direct investment, and of other forms of international economic involvement (such as collaborative ventures between firms), through the medium of transnational corporation (TNC)'. [Dicken 2003b] Consistent with this, since the 1980s, there has been an increasing shift within spatial-economic planning from an exclusive focus on the amount and type of industrial land development towards the positioning of regions in an internationally competitive struggle. Regions should be attractive enough to entice those TNCs to expand or settle in the region in question. Nevertheless, evolutionary economists have recently stressed that 'although regions are increasingly becoming collective players actively responding to increasing exposure in a global networked economy, there are serious limits to enhancing the competitiveness of regions.' For instance, benchmarking practices would not be of much help, while it would stimulate policy-makers to imitate supposedly successful (institutional) models – such as the Silicon Valley or Boston Corridor model – without accounting for region-specific contexts. [Boschma 2004] Moreover, it has given rise to weakly augmented and sometimes even misplaced assumptions right from the outset. For instance, at the end of the 1980s, one could conceive imaginary pictures in Dutch governmental plans, such as that of Japanese businessmen fishing in a green, rural setting against the background of the dynamism of the south-east axis of Amsterdam. It was assumed that retaining the Green Heart would be a crucial element of a policy on international economic competition.[8] [Fourth Report on Spatial Planning, hereafter VINO, 1988] Furthermore, other images began to be used in the 1990s – such as selectively accessible A, B, and C locations – which would stimulate targeted but attractive settings for international businesses. [Fourth Report on Spatial Planning Extra, hereafter VINEX, 1991 and the actualization of VINEX, later, VINAC 1995] At the turn of the present century, the focus shifted to economic corridors [BCI 1995] or later to a 'view from the road' [Houben 2002, Ministry of Transport, Public Works and Water Management, hereafter Ministry of TPW, 2005] in order to facilitate highway locations in a responsible, (spatial-economic) theme-based fashion. At present, influenced by Richard Florida, the creation and subsidization of brownfield planning settings is proffered by the so-called 'creative herd' as the panacea for international competitiveness and a flourishing knowledge economy. [Florida 2002] Recently, albeit in a more qualified fashion and with the acknowledgement that the current knowledge economy requires more of a cluster-based approach, [Ministry of Economic Affairs, hereafter Ministry of EA, 2006] there has been a transition to spatial measures to promote 'spatial quality' (whatever is meant by that), the creation of green-red settings for knowledge workers, optimal accessibility and an attractive regional brand, so as to promote the economy. [SRE 2008]

[8] Recently this notion has even been echoed again in the Governmental white paper entitled *Randstad 2040*, [2008] which emphasizes among other points the development of metropolitan parks as a means of making this urban region in the west of the country internationally attractive and competitive.

Spatial and infrastructural determinism

It is precisely here that one finds what I have referred to elsewhere on occasion as the spatial or infrastructural determinism of spatial-economic planning. [Boelens 2009] Apart from fiscal or financial stimulation measures, pleas to boost international competitive positioning in spatial-economic policy are translated almost directly into proposals to improve (international) accessibility or measures which affect the spatial conditions; as if a high-quality living and working environment, a red-green setting, and an extra motorway or airport landing strip added in would automatically lead to improved economic competitiveness.

This becomes very clear in the mainport policy conducted in the Netherlands. Partly on the basis of a report *Schiphol op weg naar 2000*, [Van der Zwan Commission 1985] this policy took shape for the first time in the research paper *Spatial Explorations of the Main Infrastructure* or *Ruimtelijke Verkenningen Hoofdinfrastructuur*, *RUVEIN*. [the Ministry of Housing, Spatial Planning and the Environment, hereafter VROM, 1986] It was prompted by the recession into which the Dutch economy had fallen during the 1980s and the attempt to identify new spearheads on the basis of which it could profile itself effectively by comparison with the rest of Europe. Those who sought to do so had recourse to the long-prominent commercial, transport and distribution function of the Netherlands in the EuroDelta, with the seaport of Rotterdam and the airport of Amsterdam – as *primus inter pares* – being identified as the means of providing these functions with a contemporary interpretation. In addition, in consultation with the Dutch air travel sector, Schiphol was characterized as a potential *Gateway to Europe*, the primary ambition being – on account of the limited domestic market – to target above all trans-Atlantic and Japanese transfer passengers travelling to and from other destinations in Europe. For its part, the port of Rotterdam received the status of a *Mainport of Europe*, which, as well as enhancing its short sea and hinterland connections, needed to profile itself as the major hub at least in the *Le Havre-Hamburg range*. In combination with this, the national government would back the creation of multimodal transport arteries – i.e. by road, water and rail – which would meet the highest quality standards and connect the gateway and the mainport effectively with the hinterland. Thus it is from this period that the first studies for the Betuwe rail link derive: the north-eastern freight link, the high-speed lines from Schiphol towards the south, east and north, and the extension of motor and waterways so that they would even be suitable for road-trains and six-vessel push navigation. [Ministry of TPW 1986] At the same time, the brainport concept was introduced a year later: this was used during this period to refer to 'the advanced use of communication and information technology – telematics – and the creation of dedicated inland terminals in order to achieve the integration of transport and communication flows in the gateway and mainport'. [City Council of Rotterdam 1987, Zonneveld 1991] Although Schiphol lost its *gateway* prefix in *the White Paper on Spatial Perspectives* or *Nota Ruimtelijke Perspectieven*, [VROM 1986] and reference has only been made to mainports since then, these approaches were further formalized as governmental policy in the *VINO* [VROM 1987/1988] and the *Second White Paper on Traffic and Transport*. [Ministry TPW 1990] In addition, it also resulted in the creation of the semi-private *Holland International Distribution Council* or *Stichting Nederland Distributieland*, in which, besides governmental policies, the business sector also started aligning strategies more effectively with a view to 'reinforcing the international competitive position and level of knowledge of the Dutch logistical sector in the broad sense'. [NDL 1987]

Although its airports and seaports had long been seen as the mainstays of the Dutch economy, [RPD 1958, RPD 1962, PZH 1968] the mainport policy had mainly been logistical and infrastructural in nature up to that time. At most, it targeted dock and deep-sea port-related functions or derivative logistical platform-related functions in the case of the airport. In the *Fourth Report on Spatial Planning Extra* it was even explicitly stated that no office development should take place at or around Schiphol, as this would create the risk of the mainport's logistical development being impeded by uncontrolled traffic growth and hemmed in by new building. Other so-called 'top locations' in the Randstad were designated as places where this international office development could take place. [VINEX 1992] Even so, with government *White Paper on Dutch Economy Without Borders* or *Economie met open grenzen*, [Ministry of EA 1990] the interprovincial vision *The Randstad Presents Itself* or *De Randstad maakt zich op* [RORO 1990] and the growing focus on added value logistics, [A.T. Kearney et al. 1993] the significance of the mainports was already being seen in a broader, more spatio-economic perspective. Since the mid-1990s, in addition to the mainport idea, the concept of *Airport City* has been used in and around Schiphol, [Schiphol 1995] or even *Aerotropolis* [Kassarda 2000] or, at present, *Airport Corridor*. [Schiphol 2008] These terms express the idea that as well as the landing strip and the transport and distribution sites, other high-quality facilities and business, offices and residential sites are of importance as destination factors for the mainports too. Similarly, reference is now made in Rotterdam not to a Mainport but to a Gateway of Europe, including an environmental, knowledge and energy gateway, in order to express the idea that the port involves more than just logistics. [Port Authority of Rotterdam 2004, City Council of Rotterdam 2007] Even so, the picture of the development of economic prosperity based in and around major nodes of international physical infrastructure has not fundamentally altered. It is still assumed that the junctions between water, road, rail and/or air connections are obvious contributory factors for trade, the market, business development, innovation, economic prosperity, etc. In other words, spatio-economic policy is still predicated on a kind of spatial and/or infrastructural determinism for economic competitiveness and welfare. I do not deny the significance of this (international) accessibility in today's network-based world of the space of flows and the global economy. But, at the same time, I do wish to relate this idea to the new economic-geographical insights in the field of comparative advantages and competitiveness, which may lead to a shift in trends of economic related planning thought and action.

Shifting economic-geographical foundations

Recent works surveying the development of economic geography are based on at least four approaches to economic geography. [Coe/Kelly/Yeung 2007, Pellenbarg/Wever et al. 2008] In each of these approaches, the focus is not just on the significance of space and infrastructure, but also on the locational and other behaviour of economic actors such as (large) firms, banks or consumers. At the same time, there is a kind of progressive understanding in which the one approach stands on the shoulders of the other.

The first is usually identified as the most traditional and location-oriented. In this approach, the object of attention is usually the unique characteristics of the location itself – such as the presence of raw materials, cheap or suitable labour, spatial development possibilities, the cost of land, (international) accessibility and associated transport costs, distance from sale areas, etc. – which are regarded as explaining the way in which specific economic activities spread across a given area or region, or the world as a whole. [Smith 1776, Von Thünen 1826, Weber 1909 etc.] In a more modern, adapted neo-classical approach, scientific models, often derived from nature, were used to explain economic-geographical patterns and, where possible, even to forecast or plan them. [Christaller 1933, Hoover 1948, Smith 1971] Businesses are regarded here as *black boxes* which adapt their behaviour to reflect a thorough knowledge of local conditions. [Pellenbarg/Wever 2008] However, the big problem is that this has not always happened in practice, and that businesses have made surprising locational choices, despite apparently having sufficient information about supposedly superior (in terms of costs, accessibility or quality) locations. In other words, the presence of cheap, high-quality land around deep waterways or an outstanding network of flight connections has not yet been shown to lead automatically to economic concentrations and/or prosperity. Great differences have been revealed between locations, which, in logistical terms, are apparently similar. [BCI 1991]

The second approach, which emerged in the 1960s and 1970s, was the behavioural approach. In this, much more interest is taken in the precise considerations and motives of the businesses themselves. In addition to rational considerations, the human factors, normative restrictions or the mental map of the business managers themselves became prominent, which means that locational choices certainly do not always proceed rationally or locationally, as is assumed in the (neo)classical approach. [Simon 1960, Pred 1967] One wide-ranging but never substantiated assumption in the 1980s, for example, was that the attractiveness of the environment, the quality of housing, the level of facilities and/or even the preferences of the director's wife were factors in economic locational behaviour, rather than just locational factors. Even the Richard Florida *idée fixe* that a high concentration of homosexuals ensures a flourishing creative (knowledge) economy – whatever that might mean – fits with this. [Florida 2004] Be that as it may, this approach in its purest form is likewise unable to explain why certain economic regions grow, while others decline, or how this leads to a shift in spatio-economic prosperity or competitiveness. The reasons why businesses flourish or relocate turn out also to be affected by other than purely behavioural motives in addition to internal business considerations. [Porter 1990]

The third approach, which is therefore distinguished, is the structuralist approach. Usually, reference is made exclusively here to the (neo)-Marxist approaches, which regard the fundamental differences between distinctive societies as the underlying factors in capital accumulation. In turn, the struggle between capital and labour and obvious power differences would have explanatory power for the (worldwide) differences of economic development and innovativeness. [Althusser 1965, Harvey 1985, Swyngedouw 2003] However, Anthony Giddens's structuration approach, and especially his focus on the institutional conditions under which economic development takes place, also falls in my view within the scope of this more structuralist approach. [Giddens 1984] Here the emphasis shifts from the significance of the set of rules, procedures or conventions – both formal and informal and both external and internal – to the innovativeness or competitiveness of certain regions. It is not just a question of levels of taxation, the business climate or the flexibility of rules. Improper business practices or lock-in situations are very important too, since they prevent innovation. [Boschma et al. 2002] Conversely, suitable institutions can reduce so-called 'transaction costs' and hence encourage a flourishing economy. [Polyani 1944, Granovetter 1985] However, even this structuralist approach or the existing set of rules and conventions prove inadequate to explain why certain regions do so well or so poorly economically. Economic competitiveness can develop even in spite of opposition, and the reverse may also be the case.

Accordingly, since the mid-1990s, a fourth approach has emerged, which, in my view, combines the different elements of the previously mentioned approaches in a certain sense: the so-called 'new' or 'relational economic geography'. [Boggs/Rantisi 2003, Bathelt/Glückler 2003, Yeung 2004, 2005] In this approach, economic processes are not seen as separate from social developments, but social, business cultural and institutional factors are actually seen as key concepts in explaining the spatio-economic dynamics. [Coe/Kelly/Yeung 2007] Going further, this approach takes the relational significance of the current network society in the broad sense as an important starting-point. So this is not just about the spatial, institutional and cultural 'embeddedness' of specific economic sectors in a given region or business climate, [Granovetter 1985] but rather about innovation resulting from mutual relations and coalitions between and within businesses, and about exchange relations or competitiveness between places and businesses, even ones which are far removed from one another. [Taylor 2001] The starting-point here is that economic actors – such as TNCs, governments, consumers etc. – in specific (institutional, spatial or cultural) settings are capable of temporary or permanent strategic coalitions or contracts that lead to added value for all, in complex ways. Temporary or permanent clusters as fora for socio-economic innovativeness, mutual added value and innovative crossovers are crucial here, of course. But such clusters cannot be conceived just in a spatial sense. They become also active in the form of institutional, cultural, organizational and relational proximity; i.e., in specific networks over a longer distance and across sectorial or geographical boundaries. [Coe/Kelly/Yeung 2007, Boschma 2005a] In this sense, this approach is locational in view of the accessibility and entrenchment principle, behavioural in view of the emphasis on the behaviour of economic actors both within and between businesses, and structural because it includes underlying cultural, political, social and hence also institutional structures as explanatory factors in international competitiveness. Above all, though, it takes the relationship and mutual interaction between these three components as its starting point, and hence is relational in a broad sense: in relation to the unique setting of the location in which it operates, in relation to clusters of similar or mutually reinforcing business processes, and in relation to the precise institutional context (political, economic, social).

Relational spatio-economic approaches

This approach thus dovetails with the general developments in academic geography and planning already announced in chapter one. [Giddens 1995, Amin & Thrift 2001, Urry 2002, Murdoch 2006] Here, too, there is a kind of relational, actor-network approach, in which the central factor is the structure and dynamics of economic relations seen from a spatial perspective, rather than the space itself. In other words, this approach is based on the assumption that it is not really the specific properties of the place and region that determine their development or attractiveness to a company: rather, there is an iterative connection, in which primarily the companies themselves shape the material, institutional and spatial development of a region. [Bathelt and Glückler 2002] Economic action is seen here not as a type of abstract, rational or strategic action, but rather as a specific form of social action, embedded in concrete structures and related to changes which take place elsewhere in the world in the general sense and, above all, in the local region in the specific sense. [Storper et al. 1997] In this sense, the relational aspect is expressed not just in the relative economic attractiveness of and developments in one place compared to others, but in the possible institutions, associations and economic constellations – formal or informal – which are actually or potentially present and possible in the space in question. Therefore, after Massey, [1999] Boggs and Rantisi, [2003] Henry Yeung [2004] distinguishes

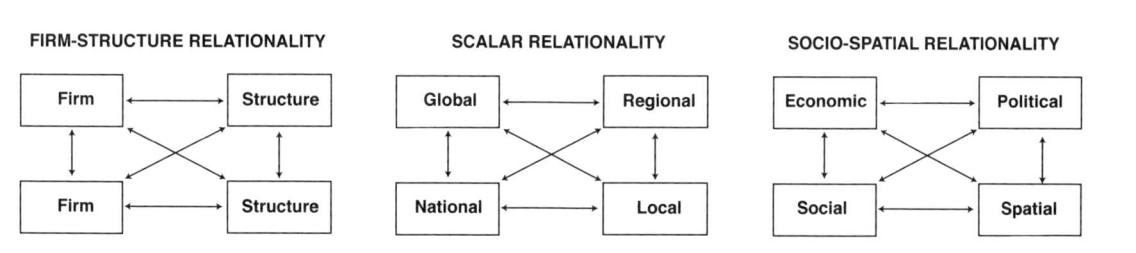

FIRM-STRUCTURE RELATIONALITY

| Firm | ↔ | Structure |
| Firm | ↔ | Structure |

SCALAR RELATIONALITY

| Global | ↔ | Regional |
| National | ↔ | Local |

SOCIO-SPATIAL RELATIONALITY

| Economic | ↔ | Political |
| Social | ↔ | Spatial |

Firm, scale and structure relationality [Yeung 2005]

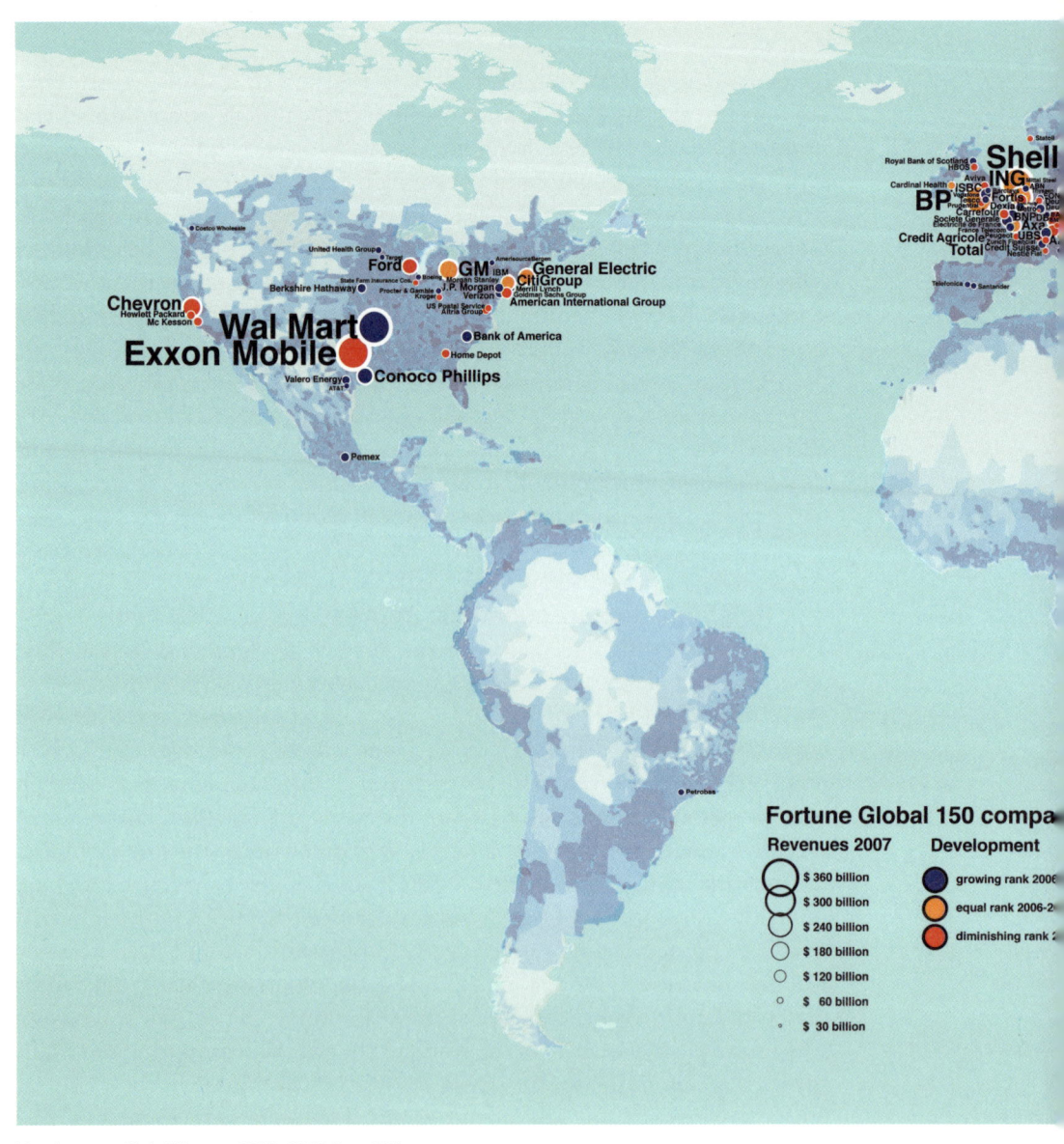

Headquarters Global Fortune 200 in 2008 [Fortune 2008]

three kinds of conceptual relational economic connections between (a) global and local scales, (b) actors or firms and structures and (c) the social and the spatial. [see figure on page 41] So what exactly is going on here?

Scalar relationality According to the relational economic geographers, the specific characteristics of a given space and national differences obviously remain important for the global economy, even though it is increasingly becoming organized in a transnational context. But this is the case in a different way – one that is far more complex, iterative and relational – than is

42   Main and brainport planning 2.0

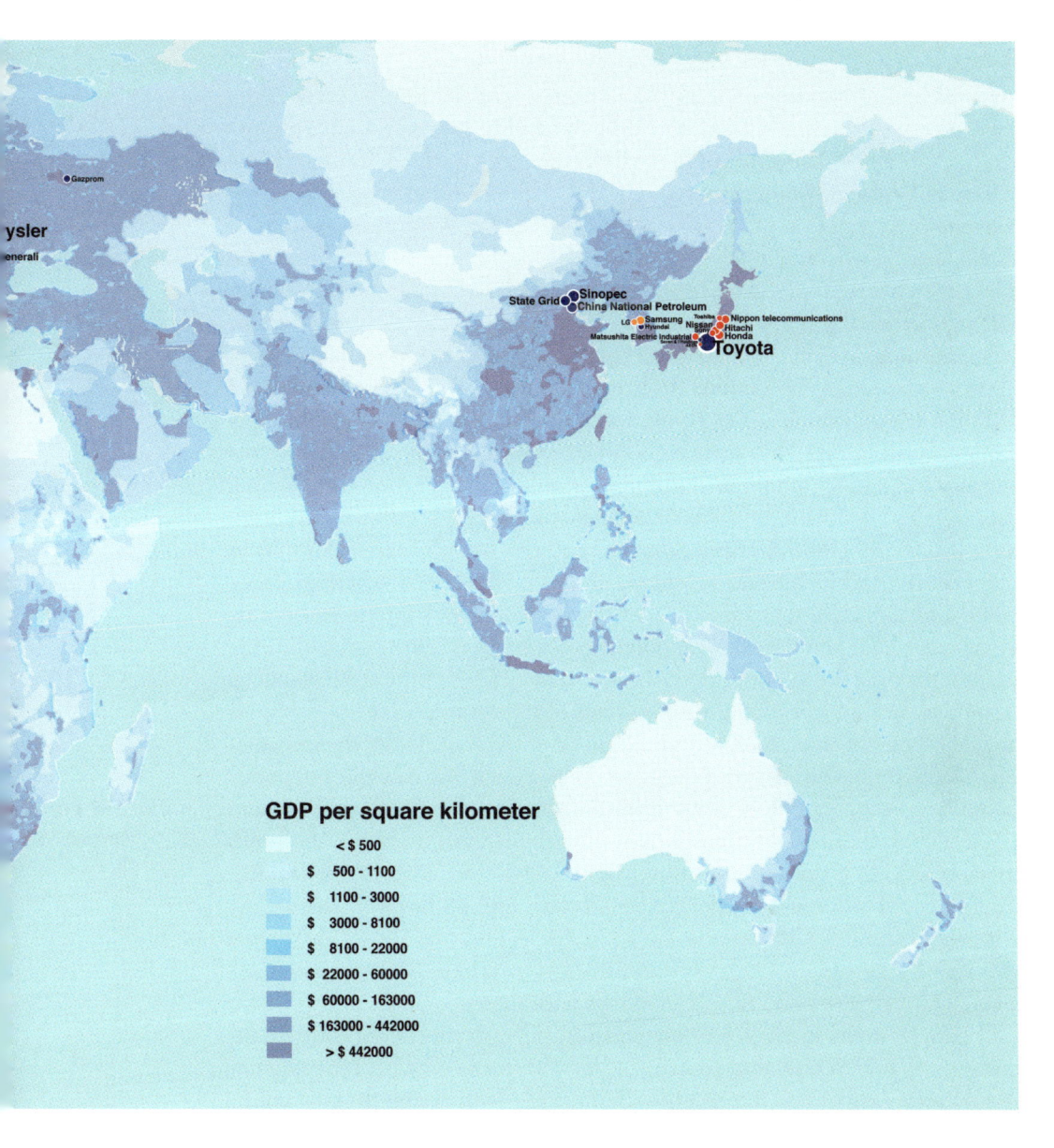

currently common in spatio-economic planning practice. Today's global economy is unmistakeably metropolitan in character. [Friedmann 1988, Sassen 1990, Castells 1996, Taylor 2004] According to the Global Fortune 500 – before the recent financial crises – over 82% of the head offices of the 500 largest transnational companies were located in metropolitan regions of more than 1 million people, and approximately 60% in metropolitan conurbations of more than 5 million people. [Global Fortune 2008, situation 2007] The same is often true, incidentally, of the other services, research & development facilities, transport & distribution arms, and production units of these TNCs. Although no more than 1/6 of the total world population live and work in these metropolitan conurbations of at least 5 million people, over 30% of total world GDP is earned here. [OECD 2006, City Mayor Statistics 2005] And the history of this development stretches back a long way.

Assisted by and building on the work of others, scholars such as Peter Taylor have described the spatio-economic development of this world-city network down through the centuries; [Taylor 2004] from the transcontinental urban archipelago of Beijing/Canton through to Bruges/Genoa around 1300, [Abu-Lughod 1989] via the North-west European Hanseatic network in the North Sea-Baltic region during the Late Middle Ages [Dollinger 1970, Brand/Muller 2007] and the developing colonial city network from the mid-16th century (see Introduction in the referential argument), through to the capitals of these colonial states, which became more prominent than those in the area around them thanks to nationalism. [Braudel 1984] According to Taylor, [2004] however, it was with the industrial and later the telecommunications revolution, and the associated functional specialization not just within but also between regions that a new transnational urban setting arose, founded on different network bases. Taylor cites (among others) John Friedmann [1986] here, who states that the new world-city networks, as well as a new global hierarchy (in the northern and southern hemispheres and between and within NAFTA, the EU and ASEAN), are also reliant on functional global-local factors. Urban-economic development has likewise become closely dependent on the extent and nature of relations with other cities, while at the same time the role and specific position that the institutional formations occupy in local contexts is, in turn, a factor of importance in the possibilities and development chances of local and regional economies. Taylor then enlarges on this place-specific relational thesis on the basis of a broad analysis of population size, economic functions, level of costs, international accessibility, physical and virtual connections, urban clustering and its intensity. He comes up with his own classification of the current world-city network, divided into leading world cities, major regional world cities and important cities on the edge. [Taylor 2004, see figure on page 45]

Many cities now respond to such rankings with their economic policy. Thus, for example, in the spatio-economic policy of the municipality of Amsterdam and even that of Schiphol, there is a considerable focus on what is happening in competing regions such as Madrid, Berlin and even London. Its own policy is then attuned or refined in the light of these observations. [Amsterdam 2007, *Nota Randstad 2040* 2008] As said previously, such benchmarks often result in a policy of copying others that are deemed successful, the desire to perform just as well as others in every respect, and the apparently ineradicable tendency to promote oneself continually at the centre of different regions and force fields, as if Christaller's central places model were still decisive. In a more sophisticated and embedded manner, however, the importance of locational factors becomes connected with a more specifically adapted economic-geographical cluster or network policy. Thus, nearly two decades ago now, Michael Porter [1990] pointed out the importance of not just factor and demand conditions, but especially of existing entrepreneurial strategies, structure and rivalry, and of related and supporting industries, which would mark the competitive position of a country or region compared to others. Ann Markussen [1996] also refers to the stickiness

	LEADING WORLD CITIES				MAJOR REGIONAL WORLD CITIES - FIRST LEAGUE				MAJOR REGIONAL WORLD CITIES - SECOND LEAGUE				
CLUSTER NUCLEUS	London New York	Frankfurt Hong Kong Paris Singapore Tokyo	Chigago Los Angeles	Amsterdam Zürich Madrid Milan São Paulo Mexico City	Bangkok Jakarta Kuala Lumpur Manila Seoul Shanghai	Atlanta Boston Dallas	Berlin Düsseldorf München	Warsaw Moscow Prague St.Petersburg	Istanbul Dubai	Caracas Bogotá	Copenhagen	Adelaide Brisbane Perth Vancouver Monteral	Calcutta Karachi Bangalore
SINGULAR MEMBERS				Sydney Buenos Aires Toronto	Beijing Taipei	Washington	Hamburg	Budapest Vienna	Mumbai Cairo	Medelin	Rome Stockholm Helsinki	Aukland Hamilton Cape Town Winnipeg Calgary Ottowa Chrsitchurch Edmonton Johannesburg Melbourne Hobart	Islamabad Chennai Dhaka Riyadh Jeddah Lahore New Delhi
HYBRID MEMBERS		Brussels —————— Barcelona ——————		——— Brussels ——— Barcelona	Miami				Dublin Lisbon Athens Amman Beirut	Miami Lima Santiago San José	Dublin Lisbon Athens Riga Vilnius Talinn Sofia Bratislava	Canberra Monterrey Gualdaljara Birmingham Manchester Southampton	Nairobi Colombo
NEAR ISOLATES								Kiev	Geneva	Curitiba	Oslo	Durban Wellington Ruwi Manama	Ho Chi Minh Bucharest

World City Network, relational clusters of cities [Taylor 2004]

of places in a global economy, as a result of locally or regionally integrated business clusters. Building on this, an economic-geographical school has also emerged in Utrecht, focusing on the importance of economic complexes, formations and clusters. [Atzema et al. 2002] This expresses the idea that in a burgeoning knowledge economy, good knowledge exchange between and within businesses is of enormous, perhaps decisive (added) value. Elaborating further, some scholars have emphasised the spatial concentration of related, mutually supportive businesses, because when it comes to product innovation, economic development and the tacit knowledge needed for that, face-to-face contacts still seemed to be still extremely relevant. [Nadvi & Schmitz 1994, Porter 1998, Enright 2001] Based on more detailed study of the conditions for industrial districts and innovative environments and a number of specifically examined cases, Thomas Brenner [2004] even came to the conclusion that the economic attractiveness of a region seems heavily dependent on 'the existence of universities and research institutes, the entrepreneurial attitude of the population, the geographic location and accessibility of a region, the availability of venture capital and the existence of firms in related or necessary industries'. In a way, these ideas have already fed through into the Dutch *White Paper on Peaks in the Delta* or *Nota Pieken in de Delta*. [the Ministry EA 2005] For the first time, this picks up on the idea of place and region-specific clusters of high-tech, food, energy, creativity, etc., whereas promoting universities everywhere, promoting R&D facilities in every city or region, or stimulating venture capital throughout the nation does seem just as unlikely as inappropriate to promote a robust competitiveness. Even so, it remains unclear exactly how this can be implemented in spatio-economic policy terms. At the same time, this only addresses relationality in the narrow sense of mutual competence, relations and networks between and within (parts of) those regions themselves. Specific economic institutional settings are also relevant. I shall return to this point later. Because here too, the companies concerned are not passive, mechanical entities, but active parties which themselves affect these clusters and institutional settings and their attractiveness. [Dicken 2004, Amin 2004]

Firm-structure relationality Instead of the customary exclusive focus on the precise characteristics, attractiveness and supposedly unique values and centrality/cluster-forming of a given place, over the past decade increasing interest has therefore been developed in the specific characteristics and structure of the (trans-national) companies themselves. [Dicken & Thrift 1992, Cowling & Stugden 1998, Bathelt & Clükler 2000] In this sense, I have already argued elsewhere in favour of a more actor-oriented perspective on spatio-economic planning and policy. [Boelens 2005, Boelens & Atzema 2006] This is partly prompted by the observation that, influenced by ongoing globalization, mobility and computer and telecommunication technology, the locational motivations of businesses – especially transnational ones – seem to be shifting from mainly external considerations to increasingly internal ones. Instead of attention being focused exclusively or primarily on the accessibility, availability or level of training of personnel or on land prices, taxation and rent levels, for example, other internal business considerations are starting to gain in importance. In chapter one, I have already pointed out the increasing outsourcing, insourcing and co-sourcing of specific businesses and business components, coupled with continuing globalization and international competition processes. On closer examination, however, these processes turn out to be far from uniform – in fact, they differ from company to company. There are various factors responsible for this.

First, a distinction can be made on the basis of business size. Take the world's ten largest companies, for example. All of them have an annual turnover that is larger than the gross national product of countries such as Malaysia, Chile, the Czech Republic, or even Singapore, Pakistan, Israel and Egypt. According to figures of 2007, the three largest (Wal-Mart, Exxon Mobil and Shell) have a larger turnover than Denmark, Finland, Ireland and Portugal. These so-called 'supranational' businesses are so large that they (apart from a few exceptions such as Wal-Mart) have full functions and/or representation virtually all over the world. The transnational businesses, which are somewhat smaller in turnover terms (around $30-100 billion per year) are often characterized by the fact that they only have specific facilities distributed around the world, whereas the multinationals, which are slightly smaller again (turnover around $5-30 billion per year) mainly have specific sites around the world. Finally, the internationals (up to around $5 billion per year) often cluster in specific continents or sometimes even work together in international service centres or logistical activity centres. [Stratagem 2006] Each of these companies accordingly requires its own (spatial) approach. [see figure on page 47]

Turnover Diversification Trans-National Corporations

	Turnover	Geography	Examples
Supra-national	> 100 billion €	Distribution of all functions over the world	Shell, ING, GM
Cross-national	10-100 billion €	Distribution of specific functions over the world	Siemens, Philips
Multi-national	1-10 billion €	Distribution of branches around the world	Telecom, Tata, Nokia
Inter-national	< 1 billion €	Distribution of products around the world	Lockheed, Bertelsmann

Turnover Diversification Trans-National Corporations [Stratagem 2007]

There is also differentiation on the basis of business sector. Thus Peter Dicken [2003] persuasively demonstrates that the textile and clothing industry has been structured on the basis of a global division of labour, in which design, tailoring and marketing are still highly concentrated in the highly developed Western countries (especially Northern Italy, France, the USA and to an extent the Netherlands), whereas sewing and garment assembly largely take place in the low-wage or developing nations and regions such as Mexico, the Caribbean, China, South-east Asia and Sri Lanka. By contrast, the Japanese and American car industry tried (unlike the European car industry) to set up autonomous, integrated production systems in the three major trading blocs (NAFTA, EU, ASEAN), whereas the semi-conductor industry consists of several large consortia, some of which are organized in a single country (Japan), while others are organized around global firms specializing in research, production and specific applications. Again, financial services were heavily concentrated in London and New York (and in fact in very specific districts of those cities) at least until mid-2008, with Tokyo, Frankfurt, Zürich, Paris and Amsterdam in the second rank, although there are also a number of new, fast-growing regional centres such as Beijing and Charlotte and numerous offshore financial centres in the niches and the virtual circuits of global capital. [see figure on page 48]

Last but not least, there is also differentiation on the basis of business culture. Henry Yeung [2002] is among those who convincingly demonstrate that, although transnational companies can be distributed all over the world, with employees working with numerous different nationalities and cultures – it still makes a difference what the national origin of such transnational corporations actually is. In Yeung's view, for example, the dominant economic ideology of Japanese and Chinese TNCs is still a kind of 'familism' or 'technonationalism', whereas those of German or American origin are more characterized by a kind of 'social partnership' or 'free enterprise liberalism' respectively. Similarly, the corporate governance structure of Chinese and Japanese companies

Sectoral Diversification Trans-National Corporations

	Main Drive	Primary	Secondary
Fashion	Global divisions of labor	Design (& cutting) in developed country	Sewing & assembly in developing country
Industry (automotive)	Integrated production in NAFTA, EU, AEAN	Regional headquarters & distribution centres	Manufacturing in low cost labour countries
ICT	Global and regional alliances	Design houses in several global centres	Assembly-production on a global basis
Finance	Global concentrations on a 24 hour basis	Concentrations in global cities	Niche-markets in peripheral regions
Logistics	Economies of scale	Mostly concentration in the mother town	(Main)ports, logistic centres, warehouses all over the world

Sectoral Diversification Trans-National Corporations [Dicken 1992]

is said to be characterized by a stable, socially related shareholder structure and/or control by family members, whereas German companies are typified by a relatively autonomous management, and companies which are American by origin are characterized by a 'short term shareholding', in which the managers' freedom of action is heavily restricted by the relevant capital markets and investors. The funds available for research and development in Japanese companies are said often to be extremely high, while those at American companies fluctuate; corporate financing for German businesses is often organized on a markedly regional basis, whereas that for American businesses is more global in its nature. [see figure on page 49] Similarly, Sally had at an earlier stage noted striking differences between French and German multinationals, and Whitley had pointed out the considerable differences between multinationals from the different Asian countries. [Sally 1994, Whitley 1999, Hall/Soskice 2001]

Socio-Spatial relationality This is not the full story, however, because as well as these locational and behavioural aspects, interest has recently been growing in the specific economic institutional settings in relation to these aspects. [Martin 1999, Boschma 2005] *Institutional settings*, refer not only to social agencies that instil a particular set of norms or attitudes in those who operate within them, but also to a certain power it confers on particular actors through an existing matrix of sanctions and institutions or through the present (im)possibility to embed or socio-economic mobilization. [Coleman 1990] Here, this is to be understood in the broad sense of a communally underwritten economic pattern of standards, values and learning, and thus also includes formal and informal networks, financial, juridical, cognitive and social networks (including those over longer distances). Partly building on this, Saskia Sassen [2006] has

Cultural Diversification Trans-National Corporations

	American	German	Chinese
Economic Institution	Decentralized, open markets	Organized markets Tiers of firms	Family-based corporate organisation
Economic Ideology	Free enterprise liberalism	Social partnership	Interpersonal relationships
Direct Investment	Extensive inward and outward	Selective/outward orientation	Extensive outward
Corporate governance	Short term share-holding	Managerial autonomy	Long term share-holding
Corporate financing	Diversified, global funding	Concentrated, regional funding	Diversified, network funding

Cultural Diversification Trans-National Corporations [Yeung 2002]

recently pointed out that, throughout history, the specific assemblages of territoriality, authority and jurisprudence have in fact also affected innovativeness, competitiveness and economic progress. In turn, Peter A. Hall and David Soskice had already earlier focused on five specific institutional spheres (industrial relations, vocational training and education, corporate governance, interfirm relations and employees relations) which, in their view, differ enormously within liberal (such as in the USA for instance) or co-ordinated market economies (such as Germany for instance). They show that firms develop different corporate strategies within these systems, in order to take advantage of institutional support, dealing with the national legal frameworks and particular modes of co-ordination, thus resulting in different patterns of economic performance. [Hall/Soskice 2001] Nevertheless, here it is not just a question of the tax climate, interest rates, whether the dominant political organizations take a liberal outlook, economic policy or legislation to stimulate the economy. Rather, it is a question of the subtle interactions between and the constellation of private and public-sector mechanisms, the reliability or corruption of the establishment, social support for developments, and so on, and of how these things find expression in a given legislative and structural order. In fact, that corresponds to the (re)appraisal of the specific 'spatial configurations of heterogeneous power relations' that Yeung [2005] advocates in his reorientation on the basis of the relational economic-geographical approach.

These configurations seem place-specific, but there is a subtle interaction between geographical-morphological conditions, endogenously developed alliances between dominant actors and specific historical 'ways of doing things' which have grown and taken root. Thus the planner Peter Hall [1998] has described the interrelationship between the development of global cities and specific civilization processes in the fields of economics, politics, jurisprudence, culture etc. Elaborating on this along with historian Ed Taverne, I recently ventured an attempt to identify with a little more precision the structural DNA of the polycentric archipelago of the Rhine-Meuse-Scheldt delta (henceforth EuroDelta) compared with nearby, more or less monocentric metropoles such as London and Paris. That DNA is determined by the age-old, changing, yet distinctive forms of mutual influence of context, actors and structure. [Boelens/Taverne 2009] For example, the greater region of Paris (Île de France) can still be described in one form or another as an 'absolutist metropolis'. Because although Paris also has countless district, municipal and regional authorities for its fundamental development and position, the nature of urban politics in Paris is still determined to this day by the model in which the state (i.e. the head of state) regards itself as the engine of urban development, at the very least, and uses its power and prestige to attract private capital and get it to behave in accordance with its plans. In support of this, one can cite not just the rule of the Capetians, the Bourbons or Napoleon I and III, but also the involvement with Paris of presidents Poincaré, De Gaulle, Pompidou and Mitterrand. Even Nicolas Sarkozy's recent initiative of giving ten prominent architects – supported by a team of planners, engineers, sociologists and philosophers – six months to come up with new plans for the development of Paris falls within this tradition. By contrast, the metropolis of London has been controlled by a municipal authority for centuries, or more recently by the Greater London Authority, which, though not uncontroversial – as its abolition during Thatcher's premiership demonstrates – nonetheless functions on the basis of a subtle equilibrium between state and local citizens (or prominent figures among them). This distinction affects not just the way in which the two metropoles are organized, but their specific physical interpretation, street pattern, image and sense of community. In a sense, despite the global network economy, this seems even to affect their economic base. Over 50% of the Global Fortune 500 head offices based in Paris are of current or former state concerns, and 2/3 have close ties with the state; whereas in London the same is true of only 10%. This also appears to be one of the reasons why in the European Union's recent *State of European Cities* report, [EU 2007] Paris is regarded as an 'established capital' while London is classified among the more dynamic 'global knowledge hubs'.

For delta metropoles – such as those in the EuroDelta – things are fundamentally different, however. Other than for short periods, this delta has never had a unified authority. As a result, the urbanization process over the centuries has been essentially bottom-up in character. In order to survive on a long-term basis in such deltas, it was advisable to work with others in the same situation in order to undertake and maintain common projects such as dike and coastal improvements and the construction of roads and waterways. For Simon Schama, this even forms the basis of what he classifies in cultural terms as a 'moral geography'. In Schama's view, the long-term, deadly serious struggle against water resulted in a profound sense of self-determination over the land that its users had made, protected or managed themselves. [Schama 1988] But this bottom-up orientation affects not just the geographical structure, institutional setting and political organization, but also the economic organization of the Delta. As is known, the great voyages of discovery and the international trade which developed from the seventeenth century onwards were – in contrast to countries such as Spain, Portugal and later England, too, to an extent – made possible and guaranteed not in a top-down approach using state funds, but primarily from the bottom up, via the joint financing of leading private merchants in different Delta cities. In fact, unlike their previously established joint stock counterparts in England – such as the Company of Merchant Adventurers or the Muscovy, Spanish, Eastland and Levant Companies – these translocal limited companies were examples of enormous economic and power-political interwovenness. The Dutch East India Company (VOC) and West India Company (WIC) existed not just for commercial purposes, but were also granted political and military powers to establish and/or consolidate Holland's commercial position around the world. [Prince 2006] Unlike capital metropoles, Delta metropoles such as the EuroDelta were thus founded in a fundamentally polycentric and 'opportunistic' manner – in the spatial, political, social and economic senses of the word – not just on a basic right of self-determination, but also and above all on a very prominent colleague/rival attitude of co-operation where necessary and competition where possible.[9] Delta metropoles have no clearly dominant public authority, and no decisive higher moral or general code of behaviour to structure the space, economics and society. Above all, they have shrewd negotiators in the civic and business society, who seek the most profitable coalitions through negotiation. Often, delta metropoles are extremely dynamic, versatile and creative to their very core, although in a bottom-up and often modest fashion, without grandeur or emotion and based on a mainly utilitarian approach.

9 Other examples here are the cities withing the Hanseatic League in the northern German, Baltic and North Sea regions and the City States in Northern Italy (see also the referential argument).

Summarizing, the relational economic geography is not just focused on one of these assemblages, but precisely on the interrelation between all these conceptual connections; that is the scalar, firm-structure and socio-spatial rationality. In fact, it concentrates on the interrelation between the specific (internal, structural) characteristics of involved (leading) firms, the specific spatial contexts and above all institutional settings and the cluster/network strategies between them, which jointly determine the robust competitiveness of a region. Spatial planning and/or governmental policies could influence or facilitate each of these factors of importance. A sophisticated and precise actor-network analysis is particularly helpful here, rather than benchmark practices or a specific ranking of places.

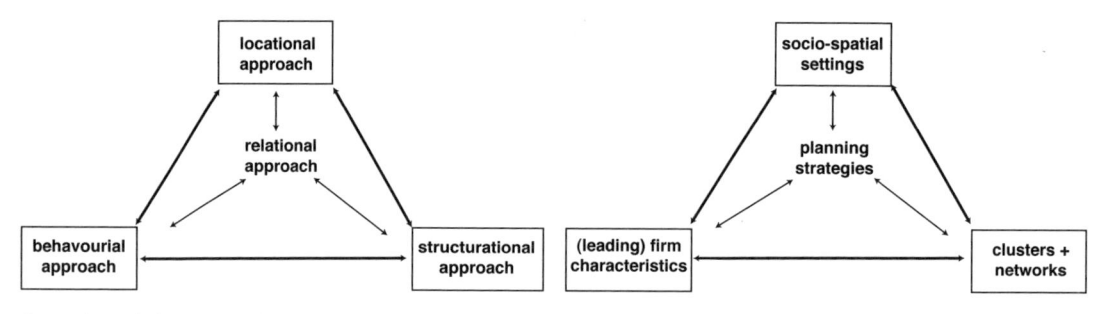

Comparison relational approach and planning strategies

Main/Brainport policy revisited

Returning to the main/brainport policy, we can discover an enormous gap between what is repeatedly proposed in spatio-economic planning practice and what is described here as a more or less generally accepted fact in engaged and sophisticated economic-geographical theory. It is now widely recognized that the international competitiveness of regions does not depend purely on better (international) accessibility, or sufficient (high-grade or otherwise) possibilities for spatial development, but is reflected in much more complex, iterative and relational assemblages than is assumed in the simple approach of spatial-infrastructural condition management. Thus international competitiveness – and especially a sticky and natural relationship with specific regions or places – is structured (not in a one-dimensional conditional sense, but in a thoroughly relational sense) around three distinct but co-dependent assemblages of a network, actor and institutional nature. These are (a) geographical competition, network and cluster-building on all scales, (b) the presence of culturally, commercially and sectorially embedded leading actors (whether already active or requiring activation) in connection with comprehensive regional ambitions in the broad sense, and (c) temporary or permanent practicable and fruitful actor-network constellations of business, public and civic stakeholders.

In point of fact, on closer examination this turns out always to have been the case in the development of the seaport of Rotterdam, the airport at Schiphol and Brainport Eindhoven (see Boxes 2.1, 2.2, 2.3). Yet spatio-economic policy with regard to these main/brainports has repeatedly been completely at odds with such an approach, and remains so. Formerly, main and brainport development was left *de facto* to the initiative of business (or at any rate to business pioneers and bold entrepreneurs), or received support exclusively of a logistical/infrastructural nature, or (as in Brabant) there is always at least a time-gap between spatio-economic policy and actual brainport development. Moreover spatial planning policy remains – even though it is sometimes actually instigated by business leaders or spokespeople (NDL, Arie van der Zwan, Philips etc.) – predominantly government-centred, and for the most part focuses exclusively on ensuring adequate infrastructure and sufficient space for development. This is the case with the Tweede Maasvlakte/A15 focus of Gateway

Rotterdam, with the Airport Corridor approach to Mainport Schiphol, and with the A2/high-grade red-green approach of the Brainport of Eindhoven. Spatio-economic policy on and around the Gateway, Mainport and Brainport accordingly remains primarily focused on the classical, location-oriented view of economic-geographical dynamics. Hence it is growth/expansion oriented, primarily in quantitative terms. In order to prepare for current and possible future economic developments in a responsible manner, increasing attention also ought to be devoted to cluster-formation, internal business considerations, the institutional settings within which businesses operate and, above all, the mutual interactions between these elements. What is more, this results in a more specific (as opposed to generic) and qualitative (as opposed to quantitative) approach, which can operate in a more discerning fashion compared with policy on other locations, and can possibly become more socio-cultural, as well as economically-instrumental sustainable, area-specific and environmentally responsible.

At the same time, different emphases are called for in the case of each individual Gateway, Mainport or Brainport.

Within the recent policies of *Gateway Rotterdam*, the focus is still almost exclusively *locational* in nature. It is true that the new port and structure plan stress themes such as the innovation port, the environmental port, the knowledge port and the energy port, in addition to the traditional exclusive focus on transit port. But beyond the confines of spatial condition management, this has had little effect on the spatio-economic mainport policy as yet. Co-siting, as explained in Box 2.1, might be a suitable instrument for this purpose, but remains predominantly spatial in nature (involving the temporary or permanent leasing/use of fallow land), or is process and environmentally oriented at best (one business's waste is another's raw materials). Closer examination reveals that this instrument is still scarcely used for broader applications such as adapting support facilities or mutually reinforcing business processes, let alone communal learning and innovation processes; nor is it used for the distriparks which have been separately created for the purpose. [Damen 2008] This could be

MAIN/BRAINPORT POLICIES	MAIN ECONOMIC-GEOGRAPHICAL VIEWS			
	Locational	Behavourial	Structural	Relational
Harbour Rotterdam	X	-	-	-
Airport Amsterdam	O	O	-	-
Brainport Eindhoven	X	X	O	-

Brainport/Mainport and relational economic view

X = primary policies
O = affliate policies
bold = explicit focus

related to the fact that the port authority's current institutional-financial setting is still very much quantitative-based. Although proposals were advanced as far back as 1998 to implement a transition from 'a landlord' to a 'mainport manager' kind of operation, [Doe/Schoenmakers in Kreukels/Wever 1998] the Port's income is still largely obtained via the issue/leasing of land and the collection of port charges. [Port Authority Rotterdam 2008] As a result the Port Authority ultimately still remains focused on more freight transits and on more or better land values. Nevertheless, at this moment, two new initiatives have arisen which seem very promising for the intended long-term transition. They also emphasize quality besides to the traditional focus on quantity. The first one is the Research, Design & Manufacturing Initiative on the former wharf of Rotterdamse Droogdok Maatschappij (RDM) involving the Albeda comprehensive school for intermediate vocational education, Rotterdam University of Applied Sciences, the Woonbron Housing Association, the local Government and the Port Authority, backed up by several innovative industries. The objective is 'to encourage a fruitful breeding ground for creative and innovative manufacturing and new energy carriers, through co-operation between companies and knowledge institutions'. [RDM Campus 2008] The second one is the Rotterdam Climate Initiative of Deltalinqs (the representative of some 600 businesses in/around the Harbour), the DCMR Environmental Protection Agency of the Rotterdam region, the local government and the Port Authority, backed up by the Delft University of Technology and the Erasmus University of Rotterdam, to set up a high-tech community for higher education, science, research and industry in the areas of energy transition, climate migration and climate adaptation. [Rotterdam Stadshavens/Rotterdam Climate Initiative 2008] But to make it work, also as a first step towards a broader transition of the whole Harbour Area on the long run, it is acknowledged that the existing structural and institutional setting has to change too. That would not only be confined to a separate status in regulatory and litigation, [Rotterdam 2008] but should also be extended to the basic incentives and incentives of the Port Authority itself. In order to go beyond generic logistical requirements in terms of adequate land and sea accessibility and take a more discriminating, area-specific approach to quality, innovation and sustainability, more of a focus is needed on facilitating cluster development in the aforementioned themes and areas. Examples might include a different income basis by raising tax on added value rather than collecting port charges. In other words co-siting, should also be reflected in co-working and therefore co-earning in order to deal with these issues. In line with the relational spatio-economic perspective, the Port's incentives will need to be placed on a more behavioural and structural footing rather than an exclusively locational one.

Something similar is going on with mainport policy on Schiphol. Here too, policy has been focused for a long time – and recently perhaps to an even greater extent – on safeguarding logistical operations (the Competitive Network) on both the air and land side of the Airport – and on promoting high-grade spatial quality, first and foremost in the transfer function (Airport City), and recently and increasingly as a destination as well (Airport Corridor). To a lesser extent than with the Gateway of Rotterdam, there seems to be a highly ambitious cluster policy here. Nevertheless, although there was initially talk of a distinction between Platform-specific, Schiphol-specific and Schiphol-oriented economic functions, this seems to have been introduced more on a spatial-logistical than on a business basis, and above all in a highly volatile and opportunistic fashion. In addition, it was primarily conceived from the viewpoint of passive, permission-based planning rather than from an active, facilitation and/or development-based planning. More so than with the Gateway of Rotterdam, however, there has been an attempt to develop governance, with an effort being made (sometimes in specific components) to conclude agreements and alliances with stakeholders in public, business and civic society. [Cerfontaine 2006] Even so, this still appears to be primarily informed by Schiphol's own agenda and/or to be government-centred and inside-out, rather than based on a genuine survey and analysis of underlying community or business motivations and the ambitions and associated strategies that these parties may have (outside-in). Thus an effective mainport policy for Schiphol seems increasingly to be falling victim to the prevailing polder mentality of the 'happy medium',[10] as well as to the bottom-up colleague/rival mentality of 'co-operation where necessary and competition where possible'. In view of the analysis in Box 2.2, an unambiguous, all-embracing vision and institutional structure model for Schiphol seems an ever-more remote necessity.

The picture looks different, and in relational terms much more promising, in the case of the spatio-economic policy for Brainport Eindhoven. Here, we can discover a carefully conceived, structurally implemented Triple Helix Planning model, involving close collaboration between government, knowledge institutions and businesses. The brainport concept is not shaped by a mainly government interpretation or concept development, but by the economic transition of a leading TNC – Philips – which, for reasons of its own survival in the harsh global competition, has exchanged a closed innovation model for an open one (see Box 2.3). Internal business strategy adaptations, spin-offs and new alliances and forms of attractiveness to other businesses (start-ups or established players) which are coupled to this have in fact led to a dynamic, self-developing spatio-economic complex that is now referred to as a *Brainport*. Building on this, the recently devised Spatial Program Brainport also expressly starts out from what it describes as a 'relational perspective'. [SRE 2008] However, what is meant by this is not defined in more detail. This is a pity, as the programme quickly reverts to the familiar classic goals of promoting adequate accessibility and ensuring a high quality of life and adequate business locations. Thus, on closer analysis the spatial programme also turns out to have been compiled on an internal government basis by an internal project group of the joint venture in conjunction with a few consultants and representatives of the relevant municipalities

---

10 Main features of this approach are, for instance, the double objective mainport policy of the reworked Fourth Report on Dutch Spatial Planning (VINAC), focusing on economic as well as ecological objectives, but in the end did neither of the two. Another one is the so-called 'compensation strategy', to compensate ongoing aviation development with new tree-planting, amenities or environmental improvements in the surroundings of the airport. It turned out to be an indulgence for unbridled economic development.

and province. The new and highly innovative *open business innovation model* of Philips, for instance, has thus been answered with a traditional, highly *closed spatial planning model* on the part of government, with all the involved lock-ins and traditional planning concepts. The main elements of the ultimate result are thus interchangeable with regional structure plans developed elsewhere, and reflect little of the area-specific dynamics contributed by the alliances between business and knowledge institutions of the Triple Helix. The innovative, competitive aspect in the relational sense used in the foregoing therefore still falls short in relation to what it could become.

Initial conclusions and recommendations

To recapitulate, it can therefore be observed that, despite new insights in (primarily) relationally inspired economic geography, and despite the seemingly new cluster approach of the *White Paper Peaks in de Delta* or *Pieken in de Delta* the current mainport and brainport planning policy in each case still relies on what I call a familiar, classic, 'spatial and infrastructural determinism'. As a result, despite good intentions, it is not just the tie-in with current shifts in the global network economy that is missed. Recent spatio-economic policies on the gateway/main/brainports also remain predominantly focused on quantity and generic growth, and less on a more area-specific and sustainable quality environment in the broad sense (economic, social, political, spatial). On the other hand, at Gateway Rotterdam, Mainport Schiphol and Brainport Eindhoven, new experiments can be pointed out which may establish promising new directions. These could include the original ambitions for the Rotterdam Stadshavens or Cityports (especially with regard to co-siting, the climate initiative and RDM), the first rudimentary steps towards an Airport University at Schiphol and the proposals for new residential and working areas on abandoned agrarian farms near Eindhoven, which have been or are to be released in the near future. For a relational, actor-oriented planning policy, such cases offer chances to come up with new and creative spatial proposals. But to make that happen effectively, a shift is needed from a primary spatial approach to a more actor-specific, cluster and network-oriented approach, with due regard for institutional settings and more facilitating relational planning strategies. Indeed, a fundamental relational turn is needed, explicitly with regard to the following concrete issues.

Develop a genuine behavioural approach of spatial-economic planning Instead of the lip service that is currently paid to the importance of economic clusters in spatial planning and therefore often results in merely a spatial differentiation of a variety of business areas on offer for specific economic sectors, [see also the Spatial Economic Structure Plan Schiphol, REVS 2008] an effective and fruitful cluster approach calls first and foremost for a much more thorough, behavioural firm-related approach. Its basic attitude must be to recognize that – in accordance with evolutionary economic approach – economic development usually hardly shows the emergence of entirely new activities. Instead, these developments are generally rooted in existing firm-related opportunities and potentials on the spot. This requires not only thorough understanding of the spatial factors of the location or node in question (the spatial quality and grade of accessibility), but also thorough insight into the exact (leading) businesses that are already present, their ambitions, goals and development progress, the potential attraction to other companies by sector, culture and size, and the added value that can be achieved in clustering etc. As noted in Box 2.1 and stated by Atzema and Visser, [2005] different orders or regimes occur over here, depending on intensity and added value, ranging from formation, through industries, complex, and alliances towards innovative milieus. Each of these regimes is in fact also asking for precise and individual corresponding 'facilitation strategies' from the part of government, spatial and economic planners, affiliate organizations or other institutions. That said, it means also that an exclusive focus on intermediate organizations (such as the Chamber of Commerce, Sector or Businesses Representatives, Confederations of Industries and Employers etc.) is generally useless or at its best facilitating. In order to stimulate a fruitful and innovative cluster-approach, the central focus is and should be on the individual (leading) firms, which are willing and capable to invest in their economic, institutional, spatial etc. surroundings; this by the way out of pure self-interest.

Refocus especially on the structural and institutional settings

Second, the previous cases make clear that, despite good intentions, they often fail to achieve their original intentions. Further research shows that this has much to do with the underlying forces, lock-ins and institutional settings in which the proposed spatial-economic developments take place. [Granovetter 1985, Boschma 2002, see also Box 2.1, 2.2 and 2.3] If the final and ultimate incentives of a particular company or organization (such as the Port of Rotterdam for example) are determined by quantitative criteria (such as the size of the flow of goods or the issuance of business areas), then an exclusive focus on quality or added value has little chance of success. The same situation applies at the mainport Schiphol Airport, but in a different way. Currently that airport company derives its revenues primarily from affiliate activities of the original core aviation businesses, and its organization has thus seen a major transition and refocus on goals and ambitions in the last few years; with all the new actor-networks and pressure on former successful regimes involved. It has resulted in a growing competition with the surrounding development departments of the municipalities of Amsterdam and in some way Haarlemmermeer and Aalsmeer. A spatial-economic strategy that is not aware of these fundamental changes and underlying driving/competing forces, or is not more precisely focused on a simultaneous transition of the involved institutional settings, will not be very effective or robust. This therefore not only concerns the regulation and litigation, law and sanctions, and/or rescaling and reordering of governments (as often proposed) but also and especially the (financial) incentives and settlements, exact responsibilities, method of dealing and wheeling, and shared norms and values in the way of doing business etc. That these settings are crucial, also in evolutionary terms, is shown by Hall and Soskice when they emphasize that Transnational Corporations aren't at all uniform, but adapt their specific organization and strategies to the situation in which they operate. [Hall/Soskice 2001, p.56] The absence of such detailed insights into the bulk of the current economic geographic planning strategies, make them hopelessly obsolete and outdated. In order to regain a potentially successful spatial-economic policy in these times of globalization and even crises, it is necessary to account more clearly for an effective interaction between the proposed strategy and the exact suitable institutional setting that should fit and support them. More than generic measures or rules, precise and targeted regimes are consistently and increasingly involved.

Reinvent the importance of spatial notions in the relational economic geography Third, it is remarkable how little spatial economic plans around the Gateway, Mainport and Brainport, but also elsewhere (such as industrial policy), reflect the actual economic insight or the ambition and drive of leading companies. That is most manifest at Brainport Eindhoven, where the open innovation model from Philips is spatially mirrored by a more or less closed, government-centric spatial planning perspective embracing old, traditional plan concepts and an abundance of seemingly no viable government ambitions. Against this background, it is not surprising that leading firms begin to consider spatial planning no longer an issue of importance; room for space is or is not available. If necessary it will be self-fulfilling (as in the case of the High-Tech Campus), otherwise, and if possible, the activities will be moved elsewhere. But that is based on criteria other than spatial ones. This is in fact detrimental to the actual relational meaning and value of space previously mentioned. Nevertheless, the connotation of place also gets its spatial appearances. Furthermore, design explorations show that it is possible to reintegrate a more behavioural approach and/or regulatory and institutional settings into new and innovative spatial planning proposals. [ACE 2005, Hauben 2007, Agro & Co 2008] At this moment, however, these explorations occur mainly in the cultural and creative niches of real economic reality. Better adherence to the underlying motives and ambitions of leading firms is needed, because then the relational turn in economic geography will be supported by the relational meaning and value of spatial proposals. In that case, however, spatial planning will become ensuing, instead of steering; it is facilitating, instead of setting conditions. It needs a proactive stance of spatial planners beyond the confines of their own expertises and an involvement in the underlying behaviours of firms, and an involvement in a new fit of institutional settings and the specific (spatial) regimes which go with that.

BOX [2.1]

Rotterdam: from staple port to mainport and further

The generation and development of the Rotterdam Mainport is often explained in terms of its location and the strategic position it occupies with regard to the developing western European hinterland. Recently, the Mainport strategy of Rotterdam was still geared to retaining its lead as the deepest seaport in Western Europe, strengthening its hinterland connections via road, water and rail, and the further development of new space for expansion: 1st Maasvlakte, 2nd Maasvlakte… However, on second thoughts, it turns out that in the history of this mainport, the extraordinary entanglement of the political elite and a larger group of enterprising citizens, as well as the institutional positions that thereby developed, were the conclusive factors. Nowadays the situation has radically changed. Large transnational corporations and globally-operating ship-owners currently dominate maritime transport & distribution, while the port authority itself is still predominantly locally structured and generates its income from issuing land and port dues. If we also wish to be able to come to a robust, supported and innovative port development in the future, then this global-local setting must be radically reviewed. A new affiliation is desired among maritime actors, the institutional context and cross-over strategies, based on quality instead of quantity incentives.

The merchant elite

Until the second half of the 19th century, just like many other ports, Rotterdam was a staple port managed by a powerful and closed merchant elite of leading entrepreneurs in trade, shipping, deposit banking and assurance. They were an essential link in the pre-industrial logistics system, where, at their own expense and risk, they purchased goods and subsequently traded them in the Netherlands and abroad. In Rotterdam, this was a well-ordered, limited number of families, which gradually took on all the characteristics of a patriarchy through marriage, business (part) interests and association memberships.[Callahan 1981] Moreover, characteristic of this merchant elite was that they – other than the traders for example – did not seek out trade but remained at the staple location because the goods flows and all buyers and sellers would come around in any case. In other words, although they were merchants, they were thoroughly rooted in that place. The international trade was heavily monopolized via the East India and West India Companies (EIC & WIC) and in the wide surroundings there were only a few well-equipped and accessible maritime ports, so this system was able to prosper. Thus they were against free Rhine transport and, after the economic downturn during the Batavian Republic, they tried to consolidate the original power base by restoring the system of the traditional staple locations. Nevertheless, the economic, political and institutional context had substantially changed in the meantime. Not only was the WIC already defunct by 1792 due to a lack of funding and falling income, the VOC was also nationalized in 1796.[Gaastra 2002] At the same time, England and Prussia – certainly after the separation of Belgium in 1830 – increasingly determined the margins of Dutch trade politics. Moreover, Western European industrialization was slowly but

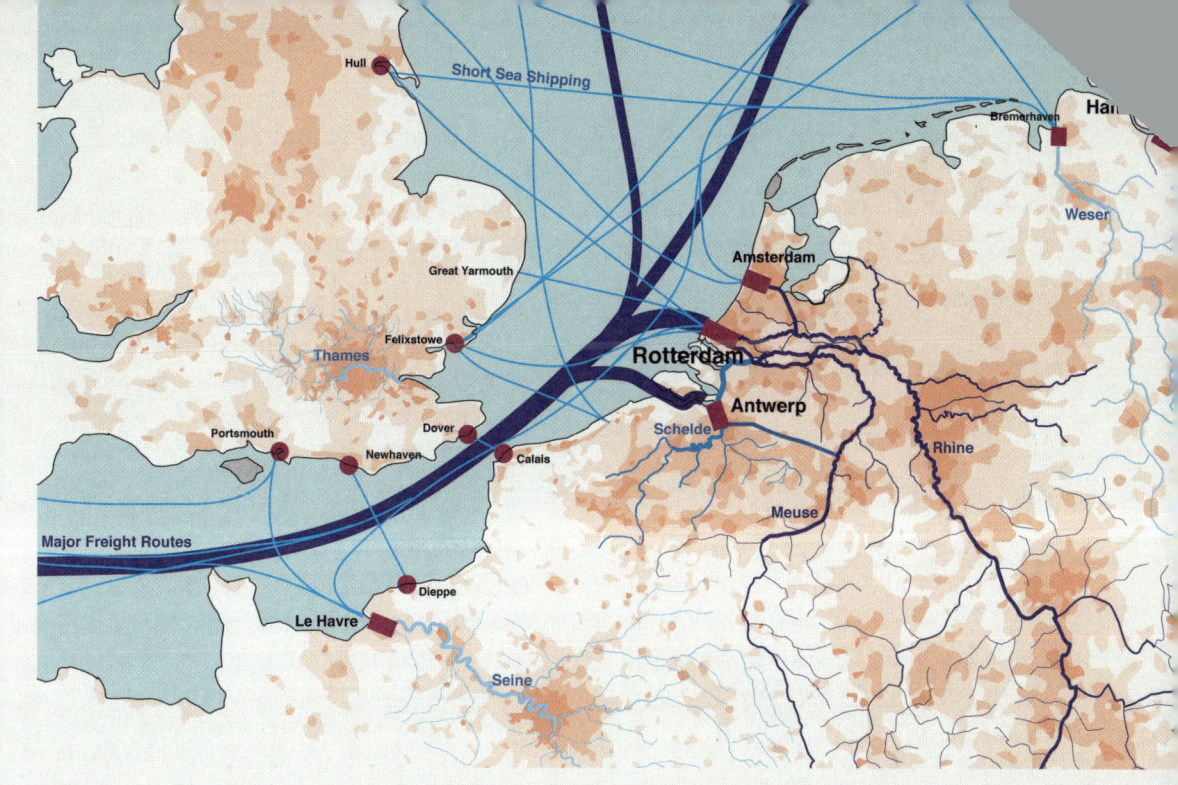

Geographical advantages of North West European harbours

surely gaining form. The obvious economic hinterland of Rotterdam increasingly began to shift from its northern orientation to the Dutch trading and production cities via the Rotte and Schie rivers, to a more eastern orientation via the Rhine and Meuse toward the upcoming industrialization in the Ruhr area and the Walloon coal basin.

In this configuration there arose new strategic actors who recognized the unique position of Rotterdam in the EuroDelta and wished to utilize it in contemporary fashion. The entrepreneurs in the upcoming German hinterland had in fact an increasing interest in transporting raw materials and end products freely and as quickly as possible to customers at home and abroad, unhindered and with as few as possible middlemen. To avoid route-dependent behaviour, new, leading entrepreneurs were again needed from outside the community. These, 'fantasy boys', as they were affectionately branded by Van der Mandele, were, in contrast to their predecessors, modern and well-educated and also newcomers to the Rotterdam economic elite: the originally east European businessman Lodewijk Pincoffs, D.G. van Beuningen from Utrecht, the accountant Willem van der Vorm from IJsselmonde, the Ouderkerk shipowner Willem Ruys, the Zegwaart bookkeeper Albert Goudriaan, etc., This does not diminish the fact that although they also received partial support from the established order (Marten Mees, the Chabot brothers, Engel Pieter de Monchy, among others) – the intended transition from staple to transit certainly did not proceed without resistance. Indeed, it had enormous economic and local political implications, where established positions were broken down and new ones developed; with at the same time an important revolution in the spatial-physical course of the city.

Spatial, economic and civic embeddedness

Broadly described, the arduous leap to Rotterdam south, ultimately also meant fraudulent practices, the bankruptcy of the building and trade monopolies in the south (Lodewijk Pincoffs, and others) and loss of face for the allied port barons, including above all Mees, Van der Mandele, Van Beuningen and others. [see for instance Van de Laar/ Jaarsveld 2004] Nonetheless, from the 1880s onwards, the first modern harbour basins were constructed at Feijenoord, where goods were first of all quickly and efficiently and transhipped from over the sea to inland navigation and *vice versa* via the wharves (Binnen, Spoor and Rijnhaven), but later also via the river (Waalhaven). At the same time, the port concentrated increasingly on petrochemicals, shipbuilding and strategic storage. In the 20th century, it grew into the largest – and is nowadays the second largest – port in the world. Three functions in particular were the foundations for this development: transit (logistics and later containers), strategic storage (of raw materials, grain, crude oil, etc.) and processing (petrochemicals, shipbuilding, etc.). Furthermore, there was a strong supporting financial sector (banking, assurance and insurance). The port of Rotterdam derived its strength from six goods flows (crude oil, coal, liquid fuels, basic chemicals, iron ore and containers). These six flows still currently constitute 90% of the supply and dispatch flows in the Rotterdam port. [Havenbedrijf Rotterdam BV 2008]

However, this development was not only due to the logistics strategy and an excellent geographic location with respect to the booming German hinterland. This would not explain why Amsterdam, Dordrecht, Vlissingen, Bergen op Zoom or other ports in the EuroDelta hardly passed through such

Physical growth of Rotterdam

a comparable development. The capacity of several leading Rotterdam port entrepreneurs to take quick initiatives and their network-oriented enterprise also played important roles. In the words of Plate: 'They were almost all enterprising, energetic chaps'. [Plate 1934] Furthermore, they were able not only to make and maintain effective relationships with their colleagues in the 'global foreshore' (like Plate himself, Rijckevorsel and Ruys), but also with those in the West European hinterland (including Van Stolk, Van Der Vorm, Van Beuningen, etc.). Whereas in Amsterdam it was primarily the line shipowners who fulfilled a crucial role and in Antwerp it was the stevedores who were a driving force, in Rotterdam, according to Paul van der Laar, this was primarily the relatively new and modern ship-brokers: entrepreneurs who were engaged in the transfer and storage of cargoes. [Van der Laar 2004] Originally, these ship-brokers were still located close to the traditional merchants, but after industrialization had brought about a separation in function between merchants and shipping companies, the ship-brokers provided mainly services to the latter. For these shipowners they organized the loading and unloading of the vessels, the storage and transport of the goods and furthermore, sometimes also provisioning, or mediating with any necessary ship repairs. The effectiveness and speed with which this occurred gave the port of Rotterdam a crucial lead over its West European competitors. Moreover, successful ship-brokers also ultimately exploited their knowledge of cargoes and navigation and they themselves occasionally combined the ship-broker's profession with a shipping company.

At the same time, the port barons were also able to embed their enterprises relatively well in the (institutional) context of Rotterdam. In the example of the traditional merchant patriarchy, this manifested itself not only in the maintenance of good relations with and inside politics and society. The modern port barons also played a prominent role in the social and cultural life of the city. Major urban projects, such as museums, the Blijdorp zoo, the Kuip (Feijenoord football stadium), the HBS and later Erasmus University, the Havenziekenhuis hospital, various (social) housing projects, fountains and plaza improvements, were realized by or with the assistance of the port barons. [see also de Goey 1990] According to Han Meyer, there was also a strong civic culture in Rotterdam as a factor in the social styling of the relations between the city and port. [Meyer 1996] Len de Klerk, in turn, emphasized the governance significance of this collective entrepreneurial mentality, where civic leadership in the areas of cultural and social welfare is also viewed as the duty of an urban and economic elite. Besides obvious economic and profit motives (a healthy and happy worker achieves better results and revolutionary tendencies are stifled at birth), according to de Klerk, this was also driven by unorthodox ideas about faith and religion, the liberal-philosophical notions of the responsible citizen, the rational-scientific belief in progress, an enlightened self-interest to do good works and the constitutional idea that collective awareness was a private and not a public matter. [De Klerk 1998] Whatever it was, due to this attitude not only economically, but also culturally, socially and psychologically, a close bond was exhibited between the port and Rotterdam society. Despite the progressive expansion of the port towards the west and progressive specialization, functional classification and fading (via computerization) employment perspectives, the port, partly due to this, was a typical *Rotterdam* port with broad support from the population and magistrates.

Unknown grain merchant in 1755

Lodewijk Pincoffs, a new harbour baron in 1866

Wei Jaifu, new CEO of Cosco Shipping in 2007

New tasks

Perhaps Len de Klerk [1998] as an objective historian did not wish to bind conclusions to this, yet he seems to establish, with some disapproval, that this broad social practice of the Rotterdam port barons after the Second World War, and particularly from the nineteen-sixties onward, began to diminish considerably. Supported by the planning structures established by the Nazi occupiers, the government now drew strongly on the social goals and legal and budgetary frameworks; and this was not only in the area of house building, but also – mindful of Milton Keynes – in many social areas. In Rotterdam, this was expressed in an increasingly greater involvement of at first the municipal and later also the national government, with the reconstruction and expansion of the port. Especially from the end of the fifties onward, many thought themselves capable of dictating the development of not only house building, but also the division of the economic activities, port development and the affliate infrastructure. [Kreukels/Wever 1998, Van de Laar/Jaarsveld 2004] This resulted in *Plan 2000+* of 1969, with extension of the port at the Hoekse Waard and Voorne-Putten, and a complete new city at Goeree Overflakkee. Meanwhile, it has nevertheless been shown that this same government has not or cannot entirely live up to these overblown expectations in the field of economic development, port activities and welfare. The *Plan 2000+* very quickly encountered wide and massive social resistance and the oil crises of the 1970s also implied a tempering of the enormous post-war transhipment growth. In the meantime, it also became clear that this government-centred reconstruction period was no more than just a temporary hiccup in a longer history of socially responsible Delta citizenship. The port authority was consequently privatized in 2004, although the municipal and national governments are still the only stockholders. This does alter the fact that that even in this situation, a return to the practices and projects of port barons cannot easily occur.

Influenced by progressive internationalization and networking, important port entrepreneurs themselves are now 'globalized' to an increasing extent (Shell, Vopak, RVS, etc.), or have become part of a larger Trans National Corporation (Maersk, Cosco, Lyondell, Huntsman, etc.). These large port concerns, which have branches all over the world, are chiefly focused on a much more globally oriented decision-making structure, or have become directly dependent on decisions taken at head offices elsewhere in the world.

Second, the port itself has increasingly become a network of sundry activities that extend ever further, beyond the formal

Local projects of the barons [Van de Laar 2002]

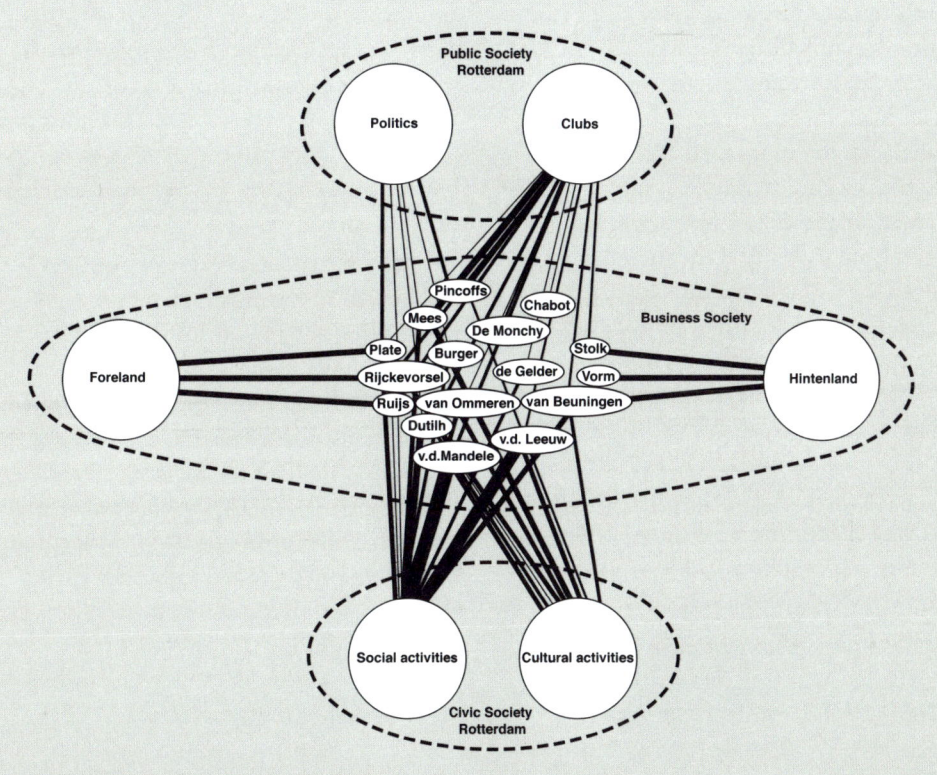

Relations of the harbour barons [Van de Laar 2002]

65

terrain managed by the port authority. Van Klink [1995] refers to the enormous hinterland networks of the port and to participations or representations elsewhere in the world. However, on the other hand, the shipping companies have themselves become huge due to mergers, strategic purchases and evolutionary development, and now have branches all over the world. The ports can consequently be played out against each other.

Third, and partly connected with this, there is talk of a managerial revolution nowadays. With this idea, which was introduced during the Second World War by James Burnham, [1941] there is an allusion to the increasing separation of managers and capital providers in large concerns. Although many of these predictions seem to be considerably exaggerated, instead of a director-owner, the power of decision over a large concern nowadays is divided among a CEO, the Board of Directors, specific stockholders (sometimes the original owners) and managers of hedge funds, which are increasingly playing a questionable role in the take-over and/or splitting up of large concerns and even in the recent financial crisis.

Finally, influenced by increasing global competition, the profit margins of logistics entrepreneurs have been greatly marginalized. There is less and less money to be earned by transit. Storage, transhipment and transit have become commodities – services that can be purchased anywhere in all their variations – due to which the transport function of the port, apart from the distribution function, no longer offers many new or unique development opportunities. [Welters & De Langen 2004]

The (direct) merits of the Rotterdam port are thus declining, the regional burdens have increased, resulting in a fading social support for its operations. In recent years, many people have also pointed out the necessity for a powerful change of course within the logistics sector, [see, among others, Van Laarhoven 2006] while the city of Rotterdam and the Port Authority, besides being a fast and safe port, seem to be increasingly aiming at themes like becoming a more all-round, sustainable, knowledge-innovative, attractive and clean port. [Gemeente Rotterdam/Havenbedrijf Rotterdam 2004] However, the Port Authority takes its income largely from leasing and/or issuing land and collecting port dues. Within the Port Authority itself, there is hardly any (financial) incentive to abandon a progressive quantity policy in favour of a more subtle quality policy. Moreover, there do not seem to be new players (the so-called 'fantasy boys' of oldtimes) immediately available to break through the present lock-in of the primarily logistics-oriented port activities; certainly not yet players who are embedded in the 'Rotterdam Delta culture'. Perhaps they are the new, upcoming players on the alternative energy market, possibly in relation to recycling or in environmental housekeeping. However, a close interrelationship with the sociocultural, sociopolitical and possibly spatial problems of the region is not (yet) in order.

Co-siting – new perspective?

This does not diminish the fact that – from the viewpoint of an effective lack of space – a new strategy has now been developed which, provided it is more widely applied, can possibly give a boost to the renewal and added value of the logistics system and thereby the international competitive strength of the port: co-siting. This strategy was originally intended to induce sitting companies to (temporarily or not) deploy their spare and optional space in lease contracts for other or new companies, in order to utilize the available space in the

port more effectively. Moreover, it can also have an environmental-hygienic effect because, due to their mutual proximity, residual or waste substances from one company can be more effectively utilized as raw materials for another. An example of this is the use of CO_2 in cultivation under glass, excess heat from the power station of EON-Benelux in, e.g., the Happy Shrimp Farm, and the mutual exchange of raw/waste materials between companies like Lyondell, Bayer, Hutchinson, etc. The question is, however, whether these mutual interactions can also ultimately obtain economic and (thereby) social embedding. According to the theory, reinforcing (vertical, diagonal, horizontal and lateral) interactions between companies may not only make a powerful contribution to the 'stickiness of the place', [Markussen 1996] but possibly (over time) may also increase mutual learning capacity and innovative strength, and result in extra added value. Five regional cluster processes are distinguished by Atzema & Visser [2005] in this case:
• *Formation*, clustering based on dominant location factors such as a quay;
• *Industrie*, clustering based on cost savings in transport, personnel, etc.;
• *Complex*, clustering based on strengthening cohesion in the production chain;
• *Alliance*, clustering also based on social, institutional and administrative bonds;
• *Milieu*, clustering based on second-order collective learning processes and innovation).

The hypothesis behind this scheme is that the further we go in the cluster process, the stronger the 'stickiness of the place', i.e., the embedding in the environment, and the greater the added value can become. The economic geographer Boschma points out, however, besides geographic proximity, the importance of cognitive, social, institutional and organizational proximity, which

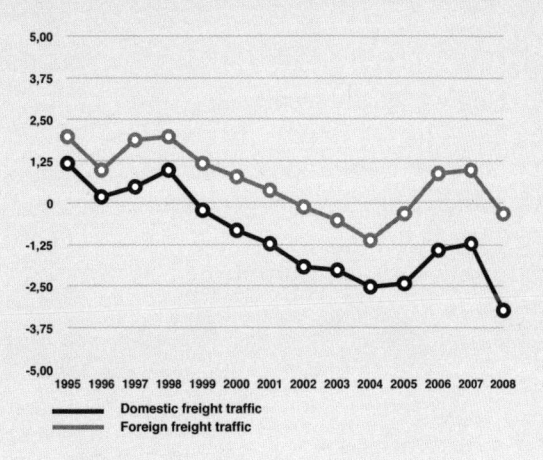

Average cost-effectiveness of Dutch road freight traffic 1995-2008 (NEA 2008)

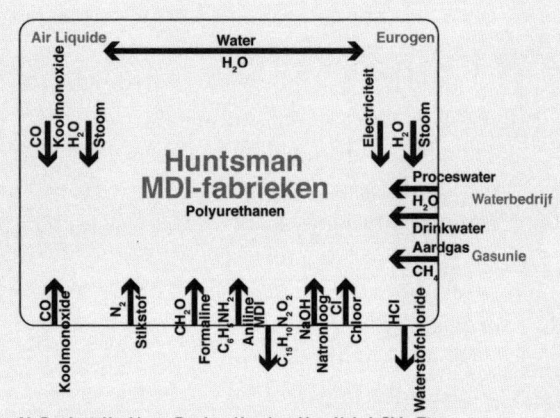

Co-siting (Industrial Imaging)

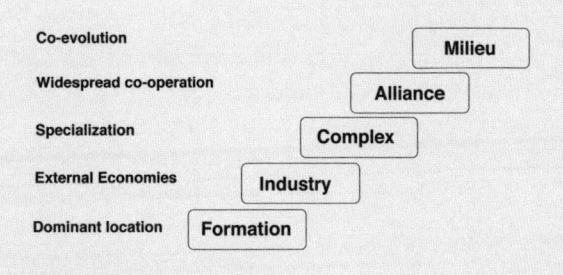

Regional cluster prototypes [Atzema 2004]

Europoort
Scheurweg
260 wp.

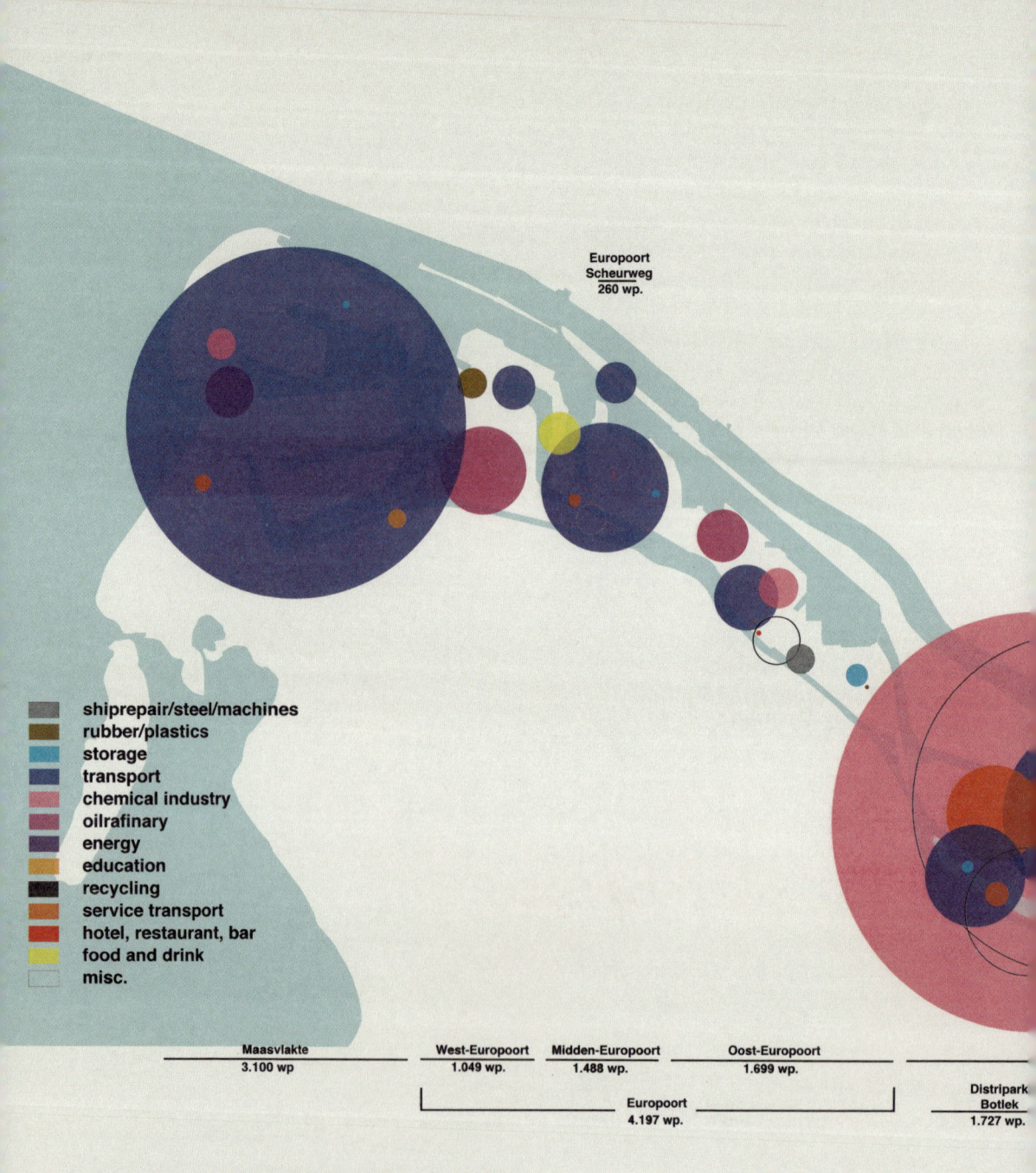

- shiprepair/steel/machines
- rubber/plastics
- storage
- transport
- chemical industry
- oilrafinary
- energy
- education
- recycling
- service transport
- hotel, restaurant, bar
- food and drink
- misc.

Maasvlakte
3.100 wp

West-Europoort
1.049 wp.

Midden-Europoort
1.488 wp.

Oost-Europoort
1.699 wp.

Europoort
4.197 wp.

Distripark
Botlek
1.727 wp.

Number of employees per sector (Bedrijvenregister Zuid-Holland)

68 **Main and brainport planning 2.0** BOX [2.1]

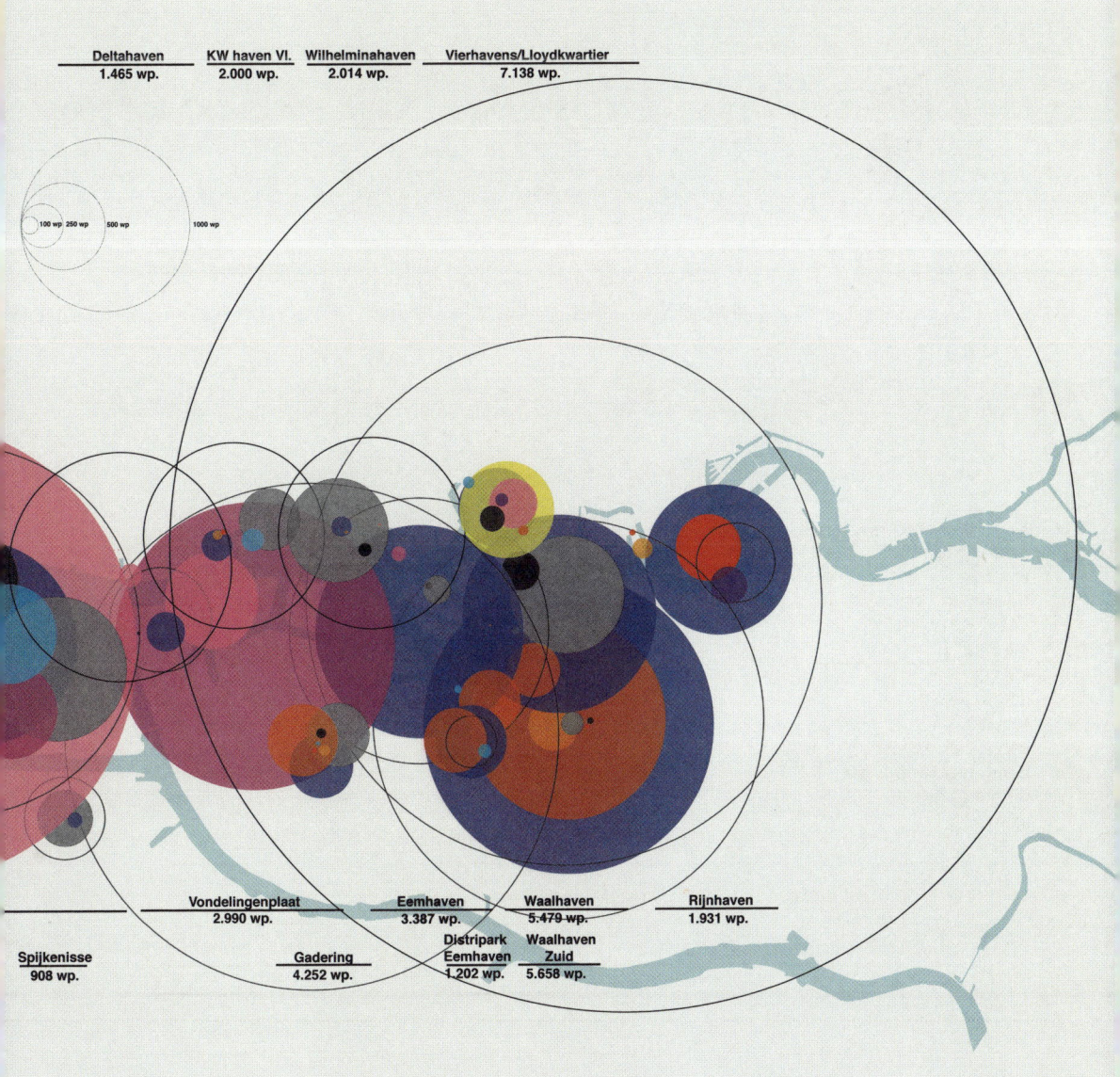

Deltahaven	KW haven VI.	Wilhelminahaven	Vierhavens/Lloydkwartier
1.465 wp.	2.000 wp.	2.014 wp.	7.138 wp.

100 wp 250 wp 500 wp 1000 wp

Spijkenisse	Vondelingenplaat	Gadering	Eemhaven	Distripark Eemhaven	Waalhaven	Waalhaven Zuid	Rijnhaven
908 wp.	2.990 wp.	4.252 wp.	3.387 wp.	1.202 wp.	5.479 wp.	5.658 wp.	1.931 wp.

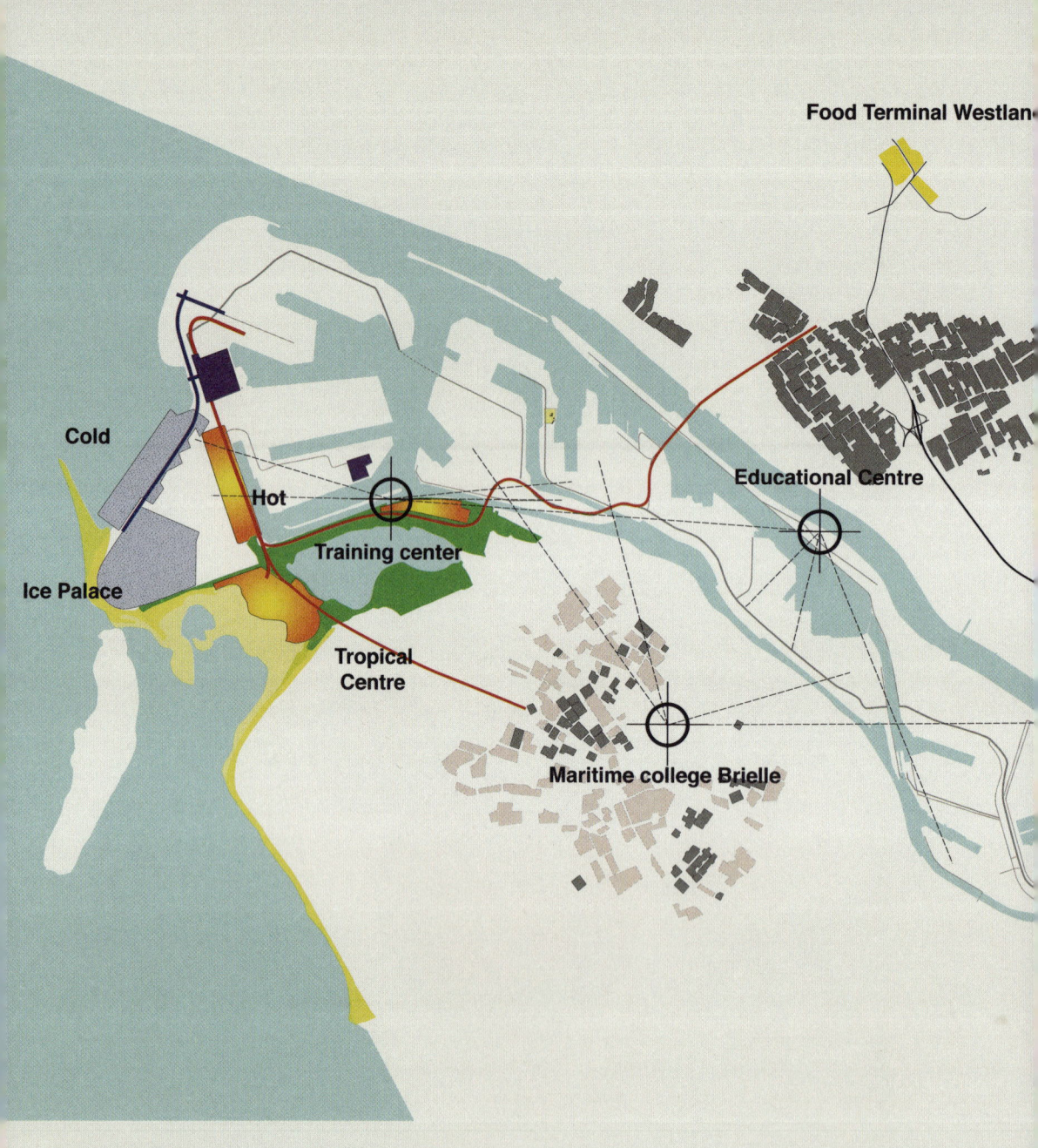

Chances for the harbour

70 **Main and brainport planning 2.0** BOX [2.1]

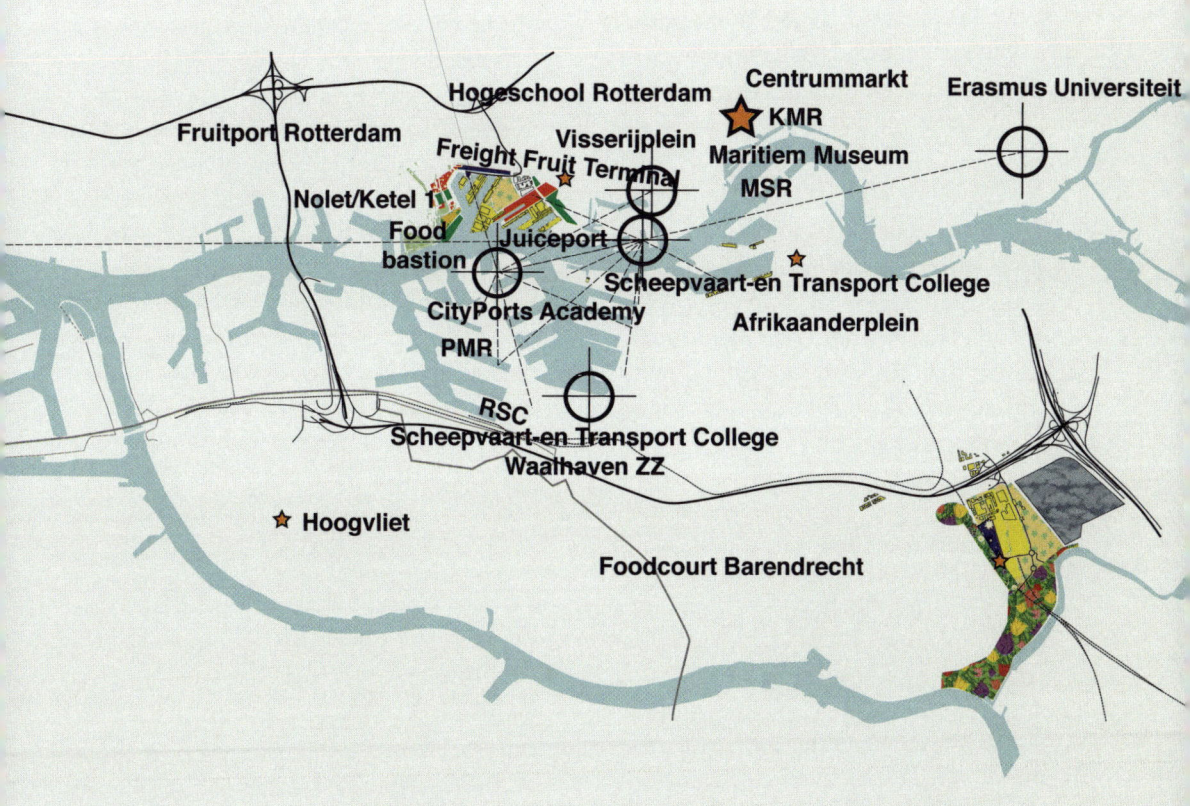

Fruitport Rotterdam
Hogeschool Rotterdam
Centrummarkt
Erasmus Universiteit
Visserijplein
KMR
Freight Fruit Terminal
Maritiem Museum
Nolet/Ketel 1
MSR
Food bastion
Juiceport
Scheepvaart-en Transport College
CityPorts Academy
Afrikaanderplein
PMR
RSC
Scheepvaart-en Transport College
Waalhaven ZZ
Hoogvliet
Foodcourt Barendrecht

Urban Docklands/Stadshavens (Stadshavens)

can be organized into networks at a distance in different ways. Too much and too little proximity between economic actors in these areas can also have a negative effect on learning and innovation, and there are always new solutions conceivable for each of these areas. [Boschma 2005a]

This does not alter the fact that further research into the intensity of collaboration between companies in the port complex of Rotterdam has shown that this often goes no further than the *complex* cluster type and often remains stuck at that of the level of *formation* or *industrie*. [Damen 2008] The ambition to make the port of Rotterdam also a knowledge-oriented, innovative and attractive port, next to a transit port, is still far from becoming reality. The sole exception to this is possibly the urban ports project of Rotterdam and particularly the proposed Research, Design & Manufacturing Campus or the Innovation Dock. On this former shipyard of the Rotterdamse Droogdok Maatschappij, the aim is to promote an innovative and creative manufacturing industry in Rotterdam via collaboration between companies and knowledge institutions, with a focus on innovations in sustainable building, mobility and sustainable energy transition. For the time being, however, this project still has to prove itself, since at the time of writing the first students from the Rotterdam Academy and the Albeda College have just moved into the Campus. The extent to which interaction between knowledge, business development and regional embeddedness can actually take place is still questionable, since the pioneering function is the central focus and a physical incentive (such as the Natlab at the High-Tech Campus, see Box 2.3) is lacking. Furthermore, the Port Authority keeps – although they for the time being claim otherwise – its financial incentives of port dues and land issue, and is therefore still focussed on quantity and not quality, via an alternative betterment levy on added value, for example. Thus, to bring about a change in the spatial-economic development of the harbour, planning of that complex seems to have possibly become less a matter for the designers and infrastructure or building fetishists, but more that of effective negotiators, alliance brokers and evolutionary (environment) embedders, supported by an adequate and thereby attached transition of the institutional system. To deal with the exisiting problems and ambitions of harbour development, spatial planning has to reinvent itself.

Impressions of new cross-overs

Constructing + exposition

Energy + leisure

Recycling + art

Chemical + lifescience

BOX [2.2]

Schiphol: Airport planning in actor-network constellations

Another example. Because, with respect to mainport Schiphol, too, we can recognize fundamental changes in actor-network relationships and hence a need to approach this mainport from another relational spatial planning perspective. Originally there was indeed a relatively simple airstrip, with a relatively clear and strong coalition of leading pioneering actors, in part associated with the public sector and local/national governments. Moreover, each of them served key components of the emerging aviation sector: industry, carrier and terminal. With the recent deregulation, privatization, networking and increasing environmental pressures, however, mutual relations became more complex and shifted fundamentally. Therefore new spatial strategies are also needed to meet these new actor-network relationships.

Pioneering actor-networks

In the pioneer stage of Schiphol Airport, there were three prominent and decisive actor networks. The first one was Anthony Fokker – the Flying Dutchman and aeroplane builder – who provided the sector with the best wooden and linen airplanes one could get around and after the First World War. At that time he owned several aircraft maintenance service buildings, with headquarters in Amsterdam, Veere and New York. In the twenties and first half of the thirties, Fokker dominated the European Market and captured 40% of the American market. Moreover, when Donald Douglas introduced his metal planes, Fokker received the right to be the first European representative for the Douglas Aircraft Company. In this way, he accomplished a prominent role in the airplane industry until he died in 1939. [Wennekes 1993]

The second one was Albert Plesman, a first lieutenant who had received his military pilot's license in 1917 and convinced his superiors to organize the First Airline Exhibition in Amsterdam in 1918. This exhibition proved to be a big success. Nearly 1 million people attended, all costs were met, and the colonial Kingdom of the Netherlands presented itself as a prominent aviation nation at one fell swoop. Moreover, Plesman managed to convince attending Rotterdam harbour barons like Van Beuningen, Fentener van Vlissingen, Kröller and others to invest in the foundation of a Dutch airline. The Dutch government also backed this initiative. Queen Wilhelmina even gave this airline her royal blessing. And so it happened that in 1919 Plesman became the first CEO of the Royal Dutch Airline for the Netherlands and Colonies; in Dutch KLM. [Dierikx et al. 1999]

The third one was Jan Dellaert, a military officer like Albert Plesman. In 1921 – when the Dutch military air department moved its operation to airbase Soesterberg – Plesman convinced Dellaert to become stationmaster on behalf of KLM. Soon the new station manager started to build a finely equipped serviced airport building, air-control tower and the first paved landing strip in Europe. In the meantime, however, the municipality of Amsterdam also became interested in the airport, because it assumed that Schiphol could contribute to the economic growth of the city. As aviation is a costly business, the national government did not mind involving more investors. So in 1926 Amsterdam became responsible for the maintenance of Schiphol. This was emphasized by Dellaert's switch from stationmaster on behalf of KLM to airport manager on behalf of the capital city. With the Olympic games of 1928 being held in Amsterdam, Dellaert in turn convinced the municipality to invest a great deal of money in Schiphol, in order to strengthen its leading role within Europe even further. [Bouwens & Dierikx, 1997]

Robust Alliances?

Next to the fact that the Netherlands was still a major colonial empire with economic, political and military networks worldwide at that time, it was precisely this effective association between an aeroplane builder (Fokker), airline company (Plesman) and airport operator (Dellaert) on the one hand, and the local and national authority on the other, which made the Dutch aviation sector very prosperous. Of course they had their quarrels and disagreements, but they also recognized the mutual benefits of co-operation. Thus, during the thirties, Schiphol became one of the best equipped airports in Europe, while at the same time the Fokker company (partly in co-operation with DAC) conquered Europe and America with its aeroplanes. In turn, KLM became one of the biggest and most reliable airline companies in the world. Before the Second World War, it had already built up an extensive intercontinental network, especially on routes between Europe and South-east Asia (especially with the former colonies). Moreover, after the war, this association between aviation pioneers and local/national governments remained strong as it evolved into a driving force for the planning and building of the new Schiphol in the 1960s. It became one of the most modern and logistically effective airports in the world at the time,

Anthony Fokker

Albert Plesman

Jan Dellaert

with separate passenger flows on separate floors going in and out, central baggage claim areas, airline and custom services in the centre, and flexible airplane slabs at the gates. In the meantime, like KLM and Fokker, Schiphol had also turned into a Stock Corporation: The Schiphol Group Inc. It provided the more or less informal *aviation association* of KLM, Schiphol and Fokker, with enough playing fields to cope with upcoming globalization, backed up by the leading public authorities. The total amount of passengers grew from approximately 350,000 a year in 1950 to more than 10 million in 1980; while KLM grew to become one of the main airlines in the world, with approximately 1 million passengers a year in the 1980s.

At that time, however, the spatial-economic planners showed increasing interest in Schiphol. Before that, of course planners used different zoning regulations, issued building permits and realized several links on the landside (road and rail) in order to improve passenger flows and diminish the effect of the growing murmur from the environment on aircraft noise and air quality. But airport planning remained first and foremost a military matter, and later the subject of mainly logistical planning, driven exclusively by the Ministry of Transport and Water Management. From the mid-eighties, however, this started to change because the Netherlands was one of the first countries to express a spatial-economic policy with regard to airports, giving Schiphol – in addition to the port of Rotterdam – an important role in the development and competitive growth of the regional and national economy. Although this initiative received much aviation and business support, it remained predominantly an internally oriented governmental co-ordination strategy. This was also due to the fact that, from that moment on, the informal aviation association, which had hitherto been the driving force behind Schiphol's development, fell apart into separate actor-network arenas in the domains of airline, airport and air region.

Competitive Airline Network

A competitive airline network is the most important factor in order to maintain a central position in the world. Until recently, many nation states have been heavily involved in the development of these national and international aviation networks, still largely as the result of the Paris Convention following the First World War. This changed in 1978, when the United States of America under the Carter Administration enacted the Airline Deregulation Act on the 24th of October. [Bouwens & Dierikx, 1997] The aim of this act was to trigger competitiveness and, by doing so, reduce airfares and promote economic development. Airlines could now go for slots issued by the national government. All of a sudden prime national airlines, which could hide behind the big backs (read: *subsidies*) of national governments until that time, had to deal with a fierce competition. At a number of major carriers, it led to heavy losses and conflicts with labour unions, and in some cases even to bankruptcy and liquidation. But it also led to a reduction of airfares by approximately 30% between 1978 and 1990, and *mutatis mutandis* to an enormous rise of passenger and cargo loads especially on busy routes. [Barnum, 1998] Moreover it gave a boost to the global network economy at the same time. Therefore, after a while, the EU also decided to deregulate the market gradually. This happened from 1987 until 1997. Slowly but surely international competitiveness emerged within the aviation sector. [Hakfoort & Schaafsma, 2000, Burghouwt & Huys, 2003]

In this fierce global battle, only those airlines who were able to adapt to the new demands of the competitive aviation sector could survive. In this respect KLM and Schiphol had major advantages. As a result of the relatively small national catchment area, KLM had already set up a kind of hub and spoke system in the sixties, in order to ensure adequate support for its route coverage. In addition, KLM was the first airline to enter successfully an open skies agreement with Northwest Airlines, leading to a domination of the transatlantic market and a huge expansion of the network destinations served, while reducing costs substantially.

During the nineties, however, other carriers also started to recognize the benefits of this network co-operation and began to implement the basic principles of this hub-and-spoke system themselves. In doing so, they could also profit from scale-advantages, which in themselves promoted the development of big world alliances. At this moment, it has led to three dominating global airline alliances – Skyteam, Oneworld and Star Alliance – with a global market share of approximately 60% in 2005. To survive in this battle of global giants, KLM eventually had to merge with Air France. And although agreements have made sure that the hub status of Schiphol is temporarily assured, [van Wijk, 2006] the smooth twin-coalition Schiphol/KLM is not so obvious anymore, while KLM, like Air France, is currently becoming increasingly 'footloose' to orientate itself to a dual, triple or even multiple-hub strategy.

Moreover, no-frills airlines (so-called low-cost or low-fare carriers) entered the scene in the meantime, offering cheap point-to-point services on former niche routes. These carriers are not only less dependent on hub airports, but also provide cutthroat competition to the full-service airlines on their continental origin-destination network. As a result, besides hub-and-spoke, they introduced also point-to-point, double hub, wheel and spoke, co-ordinated chain and random schedule structures. [Burghouwt 2005] It means that the mainport Schiphol has not only lost its obvious home-carrier connection (of KLM), but also has to deal with at this moment some eighty carriers – each of them with their specific networks, slot demands and terminal strategies.

Finally, due to the deregulation and cut-down prices, the number of passengers and the number of flights to and from Schiphol also quadrupled towards some 45 million and 450,000 respectively in the last year. And although growth is showing cut-backs due to the current financial and economic crises, it has already placed a heavy environmental burden on the inhabitants and working places in the direct surroundings. In turn, these 'locals' evolved into professionally organized and sophisticated countervailing powers to an unbridled aviation development. To avoid stalemate, the government installed the so-called 'Alders tafel', in which civic and environmental parties, along with the aviation sector and involved governmental departments, make deals about the future framework of the airport. The outcome shows a wide range of specific deals with civic parties and carriers, environmental organizations and governments, between airports and/or governments and governments, each of which has an enormous impact on the future competitive network of Schiphol. [de Jong 2009, forthcoming]

Competitive Airport

Secondly, airports originally only housed a few airplane facilities for maintenance and repair; because it was indeed quite often that the planes reached the other side of the

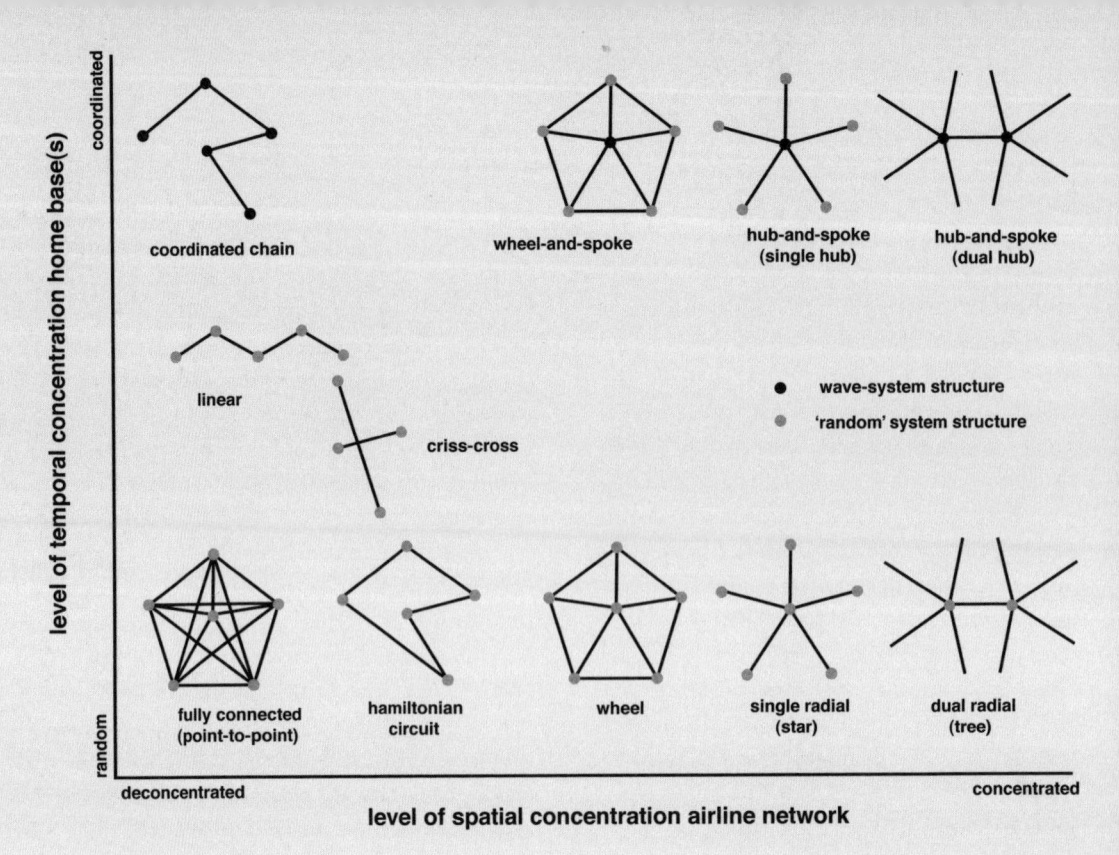

Airport systems [Burghouwt 2005]

Y-axis: level of temporal concentration home base(s) — random to coordinated
X-axis: level of spatial concentration airline network — deconcentrated to concentrated

Network types shown:
- coordinated chain
- wheel-and-spoke
- hub-and-spoke (single hub)
- hub-and-spoke (dual hub)
- linear
- criss-cross
- fully connected (point-to-point)
- hamiltonian circuit
- wheel
- single radial (star)
- dual radial (tree)

Legend: ● wave-system structure; ○ 'random' system structure

---

trip battered and needed repair on the spot. In that sense, right from the beginning there was a close co-operation at Schiphol with Fokker, who, as mentioned, became the biggest airplane builder in the world during the thirties, as well as the European representative of the new McDonnell Douglas planes before and after the Second World War. This mutual interaction survived until the bankruptcy of Fokker in 1996 and the takeover of McDonell Douglas by Boeing in 1997. At this time, the airplane industry is actually concentrated into two large conglomerates, namely Boeing and Airbus. At specialized locations, they produce different kinds of aeroplanes focused on different kinds of markets and even different network configurations (Dreamliner and Airbus 380). At the same time, the maintenance of airplanes has become so standardized and marginal that it takes place decentrally at virtually any airport around the globe. The presence of an aviation industry at an airport is therefore hardly distinctive anymore; it has become a commodity.

In addition, the development of the airport into a hub also needed other amenities, as the development of the hub-and-spoke system not only meant an increasing amount of air cargo and additional logistic functions, but also an increasing number of passengers lingering during the transition from one airplane to another. Apart from that, the Schiphol Group soon realized, to its dismay, that the aviation sector had become very volatile due to the deregulation act and due to political, economic or oil crises. To assure future businesses, it decided to diversify its income basis. Here, especially non-aviation revenues gained

Proposal for an airport region

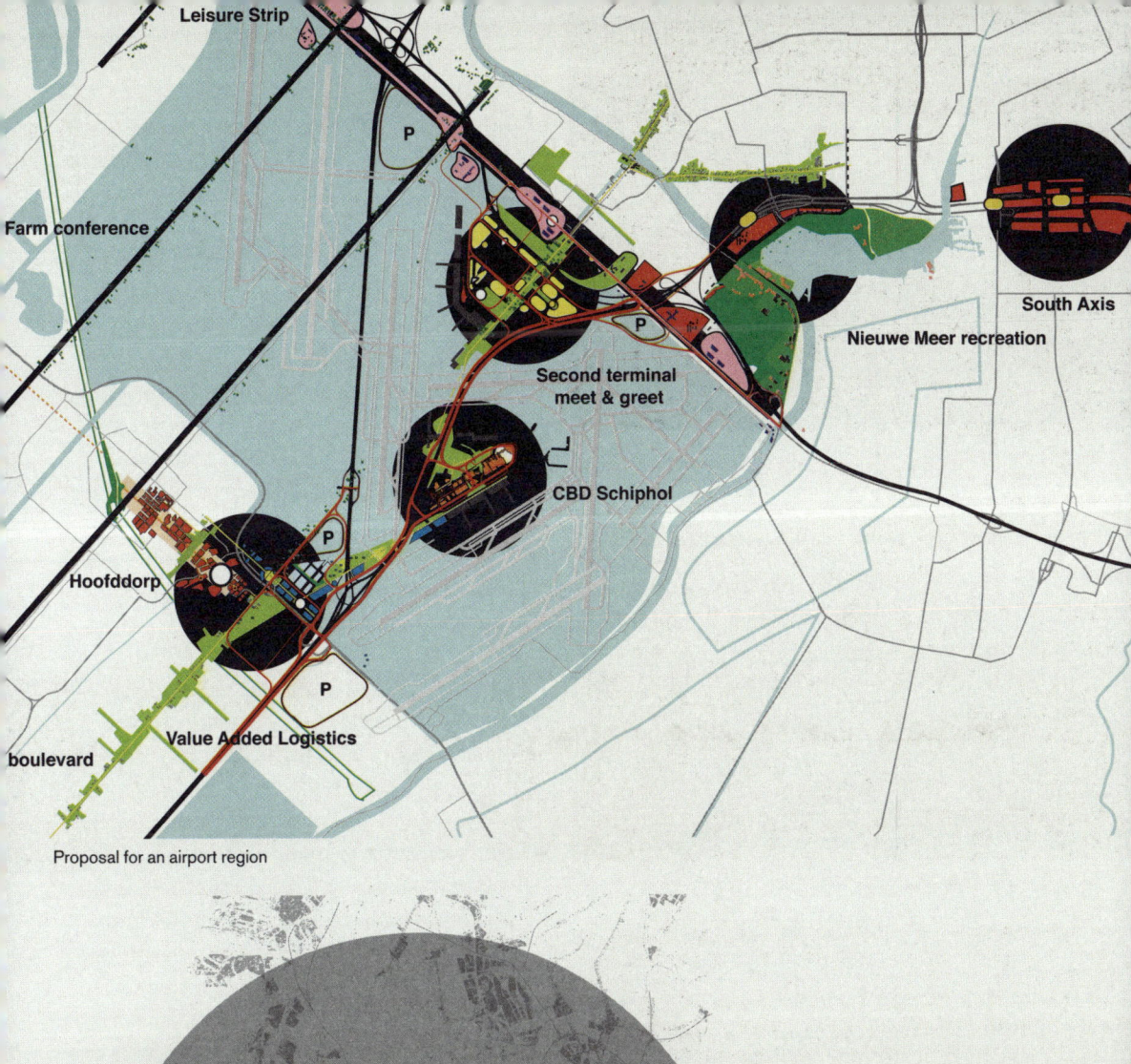

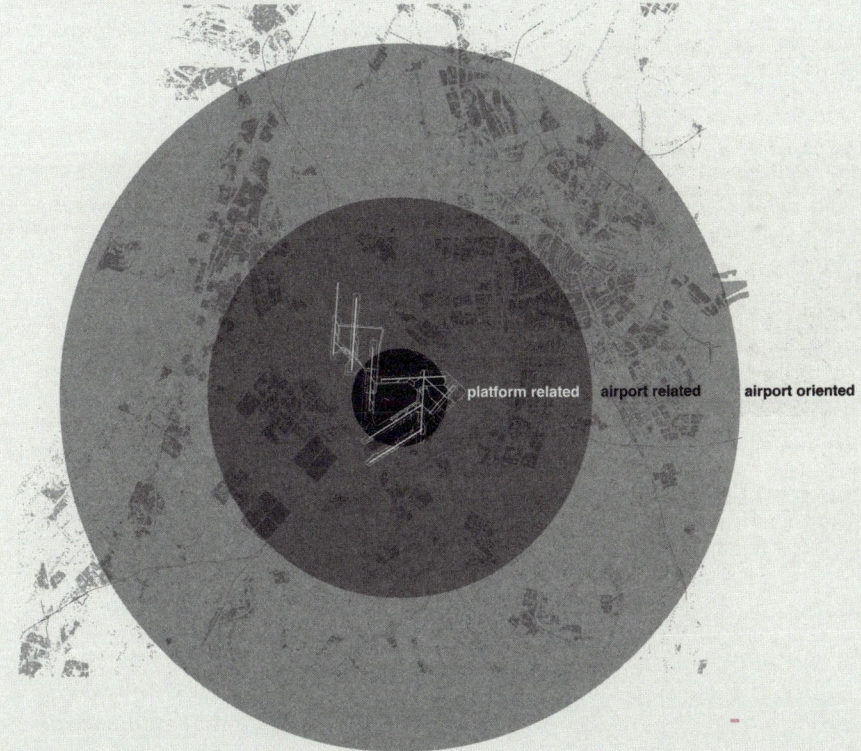

Platformrelated, airportrelated, airportoriented activities

79

Airport City

Impression of an innovative Airport University

Impression of High Value Added Logistics

importance. On the basis of this idea, Schiphol was one of the first to implement the so-called 'Airport city' concept. In this concept, the airport is viewed as a perfect stop-over in air travel, as it offers hotels, working places, shops, restaurants, casinos, recreational facilities, museums, conference facilities, swimming pools and even churches. From the mid-nineties onwards, it began to offer more and more of these 'urban' services. The airport became so effective at it that consumers and real estate now account for 81% of the operational results. [Schiphol 2008] Moreover, Schiphol also rolled out this airport city formula internationally, having shares and joint ventures in JFK International New York, Brisbane Airport, Vienna International Airport, Tradeport Hong Kong, Aruba Airport, Angkasa Pura Jakarta, Stockholm and Milan Malpensa. [Boelens & de Jong 2006] Thus, landside revenues and their (real estate, consumers, alliances & participations) business units and affiliate actors gained importance, precisely because these became the most profitable businesses for the airport. [van Wijk 2006] But it also meant new (latent) enemies.

Although the City of Amsterdam, next to the State of the Netherlands (75.8%) and the Municipality of Rotterdam (2.4%), owned 21.8% of the shares of Schiphol Group, it did not like the fact that some functions were established in and around the Airport City, while it actually wanted them to settle in the city (and especially on the South Axis of Amsterdam) themselves. When the privatization of Schiphol became a major issue, in addition to the carriers (who were afraid of higher airport charges), especially social-democratic politicians of the national government [Duivesteijn 2005] and those of the city of Amsterdam did not want the deal to go through. On the one hand, they didn't want to lose influence on the largest provider of regional employment and added value, and on the other hand they also wanted to keep some influence on its consumer and real estate strategies. The Deputy Mayor of Amsterdam – Lodewijk Asscher – even went as far as to bid for 29% of the national shares of Schiphol in mid-2006, in order to get a majority vote. The government refused the offer and since then the privatization issue has been swept from the table. Nevertheless, the traditional smooth actor-network constellation between Schiphol, Amsterdam and the State has suffered from this impasse.

Competitive Region

This brings me to the Competitive Region, the third element of Schiphol's mainport strategy. Next to being transfer point, Schiphol and its surroundings should also become a destination area in order to maintain its future position. Originally there was strong interaction between the airport and the surrounding local, regional and national authorities, based on a sharp spatio-economic zoning. One could distinguish platform-related, Schiphol-related and Schiphol-oriented economic activities. This distinction was mostly motivated by the consideration to use the scarce land around Schiphol exclusively for aviation and primarily aviation-related functions, to increase the competitiveness of the region as a whole and prevent unnecessary congestion at the landside of the airport. [Province of Noord-Holland, 2007]

The airport itself was made responsible for the first platform-related activities. For that purpose, the airport established a specific Schiphol Real Estate branch in 1997 to develop and exploit the (originally intended platform-related) buildings at the airport area itself. But, as mentioned previously, the Schiphol Group itself soon started to extend this mission towards a broader Airport City concept. However, for the second category – that of the Schiphol-related economic activities – the region was made responsible. For that reason, the Schiphol Area Development Company (SADC) was established in 1987, in which not only the airport itself (33.3%), but also the municipalities of Haarlemmermeer and Amsterdam (each 24.3%) participated, as well as the province of Noord-Holland (18.1%), with land, resources and expertise. In this way, the SADC is currently responsible for the development and exploitation of roughly twelve industrial and business areas within 2 miles around the airport. It serves the interests of all its shareholders in the Directors Forum Schiphol (the *Bestuurs Forum Schiphol*, hereafter BSF), and competes with the private entrepreneurs operational in this area, such as Chipshol for instance. The last category (that of the Schiphol-oriented activities) focuses on high-quality locations for different types of business-like services and logistics in a wider area. The surrounding municipalities within the framework of the general spatial policy of the national and provincial authorities are responsible for the realization of these Schiphol-oriented areas.

Since the inauguration of the mainport concept, this distinction and spatio-economic zoning has proven to be very successful. In the 1990s, the Schiphol area as a whole proved to house the biggest number of American and Japanese Continental Headquarters and Distribution Centres of all the airport regions in Europe. Therefore it was legally reaffirmed in planning documents over and over again. Nevertheless, in recent years, striking cracks in the unified regional association have seemed to appear. First, as mentioned previously, several municipalities such as Amsterdam and the Haarlemmermeer are beginning to perceive the Airport City concept as an increasing threat to their own (metropolitan) strategies. Second, the Schiphol Group itself is wondering whether the SADC is the most effective platform when it comes to developing Schiphol-related projects. Schiphol emphasized that it believes that its own Schiphol Real Estate branch is more effective in this respect, as SADC is perceived as an intricate and viscous organization, seemingly unable to cope with the increasing volatile airport business. For the moment this discussion about breaking-up SADC is passed by. Nevertheless, thirdly, Schiphol Real Estate itself has been selected to participate in the scheduled auction of lucrative Amsterdam South Axis Enterprise shares. This not only broke the tacitly accepted boundaries of the above mentioned spatio-economic zoning rings, but also gave way to a schizophrenic situation in which Amsterdam as shareholder of the Schiphol Group is being offered at its own auction. Nevertheless, everyone needs each other in order to advance further. So, in order to obtain some common ground between the partners united in BSF, a Regional Economic Outlook for Schiphol is now being developed, to promote joint investments in the area. As a first interim result, an Airport Corridor concept has been put forward between Hoofddorp and the South Axis of Amsterdam. The emphasis remains, however, on an infrastructural and spatially dominated vision for this corridor, because, as stated, in a network society, the economic well being of a region should rely heavily on connectivity to other regions. And airport development should remain a main focus of its spatial strategy, integrated with its broader regional potentials to become a major destination area in a global network development. [Schaafsma et al. 2008]

Beyond the plan – towards new actor-network constellations

Thus, what at first seemed to be a fairly straightforward association responsible for the prosperous development of Schiphol (namely the aviation industry, terminal operator and a home carrier, backed up by national an local authorities), has evolved more recently into a more complex set of (sometimes even competing) associations between an ever-growing and diversifying set of actors, due to the above-described developments. It has even split up into at least three arenas – the airline network, the Airport City and Airport Region – each with its own dynamics, ambitions and relevant and/or leading actors. So, in speaking about the future development planning of Schiphol, it is no longer sufficient to come up with one government-oriented, spatio-economic plan. At least three simultaneous relational planning strategies are needed to enter the complex global-local constellation that is Schiphol. Furthermore – although it repeatedly concerns the airport, its development, restrictions and possibilities itself – it also appears that, in each of these arenas, actors other than the Schiphol Group itself are leading or dominant, such as the Air France/KLM Group, the Municipality of Amsterdam, the civic environmental organizations, respectively leading TransNational Corporations in the surrounding area, etc.

The development of a competitive worldwide network seems to be primarily dependent on an effective coalition between global airline alliances (here primarily Skyteam) on the one hand, and the professionally organized residents and environmentalists on the other. What are the latter willing to admit, under which conditions and guarantees and to what extent are the first willing to adapt their strategic network in time and space (possibly also in a multi-airport or

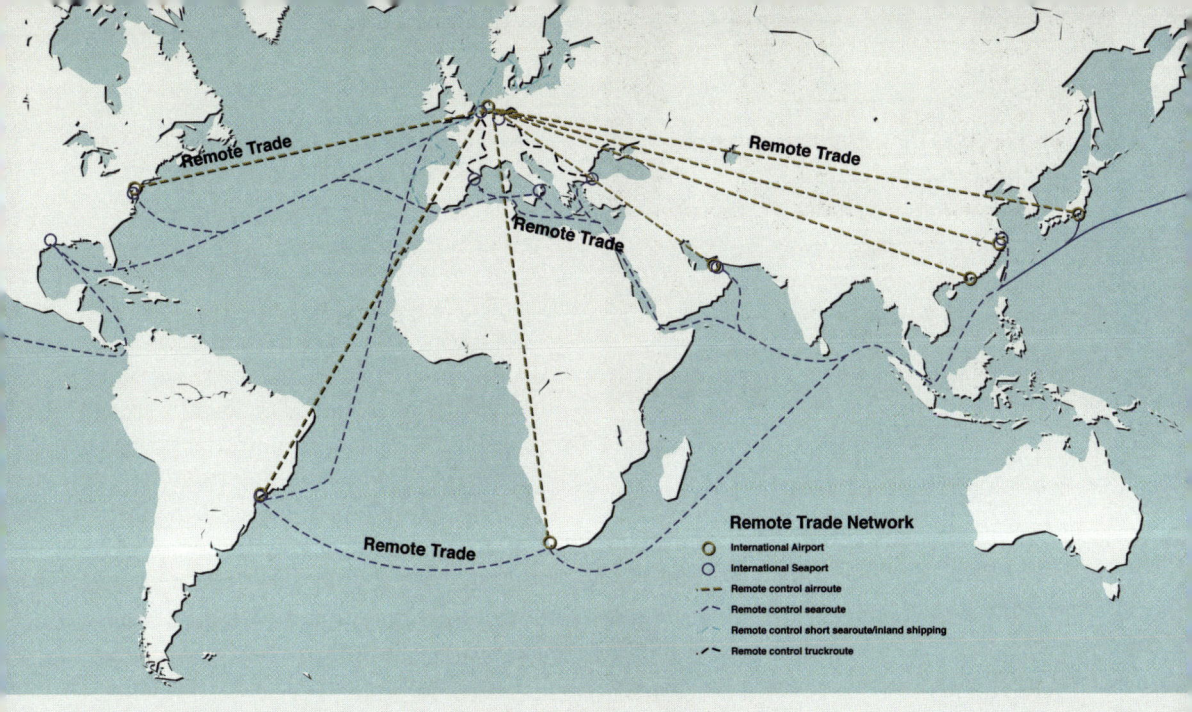

Remote Trade Network
○ International Airport
○ International Seaport
-- Remote control airroute
-- Remote control searoute
-- Remote control short searoute/inland shipping
-- Remote control truckroute

Schiphol Global Remote Trade Zone

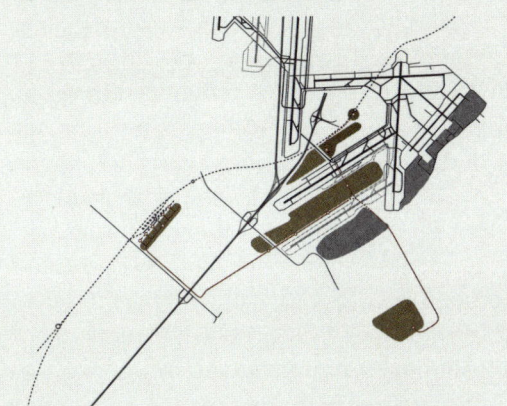

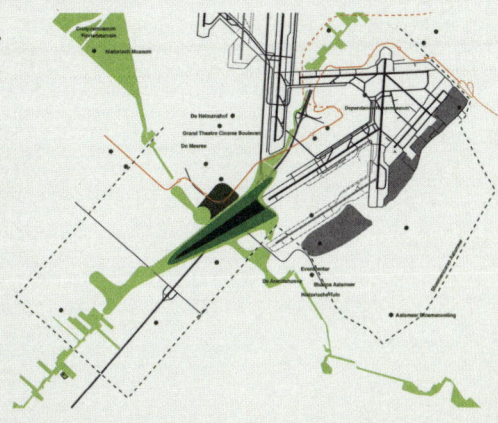

Proposal for trade zones in an Airport region

Fast Trade Zone

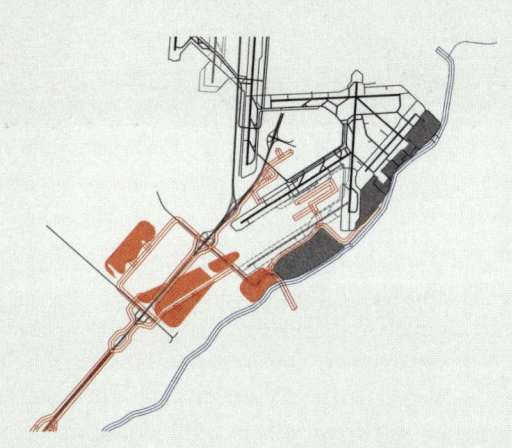

Safe Trade Zone

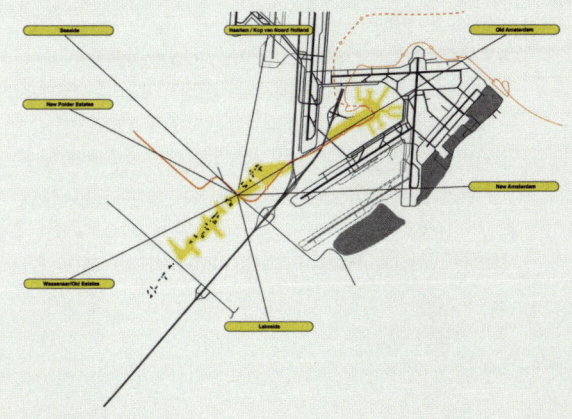

Remote Trade Zone

Premium Trade Zone

Impression of an international consumer hub

Impression of an innovative park

multi-hub setting). The airport itself can only be a facilitator over here, giving preferential benefits to the carriers it wants to keep for sure and 'smoothening' the environmental burdens for the residents with new pleasures, reliefs and spatial qualities.

In effect, it seems to be similar for the planning of the future Airport City concept. More than a new spatial concept, it seems to need a tactical and innovative strategy of the Schiphol Group with regard to its main stake and shareholders, in order to reinvent a mutually complementary economic and financial organization. How can the future development of the Airport City (read: real estate development) be repositioned in a way that is complementary to the metropolitan (real estate) strategy of Amsterdam while dovetailing with the ground policies of the Municipality of the Haarlemmermeer?

And finally, given the evolutionary economic approach, it is debatable whether the (semi-)governments united in the BSF will be able to achieve a sound positioning of the Schiphol region as a worldwide destination area. Although window-dressing is put forward with respect to the clustering concept, the interim plan of these governments remains classically-oriented towards infrastructural and spatial development planning. A prominent interaction with, for instance, the ambitions of the leading TNCs – such as ING, Philips, Cisco, ABN-AMRO, Microsoft, TomTom, etc. – remains out of sight; at least for the moment. Indeed, the outgoing CEO of Schiphol, Cerfontaine, recognizes the importance of innovation and knowledge improvement in this destination strategy. [Cerfontaine 2008] A strong and developed interaction and affliate mutual learning processes, repectively innovation between the business, public and scientific society, as in Eindhoven-Brainport are still a long way off.

BOX [2.3]

Brainport: economy versus spatial planning

Therefore the third case. It has a long history too. While the Brainport concept was originally reserved for trying to bring the basic logistics processes of the mainport of Rotterdam to a higher (knowledge) level via *value-added logistics* and *third, fourth* or possibly even *fifth-party logistics*. [Richardson 2005] These days, however, it is also applied to position the region of Eindhoven and its surrounding area – in this case south-east Brabant – as a high-tech region. It is the only region in the Netherlands and one of the few regions in Europe that complies with the *Barcelona standard* from the EC *Lisbon agenda*. In this case, the annual investment in Research & Development is at least 3% of the gross regional product and there is worker-participation of at least 70%. The region would thereby contribute as much as 16.9% to the Gross National Product, as opposed to 11.7% in Greater Amsterdam and 8.8% in Greater Rijnmond. [CBS 2004, op cit. in SRE 2008] Almost 40% of the private spending on Research & Development in the Netherlands is done in Brainport and the most patent applications come from companies in this region. [Sistermans 2005] In this way, the region attempts to scale itself internationally to other top technology regions in Europe, such as Stockholm, Helsinki, Stuttgart, Munich, Västerig and Braunschweig. To achieve sufficient critical mass, the region has made border-crossing collaboration agreements since 2004 with the TU Eindhoven, the city of Louvain, the Catholic University of Louvain, Leuven Inc., the city of Aken, AGIT mbh, RWTH Aken and Lifetec Aken Jülich. This has been done with the aim of effectively supporting the already developed transregional collaboration of knowledge institutions and high-tech companies in this so-called Eindhoven-Leuven-Aken triangle (ELAt) and this region, partly because of its central location and available knowledge competences and its development into the largest knowledge region in Europe. [Stichting Brainport 2008] Recently, a joint innovation strategy, comprising the following elements, has been developed:
• to stimulate new knowledge and innovation in areas where ELAt has the potential to be competitive
• to develop efficient transnational knowledge and technology transfer
• to improve regional attractiveness
• to increase efficiency in socalled triple-helix contacts (contacts between businesses, public sector and universities or affliate research instistutions, see furtheron), and
• to establish and support existing and new scientific networks and clusters in a cross-border region. [ELAt 2008]

The birth

However, the birth of this Brainport occurred more than a hundred years ago, when two brothers from Amsterdam – Gerard and later Anton Philips – decided to establish a light-bulb factory in an abandoned textile mill on the outskirts of the Brabant village of Eindhoven at the end of the 19th century. The motive for this choice of place of business was not only the construction of the Zuid-Willemsvaart (1823) canal and the Eindhoven Canal (1846) by the first Dutch king-entrepreneur Willem 1, and/or the construction of the railway that connected Eindhoven to Rotterdam/Utrecht, Venlo/the Ruhr and also Turnhout/Antwerp (1866), but also primarily the presence of a large number of unskilled, cheap and handicraft-driven labour force, which could easily be deployed in the production process. Because of the poor farming land, this region was traditionally an area where a farming existence was combined with home industry. After the arrival of the Philips brothers, the cigar manufacturer Van Abbe, the Frisian grocers Ebben, Damens, Aukes and Ettema (EDAH) and the mechanical engineer Gustav Brückenhaus (the later Royal Begemann Group) and others, only the original accent shifted: for many, agriculture now became a secondary source of income, beside their income from industrial work. [Janssen 2006] This also explains the predominantly rural, village character of the first industrialization in south-east Brabant. This does not alter the fact that the Amsterdam Philips brothers had huge plans for their enterprise and soon became the number 1 in the Dutch light-bulb sector, partly via a cartel with the German AEG concern. To get around import restrictions, it quickly set up branches in Belgium, the UK and Spain, thus becoming an early international enterprise. At the same time, the concern expanded its product portfolio with radio tubes and later whole radio sets as well. This branch developed enormously, especially after the foundation of the famous Natlab in 1914. In the 1920s, there soon followed argon gas bulbs, sodium vapour lamps, X-ray tubes and also the first forerunners of the gramophone. [Atzema et al. 2008] To make this expansion possible in terms of production, Philips consciously invested in the migration of skilled agricultural workers to the region (largely from Drenthe and the east Netherlands) and, faced by a lack of decisiveness on the part of the local councils, started house building activities in Eindhoven's satellite towns. Plans were made for 'garden-city type districts' of small farms and dwellings with spacious gardens of about 400 to 700 m², in order to keep the intended socio-economic structure based on so-called 'flexible familism'[11] and to smother communism and the class struggle at birth via a supplementary organized club life and community-boosting facilities. [Otten 1991, op cit. in Janssen 2006] Nonetheless, to operate more effectively – partly at the instigation of Philips – five satellite villages were annexed in 1920 and turned into a metropolitan administrative unit with the village of Eindhoven. From that time until well after the Second World War, it had all the characteristics of a company town composed of separate villages and districts. [Hauben et al. 2007]

Spatial Planning versus Economic Development

Despite Philips thus doing its best to match (international) production ambitions with the regional identity and socio-economic structure as well as possible, and receiving every assistance from the young planner and Eindhoven city architect De Casseres, this assumed 'metropolitan, megalomaniac development' was not well received by the existing elite: the traditional administrators, status organizations and last but not least, the clergy. From the beginning of the 1930s onward, under the banner of 'Brabantia Nostra', there was open distancing from the socalled 'generic alienation' that was coupled with the Philips modernization process. The loss of regional identity was opposed and the retention of the old Catholic identity was promoted, which in Brabant – according to Brabantia Nostra's absolute conviction – would be equal to the transparent, primarily peasantry-based structures of villages

11 This concept implies that the whole family guarantees part of its own food needs via agricultural activities as well as partly from industry and industrial labour.

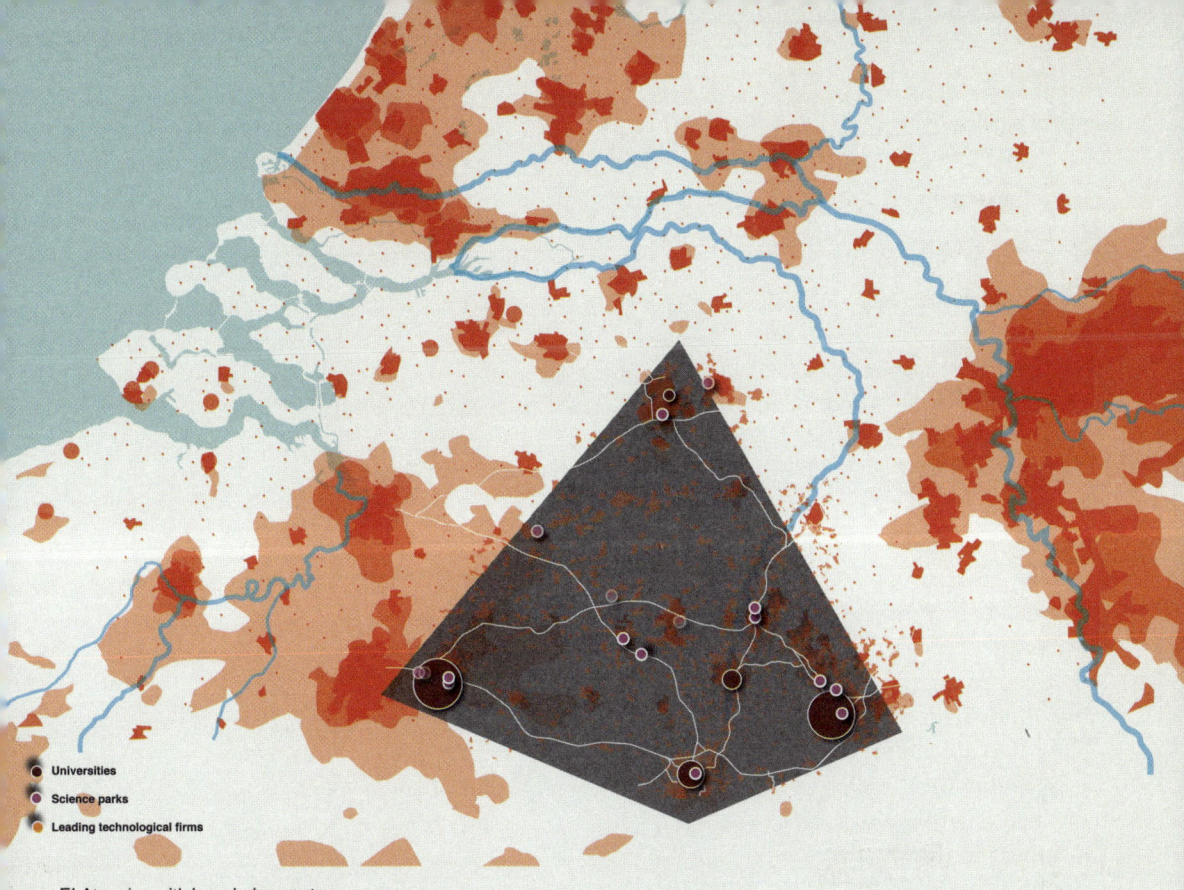

- Universities
- Science parks
- Leading technological firms

ELAt region with knowledge centers

and parishes. [Van Oudheusden 1996] This was directly translated into the closed parochial town and village image of the Delft School of Granpré Molière and Verhaagen, which was diametrically opposed to the open, modern and social-democratic approach of De Casseres, among others, although also based on garden estates. [Kuiper 1991] Nevertheless that vision was asumed to be a threat of the real Brabant identity. So after the Second World War, the decision was definitely taken with the welfare plan for Brabant set up under the supervision of the Queen's Commissioner De Quay, which was also based on the Catholic organization of social and economic life, with its social and urban planning expressed in parishes. In opposition to upcoming cosmopolitan liberalism, the restoration of small communities and the decentralization of industry were preferred, limiting the government's task to plan and regulate and allowing more space for traditional institutions and social groups, which had supported and controlled socio-economic space until then. It formed the basis for a strong corporative planning model, in which the emphasis was on informal consultation structures, which ensured substantive and organizational co-ordination between government and (status) organizations. [Janssen 2006]

This does not alter the fact that despite, or possibly even partly because of these regional difficulties, Philips went its own way. It persevered in its international development, particularly during the economic recession of the thirties and after the Second World War. Between 1930 and 1970, although the total grew, the proportion

1970

number of employees
- up to 100
- 100-500
- 500-1000
- 1000-2000
- 2000-3000
- 3000-4000

Eindhoven
42,300

1994

Eindhoven
18,5

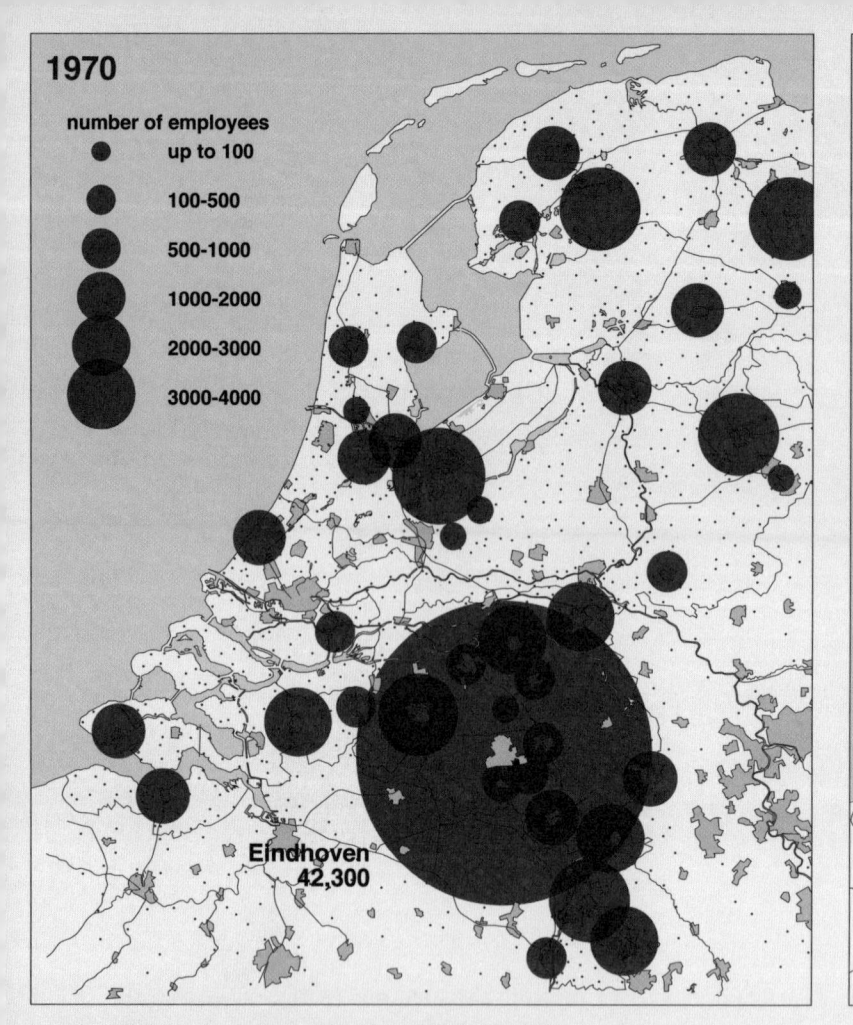

Location of Philips business sites in 1970, 1994 and 2004 [Atzema 2005]

2004

Eindhoven
15,000

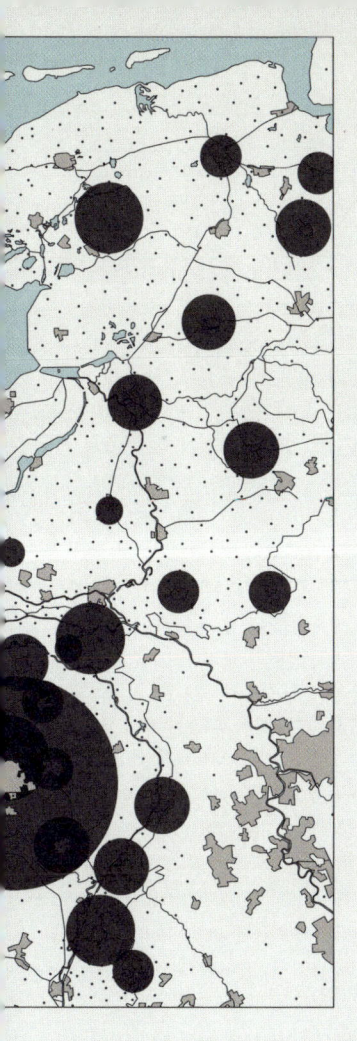

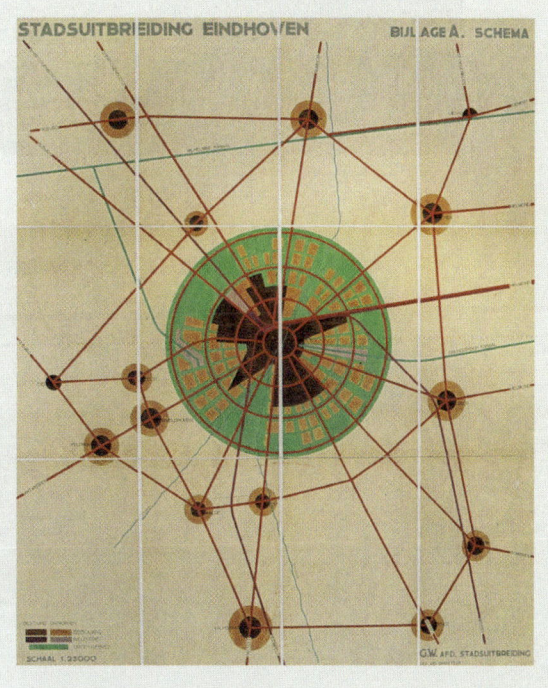

STADSUITBREIDING EINDHOVEN BIJLAGE A. SCHEMA

Eindhoven City plan [De Casseres, Bosma 2003]

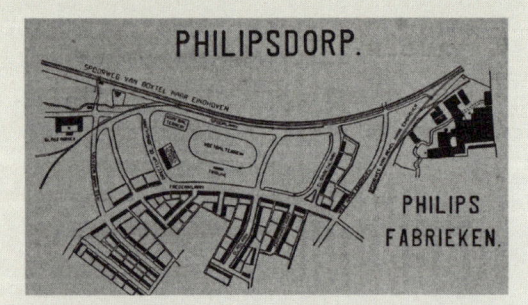

Philipsdorp company town (G.J. De Jongh)

Evoluon

High Tech Campus (Patrick Meis/High Tech Campus)

of Dutch Philips employees fell from 70% to 28% for example, and sales abroad increased from fewer than 30% to more than 90%. [Atzema et al. 2008] At the same time, the company persevered in its building activities in the region for its still-growing number of regional employees: the Philips estate (1928), the Drenthe village (1930), Woensel West (1930-40), the Airey dwellings (1949), the Polynorm dwellings (1950), the building of the TU Eindhoven (1956), the Evoluon (1968) etc. Since the reconstruction period, Eindhoven and Philips have thus become almost synonymous concepts.

The first cracks in an interactive economic-regional bastion

Nevertheless, precisely when, with the provincial *Welfare Balance* and the *Development Plan* in the mid-sixties, Brabant was also ultimately geared to facilitating this development on a regional basis, with modern planning attuned to the needs of the (large) urban society, Philips began to take a different route. Although it could be considered an early international company, the Philips business culture had in fact had a primarily Dutch orientation with a paternalistic attitude until the seventies. Employees at Philips were cared for from cradle to grave. Due to the increasing internationalization of its workforce and the increasing globalization of its business processes, this was no longer tenable. Apart from the CEO (even today he is still a Dutchman), the whole corporate management became increasingly international and the company operated on a more effective, business-rational level.

At the same time, it turned out that the local-for-local production politics from time immemorial – often to get round import restrictions – was no longer necessary or effective. In fact, it had stimulated strongly independent business units, which often did double work, collaborated insufficiently transnationally, and showed little corporate cohesion. More direction from the top became vital. Finally, under pressure from rising global competition, Philips was forced to redefine its core business from the end of the seventies/beginning of the eighties. Here, a distinction was made between interlinked (e.g., those concerning consumer electronics, components and telecommunication & data systems) and stand-alone activities. Outside the lighting department, all stand-alone activities were initially not counted as the core business of Philips and an attempt was made (with or without shareholding) to contract them out or sell them. Although Atzema, Wever and Krol indicate that between the different 'governing periods' of the CEOs Dekker (1982-86), Van der Klugt (1986-90), Timmer (1990-96), Boonstra (1996-2001) and Kleisterlee (2001-present) there were also different ideas about this, it had huge consequences for the presence of Philips in the Netherlands. For the first time, the number of Dutch employees of Philips declined also in absolute terms from around 100,000 in 1970 to fewer than 30,000 at present; at the same time, the number of business sites in the Netherlands fell from almost 100 in 1994 to fewer than 40 in 2004. [Atzema et al. 2008] With essential changes, during the last three decades of the previous century, the interference of the concern in regional spatial planning fell to near enough zero. Even more, Philips sold its housing assets, closed or even abandoned a number of prominent and socially appealing components (such as the Witte Dame, Strijp S, or the Evoluon) and between 1998 and 2001 even moved its head office in phases from Eindhoven to Amsterdam.

From a closed to an open innovation model

This does not mean that Philips is completely dismantling its position in and around Eindhoven, however. It is rather redefining it. In imitation of Chesbrough, [2003] among others, it now pursues primarily an open innovation model instead of a closed one. As a consequence of the ever-greater turnover rate of innovations, their increasing costs and the increasing mobility of the highly-trained knowledge workers and thereby ever more widely available knowledge of new technologies, the development of innovations within the company – *intra muros* – has become increasingly difficult. Furthermore, innovations are more often stimulated by other players in the chain – e.g., the knowledge institutions, suppliers or clients – and discoveries and inventions also arise, whether intended or not, during innovation processes, which do not directly fit within the corporate strategy and can be best further developed outside that strategy. Consequently, two movements developed within the open innovation model: inside-out and outside-in. [Chesbrough 2003 and Van de Vrande 2007]

With the inside-out movement, promising new innovations that do not (or no longer) fit within the corporate strategy or business portfolio are brought to new markets via launching new companies (spin-offs) and/or selling knowledge and technology in the form of licences. Myrke van der Meer [2008] shows convincingly that Philips has applied this strategy several times in past decades. From these arose ASML, NXP, Irex, Anteryon, Liquavista, Polymer Vision, Silicon Hive, FEI Company, Handshake Solutions and amBX, among others. These companies are all still established in the region and all in one way or another (via shareholding, licences or patent distribution, etc.) still connected to Philips.

With the outside-in movement, Philips attempts to gain access to knowledge development and innovations from external sources. This can be through *corporate venturing*, where Philips invests in other, usually new, small enterprises. A prominent example of this is the High-tech Campus, not only to boost technological collaboration and knowledge exchange, but also the place where Philips opens its *clean rooms* in the famous NATlab to others, for nothing or for a small rent, in exchange for a share in or an option on the possibly resulting innovations. Furthermore, in past years there have been growing strategic alliances with universities, technological institutes, governments, subcontractors, clients and even (former) competitors; directed by the Brainport Foundation, among others. This is called the Triple Helix model,[12] which, in imitation of Leydesdorff & Etzkowitz, [2000] focuses on effective collaboration within and among government, companies and knowledge institutions on regional innovation systems, with the emphasis on knowledge transfer mechanisms, absorptive capacity and the entrepreneurship of companies, and the appropriate condition-creating role of government. [SRE 2005, Van den Bosch 2007]

Parallel to this, there is also close collaboration between Philips and IMEC, Alcatel Microelectronics, Eonic Systems, Frontier Design, the Catholic University of Louvain, the State University of Ghent and the Free University of Brussels in the *Digital Signal Processing (DSP) Valley* in Louvain [Larosse et al. 2001] and with DSM, Medtronic, Anaxis, the Technical University of Eindhoven, the University of Maastricht and the Academic Hospitals of Maastricht and Aken in the framework of *Life Tec A2*. [LIOF 2007] In conjunction with the *IMEC cluster* in Louvain, the *Chema-Energy Valley* under the direction of DSM, the *Flanders Multimedia Valley* in Hasselt, the *Graphics Valley* in Turnhout and the *Dutch Design Cluster* in Eindhoven or the recent *Automotive Cluster* in Helmond/Lommel/Borne, the image of this border-crossing, open, high-tech innovation region acquires new allure: in this case, it is the Eindhoven-Louvain-Aken Triangle (ELAt).

Brainport revisited

Against this background, we can return to the actual spatial organization in and around Brainport. It can be established that the spatial planners are trying more than previously to find effective connections to this spatial-economic path to development. Next to the domains of People, Technology and Business, a matching spatial organization is also seen as an essential link for an effective Brainport development. [Sistermans 2005] It is remarkable, however, that the involved planners immediately fall back on old classical instruments like the improvement of accessibility, the reinforcement of a high-quality working and living environment and image-building of the region. In line with a limited study largely performed by the personnel of the UvA by Rob Engelsdorp-Gastelaars, which found that beta scientists prefer a green and sportive setting [Engelsdorp-Gastelaars 2007] in contrast to alpha and gamma scientists (urban orientation), the designers

---

[12] The 'triple helix' is a spiral model of innovation that captures multiple reciprocal relationships at different points in the process of knowledge capitalization between Industries, Government and Knowledge Institutions. It focuses on the internal transformation in each of the helices (Industry, Government, Knowledge Institutions) themselves – such as the development of lateral ties among companies through strategic alliances or an assumption of an economic development mission by universities, respectively the role of the federal or local government in instituting an indirect industrial policy – as on the creation of a new overlay of trilateral networks and organizations from the interaction among the three helices, in order to develop new ideas and formats for high-tech development.

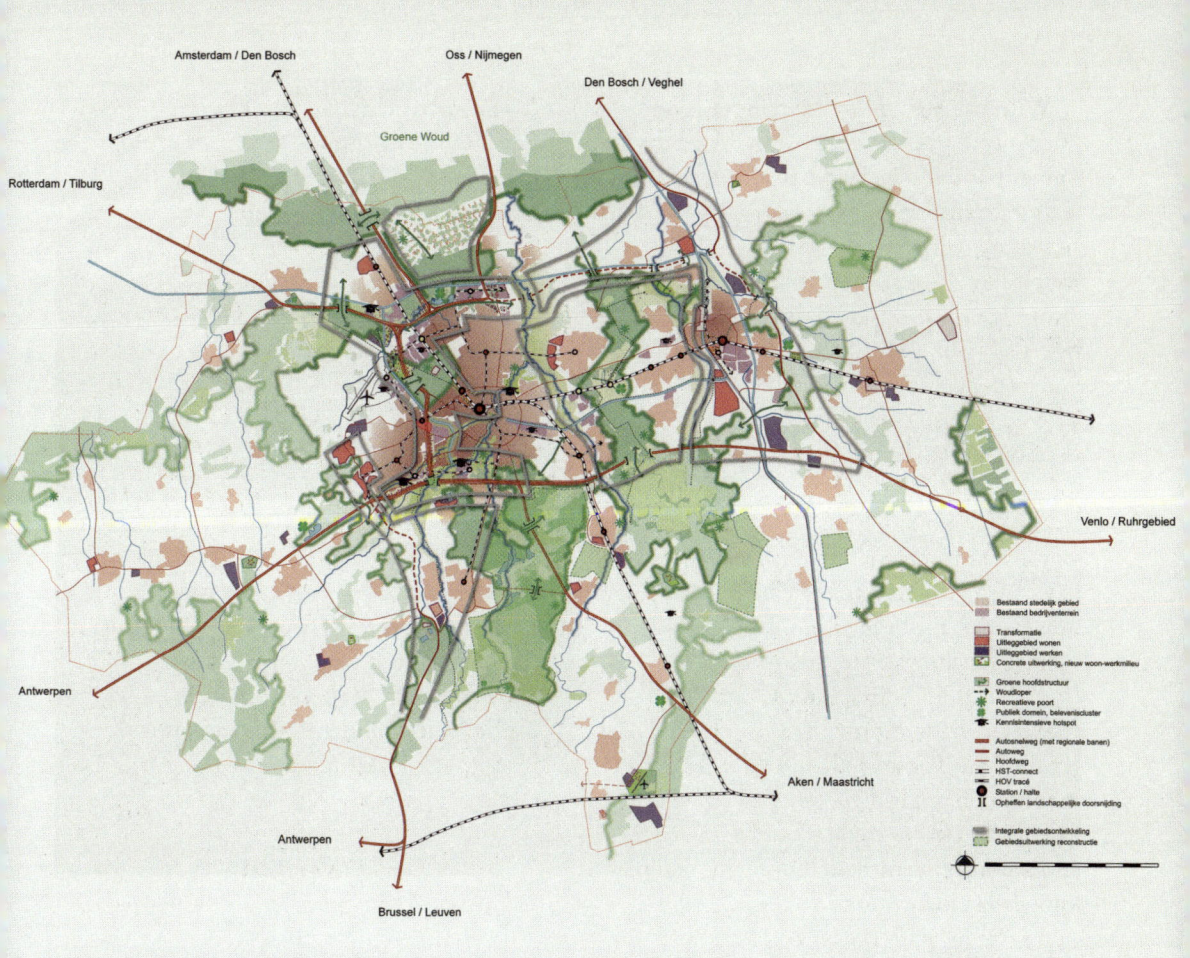

Regional strategic plan of Eindhoven (SRE)

opted for the 'Super village concept' and the so-called 'Genius Landscape' for example, for the extension of the scenic landscape of Brabant, based on a simple red-for-green rule: all agricultural land released for the reconstruction could be built on, provided that at least half of the building plot is used for trees and shrubbery. [ACE 2005, Hauben 2007]
In line with this, the recent Brainport Eindhoven Spatial Programme has opted for 'the creation of an internationally favourable climate for setting up a business by means of synergy between the centrally located dynamics and the surrounding finely-meshed village-urban network, in combination with good accessibility'. [SRE 2008] This has been elaborated in six pillars, including (a) the development of a regional landscape park, (b) an experimental green residential landscape, entitled 'The New Forest', (c) interweaving the green and red in rural areas, next to (d) the extension of the Eindhoven A2 zone, (e) the development of the Helmond north-east corridor, and (f) the extension of the so-called N69 Border Corridor.

It is furthermore remarkable that despite the Triple Helix Model being endorsed as a goal, this spatial strategy has been created within and with the various authorities; not with the involved businesses and/or research institutions. The question therefore still remains as to whether the total image obtained actually functions discrimi-

High Tech Yard, inside

High Tech Yard, outside

nately or makes an adequate, conditioned or facilitating contribution to the previously described innovation dynamics. Besides the classic means in the areas of business location policy and accessibility, the VROM council earlier pointed out the necessity for specific policy directed at 'increasing the degree of agglomeration by increasing support' and 'increasing the degree of agglomeration by the addition of specific top facilities'. [VROM council 2004] Apart from the question as to whether this is very highly directed at the restoration of the archaic Christaller centrality model, and apart from the question if this is or will be done sufficiently, one can also conclude that the open source transition of Eindhovens business model is in fact mirrored by an old, traditional and closed model of planning; as well with respect to the actors involved as with respect to the contents developed. The spatial plan of the region Eindhoven is still developed governmental inside-out and top-down; despite its prominent tradition in self-organisation and bottom-up rural-urban development. The content is still focussed on organising and at its best assumingly facilitating innovative businesses, without being creative or innovative by itself. Nevertheless under the banner of the Brabant rural area developer Agro&Co, there have been experiments in this region with a defined actor-oriented, relational approach. Although these proposals were developed in dialogue with stakeholders, developers, knowledge institutions and affiliate businesses, they give a glimp of a new kind of open planning, mirroring the transition made by the Eindhovens business society itself towards innovative open source management. In fact it is an open source model in itself, inviting new ideas and options from the outset in an organic and creative way and could therefore proof to be better equipped for the next economy to come. Instead of returning to the old inside-out ways of planning, these options and possibilities need to be further extended and developed.

[3]

Transnational communities
A comparison of neighbourhood development in Randstad Holland, Buenos Aires and São Paulo

In 2007 the Dutch Minister for Housing, Neighbourhoods and Integration Vogelaar placed 40 selected districts in a number of Dutch cities on the national agenda, assigning them special attention. These districts were selected in view of the fact that they have to cope with a number of persistent spatial, economic and social problems in the field of outdated housing, high unemployment, degradation of public spaces, vandalism and consequently feelings of insecurity. They were also chosen because the population of those districts was regarded as 'underprivileged' in the field of education and social development. [Ministry of Housing, Spatial Planning and the Environment, 2007] In total, these neighbourhoods account for around 775,000 residents, approximately 5% of the Dutch population. [Central Office for Statistics, CBS, 2008] In addition, this population also appears to contain relatively high concentrations of first and second-generation non-native residents, or in Dutch: *allochtonen*.[13] Almost a quarter of all non-Western immigrants in the Netherlands live in these neighbourhoods. Some neighbourhoods even have predominantly non-native populations, stretching up to as much as 90%. This conclusion lay at the root of what is, as far as Dutch concepts are concerned, a unique approach to neighbourhood revitalization. Here, neighbourhood development was expressly linked to that of social-cultural integration and it was included for the first time in one portfolio at ministerial level. The reason behind this was not only the increasing tension in Western societies between the (traditionally) native Christian Occidental inhabitants and the (sometimes fundamentalist or oppressed) Muslim immigrants. [Habermas, 2008] Additionally, the excessive unrest in impoverished workers' districts, such as in the Paris *banlieux* in 2005 and 2007, also mirrored the potential social unrest created in such deprived and tense areas. [Reinders 2006] Comparably, albeit to a less excessive degree, the Netherlands had been confronted with unrest in disadvantaged neighbourhoods. These occurred not only in the traditionally agitated neighbourhoods of big cities such as Amsterdam or Rotterdam. Increasingly they also developed in smaller traditional quiet, provincial districts such as in the Graaftsewijk in the city of Den Bosch after a local football team supporter was shot dead by the police (16/12/00) and when television channel SBS 6 exposed the sexual abuse of a female resident by her stepfather (14/12/05). The disturbances in the Veldhuizen Ede district after the New York terrorist attacks (11/09/2001), the turmoil in Ondiep Utrecht, again after a resident had been shot dead by the police (11/03/07) and recently the decision of a bus company to avoid the district of Oosterwei in Gouda after problems with mainly Moroccan boys (14/09/08) are comparable examples.

Desired help from the public authorities in the avoidance of neighbourhood excesses and the accompanying pressure from parliament to do something about the integration of immigrants in the so-called Dutch society explain the national government's involvement in a matter, which up until recently had largely been left to local councils and the associations responsible for social

13 Non-native Dutch populations, especially 'non-Western' migrants. According to the definition used by the Dutch Central Office of Statistics (CBS) a person is considered an *allochtoon* up to the second generation. This means that people with one parent born in a foreign country are considered to be *allochtonen*. In everyday life, the term *allochtoon* has acquired a slightly pejorative bias and is, in fact, associated with persons of a non-European appearance or with non-European habits. Although Germans are in fact the largest *allochtoon* group in the Netherlands, the epithet is more widely used in relation to immigrants of Turkish, Moroccan and Antillean origin.

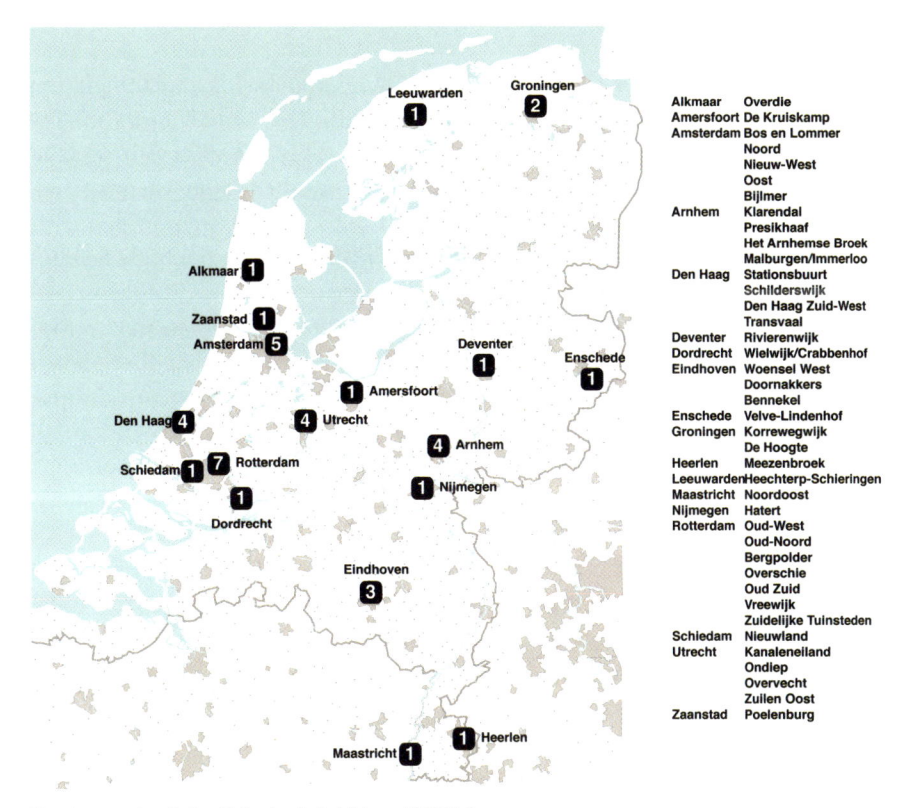

Vogelaar quarters in the Netherlands (ministery of VROM)

Alkmaar	Overdie
Amersfoort	De Kruiskamp
Amsterdam	Bos en Lommer
	Noord
	Nieuw-West
	Oost
	Bijlmer
Arnhem	Klarendal
	Presikhaaf
	Het Arnhemse Broek
	Malburgen/Immerloo
Den Haag	Stationsbuurt
	Schilderswijk
	Den Haag Zuid-West
	Transvaal
Deventer	Rivierenwijk
Dordrecht	Wielwijk/Crabbenhof
Eindhoven	Woensel West
	Doornakkers
	Bennekel
Enschede	Velve-Lindenhof
Groningen	Korrewegwijk
	De Hoogte
Heerlen	Meezenbroek
Leeuwarden	Heechterp-Schieringen
Maastricht	Noordoost
Nijmegen	Hatert
Rotterdam	Oud-West
	Oud-Noord
	Bergpolder
	Overschie
	Oud Zuid
	Vreewijk
	Zuidelijke Tuinsteden
Schiedam	Nieuwland
Utrecht	Kanaleneiland
	Ondiep
	Overvecht
	Zuilen Oost
Zaanstad	Poelenburg

housing in the Netherlands. During the formation of the current national government (the fourth Balkenende administration) in 2007, there was still talk of a separate Minister for Integration. But during the formation of the cabinet, it was decided to have Housing and Neighbourhood Improvement linked to the portfolio. Given the aforementioned views, this linking would fit better into the Minister's convened set of responsibilities. In accordance with the new cabinet's motto of 'working together, living together', the aim was to curb the persistent and sometimes growing discrepancy between the native and non-native populations and promote a sound integration of all ethnic groups, in economic, social, and spatial respects.

The policy approach adopted here was based on the assumption that the intended integration could be best organized by means of improvements in the immediate day-to-day spatial environment; namely the neighbourhood. Along with other national departments (those of Economic Affairs, Internal Affairs, Education and Culture and the Justice Department), involved municipalities, housing associations, residents, schools and other cultural institutions, the Minister aimed to convert the forty problem districts into so-called *krachtwijken* or *power districts*, by making them again 'pleasant places to live in'. The residents should be given better prospects for participation in the labour market and social improvement, and neighbours from different ethnic and religious backgrounds should be more closely involved in community building within the neighbourhoods. [Ministry of VROM 2008] To this end, the intention was to set up a Public Investment Fund for 'Pleasant Districts' with the housing associations and local homeowners. This Fund would be used to finance a wide-ranging programme, not only for home improvement but also with respect to social and economic improvements, revitalization of public areas and quality of life. The intention is to promote residential careers in these neighbourhoods, district-linked entrepreneurship, extra commitment to comprehensive schools focusing not only on education but also on community-building and after-school facilities, social work placements for advanced pupils, integration or reintegration courses, (stimulated) women's voluntary work, as well as strengthened presence of police, etc.

Misconceptions

Apart from the obvious problems the Ministry had in setting up the Public Investment Fund, this approach also appears to be based on three prominent but often equally persistent misconceptions.

First, although the policy seems to be founded on a broad approach – addressing not only physical questions, but also economic, social, cultural and institutional ones – it is still linked to the ancient and well-known structuralist approach from the past. [De Saussure, 1916] The forty districts are chosen on the basis of putative underlying factors and processes that are deemed to be generally characteristic of and structurally determining for a disadvantaged or underprivileged area. Therefore, general structural measures are also proposed to improve those conditions.

However, in the last few decades it has been more widely acknowledged that these measures do not always have the expected effect, and are sometimes even counter-productive. [Murdoch, 2006] In their place, a relational approach is increasingly being promoted, in which primary importance is attached not only to the increasing relations between the district or neighbourhood in question and other districts and neighbourhoods somehow connected to it, but also the relational implication of the specific meaning and measures taken in the space vis-à-vis the players inhabiting it are crucial elements for this approach. [Graham/Healey, 1999; Boelens, 2006]

This calls for a much more in-depth reflection on the conditioning processes of players and networks concerned than is advocated in Minister Vogelaar's approach. [Callon, 1986; Law, 2004; Latour 2005] What is at stake is:
a a strong inter-relationship between formally or informally established institutional networks (in the broad sense of the word) as well as
b heterogeneous actors in the activation of processes and
c spatial strategies connected to these. If one of these three factors does not match with the others, the policy will not be effective.

Second, the policy proposal is based on the equally old and persistent idea of districts and neighbourhoods. That model, was presented by Clarence Perry as a social ideal in the nineteen twenties, [Perry, 1929] further refined by Walter Christaller in functional and planning terms [Christaller, 1933] and subsequently introduced in the Netherlands *inter alia* by Granpré Molière and the Bos group in a Catholic or socialist variant around the time of the Second World War. [Bos Study Group, 1946] Nevertheless it has already been fundamentally demystified by Van Doorn, [1955] Gans, [1962] Murray, [1984] Doevendans, [1988] Reijndorp et al. [1998] amongst others. In our increasingly networked society, communities would also, and increasingly, come into being beyond districts and neighbourhoods. Social cohesion would be layered and be a matter for discussion at several scale levels and settings. [Blokland-Potters, 1998] Especially with regard to immigrant communities, more than thirty years ago, Edward Said even strongly contested the idea that there should be an intensive connection between territory and identity or social cohesion. In fact, he proclaimed those ideas that present identity formation as a process of controlling boundaries and maintaining the territorial integrity of communities or selves as the expression of the old ideology of colonial power and administration. Instead, he opted for a form of 'imaginative geography' in which identity is more socially and thematically constructed in relation to other identities of places, people and landscapes, representing the ways these imaginings reflect the preconceptions and desires of oneself and/or the other. [Said 1978] In this sense, the idea of districts and neighbourhoods does trigger more physically deterministic assertions, which are probably self-fulfilling prophecies according to Wellman, and would not explain the multitude of social connections and cohesion that are currently coming into being beyond those geographical boundaries. [Wellman, 2001]

Finally, and partly following the same logic, the native/non-native dichotomy and the view that integration is deemed necessary have also come under fire. The idea that something like a national (Dutch) community can be distinguished from others as a 'named population sharing a historic territory, common myths and historical memories, a mass public culture, a common economy and common legal rights and duties for its members' [Smith, 1986; Hastings, 1997] is beginning to lose its meaning under the influence of increasing globalization and the fragmentation and regionalization that go with it. In that respect, Princess Maxima of Orange-Zorreguieta was absolutely right when she said, during the presentation of the Scientific Government Policy Council *Identification report* that she did not know exactly what that single Dutch identity actually meant. [Elsevier, 24 September 2007] In its place, more and more thematic ties, either temporary or permanent, either overlapping or intersecting, are coming to view. These can be ethnic, political, religious, economic, cultural, spatial or local, or transnational and multinational. [Gellner, 1983; Weber, 1976] Political geographer Peter Taylor even suggests the creation of a kind of network of cosmopolitanism organized around the new ICT resources, with representatives and members in assorted world cities. such as a Jewish representative in New

York, Tel Aviv, Amsterdam, Antwerp and Brussels, a German one in assorted East European cities, various Muslim communities in the major cities of the western *guest worker* host countries, etc. [Taylor, 2004] To this extent, Manuel Castells also conceded in his *Power of Identity* that identities do not exist in advance, but are constructed. Identities are only real when they are internalized by people and meaning is given to them. [Castells, 1997]

Similarly, in his brilliant *Exegeses on nationalism,* [The Nation, 1991] Benedict Anderson had unmasked the nation as a cultural artefact – as 'an imagined political community'. In his view, such a thing as a national community or identity is imaginary, not only because even in the smallest state its members can never know all of their fellow members, but also because supposed sovereignty and such horizontal companionships as fraternity do not in fact exist. [Anderson, 1983] That does not mean that a nation is unreal or must be distinguished from *true* (unimagined) communities, but that a nation is constructed and is losing ground in current everyday life. Indeed, Anderson comes to the conclusion that the two factors that have been decisive time and again for the emergence and operation of national communities (i.e., a clear, delineated territory and a shared language) are losing importance on account of increasing globalization, multimedia and use of the Internet. After all, the international language is (undeniably) English for the time being, whilst at the same time the Internet and continuing globalization are dissolving traditional borders more and more markedly. [Anderson, 1998]

However, the issue here is not a development towards a new unambiguous global community and culture. Peter Michael Smith describes current globalizing developments chiefly as a complex and multilayered process, which, alongside international structures and developments, is also strongly dominated by local and national agencies. Instead of fruitless binary oppositions putting global against local, Smith therefore opts for a middle of the road approach, from a transnational perspective. He understands this as being an approach that also takes into account, of all things, social formations with respect to 'how they become localized in single places, articulated with other places in translocal communication circuits and spread out across societies and national borders'. [Smith, 2001] In the meantime, similar transnational studies as well as studies on immigrants, have also found their way into 'studies on the politics of transnational social movements, the proselytizing activity of organized religions, the economic connections of commodity chains, and the machinations of transnational terrorist networks'. [Kyle et al, 2001; Mandaville, 2001; Sklair, 2000] Better than an unambiguous 'shrinking space, global city or post-national approach', [Harvey, 1990; Sassen, 1991; Habermas, 2001] this approach enables us in Smith's opinion:

a to embed a historically conditioned agency perspective in considerations on international developments,
b to see the (trans)local, regional and national as cultural fields in which global restructuring takes place,

c see ordinary citizens as creative players in transnational organizations and geopolitical behaviour, and
d still to give considerable prominence, albeit a less dominant position, to national and regional institutions in cross-border relations.

On this point, Smith seems to be indebted to Arjen Appadurai, too, who had previously recognized a development whereby community formation and the collective expressions and standard and value systems that go with it come into being particularly by means of the new (multi-)media techniques. He distinguishes different global cultural dimensions, which appear in layer form, as it were, alongside each other, such as ethnoscapes, mediascapes, technoscapes, financescapes and ideoscapes. [Appadurai, 1996] In this way, someone can be a member of various communities in varying groups, which in fact exist alongside each other, but have different goals, ambitions and even strategies, actors and spatial settings. That approach delivers a new view on the native/non-native dichotomy. Because indeed, thanks to the new tools enabling us to hear, see and act at a distance (Internet, mobile phone traffic, satellite dishes, etc.) people are even more able than in the past to maintain and further develop original cultural, social and even political expressions in a foreign country, and are sometimes even able to do so with greater effect than in their home country. [Appadurai, 1991]

Whatever the case, against this backdrop we may assert that the link between integration and social cohesion and that of districts and district improvement is less unambiguous and/or self-evident than the Action Plan for Power Districts of the Dutch government supposes. Indeed, despite all good intentions, it could even be well wide of the mark and at best might only cause a temporary mystification or shifting of questions. The issue of integration, social cohesion, safety and development goes further than what has been announced in the Dutch policy for districts. Accordingly, the proposed policy actions require special (re)attention. Rather, a much stronger social transnational and planning-based relational approach is required, which is based on actual strong or weak links in society and a policy that could possibly be grafted onto them; spatial, social, economic, institutional or of any other kind of policy. [Healey, 2007; Boelens, 2006, 2008]

For that matter, this also dovetails with the above-mentioned report by the Dutch Scientific Council for Government Policy (Wetenschappelijke Raad voor het Regeringsbeleid) on *Identification with the Netherlands*. [WRR, 2007] The report concludes that the issue of districts requiring special attention is not so much a matter of integration but rather a community question. This therefore implies that the policy focus and chosen direction for solutions should be a different one. Instead of promoting a hypothetically single Dutch identity, and the related directions taken for solutions in respect of national and local ties, broad participation in education, district work, etc., the Council advocates using various processes of identification with the Netherlands and/or specific neighbourhoods as a point of departure. The Council considers this a dynamic process of forming, maintaining and breaking connections, if necessary, and possibly also chiefly, outside the neighbourhood or the national borders. After all, in conditions of globalization this plurality and transnationality has become one of the Netherlands' permanent characteristics, according to the Council. Here the WRR makes distinctions according to processes of functional, normative and emotional identification, which tend to appear independently and alongside one another, but jointly constitute the degree of involvement in a community. [WRR, 2007]

Using this background, my aim in this chapter is to work out, how such forms of identification might come into being, and how these can be facilitated from a spatial and/or planning point of view. With the WRR, I understand *functional identification* to be a form of community-building that mainly appears via functional relationships, such as work, sport, political participation or otherwise. *Normative identification* then relates to processes promoting the creation of a jointly accepted system of standards and values and establishing these in official or unofficial institutions. *Emotional identification* relates to the sense of belonging, which comes into being through endogenous or exogenous processes. Taken altogether, they determine the spatial identification on a local and regional, and on a national and global level as well. My main objective is, according to the arguments introduced previously, to focus on transnational communities. These are social groups with participating actors and/or members, which are engaged in interactions sufficiently close, although also over longer cross-border distances to some degree, which display a shared transnational identity, interest, culture, project or episteme. Transnational communities retain ties to their communities of origins (by the growing amount of remittances, multimedia connections, improved transportation etc.), and establish new (mostly also trans-neighbourhood and inter-neighbourhood) communities in the host country or host town in question. It seems that these people – more extreme than the original residents – belong to a kind of community or communities that exist in different locations. Moreover, further research shows that one can distinguish at least three kinds of transnational communities based on their prime motive: the so called classic (refugees), modern (guest workers) and post-modern transnational communities (expats). For these groups, I shall briefly analyse the form and degree of functional, normative and emotional identification (local or transnational) in three cases, in Buenos Aires, São Paulo and the Randstad Holland. The aim is to compare the degree of transnationality and/or local relationship more precisely as a degree of single, double or perhaps even multiple relationship. From here, some conclusions and recommendations will be drawn concerning migrant areas in general, and Dutch policy of deprived neighbourhoods in particular.

Migrant communities

The United Nations estimates that there are currently around 190 million migrants worldwide, around 3% of the total world population. [United Nations, 2005] Migrants are defined here as people who live, work or reside in a country other than that in which they were born. However, following Castells, it can be observed that this view does not seem very concerned with the boom in the world economy and its highly inter-related nature. Whereas foreign direct investment has become the driving force of globalization, and global trade has become a main conductor of transborder interdependence, only 1.5% of the global labour force worked outside their native country during the mid-1990s. [Castells, 1996, p.232] But in comparison with 1960 the figure for labour migrants has tripled. In addition, the number of migrants with double passports has grown enormously; in the Netherlands, it almost tripled in the last twenty years. [CBS, 2008] Moreover, there is an increasing convergence between inflows and outflows. [OECD, 2007] Whereas in the 1960s it was mainly immigration into OECD countries that predominated,[14] emigration from these countries has now become almost as high. In other words, globally speaking, a reciprocal migration to, from, and between these OECD countries is evolving.

[14] Further information can be found in the study reports of the research journey, available on demand at the University of Utrecht, Faculty of Geosciences Department of Social Geography and Spatial Planning.

The variety of migrants has increased considerably, too. Whereas formerly migration occurred out of necessity, for political or religious reasons, in the last few decades there has been a marked increase in voluntary migration based on social or economic motives. Here one can also distinguish between more or less forced migration (due to poverty, unemployment or family-led migration) or more or less voluntary, career-driven migration (by scientific, highbrow blue collar workers, high-technicians etc.) In a matrix of voluntary and forced migration, accounted for by socio-political and economic reasons respectively, Richmond and Boyle et al. distinguish 19 to 20 different kinds of migrant communities. [Richmond, 1988; Boyle et al., 1998] However, the numerical distinction is not yet easy to determine based on the available data. Thus, for example, the Netherlands now has around 3.2 million non-native residents (almost 20% of the total number of the Dutch population). Almost 1.5 million non-native residents are of Western origin, while almost 600,000 people came from the former colonies and are therefore Dutch in juridical terms. Moreover approximately 200,000 of the Western non-native residents are from the former Eastern European countries, and a large number of these are in the Netherlands to work as 'seasonal workers'. [CBS 2008] Therefore depending on the definition, only 5-10% of the Dutch population could be characterized as immigrants from so called 'oriental, non-Western cultures', more or less forced to migrate out of poverty and/or economic reasons.

At the same time, however, the transnational orientation has also grown enormously within these immigrant groups. This is apparent not only from the marked increase in Internet and multimedia traffic between the host country

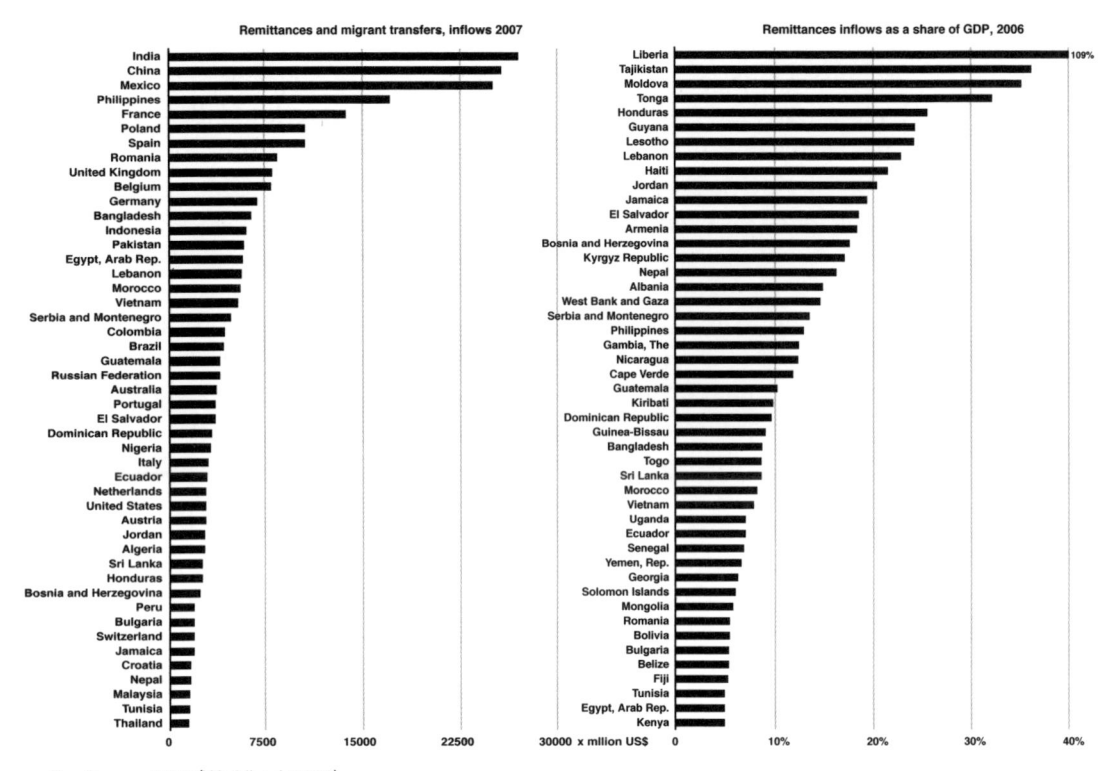

Remittances 2008 (Worldbank 2008)

and mother country, or the above-mentioned increase in double passports, but principally also from the marked increase in the volume of remittances. The total volume of remittances worldwide to developing countries has more than quadrupled in the past 15 years, to around $206 billion per year. This is almost as much as the total amount of foreign direct investment and almost four times the figure for official national development aid to third world countries. [World Bank 2007] The contribution made by remittances to the gross national product of a country such as Tonga is more than 40%, whilst it accounts for as much as 15% in the case of more populous countries such as Albania, Jamaica and Bosnia-Herzegovina, and almost 10% in the case of the Philippines, Pakistan and Morocco.

The reasons for these remittance growth appear not to lie purely in self-interest in the form of investments in the mother country (with a view to retirement prospects for instance) or temporary forms of savings and lending in that country. The sending of money back to the country of origin is also inspired by altruism or conscious family planning, whereby the migrant abroad has to support his own relatives in his home country. The countries of origin also pursue deliberate incentive policies, precisely aimed at increasing the contribution to GDP. [Stark, 1991; Ratha, 2003; Lucas, 2004]

For that matter, transnationalism of the kind referred to above, is in itself not a new phenomenon. Its origins go back to the exodus of the Jews from the

Promised Land of Judea after the conquest of the Kingdom of Israel in 722 BC, and later more definitively in the wake of the Great Jewish Revolt and the Bar Kokhba Revolt, which were put down by the Romans in 70 and 135 AD respectively. The scattering of Jews across the surrounding regions as a result of this, and the explicitly cultivated desire for a bond with the customs and traditions of the region of origin whilst residing somewhere else, is called Diaspora. However, nowadays it has taken on much more wide-ranging forms, also encompassing other peoples. Therefore one now talks of *New, Sustained* or even *Global Diasporas*. [Cohen, 1997; Van Hear, 1998; Braziel et al, 2003] Following these contributions and for the purposes of this study, we distinguish three kinds of transnational communities and diasporas:

- the more or less *classic forms* of diasporic communities which were virtually (politically or religiously) forced out of their country of origin and went to live elsewhere, often regrouping (at least initially), such as the aforementioned Jewish communities in all their capacities, the Flemish in the Netherlands after the retake of Antwerp, Bruges, Gent, Brussels etc. by the Spanish in the 16th century, or more recently the Amish in the USA and Canada, the Malaccans after the Dutch retreat out of Indonesia, etc.
- the growing groups of *immigrant workers*, including (from as early as the 18th century onwards) the Chinese, the Irish, Spanish, Italians, Moroccans, Turks and others. It was initially expected that these groups would return to their country of origin once their working life had ended. Some did, others still plan to, whilst others assume that they might never go back. Here we therefore often seem to see a diversified dual relationship.
- *the expatriates*, a group that is commonly more well-to-do, and over the years may have developed a multiple, global relationship with all kind of cultures rather than a bilateral one. Among this group of people, temporary residence has developed as a way of life, whereby transnationalism is cultivated in a somewhat 'zap'-like behaviour. Nonetheless, this transnational community is also made up of people and households of all sorts and conditions, displaying mutually different forms of relationship with the host country.

Diasporic metropoles – introducing Buenos Aires and São Paulo

This compound orientation of these three distinct transnational communities was the subject of further analysis in Latin America, in the framework of a study trip with 15 students and housing professionals in the spring of 2008. During three months we have investigated the context and historical background of the transnational and diasporic communities mentioned above, interviewed stake- and shareholders at the spot and executed additional data research to backup the conclusions. The results of this analysis were then compared to the situation in the urban agglomeration of Western Holland (the Randstad). Buenos Aires became a case city, while it could be termed the immigrants' metropolis *par excellence*. Less than 2 per cent of the current

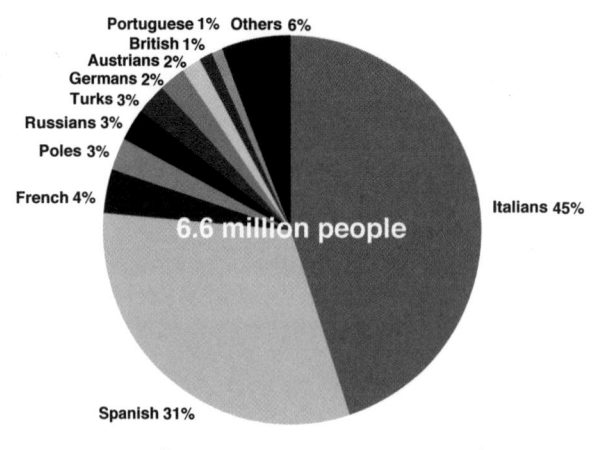

Immigration in Argentina 1857-1940 (Dirección Nacional de Migraciones,1970)

population is descended from the original Amerindians. Instead, Buenos Aires was founded by the Spanish in the 16th century and after Argentina's independence, was inhabited, especially in the second half of the 19th century, by migrants from Europe, mainly from Italy and Spain, but also from France, Poland, Russia, Turkey, Germany, Austria, etc. Apart from that, with 250,000 people, Buenos Aires also has the largest Jewish community in Latin America. [Keeling, 1992; Alamandoz, 2002] However, in the last few decades of the 20th century Buenos Aires mainly experienced migrations from Asia (China, Korea, and Taiwan) and its immediate neighbouring countries (Bolivia, Peru and Paraguay). The *porteños* therefore currently consist of relatively large groups of migrants of more than a hundred different ethnic groups. [Avni, 2005] The proportion of the original Criollo and Mestizo (descendants of the Spanish colonists) is extremely small.

The situation in the Brazilian metropolis São Paulo is comparable to a degree, although dissimilar on some points. Like Buenos Aires, it was founded as an advanced mission and trading post during the colonial era; though in this case by the Portuguese. Like Buenos Aires, it was a fairly insignificant city until the middle of the 19th century. After the abolition of slavery in 1888, large numbers of people started to migrate from Europe to São Paulo, albeit to a lesser degree than to Buenos Aires. The presence of the world's largest Japanese community outside Japan (in excess of 300,000 people) also dates from this period. Unlike Buenos Aires, however, São Paulo experienced its greatest development after the Second World War, particularly when the economic sector in the USA was looking for new possibilities for expansion, in the automobile industry and textiles *inter alia*, and with the import substitution policy pursued by the State after the Second World War. That in turn led to European and Japanese migration again (albeit in this case amongst the more highly educated groups) and in particular to a sizeable migration of *nordestinos* from the rural areas of north-eastern Brazil to the city. In addition to these large groups of poor Brazilians, Greater São Paulo is now home to around

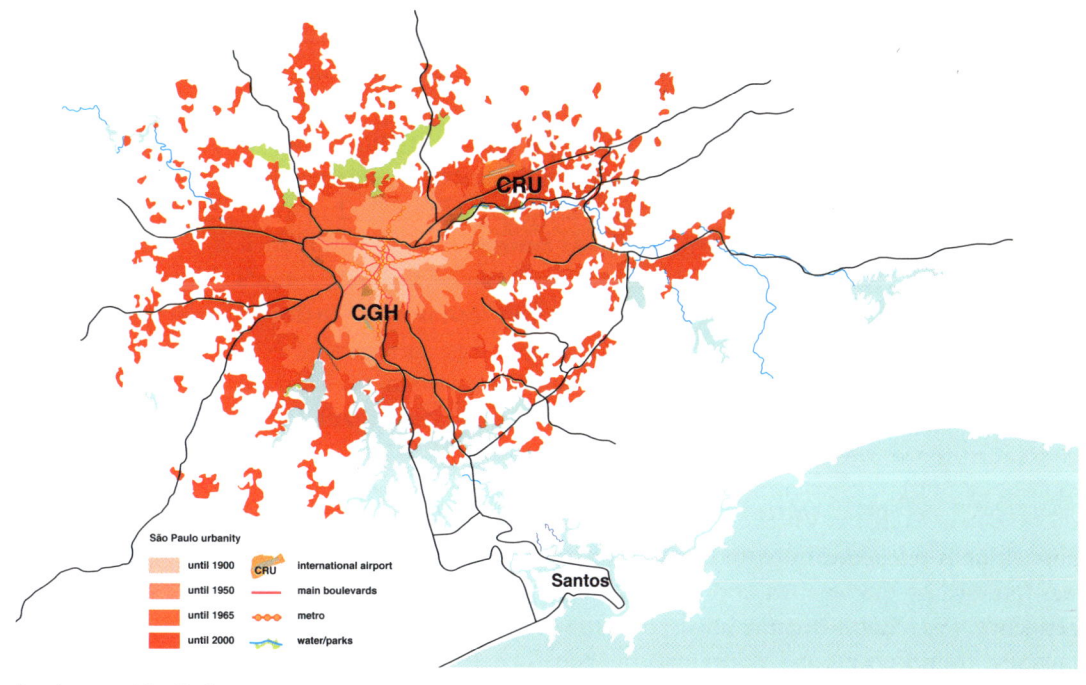

Development of São Paulo

6 million original Italians, 3 million original Portuguese, 3 million Africans and 1 million Arabs and approximately 1.5 million people from various other nations. Here, too, migration from Asia (especially Korea and China) has grown markedly, in alternating waves, in recent decades. This has made São Paulo, at least ethnically speaking, the most diverse city in Brazil. [Wirth, 1978; Instituto Brasileiro de Geografia e Estat'stica, 2007]

However, both Argentina/Buenos Aires and Brazil/São Paulo have an extremely relaxed and liberal immigration policy. Therefore, integration tends to pass through channels other than ethnic ones (for example functional or social). Most ethnic groups quickly feel Argentinean or Brazilian (respectively *porteños* or *paulistas*), although this does not detract from the fact that, in the transnational communities distinguished above, some clear prominent differences and spatial identification patterns can indeed be ascertained. Because of space considerations, we shall only deal with a few of the most striking cases of these in this chapter.[15]

15 Although this distinction has some links with the distinction made by Patsy Healey in Collaborative Planning [1997] between Representative democracy, Pluralist democracy, Corporatism and Clientilism, Purcell takes a more critical and normative stance here, while Healey seems to assess all four alternatives suitable for collaborative governance.

Liberdade, São Paulo – the classic diaspora The development of the aforementioned Japanese community in São Paulo, for example, has a long and turbulent history. The first Japanese came to Brazil about a hundred years ago, as the result of the collapse of the traditional agricultural economy in Japan and the need for new farm labourers in the coffee plantations in Brazil, particularly in the province of São Paulo after the abolition of slavery.

However, the housing, working and living conditions on these plantations were generally still so primitive that many soon decided to leave them. [Cardoso, 1998] With not enough money to go back to Japan, but enough to buy new land, some started up a farm of their own on a new plot of land. To be independent of the still poorly functioning distribution channels in Brazil and to avoid fraud, these pioneers simultaneously established farming corporations of their own, which regulated purchases and sales and maintained the community's level of welfare. These were so successful that they in turn not only attracted other Japanese immigrants, but also introduced new crops and farming techniques to Brazil. Partly with the help of the Japanese government, which in this way attempted to foster Japanese nationalism among the migrants, other cultural amenities, such as Japanese schools, were established in these communities. In 1938, there were around 187 schools of this kind, accommodating some 10,000 students, which thus maintained an important link with the mother country and Japan's own original culture. [Ameniya, 1998]

However, when Brazil became involved in the Second World War, the local Japanese community came under pressure too. The Japanese schools were closed, the farming associations dissolved, and the Japanese estates nationalized. At this time, there was also a ban on speaking Japanese in public. The community now also had to do without the financial support it had still been receiving before the Second World War from Japan for the maintenance of the economic, political and socio-cultural amenities. At this point many left for the big city of São Paulo, particularly the district of Liberdade, a slightly dilapidated but originally inexpensive Italian district directly south of the city's old Central Business District. It offered the best chance for these immigrants to ensure their further development in the city. When relations were normalized again after the Second Word War, other Brazilian Japanese and new Japanese refugees (this time mainly more highly educated and more urban-oriented people) also saw the neighbourhood as a good operating base to settle. Therefore the Japanese community in Liberdade experienced its hey-day in the 1950s and 1960s. [Nihonline, 2002] Japanese culture flourished, specific hotels and apartments quickly spread, and the Japanese retail sector, hotel, and catering industry developed rapidly.

Meanwhile, the third and sometimes even fourth generation of Japanese has become well assimilated in the general Brazilian and Paulista community. The level of education has risen, original economic activities have broadened to take in urban activities, and a growing number of inter-racial marriages are occurring. Moreover, Japanese who wanted to return to the original mother country were regarded as second-rate citizens there. This prompted the decision of many to stay permanently in São Paulo. Since then, the development of the Japanese in Brazil is regarded as a success story. [Hastings, 1969] Thanks to their training and work ethics, the Brazilian Japanese have permeated into practically every layer of Brazilian civic, public and business society. In consequence,

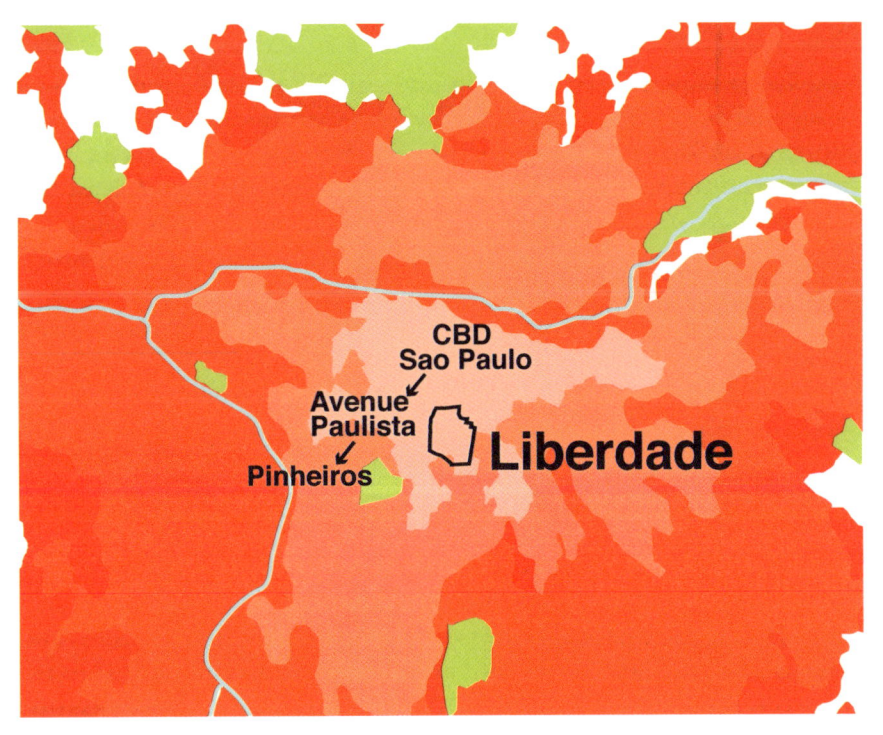

Location of Liberdade in São Paulo

people from Liberdade have also moved to better neighbourhoods, spread all over São Paulo. Their place has been taken first by Koreans, and later by Chinese. Despite this assimilation behaviour, however, Liberdade still functions as a cultural home-base for many Japanese Brazilians. Here is where they still find their cultural, religious and culinary facilities, the karaoke bars, shops, hairdressers, and so on. Therefore, they return regularly to inhale something of their original culture. In fact, the Brazilian Japanese return to a 'mother district' rather than to a mother country. [Nihonline, 2002]

The transnational character of the Japanese community in São Paulo has therefore evolved considerably over the decades from a functional and normative identification to what might be termed an emotional identification. The Japanese are now soundly integrated into the Brazilian and Paulista community, their functional network is broad and not specifically Japanese, and hardly any of the Brazilian Japanese consider returning to the original native country at some point. [Besemer et al, 2008] The Japanese Embassy in Brazil still has an annual budget of around 1 million Reais (approx. €375,000) for investment in national projects. But these are no longer aimed by definition at the Brazilian Japanese, but at activities linked to their institutions. [Sato, 2008] For all that, Brazilian Japanese youth once again displays a great interest in specifically Japanese PopArt and related multimedia. [Sato, 2003] What is more, the community (even though there are hardly any Japanese actually living there any more) is still attached to Liberdade and most of the Brazilian Japanese amenities, retail, hotel and catering and cultural institutions, such as the Association Cultural Assistencial da Liberdade (ACAL), the *Sociedade Brasileira de Cultura Japonesa* (BUNKYO) and the Japanese Immigration Museum, are still established in the district. This means that people constantly return to the area. Against this background, professor Lopion, in co-operation with ACAL, has conceived the plan to maintain and further develop the Japanese character of the district, along with the Chinese and Korean communities now living there. Each of the three existing flyovers in the neighbourhood, and the streets and squares pertaining to them, has been given an East-Asian cultural feel of its own: Japanese, Chinese and Korean. The plan is supported not only by representatives in the federal parliament and the Japanese community, but also by major Chinese and Korean multinationals that want to elevate the image of their communities in Brazilian society. [Woo, 2008]

Villa 31, Buenos Aires – the modern diaspora A different case is that with respect of the immigrant workers and migrants in Villa 31, Buenos Aires in Argentina. This district developed in the economic crisis of 1929, when the dockworkers lost their jobs and, for lack of financial resources, went to settle with their families in this adjacent area. It was one of the first *Villa Miserias* (literally: place of great misery), where an informal economy, organization and spatial management developed from the very outset. However, the district is centrally located near the *Estación Retiro* (Buenos Aires' main train station) and the *Terminal de Omnibus* (the terminus station for long-distance buses and coaches). Furthermore, Buenos Aires' Central Business District, Plaza San Martin, with its luxury palaces and hotels, and the more chic San Telmo are within walking distance. This offered the residents of Villa 31 not only an excellent operating base from which they could ply their (odd-job) services and trades in these neighbouring districts, but it also gave their children the chance to attend the relatively good primary public schools; still considered to be of high-quality in Argentina. Therefore this Villa – more than the other immigrant districts – has always acted as a magnet for migrant labourers. Currently and in addition to large migrant numbers from the north-east of Argentina, the Villa is mainly populated by Paraguayans, Bolivians and Peruvians. [Maguid, 2004] The latter are here illegally, incidentally, since Peru is not a member of MERCOSUR.

In the 1960s and early 1970s, the district was home of between 45,000 and 60,000 people, mainly tradesmen working in the building and construction sector. By that time, a solid organization had developed in the neighbourhood, partly due to the influence of Padre Mujica, who advocated the Catholic doctrine of the 'Liberation theology'. This theology views social repression, inequality and injustice as earthly sins, and Jesus' love for humankind and devotion to the poor as the basis for a radical Christian socialist movement. [Berryman, 1987; Smith, 1991] Whatever the case may be, under Padre Mujica's influence,

Villa 31 in Buenos Aires

the residents of the Villa began to organize themselves more effectively and set up a kind of democratic council. Conditions were collectively improved, with facilities such as water, gas, electricity and sewerage. Co-operatives for the provision and distribution of food were also set up. [IAI, 2008]

However, during the military dictatorship of 1976-83, strong-arm tactics were used to deal with this (potential) 'hotbed of resistance', and virtually all families were forcibly evicted. At the beginning of the 1980s, only 180 to 200 people were still living in the area. However, with the restoration of democracy, migrants (both old and new) soon came back, and by the mid-1980s, the area's population had already risen to 12,000. Today there are 23,000 people living here. All the same, in the mid-1990s, the local council had other infrastructure and river-front plans with the area, and used 'golden handshakes' in an attempt to incite the residents to move. This was partly successful and the council proved capable of building one of the missing links in the motorway network right through the district. However, due to the strategic location of the Villa, the residents affected often did a U-turn and ended up coming back to other parts of the area. At the same time, a more professional approach was now adopted towards the district residents' organization, with the help of NGOs, contributions and voluntary work. At the heart of the organization is a co-ordinating committee, made up of representatives of each of the six sub-neighbourhoods (Inmigrantes, Güemes, YPF, Communicaciones, Autopista and 31 II), who are elected every two years. They organize the daily routine, but there are also community restaurants, neighbourhood associations and sports clubs, as well as education and supplementary care and childcare facilities. There is also a specific security service for the district, a kind of co-operative construction company and property administration; in a nutshell, something approaching a state within a state. [Bos et al, 2008]

However, the land on which Villa 31 stands is almost entirely owned by the federal government. At the same time, the consortium responsible for the successful harbour-front development of Puerto Madero is eager to develop Villa 31 along similar lines, and has already drawn up an investment plan of around $460 million to this end: Puerto Madero II. For the time being, though, the federal government (the landowner) and the local municipal authority (the body responsible for planning) have hitherto failed to reach agreement on the scale and manner of the redevelopment. This situation has been seized upon by the Villa 31 residents' organization, which is stressing its 75-year residential history in the area, explicitly requesting better integration in the environment and formalization of the area's own amenities, and calling for the right to take part in the ongoing planning process. [IAI, 2008] Because of the increasing support it is receiving from wider layers of the *porteño* population, there appears to be a stalemate. This could be a prelude to the introduction of a more interactive, participatory planning of the area, with which the São Paulo city council, for instance, is currently creating a furore in the city's favellas. [Bos et al, 2008]

Although Villa 31 thus consists of an extremely varied, alternating and temporary population (rooms and even beds are sometimes rented by the hour or part of a day), it also constitutes a very tightly-knit community. The reason for this lies not so much in ethnic, social or emotional factors, but mainly on the grounds of a functional relationship. Much more so than the other Villas, Retiro 31 enjoys an extremely strategic location in Buenos Aires. Moreover, with the recent government subsidy for the transport of the poor coming to an end, a central housing has virtually become a necessity for survival of the immigrants. Furthermore, the (informal) collective is crucial in order for a stand to be made against the strong endogenous forces acting upon the district (land ownership, planning powers and investment). Should the composition of the community change and other migrants manage to come and live in Villa 31, they too, should immediately be included in the community and asked to make their own contribution, based on a strategy of pure self-preservation. The only exception to this is perhaps the Peruvians, who are actually ignored by the other villa residents because of their violent behaviour and extra-MERCOSUR and thus illegal status. International Mafia gangs are suspected here. But this does not apply to the other migrants (such as the Bolivians and Paraguayans for example) who – although they still have strong ties with the native country (in the form of remittances for example) are an integral part of the migrant community. Transnationalism here is thus no obstacle to local cohesion. In fact, it has nothing to do with it. Indeed, the driving forces behind the Villa 31 community (first Padre Mujica, then the Villa 31 co-ordinating committee, and now also the José Valenzuela's group which supports the migrants' spatial integration objective) are seeking as much support as possible precisely from related NGOs, contributors, spatial experts, planning experts and (if necessary) socio-cultural institutions. All networks, including virtual ones, are being used for this purpose. And in this respect, the strategy also looks similar to that of the Zapatistas, described by Manuel Castells in *The City and the Grassroots* and *The Power and Identity* [Castells, 1997] *inter alia*. The Internet is also being used here to garner external support for community's own goals, suppressed desires, and interests.

Expat networks – the post-modern diaspora For that matter, Internet also turns out to be a crucial cohesive factor for the third transnational community studied in Buenos Aires and São Paulo, namely the expatriate community. This is probably the most diversified and mobile of all three groups, and the least univocal. After all, who exactly are we to understand by the term? The wictionary gives the following definition: '*persons temporarily or permanently residing in a country and culture other than that of the person's upbringing or legal residence*'. [Wictionary, 2008] However, that refers also to the classic and modern diaspora described above. Therefore the term is mostly taken to encompass those people who are posted by a transnational corporation (TNC), on a voluntary basis, to a country other than that from which the company originates, in order to represent the company's interests on a temporary or permanent basis. The costs involved in such postings mean they usually involve people holding quite senior functions in corporate or governmental upper echelons; or those who are not so easily replaced by local staff. [Shell, 2007] The OECD distinguishes various and broader segments, such as *trainees, working holiday makers, seasonal workers, intra-company transfers* and *other temporary workers*. In 2005 these categories accounted for around 1.8 million people in the 17 OECD countries, representing growth of some 7% vis-à-vis the previous year. [OECD, 2007] Moreover, according to a recent Regioplan study carried out for the Dutch Ministry of VROM, it does make a difference if one is referring to young or older people, singles or families, or people from a specific cultural background. For example, Asian expats abroad are found to behave in a completely different way to their colleagues of American or European origin, and this includes senior posts too. [Regioplan, 2005]

To increase comparability between them, as well as guaranteeing the simplest access, we therefore limited ourselves in Buenos Aires and São Paulo to the Dutch expats, with the British expats as a reference group. They were approached in advance with a survey, and some of them were then consulted later in greater detail in an in-depth interview, and placed in a broader context by means of an additional study of literature and stake-holders. [Meier et al. 2008]

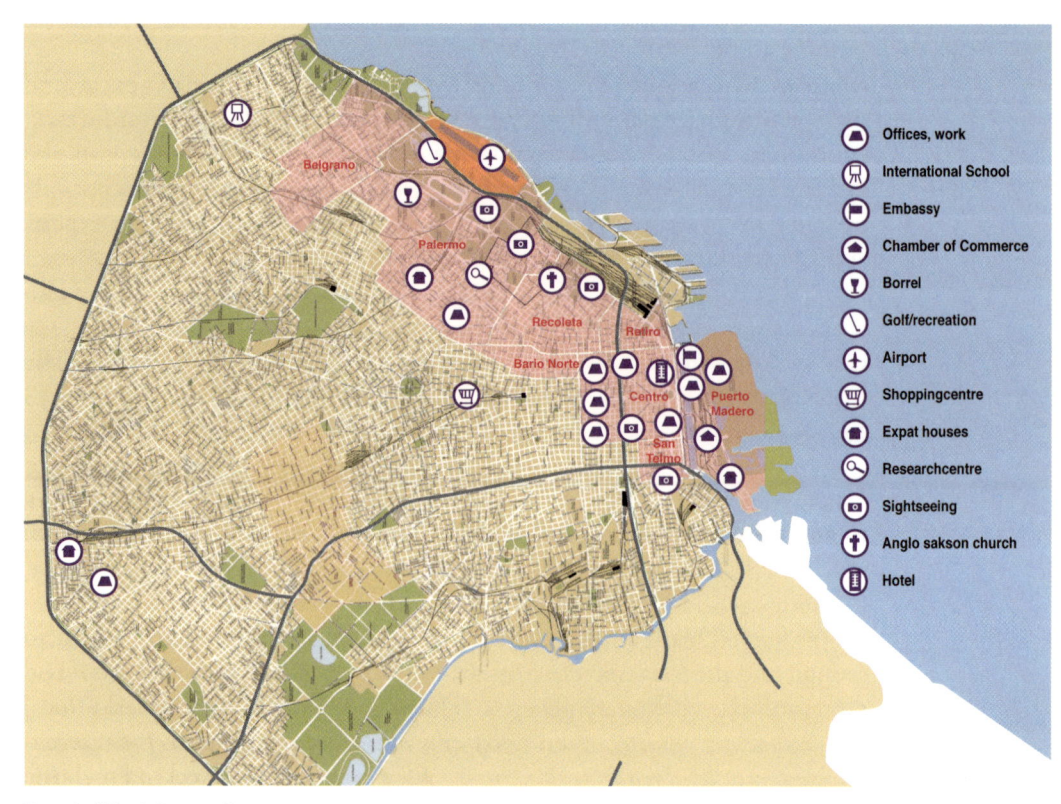

Expat facilities in Buenos Aires

This study reveals that expats in Buenos Aires mainly live in the districts of Palermo, San Telmo, Recoleta and Barrio Norte. In São Paulo they live in the residential quarters of Itaim Bibi, Alto da Boa Vista and Vila Nova Conceição. The study also reveals that expats with a family more often look for low-rise buildings and walled communities, somewhat further removed from the busy city centre, and commonly in a nice green environment. Singles or couples in Buenos Aires tend to prefer to live in the city itself. In São Paulo, on the other hand, hardly any single were noted among the Dutch and British expats. Important factors for those single expats are trendy neighbourhoods, with a good environment for going out and long opening hours, such as, for example, Palermo, San Telmo, Recoleta and Barrio Norte in Buenos Aires. For São Paulo, less unambiguous conclusions can be drawn on this issue because of the small population of single expats assessed.

It also appears that expat families, in particular, regard it as very important to be near a good international school (if possible an integrated primary, secondary and high school). It is important for these schools to be AAIE-accredited, which guarantees a more or less comparable worldwide programme, so that in the event of an unavoidable move to another country, the children can take up their studies again elsewhere without having to make too many adjustments. These schools often also provide these students with interesting cultural and sporting exchange programmes with other AAIE schools in the continent in question. They also offer possibilities for the expat's partner to make contact with others. Outside the international school, the Anglo-Saxon church also seems to play an important role for the British when it comes to making contacts. For the Dutch, it is often the Dutch culture club abroad or the monthly business drinks reception organized by the embassy or consulate.

In all cases, the survey, follow-up in-depth interviews and study of the literature all reveal that contact with neighbours barely plays any meaningful role. Outside their work, expats seek social contact chiefly with their fellow compatriots, other expats (in the context of clubs and societies), or especially friends and family in the homeland (whether these come over to visit or not). The Internet and mobile phone traffic is vitally important here. Only single people and couples have frequent or some contact with local acquaintances or friends at work. Relations at work and consequently ease of access in getting to and from the place of work are therefore vital, perhaps much more so in São Paulo than in Buenos Aires. [Meier et al. 2008]

Of the three communities studied, the expatriates therefore perhaps appear to be the most transnational. Both in their functional orientation, and social and emotional ties, their community is organized chiefly through networks (local and transnational). A number of hubs are relevant here, such as the international school, the Anglo-Saxon church, the sports club, the weekend nightlife scene or the monthly business drinks reception. However, as long as the immediate working, housing and living conditions fulfil a number of basic, often generic conditions, one particular environment can apparently be exchanged for another. In this regard, this lifestyle can indeed to some degree be called 'post-modern'. However, it was further observed that this is mainly the vogue for West European and American expatriates. After all, a further study of literature clearly reveals that Asian expats attach greater importance to mutual contact and specific environmental conditions. [Regioplan, 2005] Moreover, our study of expats in Buenos Aires and São Paulo revealed that the numbers of expats being posted by companies is declining. For cost considerations, they are being replaced more and more often by local employees, who are also increasingly more highly trained and qualified than before.

Back to the Netherlands
It is striking that in comparison with these cases, there is quite a distorted image of the so-called migrant movements in the Netherlands. First of all, and even more than in Argentina and Brazil, we can note that the Netherlands also has a massive and extensive history in the field of migration. As far back as the 16th, 17th and even the 18th centuries, the Dutch Republic was the centre of attention for the largest migrating share of the population in the North Sea Region. [Lucassen 1987, 1993, 2002] Between 1550 and 1800 it received approximately three quarter of all the migrants in the North Sea regions. As a result, in the mid-17th century for example, 40% of the population of Amsterdam

had been born abroad. Pre-modern industrial cities like Leiden and Haarlem even acquired populations with over 50 per cent of foreign-born residents. This was partly due to the retake by the Catholic Spanish general De Farnese of the 'rebellious' Protestant trade cities in Flanders – such as Bruges (April 1584), Ghent (September 1584), Brussels (March 1585), Mechelen (July 1585) and Antwerp (August 1585) – the subsequent closure of the Scheldt by the Dutch and the massive exodus of Flemish towards the more liberal trading cities in the emerging Dutch Republic. [Briels 1976, Asaert 2004] In addition, Van Lottum points at the enormous demographic discrepancies and wage gaps between the North Sea regions, which resulted in an additional migration flow from especially the Norwegian and German regions towards the prosperous cities in Holland. [Van Lottum 2007] After the mid-17th century, these were also used as temporarily in-between stops underway towards the newly discovered regions in the Americas. From the start of the 18th century however, the capital city of London in particular assumed this role. But, even in the 20th century, in the decolonization years after the Second World War, the Netherlands still received massive migrant flows from abroad; such as some 300,000 Dutch-Indonesians and some 350,000 Dutch-Surinamese for instance from the 1950s until the 1970s. So from its earliest start, the Dutch Republic could be characterized by its multinational and even multicultural population. Moreover, it was even admired for and it prospered amply from its open, liberal and tolerant attitude towards foreigners.

Nevertheless present migrant movements seem to differ in three major areas from these age-old migration processes. First of all, migrant flows in the last fifty years have seemed to evolve exclusively or predominantly out of economic motives. While (at least also) religious, ideological or political motives were dominant during Dutch migrant history, the massive Mediterranean migrants from the 1960s onwards could be characterized as exclusive labour migrants. This became particularly a problem, when the provisional end to the tremendous post-war economic growth during the 1970s paralleled the more or less simultaneously trend towards migrant family reunification. Especially these migrants became the first victims of the economic recession. And although a new economic upswing occurred in the nineties, Engbersen (amongst others) indicates that a structural underclass has evolved since then that is apparently unable to make the transition from the industrial to the post-industrial requirements. According to Engbersen, neither the welfare policies from the previous century nor the neo-liberal policies of the twenty-first century developed an adequate solution for that problem. As a result, the problem evolved into a situation where the drop-out effects are reinforcing themselves more and more. To turn the negative spiral around, a more intelligent and major institutional innovation is needed to cross the sectorial columns of employment, welfare, education, housing, spatial planning and so on. [Dahrendorf 1987, Engbersen 2006]

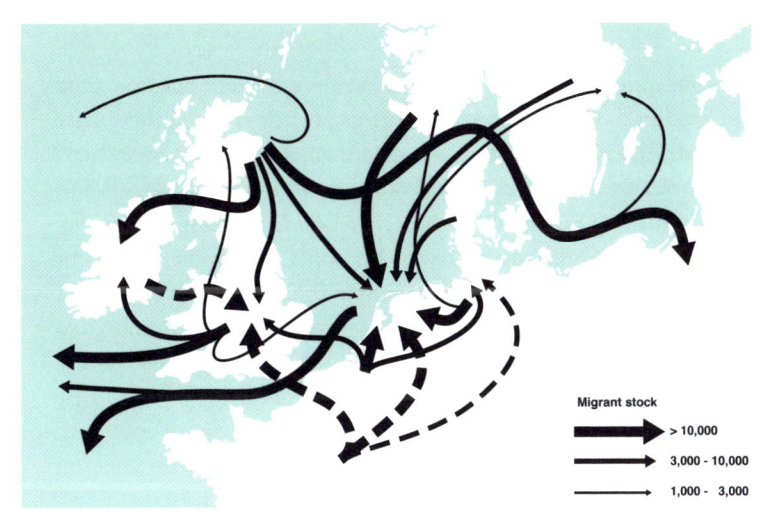

Immigration in the Netherlands 1650 [Van Lottum 2007]

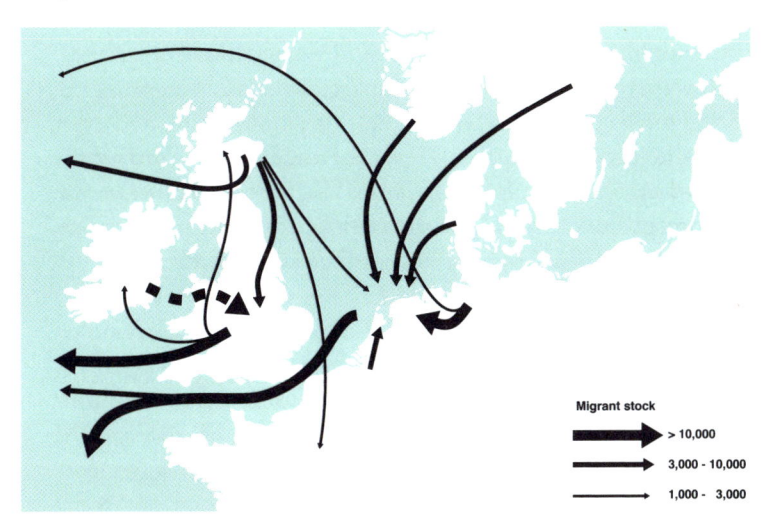

Immigration in the Netherlands 1750 [Van Lottum 2007]

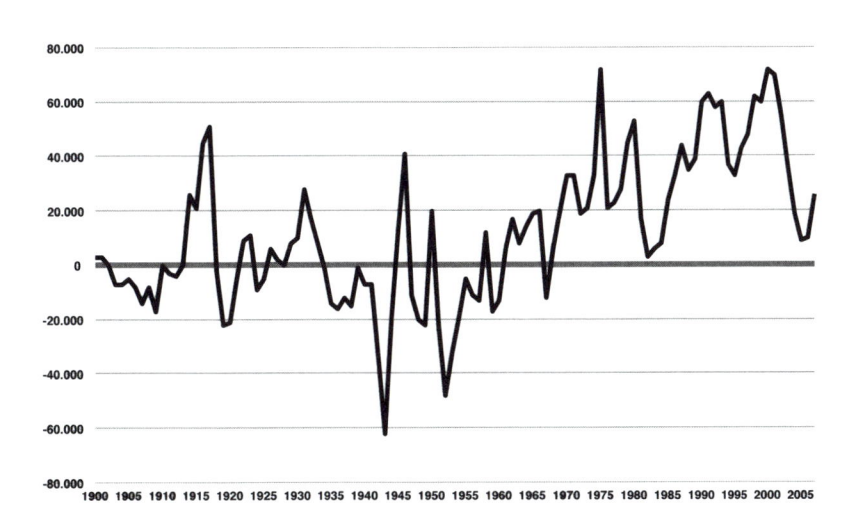

Migrant stock
→ > 10,000
→ 3,000 - 10,000
→ 1,000 - 3,000

Migration balance 1900-2007 in the Netherlands (CBS 2008)

Second, and as mentioned above, this contradiction between the so-called 'upper-class' and 'under-class' also takes the form of and/or is strengthened by the recent clashes of the Christian Occident and Islamic cultures. [Habermas 2008] That means that the setting of the 'deprived districts' in the Netherlands and elsewhere in Western Europe (where most of the '21st-century under-class' live) is more heavily charged, or perhaps more to the point, charged in an ideological way. While in Latin America one can mainly identify an economic contrast between rich and poor migrants, this is perhaps a fact in Europe to a lesser degree, but has evolved here, on the other hand, seemingly also into a more fundamental, structural and cultural contrast between opposing value patterns. Especially after 9/11 and the so-called 'final breakdown' of a smooth multicultural society, it has burdened the migration and integration question ostensibly.

And last but not least, in contrast to the age-old processes, actual migration flows are also increasingly taking part in reciprocal transnational structures. This said, I do not want to stress that transnational ties weren't there from the beginning. But due to the new means of hearing, speaking, acting and even banking at distance (telecommunication), it has become easier for migrants to retain ties to communities and cultures of origin. Since the mid-nineties, the concept of transnationalism has therefore become a key concept in migration studies and has also resulted in a rich harvest of focused research. [see for instance www.transcomm.ox.ac.uk] At the same time, however, it has also drawn new (political) attention to the question of identification. In this context, mainly populist politicians suppose that the more one identifies hem/herself with compatriots living outside the country, the less he or she is integrated in the host country and the less he or is able to participate in the socio-economic life of that host country. Nevertheless, recent research amongst a variety of migrants (Moroccans, Antilleans, former Yugoslavians, Iraqi, Japanese and Americans) in the Netherlands has shown that there is a positive relationship between identification with the native Dutch and the international migrant diaspora. Respondents who strongly identify with indigenous Dutchmen, also identify themselves strongly with compatriots in the homeland or in other immigration countries. Conversely, migrants in a weak socio-economic position, do not undertake more trans-national activities, but rather identify themselves more with the culture and customs of compatriots in the host country and thus, when here, increasingly develop an own and in fact separate aversion to the culture of that host country. [Snel et al. 2004, Engbersen et al 2006]

Returning to the deprived neighbourhoods or the 'power districts' as they are called in the Netherlands, as well as to the distinction between the functional, normative and emotional identification as mentioned in paragraph 3.1, here and in Europe or elsewhere, it can be reported that identification with the place and/or the formation of groups abroad is a complex, polymorphous and certainly not unambiguous process. It is heavily dependent on the institutional

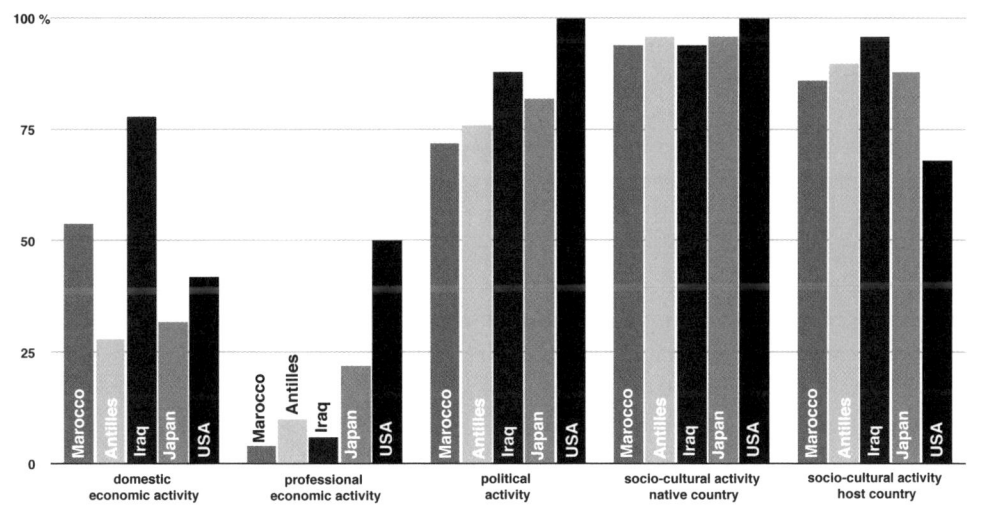

(Trans)national activities of Dutch immigrants [Snel, Engbersen, Leerkes 2004]

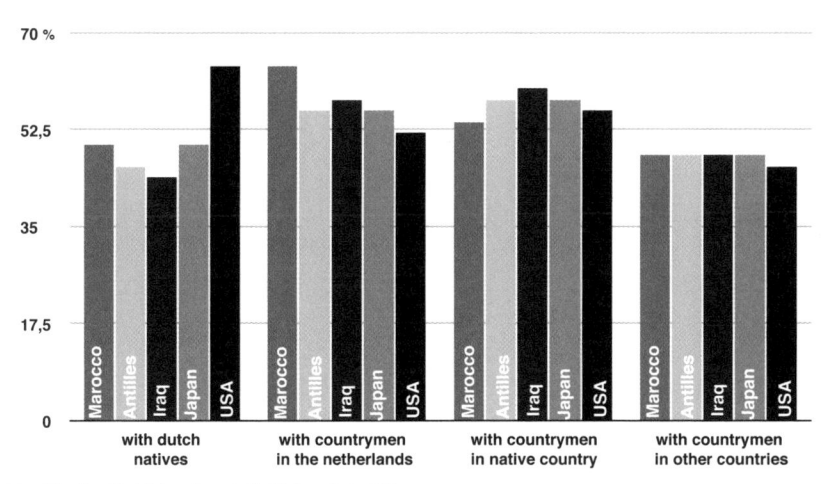

Identification Dutch immigrants [Snel, Engbersen, Leerkes, 2004]

and spatial setting, the target groups concerned and the (leading) actors operating within them. It is therefore relational in every sense. In some cases it even changes substantially over time. Whilst in the case of the Japanese migrants in Latin America the formation of groups and/or identification with the place originally found *functional expression* mainly in locally established production and trading corporations, during the Second Word War it shifted more towards a *normative identification*, also for the integration and housing of the new Japanese migrants who were arriving at the time. At this time, however, there is more a *cultural, emotional bond* with the district of Liberdade, due to the existing Japanese temples, culture, retail and the restaurants in the area.

At the same time, in other cases – such as the Jews in Buenos Aires, for example – this kind of affective shift has barely occurred over decades. Perhaps partly out of security considerations, there has actually always been identification with and a sense of feeling at home in a district when like-minded people with a comparable pattern of standards and values live there. Admittedly this is beginning to get blurred again among the youngest generations, although there is still a *permanent normative identification*, which if necessary moves right across the city, the region, or even countries. Important points of anchorage in this form of identification, such as the synagogue, school, library, etc. are simply set up anew elsewhere if necessary. The only thing that remains local, out of religious conviction, is the cemetery, where Jews literally and figuratively earn their eternal resting place.

Only in Villa 31 in Buenos Aires did we find a strong and convincing *spatial tie* with the district, irrespective of cultural background, age, religious persuasion, etc. But here, too, these connections do not depend on the superb or unique characteristics of the place itself. Rather a strong tie with the area exists because of the district's strategic position in a larger spatial context; and because of the strong bottom-up organization of the area. Nevertheless this also seems a fragile bond. For when economic centres of gravity shift across the city, the relative importance of this advantage diminishes vis-à-vis other villas or favelas, as, for example, appears in the relationship between the favelas of Heliopolis and Paraisopolis in São Paulo. Here too, there is more of a *functional bond* than a spatial one.

Similarly, no unambiguous answer can be given to the question as to whether strong transnational ties have an influence on the degree of integration and relationship with a district. As mentioned before, and according to Engbersen et al., transnational orientation could well join a local identification at the same time. In addition, Robert Merton also made the distinction fifty years ago between the locals and the cosmopolitans; whereby the former focus on the stable and fixed regimes, and the latter on the new and surprising ones. [Merton 1949] At first sight, this seems also be the case with regard to the expatriates investigated, who, instead of the specific characteristics of the neighbourhood, seem to attach more importance to generic facilities such as a secure neighbourhood (privatopias if necessary), international school, Anglo-Saxon church, standard wellness centre, shopping mall or lounge bar. On the other hand, it also emerges that among the immigrants in Villa 31, for example, despite sizeable remittances and lasting ties with the homeland, strong integration, group formation and even activism in the interests of the welfare of the district can be noted. Nevertheless, the nature of transnationality does indeed appear to have an influence on the nature and character of the local identification. After all, the Brazilian Japanese are now regarded as second-class citizens in Japan and have in fact developed a new kind of identification with their 'neighbourhood of origin' (instead of 'country of origin'). Argentinian Jews use Israel as a safety net and remigration area, when there is a danger of things going 'wrong' in the host country (such as, for example, during the military dictatorship and on the occasion of the bomb attacks in the 1990s), but return after a while to resume their activities. At the same time, there appears to be major differences in the desires, requirements and housing preferences between expatriates of Asian, West European and American origin (see Box 3.2), as well as their degree of assimilation and identification with the host country, sometimes also finding expression in transnational marriages and permanent residence. Here, instead of global floating, transnationality has in fact become locally solidified. However, it is still a dual or compound orientation, because in almost all cases, migrants, at least ostensibly, keep open the option of returning to their country of birth one day.

Initial conclusions and recommendations

If, against this background, we return to the policy initiatives regarding deprived areas (such as the Vogelaar districts), a few well-defined recommendations can be made despite these multiform and less unambiguous conclusions.

First, the Vogelaar approach focuses on the public space and the problems 'behind the front door', which is more correct than the former focus on housing supply. The exploratory Latin American study has also revealed that flourishing, coherent or attractive neighbourhoods also depend, where available, on institutional, social, cultural or even imaginary (f)actors other than a good housing supply. Extra emphasis on these (f)actors is indeed needed and developers and housing associations should heed them, instead of shifting responsibility for these issues on to other institutions. After all, it also determines the appeal and value of that home ownership (see Box 3.1).

At the same time, it can of course also be observed that the district could possibly be taken as a starting point, but at the same time it should not be the objective. It has already been asserted more comprehensively and frequently elsewhere that social ties, cohesion, integration and identification tend to run more along functional, normative, emotional and even time-dependent lines, other than spatial ones. Spatial considerations, possibilities and limitations certainly play a role, but tend to play last of all, in a conditioning or facilitating role, instead of being a central focus for special attention.

Third, and similarly, it can also be observed that the 40 *krachtwijken* or *power districts approach* and above all the conditioning criteria and considerations behind it are far too generic for practical solutions to be produced. The criteria established in the field of school drop-out, crime rate, percentage of foreigners, unemployment, educational level, etc. do say something, but mainly about the way in which planning was perpetrated and data inventoried in a top-down, structuralist manner in the past. This was and is no longer the way in which effective solutions can be brought about. To this end, each district, or rather spatial setting, is highly specific and unique, and effective spatial strategies should be produced in a more relational sense with the players involved in specific institutional and spatial contexts (see Box 3.1).

Fourth, this exploratory study shows that self-motivation plays a prominent role in the processes described here. The most integrating, coherent and binding spatial settings are those where powerful formal or informal residents' organizations or other types of organization come into being from the bottom up (see also Box 3.1). Sometimes, such as in the case of Villa 31, this is prompted by the fact that in the vicinity there are such strong and threatening forces descending on the district as to turn self-organization into a kind of (transnational) survival strategy. In other cases, those of the Heliopolis and Paraisopolis favelas in São Paulo, it is prompted by the fact that the residents are literally and figuratively given a rule-free context and/or the responsibility for fleshing out (parts of) the neighbourhood policy themselves by means of participatory budgeting. The strong district policy in the Netherlands, too, could take advantage of this more effectively – not so much by encouraging so-called 'voluntary work' in the neighbourhood from above, or even providing financial rewards for this, but rather by dovetailing much more closely with initiatives already up and running within the concerned communities themselves and stimulating the (in)formal institutional settings around that.

Fifth, the example of Liberdade shows that when a residential career in the district is not possible for the migrant groups in question, this does not immediately mean that the district is therefore doomed to be the city's or region's permanent waste pit. On the contrary, Liberdade shows that when migrant groups and transnational communities develop a strong functional and/or normative identification with the neighbourhood during their residence, and give expression to this in a cultural, functional and institutional programme, this can also lead to lasting emotional ties with the district. That goes for new-born generations too. Money, organizational power, support and new cultural expressions of transmigration then could constantly flow back to the neighbourhood itself. However, one condition for this does appear to be that new neighbourhood groups of immigrants (in the case of Liberdade with the Koreans and Chinese for instance) should have a more or less comparable system of standards and values and associated cultural expression, and should also be prepared to foster and further develop the unique characteristics they find there. In turn, this can also represent a springboard for these groups for further integration and social development. Precisely this, with the government's and housing associations' policies in mind, along with a targeted supporting cultural and events policy, could prove to be an effective strategy. However, here, too, it is anything but a magic formula for success. One will have to see by way of trial and error whether the transnational communities in question also actually grasp these opportunities.

Finally, the expat groups show specific ties and identification not so much with specific neighbourhoods or cities, but rather with specific objects, functions or housing, working and living environments. These are often extremely generic, but depending on the precise transnational background, age and household situation, specific points of emphasis can be discovered here too. Taking greater and more effective advantage of these specific expat objects, functions and housing in spatial planning does not in itself guarantee closer local ties between expat communities and the neighbourhood or city. The chiefly globally oriented economic, variable and floating identification of these groups, as well as other considerations in the case of more permanent establishment, are often still too strong for that. However, it could lead to different and unique districts, which are also very appealing to other local and native population groups as well (see Box 3.2). Spatially or even functionally integrated with deprived neighbourhoods, it could even set an intelligent and fundamental new agenda for these areas too.

BOX [3.1]

The world of Delfshaven: towards transnational housing

Many experts point out that it is difficult to distinguish between permanent and temporary migration. [Glick-Schiler et al. 1992, Staring 2001, Snel et al. 2004] The modern-day 'transmigrant' does not move from one society to another, but is someone who is at home in several worlds, speaks several languages and frequently earns his or her bread through border-crossing economic activities. This does not alter the fact that a section of the (Dutch) political establishment, supported by a significant amount of the electorate, has huge problems with this so-called transnational orientation. The persistent identification with the country of origin and/or with internationally dispersed migrant communities supposedly constitutes an obstacle to integration in the host country. For some time, the Dutch liberals (the VVD) have been a declared opponent of the possibility of dual nationality, echoed to a stronger degree by extreme right-wing parties like the Party For Freedom (PVV), Proud of the Netherlands (TON), and recently by the Leefbaar Rotterdam party, with the appointment of the mayor originating from another country (Mr Aboutaleb), who has both a Dutch and a Moroccan passport. In 2003 and 2004 this hypothesis provided a motivation for Snel, Engbersen and Leerkes to investigate how the relationship between this supposed transnational involvement and local integration actually turns out. Based on a predominantly quantitative survey, with 300 respondents divided over three migrant categories (refugees, foreign workers and new labour migrants)[16] and six ethnic communities (from former Yugoslavia, Iraq, Morocco, the Dutch Antilles, United States and Japan), these researchers found that hardly any apparent connection existed between a possibly increasing transnational orientation and declining integration into the host country. [Snel et al. 2004] In fact, the results of the survey indicated rather that the Americans showed great transnational orientation in the different fields surveyed but felt most closely drawn to the values and norms of native Dutch people (see figure on page 121). Previously – albeit not significantly – the reverse had been seen in Moroccans. They scored particularly highly on a strong mutual relationship with compatriots in the host country, the Netherlands. According to these researchers, however, much also depends on length of stay in the host country (the shorter the more transnational, the longer the more local) and the socio-economic situation. Especially those with a relatively weak socio-economic position admittedly do not develop transnational activities (because they hardly have the financial means to visit their home country regularly or send remittances) but identify themselves more with the norms and values of their country of origin and thus also with like-minded groups in the Netherlands. [Snel et al. p.98] That is in line with the results of the survey by Eda Yücesoy, [2006] who found that having a driver's licence or a car for second-generation Turkish women, even with a low income, is almost always viewed as a first vital necessity, in order to meet like-minded

[16] Comparable with the previously made three-way split between the classic, modern and post-modern Diaspora; in this case political refugees, ideological motives, labour migrants and expats.

people and friends outside their own district without accompaniment. Otherwise, social interaction is limited to the immediate neighbourhood and living environment, which seeks temporary comfort together at precise times. Exactly this last thing seems still to be the case to a significant extent in Delfshaven, an original maritime outpost of Delft on the Maas, but which has been incorporated as a borough of Rotterdam since 1886.

Pilgrim church in Delfshaven

Delfshaven

Delfshaven is the place where the Rotterdammer will still send tourists to get a hint of an authentic Dutch city: 'like it was before the war'. The narrow front and back harbour measures barely 500 metres, but also represents a piece of primal Dutch history. This was where people sailed from on their trips to catch herring or whales. Piet Hein, a maritime hero of the West Indian Company, was born there and the Pilgrim Fathers left here on the Mayflower for America via Southampton. In the meantime, this historic Delfshaven has been entirely annexed by the city of Rotterdam and is surrounded by the migrant districts of Bospolder Tussendijken and the Nieuwe Westen. Delfshaven has thus already seen many foreigners come, go and stay in its 650-year history: first the people from Delft, later the Flemish and also even the Spanish and English separatists, then Rotterdammers itself, and nowadays new migrants. The borough of Delfshaven currently has about 71% so-called 'foreign residents', of whom 15% are Turkish, 13% Moroccans, 13% Surinamers, 8% Cape Verdans and 5% Antilleans. The largest concentrations are found in the neighbourhoods of Spangen, Bospolder and Tussendijken. [Buurtmonitor Rotterdam 2009]

Transnational use of original local housing

None of this can be inferred from the structure of the streets and buildings. They are still based on the original extension plan to a significant extent, and were built at the beginning of the 20th century after the example of the Paris of Haussmann, complete with city boulevards, canals and majestic squares, albeit with a significant emphasis on fulfilling the demand for workman's dwellings. [De Klerk et al. 2008] Their use, however, has been radically transformed. This is shown not only by the people walking or driving there – seldom cycling – but also by the fact that the previously mentioned neighbourhoods were formerly rather introverted and nowadays manifest themselves primarily along the former border (main) streets: Vierambachtstraat, Mathenesserweg, Mathenesserlaan, etc. [Urban Unlimited 2007b] This is where the oriental shops and catering establishments with exotic odours, colours and sounds, the telephone shops, the library, money transfers, travel bureaus, transport companies, radio stations and media providers are located, as expressions of the transnational orientation of the residents. The most important meeting places, such as party halls, schools, sports halls, neighbourhood houses, coffee houses or tea gardens, bathhouses, squares, parks and mosques are nowadays found primarily in the neighbourhoods themselves, or in concentrated locations in and around the district. The facilities for local integration and transnational interaction are thus available within walking distance from home and are actually hardly to be found in the centre of Rotterdam.

In the meantime, in view of its renewed use, however, the built stock is beginning slowly but surely to change 'acupuncturally', driven both bottom-up and partly also top-down. In addition to the realized *Development Diamonds*,[17] one could think of the Kluswoningen/Dichterlijke Vrijheid by members of the creative sector but especially of the Biz Botuluyuz and Le Medi projects, each expressing these two administrative variants in their own way.

Biz Botuluyuz

Biz Botuluyuz (Turkish for 'we from Bospolder Tussendijken') arose because of the declaration of uninhabitability and the necessary demolition of twenty dwellings in Bospolder. The occupants, largely Turkish residents, consequently should have moved but very much wanted to remain living in the neighbourhood. Current policy was nevertheless to replace them with expensive and medium-priced dwellings in this so-called 'deprived neighbourhood' in order to obtain a better mixture of different residents. The ex-residents were disappointed about this and organized themselves into a collective with the above-mentioned Turkish title. They were supported by the Delphi social welfare organization present in the neighbourhood and an expert with a great deal of experience in collective self-development, obtained particularly in Amsterdam (Jaap Draaisma). In the spring, a provisional plan to build affordable dwellings was drawn up by the group. Initially, there was little sympathy for this and the city considered that the housing corporation Com.Wonen, which was active in the district, could excellently fulfil this task. However, after the approval of a subsidy which has been requested by the residents group in the

---

17 The Development Diamonds were given form in 2002 by the Rotterdam mayor and aldermen on the initiative of city councillor Marco Pastors. A development diamond is a promising place in the city, which, due to private initiative and the support of municipal resources and knowledge, can grow into a location where neighbourhood residents can benefit in one or more ways. The initiative is intended to bring back the small scale to the big city (see www.kei.nl).

Original external orientation towards harbour and canal

Internal orientation towards oriental shops

Do it yourself Housing

Biz Botuluyuz turkish community

Le Medi maroccan style housing

framework of the 'Innovation Programme for Urban Renewal' (IPSV) and promised support from the 'Structure Group for Experimental Housing' (SEV), the corporation changed its mind and made a purchase guarantee arrangement possible. After this, the city could not refuse to commit itself. [Interview Draaisma 19-12-2008] This does not alter the fact that the development process was long and difficult. There were doubts about the affluence of the intended owner-occupiers (with annual incomes from €25 to €30,000.00), while the process – as is often the case with collective private commissions – had to gradually invent itself, all the more because this was one of the first projects in the Netherlands with immigrant clients. [Van Duyn 2007] Only four of the original 15 to 30 initiators went through the whole process, others withdrew over time. They were, however, replaced by other Turkish candidates from the district. It therefore remained a Turkish initiative. The dwellings, ultimately completed in March 2007, admittedly have some specific Turkish characteristics in terms of layout (the toilet and bathroom are separate and the kitchen is larger than regular in the Netherlands) but in general they have a predominantly Dutch appearance.

Le Medi

Le Medi was set up much more on the basis of a Moroccan identity, with a design that refers to a *Kasbah*. The project was initiated by two Moroccan entrepreneurs Abderrahman Hassani Idrissi and Abdel Salhi from Ex-Ante Consultancy, and continued by the housing corporations Com.Wonen, Woonbron and later also ERA-Bouw. The project of almost a hundred dwellings was set up with an architecture that refers to Mediterranean countries and to the structure of a so-called *ksar*; a circumvallated Moroccan district where families live together and life takes place behind the walls, among other places, on a central internal plaza. Just like a *ksar*, the project has a main gate and various secondary gates, which can be closed (in the evening hours) if desired. [KEI 2008] The project was consequently also the subject of much political discussion about whether this would not become too much a Moroccan enclave. However, after completion, this turned out to be a superfluous concern: the purchasers turned out not to be so much attracted by the idea of living a Moroccan lifestyle, but could primarily identify with the appealing, special nature of the project. Moreover the dwellings were characterized by growth possibilities, since over time the residents could build a second residential layer, if desired. Such good and flexible housing designed with attention and with qualities like a lockable plaza, mosaics and special architecture has not been built in this part of the city for about 100 years. And this attracted Moroccans and other immigrants (approx. a quarter), but even more native Dutch (approx. three quarters). The dwellings (for just under €200,000.00) have all been sold. Given this success, the Moroccan initiative-takers have proposed a second, comparable project; now called Le Riad, numbering some 200 dwellings and possibly in collaboration with Humanitas. [Algemeen Dagblad 9-12-2008]

Epilogue

Although experience has and is also being gained in the Netherlands in Enschede and Almere with 'the self-built city'. [see, among others, Kuenzli/Lengkeek 2004, Taverne 2008] It is still too early to evaluate both projects, exactly because they represent the first forms of multicultural self-building in the Netherlands. However, in going through the realization processes, the stakeholders have certainly learned and shared a lot of lessons for future projects. First, this new culture-specific construction has moved the focus from top-down urban renewal to a cautious bottom-up development, where the city and the housing corporations are rather enablers than directors. It perhaps will not lead to world-changing projects but has provided an active form of participation and identification, also with Le Medi. In addition, one striking difference between the two projects is apparent. Where Biz Botuluyuz strongly refers to the conclusion of Snel et al. that socio-economically weak migrants are inclined to unite and identify with like-minded people in the Netherlands, in Le Medi there is rather a reverse cultural assimilation. Here native residents are increasingly inclined to identify more with the Mediterranean building style and possibly even lifestyle.

Second, it is remarkable that the wishes of immigrants in terms of the dwelling and immediate living environment do not differ very much from the wishes of native Dutch people. Both the functional layout and the identification with Biz Botuluyuz and Le Medi are apparently valued just as much by the native Dutch as by the immigrants. This is partly derived from the limited budgets and cautious market positioning, but it can nevertheless be observed that crucial details and a specific, distinctive image is generally desired and also considered important, especially in the last case.

Finally, it is remarkable that up to now there has been hardly any discussion within the projects about facilities for transnational activities. One could think of a collective satellite connection, glass fibre, transport account, Turkish newspaper or web site. There are guest rooms available. In the new project by the Moroccan initiative-takers of Le Medi there is now, however, further discussion of a 'Moroccan House of Cultures', which will probably be co-funded by the Moroccan government. With this a facility would arise such as already exists with the Alliance Francaise, the Goethe Institute, the Chinese European Centre in Rotterdam and the House of the Neighbours (Flanders – the Netherlands). Cultural anchor points and language and knowledge exchange points have something to offer people both from the country of origin and from the Netherlands. Actual transnational living would thereby be able to gain form. Given the resistance to 'another extra Islamization', which the Leefbaar Rotterdam party has spoken about in the city council, it remains the question for the time being, however, whether these extra facilities in Le Riad will be realized. This does not alter the fact that cross-over native-immigrant building are expected to gain an extra boost in a more open society with focus on new and unique aspects. Le Medi is the proof of the pudding that also Dutch natives are attracted to multi-cultural building activities.

BOX [3.2]

Randstad Holland: the EURO, USA and ASIA Housing

Although Manuel Castells [1996] explicitly refuses to speak of a 'global workforce' – and on the contrary, precisely signals an enormous paradox in the development of the increasingly borderless capital on the one hand and the still predominantly location-bound work on the other, even in borderless Europe – it still has all the appearance that with the rapid growth of the Trans National Corporations (TNCs) in last quarter of the 20th century,[18] the number of expatriates has also sharply increased. Precise numbers are lacking because the term is also not unequivocally and clearly defined. The word expatriate – a combination of the Latin 'ex' (out of) and 'patria' (motherland) – is often understood to mean 'someone who remains temporarily or permanently in a country with a different culture than that with which he/she was raised'. [Wikipedia 2008] This characterisation of an expat is too vague, however and is not so much distingued from a traditional immigrant for instance. To bring more clarity, an immigrant is often supposed to be someone who goes somewhere to permanently establish him/herself, while the expatriate (abbreviated to expat) often sees himself as a temporary resident of a foreign country and is often regarded as such by his/her surroundings. In this sense, expats are also defined as 'people who are located in a foreign country

[18] From around 7000 in 1970 to around 37000 in 1993. [Castells 1996, p.235]

for a shorter or longer period, particularly employees who are stationed abroad by an internationally operating organization, concern, university or other scientific institution'. [Ernst & Young & ILAS 2005] In this context, a TNC like Shell speaks for example of 'a person who works under expat conditions outside his/her country of birth, beginning from if the posting will continue for more than 6 to 12 months – dependent on the location'. [Shell 2008] In this capacity, around 40-50,000 temporary work permits are issued annually in the Netherlands. Almost half of them go to the agriculture and market gardening sector and can thus be defined as being for seasonal workers. Around 15,000 go to sectors like business services, education, research and sociocultural institutions, of which more than 6000 are university-educated. [CBS 2008] These then tend to approach the above definition. Others define an expat in much broader terms, however, and rank among them not only those with a foreign nationality working for an originally foreign TNC, but also 'foreign entrepreneurs with their own business in the country in question (the so-called 'maverick'), foreign students and finally, the (following) partners and children of these communities'. [ARCUSplus 2007] In this form, in Amsterdam alone the number of expats with a foreign passport and a temporary or permanent residency/work permit is estimated at 120,000. It is particularly this group of people – despite the fact that they are often temporarily present or very volatile – that can also look forward to the increasing interest of the metropolitan authorities. They in fact give expression to the cosmopolitan character of a large city and thereby also an indication of its position in the global citizens network. [Carter 2001] It is recognized that the specific living environment, climate, facilities, culture and range of amenities for this group of people often leaves much to be desired. [TNO 2004, Cushman & Wakefield et al. 2004, Regioplan 2005] This was why the project developer Blauwhoed Eurowoningen began to look into this and consider whether it was also possible to organize a living environment characterized by a certain amount of communality, individuality, but also openness and network development, [Blauwhoed Eurowoningen, 2008] for this upcoming group of people.

Target groups

Leaving aside the Dutch nationals from the (former) crown colonies and the traditional foreign workers from Morocco and Turkey, the largest foreign communities established in the Netherlands come from the neighbouring countries of Germany, Belgium and to a lesser extent the UK and France. The first two are particularly concentrated in the border areas. Here, Germans or Belgians who live in the Netherlands, but still work in their own countries and *vice versa*, travel back and forth crossborder. Moreover, since the beginning of the 1990s, there are also primarily East Europeans temporarily working in housekeeping, construction and the farming and market-gardening sectors, and in the last few years the Chinese above all have become a strongly upcoming group of foreigners with a (temporary) employment or residence permit. They have displaced the Americans from second place, although these still constitute a large and stable factor of the foreign expat community in the Netherlands. Nonetheless, the Chinese head the lists in the science sector for example, before the Indians, Russians and Americans. [CWI 2005] Besides China, India, the UK, USA and Russia, also Canadian, South African and Japanese expats are strongly represented in the Netherlands.

Housing behaviour

These expats in the Randstad conurbation are primarily housed in the centre of Amsterdam, with tendrils towards Amstelveen and around The Hague, the government centre of the Netherlands. Principally in some neighbourhoods of Wassenaar – a chic residential area of The Hague – there are expat concentrations of sometimes as much as 40% of the residents. This is also reflected – although less extremely – in concentrations of British, Americans and Canadians, for example. They live primarily in the high-quality, inner-dune, peripheral zones of the Randstad (in the strip from The Hague via Wassenaar and Leiden to Heemstede, Bloemendaal and Haarlem), the centre of Amsterdam and het Gooi. This is different for Asian expats. The Japanese, for example, have remarkable concentrations living in Amstelveen (partly as a consequence of the Japanese school located there), the Taiwanese reside in Capelle aan den IJssel, while the Chinese, in both the absolute and relative sense, are primarily established in Rotterdam and then Delft. Here it is possibly also relevant that since 2000, the most important migration motive of the Chinese has changed from 'asylum' to 'study'. Particularly the β-studies at the Delft University of Technology and the Erasmus University in Rotterdam (economy) score highly in this.

However, these differences seem to be primarily the consequence of differentiations in housing preferences. A further survey by Regioplan seems to show that the housing requirements and housing experience of expats is not only determined by their household composition and job, but above all by their cultural background and length of stay. [Regioplan 2005] Americans who come to the Netherlands often require that everything concerning their housing be prearranged – their housing, the necessary permits, service, etc. – so that they can get to work immediately. For the Americans, moreover, security is important as well as the size of the dwelling. They often consider Dutch dwellings (too) small, they think it strange that there is often only one bathroom, and annoying that the oven could just about cook a small chicken but not a decent turkey. The closeness of compatriots hardly plays a significant role; within the conditions of security and reliability, they precisely prefer a mixture of cultures and lifestyles.

For Asians, however, it is precisely the proximity of compatriots that is important. Taiwanese, Japanese and specific groups of Chinese seek each other out and like to live together in the neighbourhood. For the Asians – particularly the Chinese – the price level is also important. They often have a tighter budget and it is therefore important for them not to live too expensively. *Mutatis mutandis* they are often satisfied with a lower-quality dwelling and living environment. The traditional post-war reconstruction (Amstelveen) or suburb (Capelle aan den IJssel) is often sufficient for them. Furthermore, in contrast to the Americans, they often do not mind having to look for a house themselves when they come to the Netherlands. Much is done through the often strongly present familial structure or via friends and acquaintances. It also turns out that there is a big difference between the generations and between the stayers and temporary students/workers. Young stayers integrate, speak Dutch and try to imitate the behaviour of the Dutch. The elderly, on the other hand, organized an old-people's home, precisely because elderly Chinese women have no connection whatsoever with the native Dutch. The temporary students opt for a career in Asia and just absorb knowledge, despite the fact that some of

- Rugby
- Cricket
- Golf
- Lacrosse

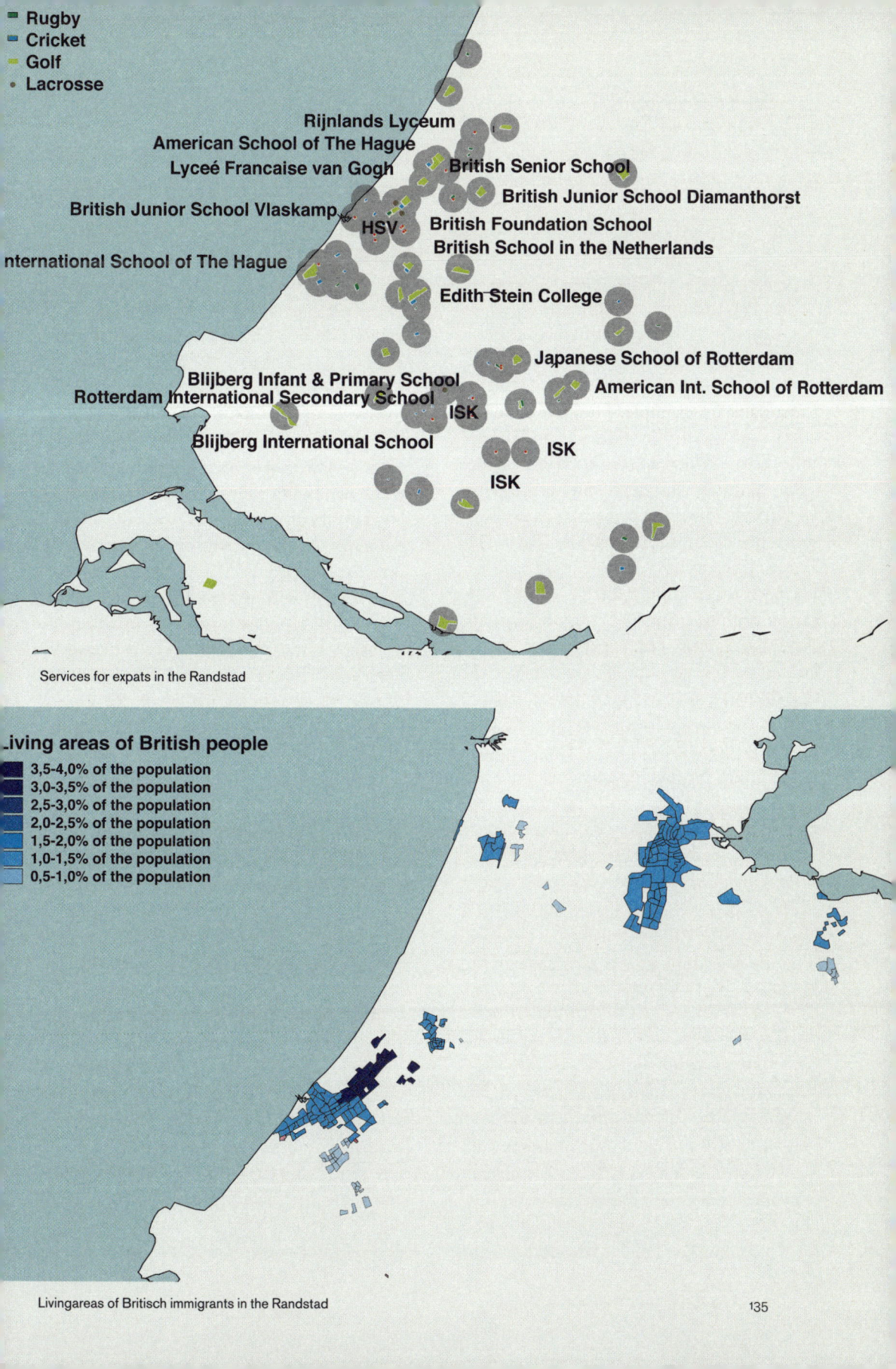

Rijnlands Lyceum
American School of The Hague
Lyceé Francaise van Gogh
British Senior School
British Junior School Vlaskamp
British Junior School Diamanthorst
HSV
British Foundation School
International School of The Hague
British School in the Netherlands
Edith Stein College
Japanese School of Rotterdam
Blijberg Infant & Primary School
Rotterdam International Secondary School
American Int. School of Rotterdam
ISK
Blijberg International School
ISK
ISK

Services for expats in the Randstad

Living areas of British people
- 3,5-4,0% of the population
- 3,0-3,5% of the population
- 2,5-3,0% of the population
- 2,0-2,5% of the population
- 1,5-2,0% of the population
- 1,0-1,5% of the population
- 0,5-1,0% of the population

Livingareas of Britisch immigrants in the Randstad

135

them have difficulties because of the language and cultural differences. [Wah Fook Wui 2008]

Moreover, obviously important differences in household composition, age and (thereby often connected) income remain important for housing preferences. Here a distinction is made between singles, expats with a partner and expats with a family, and primary (1-10 days), secondary (10-30 days) and tertiary needs (>30 days). [Arcusplus 2007] Particularly for the expat families, proximity to an international school with an ISS rating is relevant. In this way, it is possible for the scholars to take up their studies elsewhere without too much trouble, in the event of an enforced move. Excellent international accessibility and the possible presence of an Anglo-Saxon Church (for Americans), a temple (for Chinese and Taiwanese) and good own restaurants or a fresh fish market (for Japanese) are relevant. For younger singles on the other hand, precisely an inner-city location is preferable, with retail shops and possibly specific facilities with long (if possible all-night) opening times, good public transport and fitness or sports facilities with the possibility of temporary membership. For all groups, further internationalization of the cultural facilities – such as libraries, opera, concerts, dance hall, etc. – is strongly appreciated. There is also a need for more clarity in the legislation and the development of a physical expat desk. [Regioplan 2005, Meier et al. 2008]

USA Housing
Proposals were developed from this background for repositioning the existing airport at Rotterdam. At the moment this airport fulfils a role particularly for several European lines and holiday charters. Because of the increasingly larger aircraft and beginning/end of the day connections, the airport is creating a continuously increasing nuisance for the surrounding area. In the past few years it has been fined for this several times. [Inspectie Verkeer & Waterstaat 2005/2006] Consequently, transforming this airport into a general aviation airport is under consideration. Smaller aircraft will then be admitted, with a drastic reduction of the nuisance for the surrounding area and less burden on the environment. At the same time, however, there is the possibility to develop the airport as a residential-work-business airport, with new opportunities for spatial development in the immediate vicinity. Due to the presence of a spacious and green living environment, splendid lakes on the original River Rotte in Rotterdam and the close proximity of several international English-language and Japanese schools with RSS ratings at both primary and secondary levels, the proximity of internationally recognized universities like the EUR and the TUD, the head offices of TNCs like Unilever, Shell, Mittal, ING, etc., the government centre and a selection of international sports facilities for (disc) golf, rugby, baseball, cricket, lacrosse and equestrian sports, lend themselves excellently for expat housing at a high-quality, surplus level. The excellent international accessibility of the location via several transport modes is guaranteed not only due to the possibility to land one's own (business) aircraft at a short (walking) distance, but also due to the direct connections, via Randstad rail or possibly an extra station to the adjacent rail track for the High-Speed Train (HST). At the location itself, about 200 'Wassenaar worthy' villas and condominiums could be constructed, in a high-quality so-called 'Hillegersberg water environment' at a short, slow-travelling traffic distance from the primary, secondary and tertiary international facilities, with private-public and/or semi-private terminals

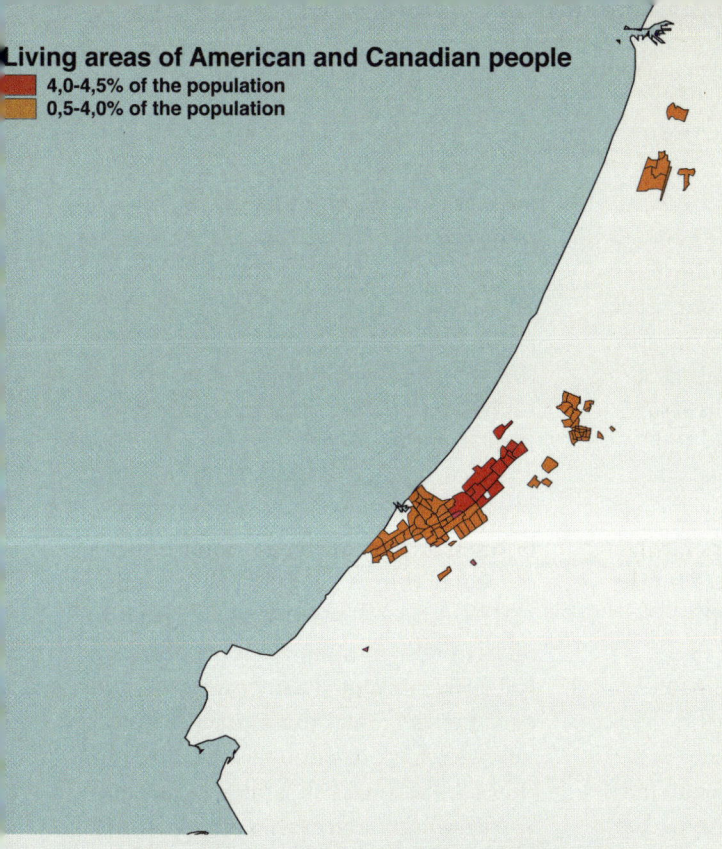

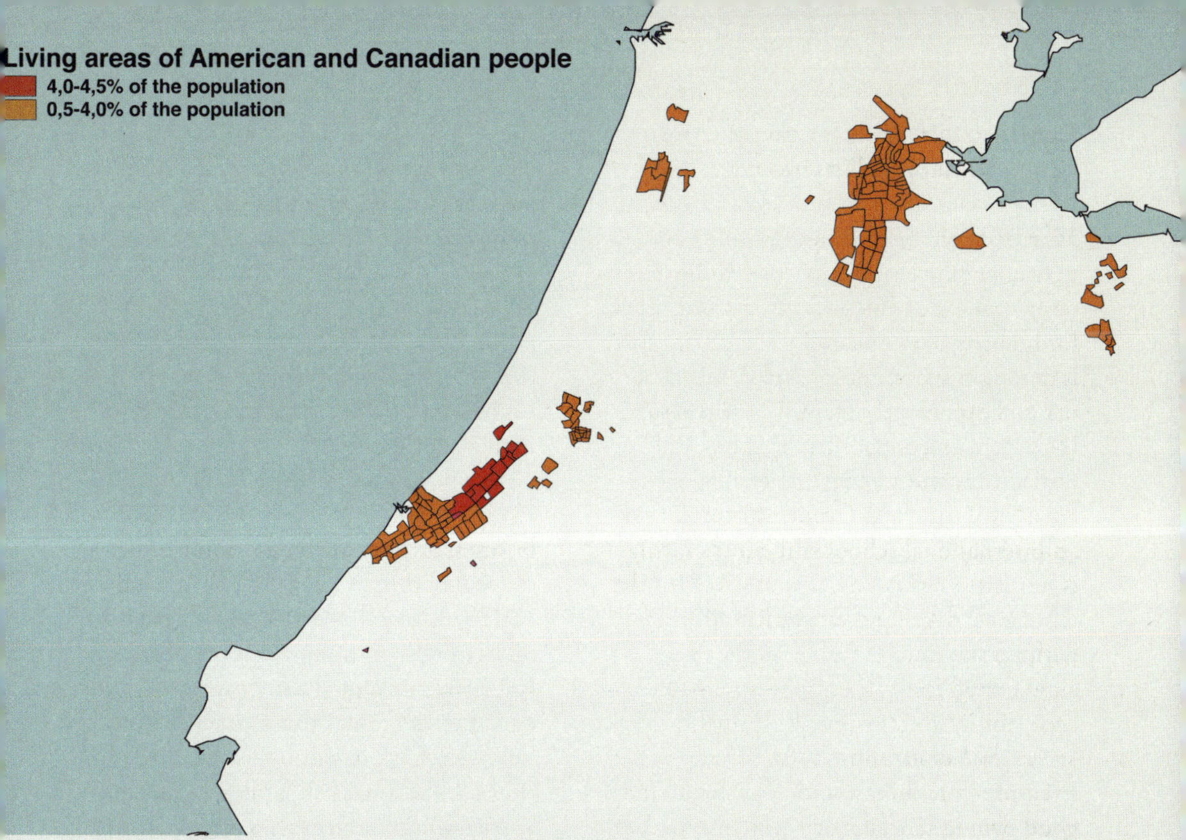

Living areas of American and Canadian people
- 4,0-4,5% of the population
- 0,5-4,0% of the population

Livingareas of American and Canadian immigrants in the Randstad

Living areas of Asian people
- 1,0-1,5% of the population
- 0,5-1,0% of the population

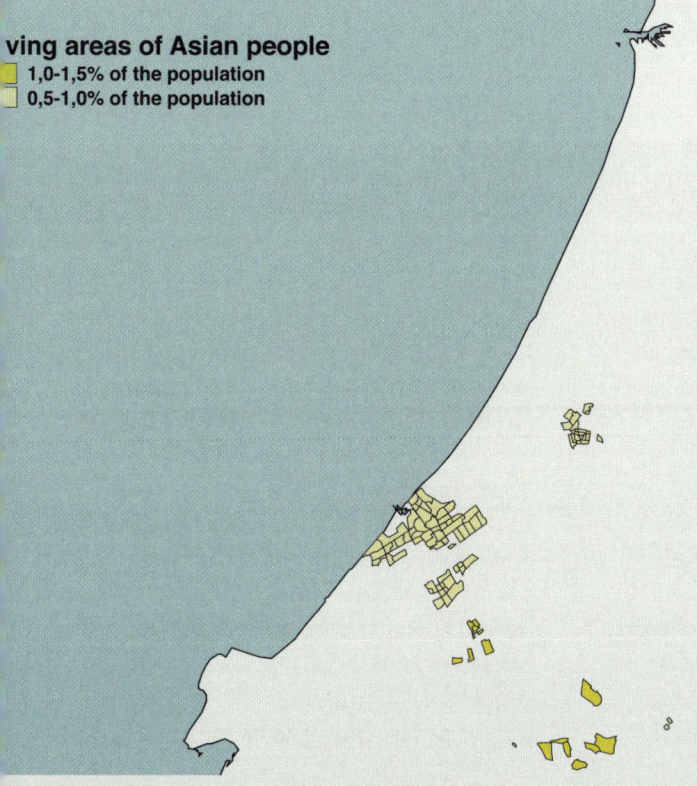

Livingareas of Asian immigrants in the Randstad

for business jets in the 'back garden', as it were, of these villas. This would provide an important contribution to the required reinforcement of the international competitiveness of the city and the desired additional quality of Rotterdam's housing stock for highly-trained people. [Rotterdam 2006] At this moment of economic downfall, however, the prospect seems utopian. Furthermore, the competent government agency (specifically the Ministry of Transport), the Schiphol Group (major stockholder of Airport Rotterdam) and the competent slot issuer (the Civil Aircraft Authority) should determine their current reorientation on Dutch aviation.

ASIA Housing

Even more than the Americans, Blauwhoed Eurowoningen, particularly with regard to Asian (and then particularly Chinese) people and households, is a promising target group, which can contribute in social/cultural as well economic terms to the city of Rotterdam. [Blauwhoed 2008] The Asians already comprise a prominent, large and varied community in Rotterdam: singles, double-income households and/or families, with, besides the elderly, increasing numbers of young people in the age category from 20-30 years. Among them are also increasing numbers of high potentials with specific desires with regard to living, working, facilities and leisure in the city. It is desirable to retain these high potentials for the city (after their studies). Blauwhoed Eurowoningen wanted to investigate from the bottom-up, in an actor-oriented manner with relevant contacts in the community and work out programmes that have a specific value for the Chinese and strongly bind them to Rotterdam. Based on discussions with these leading contacts in the Chinese civic and business community, these environments for this community are not interpreted as one spatial neighbourhood or unit (something like the often-tourist China towns), but rather built around a network and alliance in which all important places and facilities for this group are comfortably developed. From existing motives, new initiatives and opportunities in the city, there are four clusters and/or urban acupunctures under discussion.

- The first concerns the already existing Chinese residential retail-food cluster around the Kruisplein, close to the central railway station in Rotterdam.
- The second concerns the Chinese residential showroom-business cluster at Katendrecht/Rijnhaven, now under construction under the supervision of the Shanghai Construction Group and Volker Wessels: the European Chinese Centre (ECC).
- The third concerns a possible new Chinese residential culture-temple cluster around the Euromast and Parkhaven, as part of the much larger international 'Seaman's Churches route' along the Westzeedijk.
- Finally, the fourth new cluster concerns a possible Chinese residential education-gaming cluster on the Heijplaat, in tune with the development of the new education and research & development facilities already there.

A super-fast Chinese boat/land taxi mutually connects these clusters to each other. In a dialogue with the actors involved within the Chinese community, it is intended to develop housing on and between these clusters, in moderate price classes in the owner-occupier and rental sector, as well as short-stay facilities around courts and small gardens of the appurtenant additional facilities for these clusters. This is all in accordance with the specific cultural pattern of housing that is both common and desired in China. [Sunyoung Yoon & Kyungran Choi 2002]

Epilogue

Whereas with USA housing it is rather of matter of supply-oriented planning – partly dependent on the efforts of some major actors in the aviation sector – this is emphatically reversed in the case of ASIA housing, which occurs via the explicit collaboration of leading (f)actors in the community itself. In both cases, however, it is no longer about achieving a neighbourhood identity, but much more a possible communal theme identity, which is much sooner organized into networks around different (anthropological) cultures and lifestyles. Various nodes or acupunctures are always crucial certainly: such as a broad or international school, a specific church or temple, specific dining cultures, an expat supermarket, ways of doing business, sports or leisure facilities such as gaming or karaoke. However, these spatial, residential, cultural networks also become interesting and attractive to other communities and they organize specific cohesion around this lifestyle. In contrast to 'gated communities' there are consequently explicit, open networks, admittedly grafted onto, but straight through different entities. This is in line with the conclusion drawn by Robert Merton almost 60 years ago, based on his research into *locals and cosmopolitans* in Rovere New Jersey: 'while the locals wanted to know everyone in town and took positions to enhance that locality, the cosmopolitans wanted to meet the unexpected and the uniqueness'. [Merton 1949] Actually, here the cosmopolitans have a need for 'social real-estate' which can facilitate the heterogeneous, hybrid and multicultural society of tomorrow in a new fashion. It can also become the motive for a wider 'international construction' in a global network; beyond China town.

Impression of a dynamic Asian milieu

Impression of a spiritual Asian milieu

Proposal for an American milieu at Rotterdam Airport

Gate 16.3
Gate 16.2
Gate 16.1

Golfcentrum Rotterdam

Pakistan Cricket Club
Fiet Cricket Club

Blijberg Infant & Primary School

Rotterdam International Secondary School

Neptunes Baseball
Disc Golf

Cricketclub

**Baseball Duijvestein
Rotterdamse Rugby Club
American Int. School of Rotterdam
Japanese School of Rotterdam**

**Golfclub
De Hoge Berghse**

141

易
Change

New Chinese
Hou

Maritime workstation
RDM Campus
Quarantaine terrain
City harbour and academy
The China Crew
Concept living

活 Life — **Kruiskade Chinatown**

金 Gold — **European Chinese Cen**

- restaurants • culture • education • care •

watertaxi ⌒ extra w

Proposal for Asian milieus in the Rotterdam Harbour

活 Life

金 Gold

Replacing the small pagode
Tai chi on Sunday
Chinese teagarden

European China Center

平 Peace — Chinese Garden

易 Change — Chinese New Generation

• seamen churches (non Chinese)

taxi   walking routes

[4]

Institutional order via association
Towards greater, more relational democracy

The Dutch government's current *White Paper on National Spatial Planning* or *Nota Ruimte* [Ministry of VROM 2006] has as its slogan: 'Centralize what you must, decentralize whatever you can!' That was the guiding principle as well of the New Spatial Planning Act in the Netherlands, which was adopted in July 2008. Here, too, the most important criterion of spatial planning should be that it had to be exercised at the correct governmental level – preferably the lowest – to oversee all the effects of a particular decision. This would require less national supervision and give local authorities more freedom to interpret policy to their best ability. [Nieuwe Wet op de Ruimtelijke Ordening 2008] According to the proposals of the Dutch Scientific Council for Government Policy (WRR), which were presented ten years earlier, a new type of spatial order was necessary, one that would pay more attention to regional co-ordination through active involvement of a number of actors, or stakeholders. They stressed that in the present administrative situation of multi-level and multi-actor governance, it would be wise to shift planning – where possible – from 'an internal co-ordination of government policy towards an effective creation of social coalitions'. The Scientific Council distinguished three different regimes in this regard:
a the basic areas, mainly governed on a local level, for which it would suffice at the national level to formulate basic quality demands and development options;
b the developmental areas, for which national government could formulate some guiding principles, but the precise details would be worked out with partners under provincial oversight, and
c national projects, for which, in light of the National Spatial Framework, protection was deemed to be of national importance, or measures would have to be taken at that level. [WRR 1998]

Apparently this shift in planning should have a significant effect on Dutch planning practice, long dominated by the precise regulation of spatial development and vertical structured planning communities. It resembled ideas on relational collaborative planning, which were also promoted elsewhere. [Fainstein 1986, Stoker 1995, 2000, Healey 1997, 2007] Nevertheless, for many people it is still unclear what exactly can be dealt with centrally (nationally) and what at decentralized levels (locally). Also for politicians it seems to be still unclear what exactly includes the competence of the state and what exactly can be left up to other public, civic and/or business organizations. For instance during the debate on the *White Paper on National Spatial Planning*, a motion was introduced by Derk Lemstra, member of the Upper House of the Dutch parliament, calling for a more integrated long-term vision and related strategy, and one outlining in particular the long-term tasks of the national urban networks and the Randstad conurbation (January 2006). This resulted in a more or less traditional *Randstad Strategic Agenda 2040* [VROM 2008] drawn up under the supervision of the Ministry of VROM. Moreover, other development oriented scholars were very careful in making it clear that – in spite of widespread support in neo-liberal circles – they were opting explicitly in favour of a more centrally planned (Westphalian) Germanic model rather than for an open, neo-liberal Anglo-

Saxon one. [Hajer/Sijmons 2006] With the international financial crisis of 2008 in everyone's mind at the moment of writing, this position is enjoying increased interest among social democrats again. The so called 'right wing' suddenly found itself ideologically helpless to solve the financial crisis, and powerful leftist action and state regulation is demanded. [Giesen 2008] Beyond the implicit, self-satisfied rhetoric, which was concealed behind this view, this triumphalist welcoming of the 'restoration of an old state-controlled era' falls into the same trap as the one that had previously led Francis Fukuyama [1989, 2008] to proclaim the end of history. There can be no return to centralized state management, or to an updated version of a Keynesian state economy. Rather, there needs to be a form of state intervention that follows the rules of what has now become a globalized capitalism, but still tries to reconnect those interventions with what is going on in everyday life. It represents recent ideas about the pluralization of democracy, under conditions going beyond the apparent problems of unbridled individualism on the one hand, and those of state-controlled social democracy on the other.

Resetting democracy

The critique of neo-liberalism – based on its principle of the free market economy, the elimination of trade barriers and a decentralized decision-making – is nothing new and was proclaimed even long before the economic and financial crises of the beginning of the 21st century began to manifest themselves. Prominent economic geographers such as David Harvey, [2000] Robert Polin, [2003] Richard Wilkinson [2003] and Daniel Brook, [2007] among others, have already shown convincingly that, contrary to what it promises, neo-liberalism has not led to more freedom anywhere in the world, but rather to ever-greater inequality, as well as to serious political, social, environmental and ultimately even economic problems. David Harvey [2005] even goes as far as to emphasize that neo-liberalism is not much more than yet another 'global capitalist power restoration project' that primarily protects private property rights and sells off public assets. From a less ideological or economic perspective, certain political scientists have also noted the major democratic deficits of neo-liberalism. In the early years above all, the introduction of neo-liberalism went hand in hand with the installation of dictatorial regimes – some of them military – such as in Chile, Argentina, Iran, South Korea, Singapore, Taiwan, etc. Moreover, in a more structural, implicit manner, the growing worldwide hegemony of neo-liberalism was also partly based on, or gave rise to, institutions that gained more and more power, but were for the most part not subject to democratic principles, such as the WTO, the IMF, the World Bank, etc. [Dryzek 1996] Martin Kohr [1999] even stresses that these institutions offered the rich countries effective vehicles for increasingly excluding and oppressing the Second and Third worlds. Put even more strongly, at a local level these bodies gave rise to anti-democratic processes, by pushing economic growth on the basis of complicated but general propositions regarding the inevitable and ongoing process of globalization. [Brenner 1999] Not only has all this development come at the expense of social cohesion and effectively turned individuals into consumers rather than citizens, [Larner 1997] but even before the financial crisis this tendency prompted the Washington political scientist Mark Purcell [2008] to call for a way out of this 'terror of neo-liberalization'. Unlike many others, Purcell sees this call not simply as an appeal for a return to the warmth of state control – redistribution and/or welfare guarantees. For in addition to (neo)liberal democracy, with its emphasis on individual freedom, tolerance, pluralism, separation of private and public spheres and the principle of formal political equality in the latter, Purcell rightly points out that there are numerous other democratic traditions that opt for another way out of the current democratic malaise. In the process, he takes aim not only at the difference between representative democracy and more direct forms of popular democracy, [Cabannes 2004, see below] but primarily at the distinction between the deliberative, participatory, revolutionary and radical pluralist traditions.[19]

Deliberative or discursive democracy leads Purcell back to the communication theory developed by the philosopher and sociologist Jürgen Habermas, [1984] and especially to the enthusiastic elaboration of the latter's theory by Judith Innes [1995] and Patsy Healey, [1997] among others, in their communicative and collaborative approaches to planning. A central feature of this model is the promotion of intersubjective consensus-building among stakeholders, whether in business or in civil and public society, by means of deliberative processes that ideally should be as free as possible from power relations (freedom of speech). In theory, no one can be excluded from this kind of process. Its form and structure become more crucial than its contents. [Dryzek 1990] While Judith Innes still stresses the need for collective planning action through interaction, through debate, Patsy Healey stressed at that time the collaborative planning action of various stakeholders in the broadest possible sense, including the natural environment and future generations. Next to the fact that Jürgen Habermas has always stressed the idealistic, perhaps non-realistic features of his communicative model, although necessary to mirror and possibly improve the daily affairs of social action, [Boelens 1990] such a process also leads to lengthy discussions, debates and exchanges of arguments without achieving extraordinary results. At best, the results are often quite modest and familiar. As Harald Weinrich has pointed out, quite apart from the lock-in that often emerges even in the most ideal power-free situations, the lengthy deliberations can often mean that, in the end, the one who holds out the longest gets his or her way. [Weinrich, *System, Diskurs, Didaktik und die Diktatur des Sitzfleisches* 1973] This was exactly the case in the procedural and process-oriented planning approaches during the 1970s and early 1980s in the Netherlands. Here the discursive approach shot itself in the foot.

Participatory democracy in fact dates back to Aristotle's notion of self-development, according to which citizens evolve socially by taking part in public

[19] Although this distinction has some links with the distinction made by Patsy Healey in Collaborative Planning [1997] between Representative democracy, Pluralist democracy, Corporatism and Clientilism, Purcell takes a more critical and normative stance here, while Healey seems to assess all four alternatives suitable for collaborative governance.

affairs. But it has also been understood recently in the opposite sense, by Carole Pateman [1985] for instance, who argues that through citizen participation people grow increasingly closer to 'their best selves'. This approach opts, beyond the periodic right to vote, for more participation in all forms of collective life: the economy, the community, culture, social institutions, spatial development, etc. [Gould 1988] Where 'deliberative democrats' attach significance primarily to the purity of the way in which deliberation and decisions come about, 'participatory democrats' see participation as a good thing in itself. It gets people involved and increases their sense of self-value. Moreover, public cause might benefit from it, while improving the decisiveness, speed and realization of projects in their own right. Over the past twenty years, several Brazilian cities, for instance, have experimented widely in this regard with participatory planning and even participatory budgeting. [Cymbalista 2005, Bonduki 2008] But although this approach has met with much support and achieved results, Purcell [2008] emphasises that it also has a strategic value to the authorities in power: strengthening the base of governing, while still persisting in unjust en sometimes even amoral causes. However, this approach has also received considerable criticism from liberal democrats as well for pushing to one side the interests of the individual in the name of the common good. [Rawls 1993]

That phenomenon, which despite all good intentions ultimately turned the democratic effort into its totalitarian opposite, seems to be primarily a feature of revolutionary democracy. This approach in effect echoes the works of Karl Marx, Friedrich Engels, Rosa Luxembourg, etc., but has recently been revitalized in the work of David Harvey, [1990] Erik Swyngedouw [2004] and especially, according to Purcell, Michael Hardt and Antonio Negri. [2000/2004] At the centre of these positions is the absolute idea that democracy consists of 'the rule of everyone by everyone'. And although that seems an almost fictitious, ideal statement at first sight, Hardt and Negri affirm that this has become possible thanks to recent developments in telecommunications. The struggle for one's right to self-determination can manifest itself in highly precise and local forms, but can also be built up collectively in and through co-operative networks. These co-operative, decentred networks of radical democratic movements play a key role not only in the anti-globalization demonstrations against the WTO, the IMF, the G8, etc., but also take on a much broader social form in Internet. This is not to deny that, this approach is aimed at a radical overthrow and revolution of the dominant system, while leaving it unclear, however, what ought to take its place.

Therefore, last but not least Purcell describes the alternative to which he himself adheres: that of radical plural democracy. It is an approach that can be traced back to the work of Ernesto Laclau and Chantal Mouffe, [1985] but around which there has since emerged a wider network of proponents and followers (William Connolly, Claude Lefort, Nancy Fraser, etc.). They share with classical pluralists the conviction that society is built up not so much by individuals

	essence of democracy	role of the state	public private sphere	equality	main protagonists
(neo-)liberal	protection of the freedom of individuals	neutral guarantor of individual rights	strong division between state and non-state	formal political equality in public sphere	John Locke Jean-Jacques Rousseau Benjamin Franklin
deliberative	deliberation toward shared understanding	neutral guarantor of proper procedures	strong desire to mix public private deliberations	equality through deliberations of citizens	Jürgen Habermas John Dryzek Judith Innes
participatory	development through political participation	neutral encourager of civic political participation	desire to extend participation to all spheres of life	equality by participating: more experienced help the other	Carol Pateman Carol Gould
revolutionary	reclamation of powers that have been incorporated by particular interests	transformed or eliminated, while all people are assumed to have direct power	total democracy that has eliminated the public/private distinction	everyone is an equal member of 'the people'	Karl Marx David Harvey Antonio Negri
radical plural	irreducible difference engaged through agnostic struggles	will likely play a role in any institutionalisation of power	radically extend democratic relations to more spheres	commitment to 'radical equalization'	Ernesto Laclau Chantal Mouffe William Connolly
associative	leave as much as possible to self-reliant associations	stimulator of self-organisation and back up those things which are left over	strong involvement of private actors in public spheres on specific themes, options	equality through a stake- and shareholder model	Paul Hirst Joshua Cohen Joel Rogers

Some features of democratic traditions [Purcell 2008, Hirst 1994, 2001]

but by conflicts between various interest groups. [Madison 1987] According to Purcell, the differences between them have to do with the premise that power can only exist relationally (between the oppressors and the oppressed, the powerful and the powerless), and that power is not distributed in a diffuse way but is characterized by successive hegemonies based on convenient alliances between interest groups. [Purcell 2008, p.62] And according to radical pluralists there is no single public domain, but rather several parallel discursive arenas containing various dynamic hegemonic alliances.

Agreement and consensus are not the results of the successful neutralization of power and/or the intersubjective discovery of *win-win situations*. Rather, according to Laclau and Mouffe, [2005] the underlying clash of interests resulting from pluralism can only be temporarily unmasked, but not transcended to attain a Utopian ideal of concord. The concept of 'equivalence' is introduced in this context, which refers to a state of simultaneous difference and agreement. Commitment arises not through some sort of 'total democracy', but rather by extending that equivalence to several aspects of society. Individual interests are not supposed to be repressed, but on the contrary, they should be mobilized in competitive relations.

Although Laclau and Mouffe's alternative is engaged and discerning, it remains limited primarily to a conception of democracy, and is less fully developed into a practical view of how such a radical pluralist conception could lead to better and more legitimate democratic results. In his quest 'to recapture democracy', Mark Purcell builds on this foundation seven new democratic attitudes that are supposed to achieve a more democratic future. These range from the explicit rejection of the current hegemonic neo-liberal democracy by embracing a competitive social model of democracy, the development of a counter-hegemony based on radical democratization and 'equalization', to an engagement with the democratic discourse of human rights and an updating of Lefebvre's notion of the 'right to the city'; meaning more or less the right to a public domain with a plurality of conceptions, opinions and interests.

Nevertheless, even this 'practical application' of Laclau and Mouffe's work remains extremely abstract and vague, in my view. Purcell cannot convincingly demonstrate what it actually means and how – given the existing institutional contexts – it could be different and better. [Boelens 2008] In addition, Purcell is too quick to lump deliberative and participatory democracy together. Lengthy deliberations are particularly at issue in deliberative democracy and interactive planning, while this is not necessarily so in participatory budgeting or special district planning. Similarly, Purcell does not refer to the concept of 'associative democracy' developed among others by Hirst, Bader and Cohen in the last 15 years. Precisely because of their emphasis on the recognition of the fundamental heterogeneity of contemporary society and on the opportunities for organizing various layered, sometimes overlapping forms of associations around specific themes or issues, this approach positions itself, in my view, somewhere between participatory democracy and radical pluralism. At the same time, it offers practical alternatives to the present and customary focus on an exclusively representational democracy, by proposing in part and, where possible, more and more voluntary self-governing associations. Therefore, in what follows, I shall first go into their ideas on improving democratic institutions before returning to what this could mean for planning and spatial practices.

Associative democracy

The most important argument of the proponents of 'associative democracy' is the increasing and undeniable failings of representative democracy. This system of periodic elections and the representation of the electorate's interests by an elected deputy within the bastion of democracy is failing, besides the already mentioned neo-liberal problems, especially due to the following three reasons.

First, there is – as elected representatives are also aware – a great distance between those democratic bastions and the daily lives of citizens and businesses. This is so not only because the accountability of the deputies has become very indirect and mediated through the growing bureaucracy and 'multi-level governance'. Decisions can no longer simply be implemented (interpersonally) as in ancient Athens. Rather, decisions reach us through the mediation of the press, the media or other information services. Multimedia dissemination and populism play an important role. Next to that, there is also the complexity of the problems addressed, which demands that certain representatives be entrusted with specialist dossiers, while other deputies represent the electorate on other fronts. Moreover, representatives are often required to form coalitions, whether within or between parties. Ultimately this leads to what is referred to as an 'erosion of legal sovereignty'. [Bader 2001] For instance, the confidence of the American people in their Congress fell between 1972 and 1997 by 20 per cent to just under 22 per cent, and similar crises of confidence are to be seen in other Western countries as well. [Gans 2003, p.15]

Second, pluralism is – as we have said – on the rise in contemporary societies. Widespread higher and secondary education, greater disposable income and the relaxation of public and religious moral controls have led to a radical divergence in lifestyles. Along with increasing globalization and migration, the result has been that the most highly developed Western, Latin American and Asian countries are now culturally heterogeneous. At the same time, this individualization has led to a sort of 'new consumer consciousness' in which the various services and contributions by the state are not simply accepted as they are, but people seek to adapt them to their individual situations and specific set of demands. The 'one size fits all policies' of representative democracy are no longer considered adequate. [Hirst 2001] This applies not only to public services but also to the programmes of the representative political parties. One may sometimes agree with one another on a specific principle, while in other cases one disagrees profoundly. Meanwhile, conversely, the internet and new multimedia communications can enable bystanders to pinpoint specific items. Outside parliament, a wide range of new formal or informal links are developing that seek to fulfil common ambitions in their own way. [Held et al. 1999]

Third, as a consequence of increasing networking and globalization, social problems are often no longer addressed at the level which had traditionally been carved out in accordance with the hierarchical structures of representative democracy: international – national – regional – local. Many questions cut across those different levels or fall between different levels. Thus, as mentioned in chapter one, a constant 'rescaling and rebordering' is occurring in the institutional organization of social democracy. [Brenner 2004] In addition, extra emphasis is being place on governance instead of government with respect to spatial planning. [Salet et al 2003] Nevertheless, people continue to adhere to classic comprehensive institutionalisation with an energy worthy of a better cause. Thus prominent Dutch leaders have recently proposed the formation of an administration for the Randstad (metropolitan region), while the city of Amsterdam recently once again sought to create a new regional administrative body that would promote its metropolitan ambitions [Burgmans committee 2006, Cohen 2007, Van Poelgeest et al. 2008]

Against this background, the proponents of associative democracy are breaking with the practice of simply patching things up. Paradoxically it does not propose a radical alternative for the reigning (neo-)liberal and representative democratic tradition (as the revolutionary or radical pluralist democrats do) but it sets out an evolutionary process by means of which that democratic tradition is fundamentally supplemented by new associative initiatives. The central starting point is the normative claim that individual freedom and social welfare are best served when community affairs are governed and managed as much as possible by voluntary and democratic, self-reliant associations. [Hirst 1994] *Associationalism* seeks therefore from the outset to combine the claims for individual freedom and diversity with the public merits of collectivism. [Figgis 1913, Laski 1925]

Despite the aforementioned critiques, it is recognized that states still organize large parts of social life, spend large amounts of the gross national product, and continue to play an important role in welfare and in the general provision of public services. But at the same time, the proponents of associationalism seek to use all the niches and opportunities within that context decisively to facilitate the obvious pluralism and latent capacity for self-organization of present-day society. As said before, more than in the past, this has now become possible with the help of new means of telecommunications. The aim of these efforts is above all:
- fostering a more direct, formal or informal governance role for specific interest groups, namely where these associations offer more competencies and/or prospects of success (more efficient governance),
- promoting the organized representation of currently underrepresented interests, namely in cases where there is manifest unreasonableness and injustice (more equal political representation) and
- encouraging the formation of similar pluralist, independent associations around individual interests, especially where particularism threatens to undermine the fabric of democracy (less factionalism). [Cohen & Rogers 1992]

In order to promote the above, associationalists plead simply for an increased *pluralization* of society and for a more associative civil society at the same time. Where possible and/or desirable, voluntary self-governing associations could be encouraged to address specific social topics in both the public and the private spheres, provided that the essential requirements of democratic governance are honoured and preserved intact. Here we can think of the self-organization of the public domain, care & cure, mobility, housing and the like. Some of these may be extremely participatory, while others may be more minimalist, but all should have the fundamental right to choose their own board of directors, as well as the opportunity to exercise periodic control, hold elections and/or have the right to cancel one's membership. To this end, it is necessary first of all that the state is willing to transfer more tasks to such associations.

Secondly, the mechanisms and conditions for this process must be created, so these associations can carry out their tasks properly. They could receive the financial means of (central) government to spend under specific conditions according to their own interest, they could be made responsible for the social welfare and security in a specific district, they could organize even more fundamental physical tasks. This means guaranteeing sufficient (financial) resources, potentially the right to tax or premium payments, incentives for independence, etc. Citizens should be able to choose freely whether or not to join such associations, and to direct a part of their taxes or premium payments to these bodies instead of to the state. In exchange, they would receive voting and decision-making rights in specific associations, in areas such as education, care, public space management, etc. The involvement of citizens with specific public affairs could thus be promoted, and savings may even be realized. In case of misappropriation or unethical governance by associative democratic vote, the directors of these bodies could be dismissed, taken to court, and if members are still not satisfied, they can withhold their contributions and look for a more appropriate association.

The direct relationship between governors and governed would thus be restored, and justice could more easily be done to the diversity of desires and expectations. But at the same time, associationalists expect to restore the legitimacy of the current (representative) democracy, partly by transforming important parts of the state from a top-down bureaucracy into a more pluralist, multi-layered as well as bottom-up self-governing organization. [Hirst 2000] This approach is not limited, moreover, to the local level alone, but seeks also to develop new models for regional, national and even supranational associations, linked to more democratic variants of corporate governance, such as Doctors without Borders, or Amnesty International etc. [Engelen 2001] As mentioned before, with respect to the recent International Shipping, Air Transport, Telecommunications and Postal regime development it has even proven to be very effective to organize these beyond governments, from the bottom up, by the involved partners and businesses themselves. [Zacher/Suttton 1996] And last but not least, unlike the aforementioned variants, associative democracy is all but Utopian, for it can immediately begin to build on 'formidable trends already well under way'. [Hoekema 2001] Associative democracy in practice is not so different from the present-day hegemonic system of (neo)liberal and representative democracy, but rather supplements it, gradually and progressively repairing it with, as Hirst [2001] puts it, 'an open-ended agenda for reform'. Moreover, in rudimentary form it has already a long history. I am thinking here not only of the system of Water Boards or *Waterschappen* in the urbanized deltas, coastlines and irrigation systems of the *polders* in the Low Countries, but also for instance of the Special District system in the US, or the residential Housing Associations in the Netherlands, etc. Account can therefore be taken of the experience of the management of such associations that has been acquired over the years and in some cases, centuries. Strengths and weaknesses can be observed with regard to how they might serve as effective models for the current situation and contexts.

The first rudimentary forms of *associative democracy*

Water Boards Apart from the *huerta* irrigation systems in Spain (since 1435), the communal management of Alpine fields and forests in Switzerland (since 1483), the collective land management in local communities in Japan (1600-1867) and the irrigation associations in the Philippines (since 1630), the water boards in the Low Countries are considered by Toonen and Raadschelders [1993] to be one of the oldest and most successful *Common Pool Resource Management* (CPRM) institutions in the world. Unlike in the case of public assets that serve the common good and are largely facilitated by the state, CPRMs are primarily a local community interest and thus require a social arrangement among the stake and shareholders themselves in order to produce, maintain or develop the goods and services in question. In the case of the Dutch water boards, we are dealing with communal land reclamation, protection against flooding as well as communal management of the water level so that the land and the *polders* might be available for agrarian and urban production (see for a extensive English overview of the Dutch water management system: Van Ve 1993). Although good and trustworthy primary sources are lacking, it is generally considered that these organizations began in the Netherlands, in imitation of the Flemish Polders and Water Boards (*Waterings*), in the mid-twelfth century, when the population began to increase rapidly and the region saw the first expansion of agrarian production, trade and a money economy. The first neighbourhood associations were established at that time – the craft or guild, depending on where one lived – in order to look after the collective interests of the community, and in particular for the creation and maintenance of the waterways. This was carried out according to the principle of dike maintenance (*verhoefslaging*), according to which each complete farm (defined as an agrarian enterprise that could at least provide for its own needs) was responsible for one or more distinct parts of a ditch, dam and/or dike. [Dolfing 1993, Van Dam 2004] A bailiff (also known as a dikegrave) chosen from among the members of the association saw to it that everyone in fact fulfilled this responsibility, and he imposed penalties or fines in cases of negligence. And although the precise details of the system varied from one region to another, in the later Middle Ages the landowners (first the counts of Holland, and later also the bishop of Utrecht, the dukes of Gelderland, Brabant, etc.) also began to be more actively involved in local water management, out of self-interest. At their instigation, new regional structures were created under the authority of a bailiff, dikegrave, dike association and/or 'higher local council'. This bottom-up self-governing water system was intentionally kept more or less in place over centuries. When, in the sixteenth century, Emperor Charles v sought, after some (financial and functional) difficulties with the water management, to create an overarching water body that would centralize the appointment of dikegraves, he immediately met with resistance on the part of the local population and water boards, as well as of the provinces. [De Klerk 2008] Similarly, the more centralizing tendencies and even the creation of a new Ministry of Water Management (*Waterstaat*) under the Batavian Republic and French rule (1795-1814) were immediately reversed after the 'liberation'. With the growing ambition to create polders, the provinces, in addition to the traditional water and high local councils, were given an increasing role in the inspection of the smooth operation of the system. [Kloosterman 1993] At the beginning of the twentieth century, there were still some 2000 water boards operating in the Netherlands. These were associations organized and supported from the bottom up, and subject to democratic control on the basis of the triad of 'interest-payment-voice', that is, votes and seats were allocated in accordance with the (financial) contribution and/or interest involved. Thanks to the highly improved technical capacity for effective water management and the growing diversity in desirable

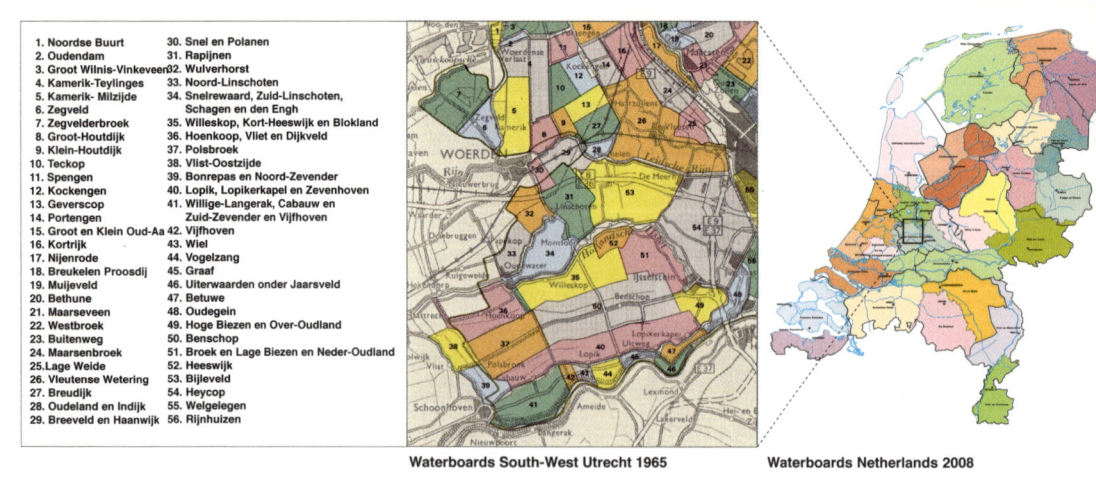

1. Noordse Buurt	30. Snel en Polanen
2. Oudendam	31. Rapijnen
3. Groot Wilnis-Vinkeveen	32. Wulverhorst
4. Kamerik-Teylinges	33. Noord-Linschoten
5. Kamerik- Milzijde	34. Snelrewaard, Zuid-Linschoten, Schagen en den Engh
6. Zegveld	
7. Zegvelderbroek	35. Willeskop, Kort-Heeswijk en Blokland
8. Groot-Houtdijk	36. Hoenkoop, Vliet en Dijkveld
9. Klein-Houtdijk	37. Polsbroek
10. Teckop	38. Vlist-Oostzijde
11. Spengen	39. Bonrepas en Noord-Zevender
12. Kockengen	40. Lopik, Lopikerkapel en Zevenhoven
13. Geverscop	41. Willige-Langerak, Cabauw en Zuid-Zevender en Vijfhoven
14. Portengen	
15. Groot en Klein Oud-Aa	42. Vijfhoven
16. Kortrijk	43. Wiel
17. Nijenrode	44. Vogelzang
18. Breukelen Proosdij	45. Graaf
19. Muijeveld	46. Uiterwaarden onder Jaarsveld
20. Bethune	47. Betuwe
21. Maarseveen	48. Oudegein
22. Westbroek	49. Hoge Biezen en Over-Oudland
23. Buitenweg	50. Benschop
24. Maarsenbroek	51. Broek en Lage Biezen en Neder-Oudland
25. Lage Weide	52. Heeswijk
26. Vleutense Wetering	53. Bijleveld
27. Breudijk	54. Heycop
28. Oudeland en Indijk	55. Welgelegen
29. Breeveld en Haanwijk	56. Rijnhuizen

Waterboards South-West Utrecht 1965   Waterboards Netherlands 2008

Waterboards in the Netherlands (Atlas van Nederland 1986, Unie van Waterschappen, 2008)

polder levels, the number of these water boards even increased in the first half of the twentieth century until there were around 2500 in 1950. There were cases where an individual stockbreeder personally represented the entire water board management as well as carrying out the tasks of the technical service. The polder archives – as far as these are available – were given pride of place on the night table in the bedroom. [IJff 1993]

Since that time, an important change in the system has gradually been introduced. In the 1960s, there were increasing demands that the water boards should take charge of managing water quality as well as quantity. Waterways and water management should be put in the hands of a single body of control as far as possible. This is why the water boards had to take increasing account of a variety of functions: not only agricultural and urban water management, but also nature preservation, recreation and landscaping. The broad expertise needed for this purpose, could no longer be supervised by the small water boards, it was thought. Since the 1950s, the water boards therefore had to upscale and merge, so that of the 2500 boards in 1950, only 800 remained in the early seventies, 120 at the beginning of the 1990s, and today there are only 27 left.

Along with their broader list of tasks and as a result of the upscaling, the water boards also underwent an enormous bureaucratization in the intervening years. Whereas in 1950 each water board employed an average of 2.5 people, this figure has since grown to around 370 per water board. [Van der Meer/Raadschelders 1993, Key data on government personnel 2008] Along with this growth, the management of the water boards has also been greatly professionalized. In fact, the originally autonomous boards slowly but surely became intertwined with the general administration of the towns, the national administration and especially the provinces. The recent Dutch Water Management Law that came into force in 2008 not only abolished the legal differences between water boards, but it altered the contribution system and established a more uniform system of governance. At the same time, the electoral procedure has been adjusted. The traditional personal system has been abolished and replaced in part by the electoral list system of representative democracy. [Ministry of Transport and Water Management 2008]

Apparently the effectiveness, integrity and scope of the water board's service provision increased considerably as a result of a simultaneous management of costs. Nevertheless, the water board has thus become increasingly remote from its stake and shareholders, now renamed 'clients'. And that is unfortunate. For where the efficiency of the water board system depended in the past on local residents' experience and of their own interest in carrying out these tasks, the identification with local water management now lies to a large extent outside him or herself, i.e. with the government or the quasi-governmental water board, increasingly endowed with all the characteristics of representative democracy. The traditional social control that has always been a strong feature of the relationship between local residents and water administrators on the old water boards [IJff 1993] has disappeared completely under the new Water Management Law. In that respect one may well ask whether the water board today is still based on something like a CPRM. Elinor Ostrom, [1990] Toonen and Raadschelders [1993] identify eight design principles governing those common pool resources: from clear boundaries and membership, appropriate rules, a recognized right to organization, adequate oversight and conflict resolution mechanisms to an appropriate system of 'graduated' sanctions, collective decision arrangements and 'nested units'. Particularly with regard to the latter criteria, the current legislation leaves much to be desired. The degree to which the stakeholders are given the opportunity to take part in decision-making has become very indirect and mediated, in keeping with representative democracy. The same is true of the degree to which people feel they share responsibility for the results and for involvement in the wider local socio-cultural setting that is distinctive to the region and the water board. According to Toonen and Raadschelders, the robustness of the water board system has suffered greatly as a consequence of that.

Special Districts Like the water boards, the Special District System in the US also has a long history. Special Districts refer her not so much to a specific geographical unit, locality or separate territorial unit, but especially to a specific item or function, which involved people like to organize collectively. And although they have been included in the constitution for more than two centuries, they took off mainly after the Second World War. The incentive for their development has been not only the enormous suburbanization in this period, but above all the increasing individualization and differentiation of all sorts of needs and wants on the part of the American people. Special districts are especially well suited to meeting significantly changing spatial patterns. Moreover, these districts fit in extremely well within the American governmental climate, in which it was taken for granted that power should be shared as much as possible between various forms and levels of government, in order to satisfy as much as possible the democratic need for self-fulfilment and individual autonomy. [Sharpe 1973] The most important feature of the special districts – as a governing institution – is their flexibility with regard both to territorial scope and boundaries and to the topic or problem, and/or the capacity to adapt to changing circumstances. Since the 1950s, the number of special districts in the US has nearly tripled to around 35,000. More than 85% of these are 'single function districts', established in order to serve the shared interests of the local residents with regard to, for instance, natural resources, fire protection, water supply, housing and community development, sewerage, libraries, parks and recreation, public transport, highways or care & cure, etc. A mere 10% serve a multiple of these functions and interests. Along with the School Districts (c. 15,000), they constitute more than half of all government units in the US. [US Census Bureau 2002]

John Bollens, one of the first political scientist to write about the issue, stressed that, although there are many forms and sizes of special districts, they have a number of common characteristics too. *'They are organized entities, possessing a structural form, an official name, perpetual succession and the rights to sue and be sued, to make contracts, and to obtain and dispose of property. They have officers who are popularly elected or are chosen by other public officials. They have a high degree of public accountability. Moreover they have considerable fiscal and administrative independence from other, general purpose governments.*' [Bollens 1961, p.1] The popularity of special districts is, in his view, the result of the fact that existing local and regional government units are not always well suited to serving a specific interest, such as geographical scope (special districts can be related to a single appropriate territory, which may if necessary cross municipal, county, or state boundaries), financing and function (in special districts, resources or taxes may be made available or allocated directly to the matter at hand) or the administration and/or structure. Unlike regular government bodies, special districts can be set up specifically on the basis of their function and objectives, and their management can deal directly with those. In addition, for reasons of competition, special districts are sometimes also given a powerful stimulus by local or regional governments in order to offer better services and service provision than the neighbouring areas. In this way, they are better able to focus directly and more efficient on meeting the specific wishes of their residents. Finally, special districts have also multiplied because of the desire for autonomy or the unrestricted pursuit of the self-interest of specific interest groups or lifestyles. Special districts often develop through a bottom-up process of consultations and petitions. Sometimes, however, they are well served by the intercession on their behalf by the specific district of the day. Financing is often provided on the basis of membership, an additional property tax, the issue of bonds or shares, as well as by tax increment financing, capitalizing the expected future gains in the present.

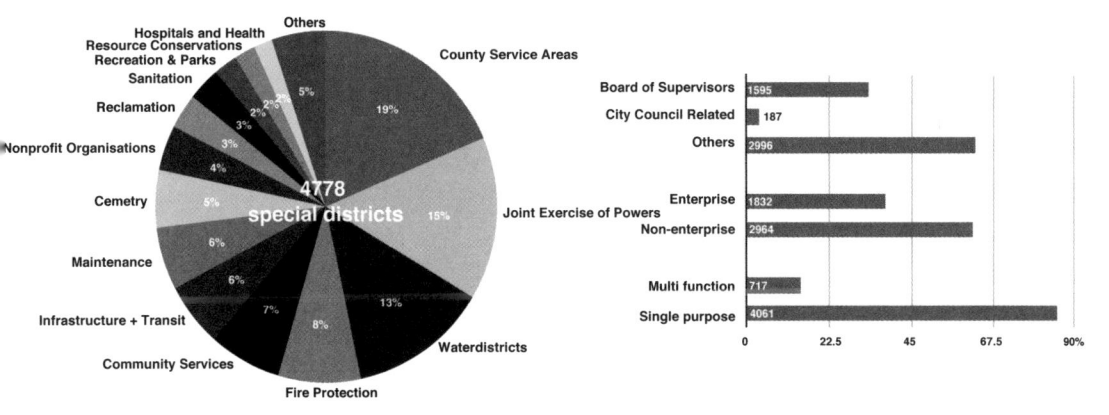

Some Features of Special Districts in the State of California USA (California State Controler Annual Report 2008)

Certainly there is initially often a strong direct involvement by residents in a special district, and therefore these can be far more effective than local or regional governments. But this is not to say that over time, dysfunctionalities or misappropriations cannot creep in. Even Bollens [1961] observed that already in the 1960s in certain regions there was a superimposition of overlapping and sometimes conflicting special districts, as a result of which oversight was lost – including that for the stakeholders themselves. Virginia Perrenod, [1984] for her part, pointed to the invisibility of some special districts in the 1980s, referring to their lack of democracy and accountability, their inefficiency and duplication of functions and the competition for tax dollars. In line with Woodworth, Tees and Anderson, she advised that some districts should merge into larger units, while others should be abolished and/or their functions transferred to the regular local or regional governments. Similarly, the Little Hoover Commission, [2000] established by the State of California, issued a report on the special district system in 2000 stating that 'independent special districts often lack the kind of oversight and citizen involvement that is necessary to promote their efficient operation and evolution'. Without the stakeholders, let alone the managers, realizing it, some independent special districts held more than 2.5 times their annual revenues in reserve (in total nearly $20 billion), while 24 health care districts in California no longer operated a single hospital, in spite of the fact that they were still collecting property tax for this purpose. Moreover, the desired consolidation of excessively small special districts into larger units turned out not to be so simple. Therefore the commission advised among other things:
• that legislation be passed to make special districts more visible and accountable to their stakeholders, that Local Agency Formation Commissions be set up in order to serve as catalysts for a more democratic and efficient development of independent special districts,
• that special districts make their financial reserve, income and expense structures more transparent, and
• that a study be made of the desirability of certain districts retaining local property taxes in view of the services they provide.

In short, it seemed that some were calling for a prudent, rather than an unbridled development of special districts, in order to avoid overkill and to promote efficiency and transparency. Instead of a 'laissez-faire, laissez-aller' attitude, there were calls for a better adaptation of the district system to that of representative democracy, although not for abolition.

Residential Housing Associations A typically Dutch example of associative democracy is that of the residential housing associations. For although such organizations exist(ed) elsewhere as well, in the form of Housing Districts (USA), Housing Corporations (UK), *Wohnungsgesellschaften* or *Heimstätte* (Federal Republic of Germany) or *Sociale Huisvestingsgemeenschappen* (Belgium) etc., these associations seem to have been more widely institutionalized in the Netherlands than elsewhere.[20] [Vreeze, 1993] The earliest forms of socially organized housing emerged in the mid-nineteenth century, during the first industrial revolution and the accompanying move from the countryside to the city. In addition to regular private housing, where speculation and bad housing conditions were rife, Jacques Nycolaas [1980] distinguished three more idealistic initiatives focused on the 'moral elevation of the distressed and on the newly received medical insights based on the understanding that personal hygiene ultimately serves a higher general purpose', e.g.:

- social housing built by industrialists (partly out of social commitment, but also out of economic self-interest),
- the philanthropic housing of the Enlightenment thinkers (partly out of social conviction but also for speculative purposes) and
- residential housing provided by workers' associations.

In their pure form, the latter were primarily trade unions (apolitical, but socially and ideologically driven) that strove to improve the working, living and housing conditions of all workers 'without violently disrupting the existing order'. [Kruseman 1939, citing Nycolaas 1980] Thus in Amsterdam in 1868, for instance, an associative Building Society *De Bouwmaatschappij* was set up in order to help people acquire their own homes, using a system of contributions to collect enough start-up capital to develop projects that would then be rented out to members according to a lottery system. The rental income which would be earned by that would then be reinvested in new projects, etc. [Harmsen 1972] The *Vereniging tot het verschaffen van geschikte woningen aan de arbeidende klasse* or Association for acquiring suitable housing for the working class in Arnhem 1851 and the *Vereniging tot verbetering van de woningen van de arbeidende klasse* or Association for the improvement of working class housing in The Hague 1854 were predecessors of the building society and were set up in a similarly bottom-up and independent way, but sometimes financed a bit differently. Around the turn of the century, there were some 40 of such companies or associations operating in the Netherlands. [Kempen/Van Velzen 1988] Nevertheless, their output was still very limited, sometimes no more than a dozen dwellings,

20 Noud de Vreeze stipulates that in the end of the twentieth century the Dutch social rental sector comprised 44% of the housing stock while this figure amounted to 16% in former BRD %, 17% in France %, 24% in England %, 17% in Denmark % and 7% in Belgium %. [De Vreeze 1993, p.13]

scarcely a drop in the bucket of poor hygiene, abusive situations and illustrious practices of the slum landlords in working-class housing. Faced with the social riots of the late nineteenth century, an increasing number of strikes during the crisis years of the 1890s as well as the entry in 1897 of the Social Democratic Workers' Party (SDAP) into parliament, the government decided to pass a Housing Law in 1901 and to experiment with more powerful and structural support for the aforementioned housing associations. The (national and municipal) government actually began to act as financier and/or patron of co-operative housing associations to stimulate their social housing activities. [Casciato 1980] In order to be eligible, the association had not only to be officially recognized as a housing corporation, but to obtain financing as well there was a series of criteria to be met as regards the hygiene of the dwellings, (over) population, periodic upgrades, rental rates, repayment requirements, maintenance etc. In fact, this was an early, rudimentary form of what has been referred to above as 'participatory budgeting'. Government funds were made available to self-governing stakeholders, who could take part if they met the aforementioned conditions. Nevertheless it took three years before the first *Vereniging tot bevordering van de bouw van werkmanswoningen te Leiden* or Association for the promotion of the construction of working men's housing in Leiden received this status. But thereafter, progress was rapid and by the beginning of the 1920s the Netherlands had some 1340 accredited corporations. These were often organized around various local, religious, political and/or ideological interests. Their development was so rapid that by 1913 an umbrella organization was founded to promote collaboration on social housing construction – the National Housing Council – which in turn urged the national government to admit only those associations that served the improvement of social housing to the upmost, and even to abolish existing ones if they did not sufficiently serve that goal. [Kempen/Van Velzen 1988] The rules were thus made stricter on the basis of a stronger, broadly formulated social housing policy. Thus, until the Second World War, more than 160,000 social dwellings were built, representing nearly 15% of all building construction in the Netherlands. [based on statistics from the CBS and the NWR, see figure on page 162]

The Netherlands emerged from the Second World War having suffered serious damage. Besides the effects of the bombing of Rotterdam in 1940, the housing stock had fallen by nearly 100,000 dwellings, 41,000 were seriously damaged and some 400,000 had suffered slight damage. Very quickly, the new social democratic government declared the housing shortage the number one public enemy. Given the scope of the problem, the government took on a significant role in the task of rebuilding. Both the allocation and the construction and management of housing became primarily a task for the state and the municipalities. In the best case, the corporations were seen as implementing organizations for the reconstruction programme, and although they could propose candidate tenants to the municipality, the latter decided on the basis of urgency and not primarily according to ideological orientation or membership.

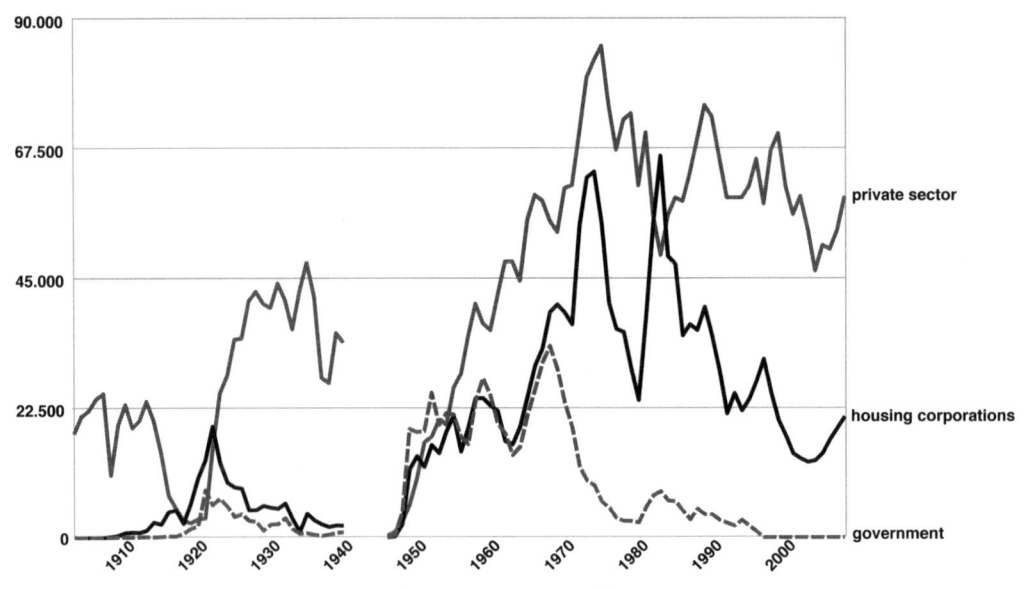

Housing production in the Netherlands 1902-2006 (NWR 1988, Aedes 2008)

Although this was presented by the first post-war administrations as a temporary emergency measure, necessary to alleviate the immediate need, there were soon voices saying that this was in fact an ideal organization for Dutch government. The authorities in fact seemed extremely effective in raising housing construction to an unprecedented level. At the same time, there came to be – partly as a result of that rapid growth – an increasing number of rules, making it necessary for corporations to be staffed by professionals. More so, this period of reconstruction saw fundamental transformations among and within the corporations too. The latter increasingly alienated themselves from their base. The relationship shifted from a board-stake/shareholder relation towards a general relationship between landlord and tenant. The question about matching 'housing culture' or 'ideology' was in fact no longer asked to candidate tenants, and thus the caring, community-building and unifying task of the corporation disappeared. According to Kempen and Van Velzen, this took place definitively in the 1960s. In its repositioning announcement, the Patrimonium housing corporation of The Hague made it crystal clear 'that the corporation no longer builds exclusively for its members. It is a service-providing social body for the benefit of local and regional society'. [Patrimonium 1966, cited in Kempen/Van Velzen 1988, see also Salet 1994] This entanglement of interests between the government and the corporations' policies consequently reached unprecedented heights in the 1970s and 1980s. And although that close entanglement, at least at the financial level, was definitively broken up with the establishment of the new Social Housing Policy of State Secretary Heerma, [Volkshuisvestingsbeleid in de jaren negentig, 1989] the original associative basis of the corporations was never restored. [Klijn 1995] Rather, the process turned into a privatization operation, in which on the one hand the government withdrew from social housing,[21] and on the other, the housing corporations themselves acted

21 This was because it was assumed that the acute housing shortage would be resolved, well-being was growing rapidly, and that a supply-driven housing market would yield to a demand-driven one. In addition, the effort to keep national expenditures on social housing manageable played an important role.

more and more like market participants, albeit carefully watched over by the public authorities, making sure they fulfilled their social task of providing social housing. Although there are still (local) differences, the intense relationship with and joint authority through their tenants and/or stakeholders never did return. Instead it was replaced by an intensive concern for (the value of) the corporation's housing stock and for its managerial accountability to government. [Bomhof 1999, Strijland 2006] In fact, every form of association has now been lost, both from the side of the tenants and from the side of the corporations themselves.

Prospects for the future

Returning from these three (historical) examples, one can conclude that in itself, *associative democracy* offers fruitful prospects in both practical and in social and political terms. Down through the centuries, it has demonstrated its functional value and power of governance. In addition to its flexibility and its specific and concrete collective objects, the most interesting aspects of these examples were their self-determination, the accompanying commitment of those concerned to the success, and the vicissitudes of *the commonweal*. Those concerned were actually entangled stakeholders rather than one-dimensional clients. Nevertheless, after the initial successes of the associative cases discussed above, all three came under great pressure in due course, and/or ended up leading to the opposite of what was intended. Remarkably enough, this has taken place in all three cases mainly during the past five decades, that is, in the period of post-World War II reconstruction and accompanying welfare state policies involving structural changes in post-industrial society and the associated neo-liberalization.

The Water Boards thus underwent an important transformation once the problem of water management became ever-more complex in the light of growing environmental pollution, and once they had to address not only quantitative but also qualitative problems. The requisite professionalization which came hand in hand with that called for upscaling, mergers, bureaucratization and, recently, an increasing integration into the electoral list system of representative democracy.

For the Special District System in the USA, one can perhaps more reasonably state that they have been the victims of their own success. The enormous increase in every manner of new and sometimes overlapping special districts – especially on the fringes of urban agglomerations – had not only led to less transparent governance, but also resulted in a fragmentation of the commitment of the stakeholders, as well as a lack of oversight of the operations of these districts.

Finally, after the Second World War the residential housing corporations had to deal with the tense relation between the included and the excluded, a question that by definition is part of all associative democracy. Although the central government insisted at the time that this would be a temporary measure only, allocation on the basis of urgency rather than of participation or membership endured longer than expected. Thus the corporations in question, like the other bodies mentioned above, became increasingly alienated from their bedrock, partly because their pre-war basis of ideological pillars and the political tendencies of the 1960s also began gradually to crumble. The privatization during the 1990s did not restore the participatory basis at all, it more or less abolished it.

So associative democracy in the twenty-first century can only be fruitful if it takes on a new form that will produce a socially responsible and politically feasible addition to the current representative types of public (spatial) planning and/or neo-liberal privatization. If we want to restore or reinvent it – and for that there are good reasons with regard to the ongoing fragmentation and alienating effects of representative democracy – it should, in my opinion, have to fulfil at least the following conditions.

First, associations should be based not so much – and certainly not in the first instance – on grand stories or ideological convictions, otherwise we would again fall in the trap of the modernists. [see also Sloterdijk 2004, Boomkens 2006] Rather, as is more or less the case in the special district system, they should be centred on specific topics or problems (such as care & cure, water management, housing, education, etc., preferably crossing sectorial borders). This is increasingly possible while the 'domestication' of contemporary means of communication has given rise to a new set of collectivisms (through shared interest, norms, values, lifestyles or other) alongside the traditional forms of neighbourliness. In my view, it is precisely these new collectivisms that can create the impetus for associative planning and democracy, rather than the other way around. [see here also Dekker 2005]

Second, associative democracy is not an alternative to, but rather an effective framework, complementing current dominant forms of representative democracy and state planning. In the US, there is perhaps a greater need for more effective monitoring or reform of the system. But elsewhere, in Western Europe – and above all in the Netherlands – there is scarcely a serious debate about such forms of self-organizing and participative democracy or planning. Unlike Hirst, [2001] I agree with Cohen and Rogers [1992] that, in this regard, the state can play an encouraging and facilitating role as well. Precisely in the area of spatial and regional planning there are new opportunities, in fact necessities, to experiment with new crossovers among and between traditional sectors and therefore to experiment in a relevant, specific and prudent manner with new, twenty-first century forms of associative democracy.

Third, this is a matter first and foremost of appropriate financing and taxation. Instead of a centralized tax collection and then a distribution by department to specific projects, it would be better to allow for more specific, decentralized project financing in crossovers from departmental and sectorial redeployment, for instance. In this context, one might consider new forms of participation and accompanying financing in areas such as transit-oriented development (road, water and rail), educational and care organizations, participatory public spatial management, red-green-blue landscape development, and/or perhaps even new forms of transnational housing corporations, etc. (see also Boxes 3.2, 5.1, 5.2). New, specific case studies are needed in order to determine and further develop specific frameworks over here, next to and in interaction with the existing forms of representative democracy.

BOX [4.1]

Unmappables: connecting people to possible worlds

By Wies Sanders

Urban planning and maps have been linked to each other from the very beginning. In comparison with architectural planning, urban and spatial planning is surely much less simple for maquettes and models. Indeed, a slightly increased scale generates not much more than a sort of 5-centimetre thick model about the size of a whole living room. Maps, on the other hand, were seen as 'a creative intervention in urban space, which styles both the physical city and urban life' right from the outset. [Cosgrove 2005] The map of Venice represented the greatness of that trading city; the fair parcelization of

Impressive Venice (Merian 1650)

Fairly divided Beemster (province 1869)

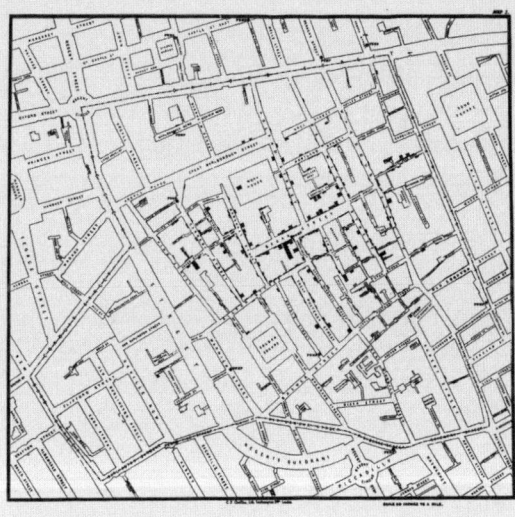

Analysed London [John Snow, 1854]

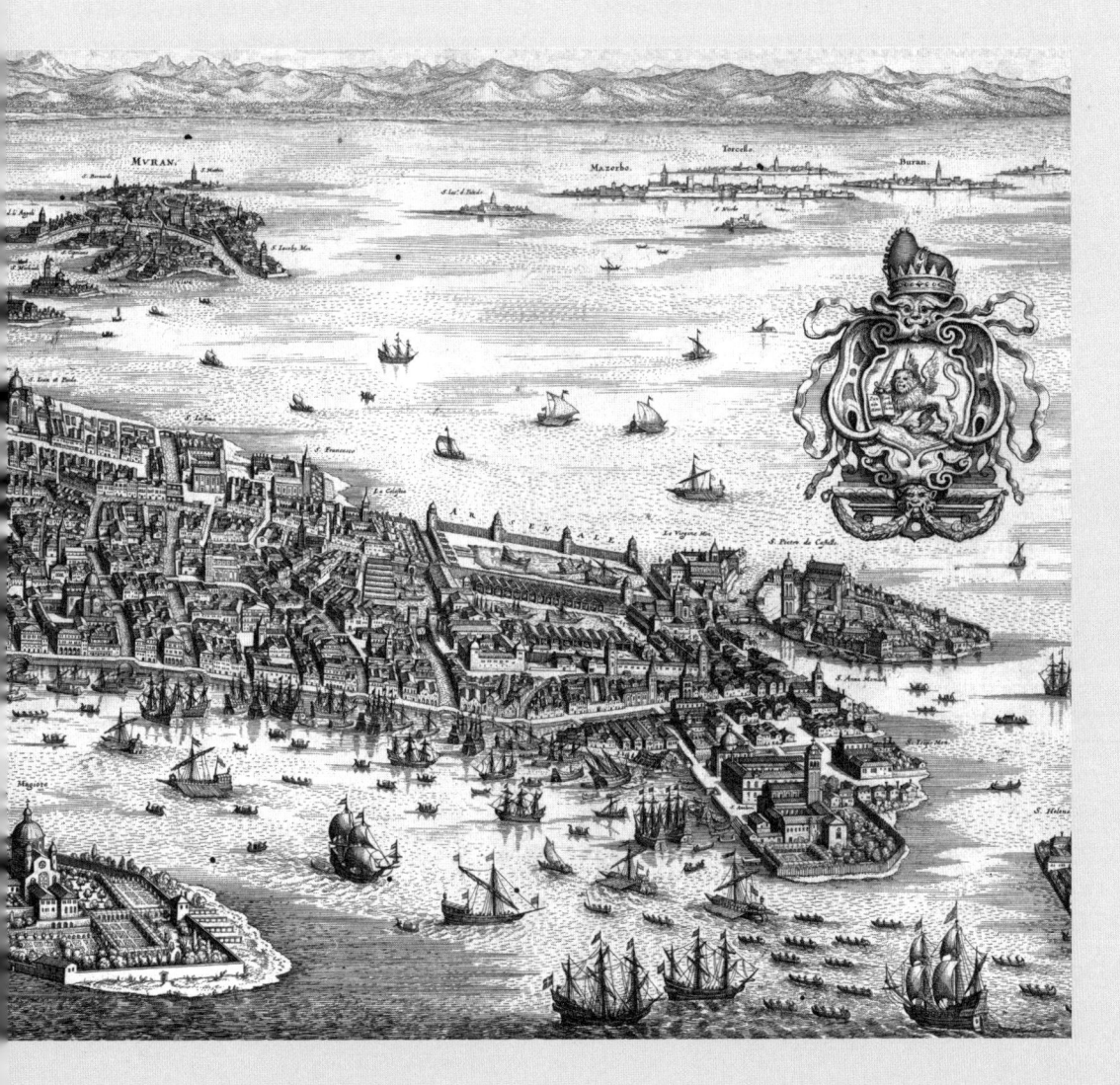

167

the drained and reclaimed areas in Holland was laid out and checked with maps, and mapping revealed the source of the cholera epidemic in London in 1854, an otherwise invisible pattern of infection. It provided cartographic proof that the disease was not spread through the air but via the drinking water. In a continuation of this, Patrick Geddes, Patrick Abercrombie, Theo van Lohuizen and others also used insight-providing maps in their 'surveys before plan'. In contrast to the often-quoted fairytale of a (low-) flying Plesman, it was precisely Van Lohuizen's cartographic analysis of the population growth in the west Netherlands in the period from 1869-1920 that invoked the image of 'a type of Randstad conurbation around a relatively open and less urbanized centre'; an image that has remained a policy until today. The power of the map is thus unmistakable, even so great that the atmosphere of objectivity around a map is sometimes misused for political purposes and propaganda, as the Nazi German propaganda maps and the coverage map of T-mobile show. Classic cartographers find the solution in a more systematic, objective and standardized working method. However, critical cartographers champion the standpoint that a map always has a cultural and anthropological context, of which the underlying strengths must be known in order to be able to estimate the value of the map. [Foucault 2003, Harley 2001] In their view, maps can never be objectified via strict professional standards; all maps are culturally selective, or 'all maps lie', as Monmonier [1991] puts it. The modern, ingrained habit of making the step from analytical maps to ideas for the future (call it planning) fits into this context. Moreover this step is often made easily and too non-committally. In itself, this does not always have to be such a bad thing. For example, the imagery in *An Inconvenient Truth* via graphics, manipulations and maps is not very well supported scientifically. However, it did evoke a general awareness, which the dryer model calculations had hardly achieved up to then. Nevertheless, precisely because of the too non-committal generation of all types of scenarios, images or ideas (which are precisely also no more than 'just ideas'), [Baudrillard 1994] it is time for the spatial planner to reconsider the value and application of his or her own mapping images and to explain them more precisely.

Opinion forming versus regulation

Nowadays, there seem to be two extreme reactions visible within urban planning. The first one is the opinion-forming of urban planning. It floats on the waves of rapid trends and hypes and is able in the short term, with the assistance of the most modern techniques, to produce unprecedented virtual speculative futures. In this capacity, however, the urban planner is overtaken by architects and animators; but let us disregard this for the moment. This part has become an independent cultural production in which complex resources are used to the full. The often over-the-top ideal planning image is modelled as attractively as possible, where the ultimate experience and the use of the realized world can actually only be a disappointment (see for example, Squint/Opera's restoration of Jeddah, MVRDV's Skycar City or the renderings of the Amsterdam South Axis). A second problem is that it has led to the inflation of views, sketches, images of the future and plans. Not only the motive, but also the status of a certain map can seldom be established and has received a shelf-life. At the time of writing (November 2008), a map has been published in newspapers and on TV of the new sports cluster and Feijenoord football stadium in Rotter-

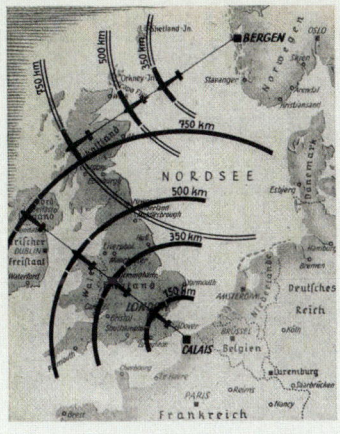

Nazi propaganda maps (Strangemaps)

T mobile coverage map and actual coverage (T-mobile, Jaap Stronks)

Al Gore suggestion of flooded areas of Holland within 50 years (An Inconvenient truth)

dam. It looks like an already-realized and inevitable situation but is actually no more than a policy intention, where all procedures and financing structures still have to be arranged. The status of this visionary urban planning is here primarily 'inspirational', but when such images are translated for participation, MER procedures (Environment Effect Reports) and calculations, then these images are an enormous obstacle. It then appears to be obscure what is variable and what is fixed, even what has already been realized or is still to come. In short, who is 'inspired' and who is not; what exactly is being 'revitalized'? Losing its status, the image begins to lead a life of its own.

The second approach is the more everyday urban planning in which complexity is avoided as much as possible in order to increase its chances of realization. Parallel to the previous inspirations, a mosaic process is set up in which the many departments and disciplines lay out their own domains:

planning areas are measured and allocated in an orderly fashion, the planning and legal processes are digitally managed in time, the actors in contracts are tightly bound and the schedule of requirements has been completed in all four dimensions. The status of technical and legal maps is usually very clear, the urban planning and image quality demands usually remain issues for discussion, as the masterplan of the Amsterdam South Axis shows, for example. [Meijer 2008 p.21] Even more important is that, as a consequence of splitting up the process, the overview and attunement in time between disciplines and in execution has become too precarious. Only in the completed situation or even in the situation where the adaptation has been recently taken into use can it be tested with regard to where it has and has not deviated from the contract, but the reason for this is difficult to establish (see the experiences with the Bos and Lommerplein in Amsterdam).[22]

Although both reactions are directly opposed, they agree in the choice of reducing urban planning in its entirety: one to an animator, the other to an organiser of subcontracts. It leads to reasonable images that function well within strictly defined locations, but where the integrating role that Van Lohuizen once allocated to urban planning work, has completely disappeared. In this way, urban planning will lack the necessary connection with the everyday practical life since it ignores essential details and dormant social processes – either consciously or not.

22 In 2006, in the night of 11 to 12 July, 190 residents had to leave their 90 houses, since the concrete structure of the parking garage upon which their houses were founded turned out not to be in order. Thereafter followed a tug-of-war among the municipality, buildings inspector, architects office, project developer, builder and insurer about who was responsible and had to pay the costs. Ultimately, the case was settled by agreement.

Four ways to navigate through complexity

In her contemplations on the work of Deleuze and Guattari – *the* philosophers who have considered complexity without wanting to reduce or further complicate it – Hillier [2008] describes the need to see spatial planning as 'strategic navigation towards a speculated future'. This is thus almost contrary to the above-mentioned planning practice. Deleuze and Guattari precisely avoid the frequently travelled paths and explore 'ready-made entities', and discover how new relationships between actors and institutions are created, how they move, how they wander the same planning pathways at certain times, and how they potentially make or could make new events happen. They propose four navigation techniques in order not to lose one's way totally in that complex process: [Deleuze/Guattari 1987]

- The *trace*, seeking out potentials,
- The *map*, mapping out the regimes that these potentials can live up to,
- The *diagram* that reflects transforming the fields of influence of the actors.
- The *agencements*, more passive elements that work bindingly on that field of influence with actors, such as laws and regulations.

It is assumed that, with these navigational systems, a planner can learn to cope with uncertainties, experiments, doubts and speculation. During the planning process, focus is placed on transformation but there is simultaneously space to learn, adapt and create. 'Embracing' this complexity ultimately leads to a possible better navigation of the planning process, while it could indicate changes, instead that a change is being looked at as an immediate disturbance of the planning process or constituting an abandonment of a principle. With this, a type of open planning process arises, which does not mean, however, that there is consequently more participation or disturbance in planning but that the choice of research, actors, proposals and rules are public, accounted for, critical and imitable. This could also possibly lead to the more effective participation of involved stakeholders and shareholders. Urban Unlimited has practised this in recent years in a relatively experimental manner. In the following, this practice is further described on the basis of the four navigation systems of Deleuze and Guattari and their value for future planning processes.

Tracing

Tracing is mapping and interpreting matters that can only be viewed retrospectively. It is both a creative and systematic way of delving into the material and unravelling from the inside exactly which conditions have formed an area, or other object of study. It literally means systematically following the tracks to the origin of an area, city or country, but also of a company, family or association, in proportion to the framework of the task. The term DNA or biography has often recently been used a great deal [Taverne/Boelens 2009] and refers to the more invisible mechanisms, though cognisable with some effort, determining how things are tackled, spatial-social ties are formed, and individual characteristic institutions exist (see also the referential argument at the back of this book). In an increasingly competitive world, these uniqueness, authenticity and recognizable characteristics seem to become important qualities in beating the competition, and being recognized as a distinctive part of the borderless world. This uniqueness can be expressed in physical things of the city and country, socio-cultural and economic structures or in an immaterial 'way of doing

Artist impression of the South Axis Amsterdam (DRO Amsterdam)

Urban plan South Axis Amsterdam (DRO Amsterdam)

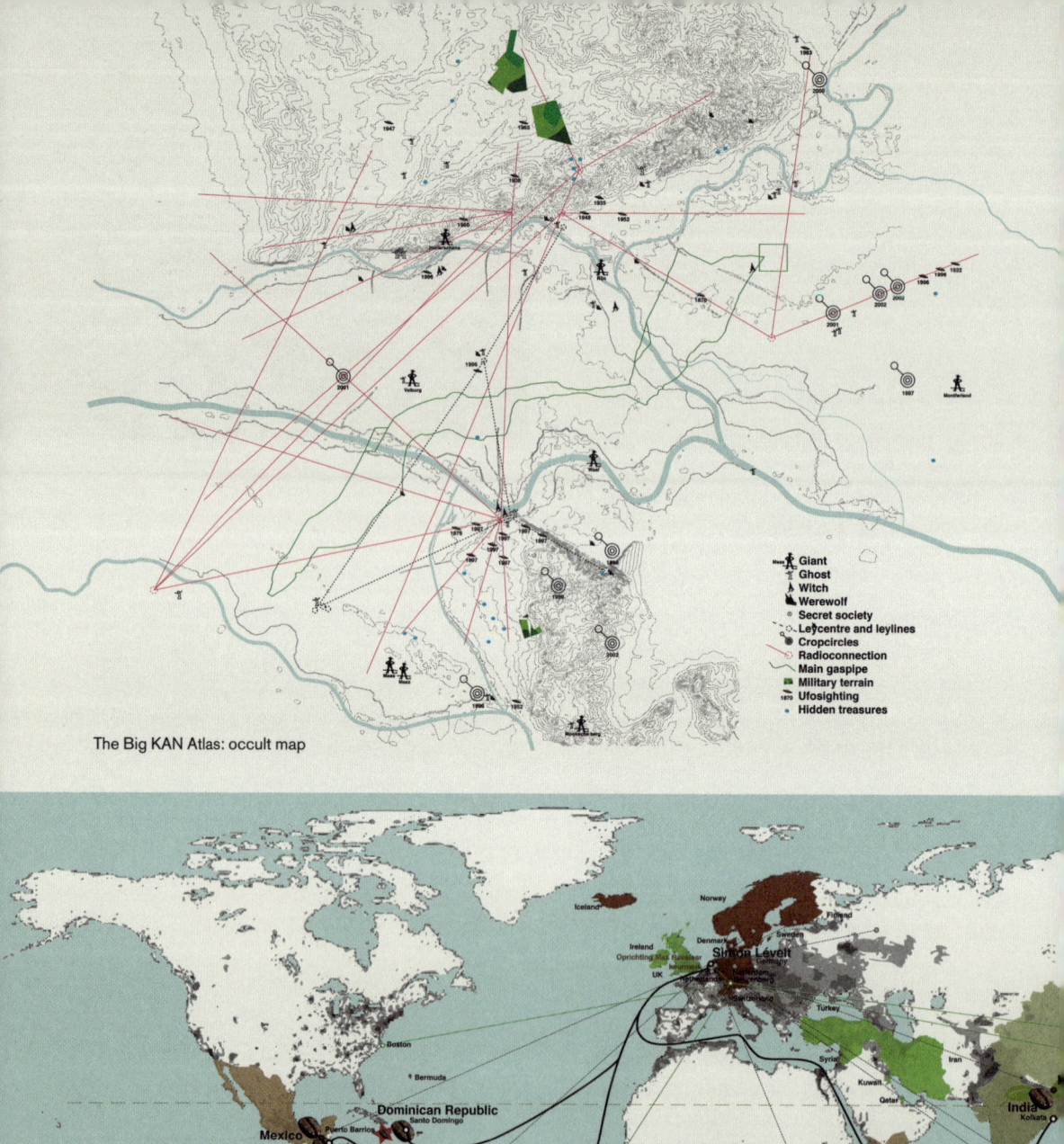

The Big KAN Atlas: occult map

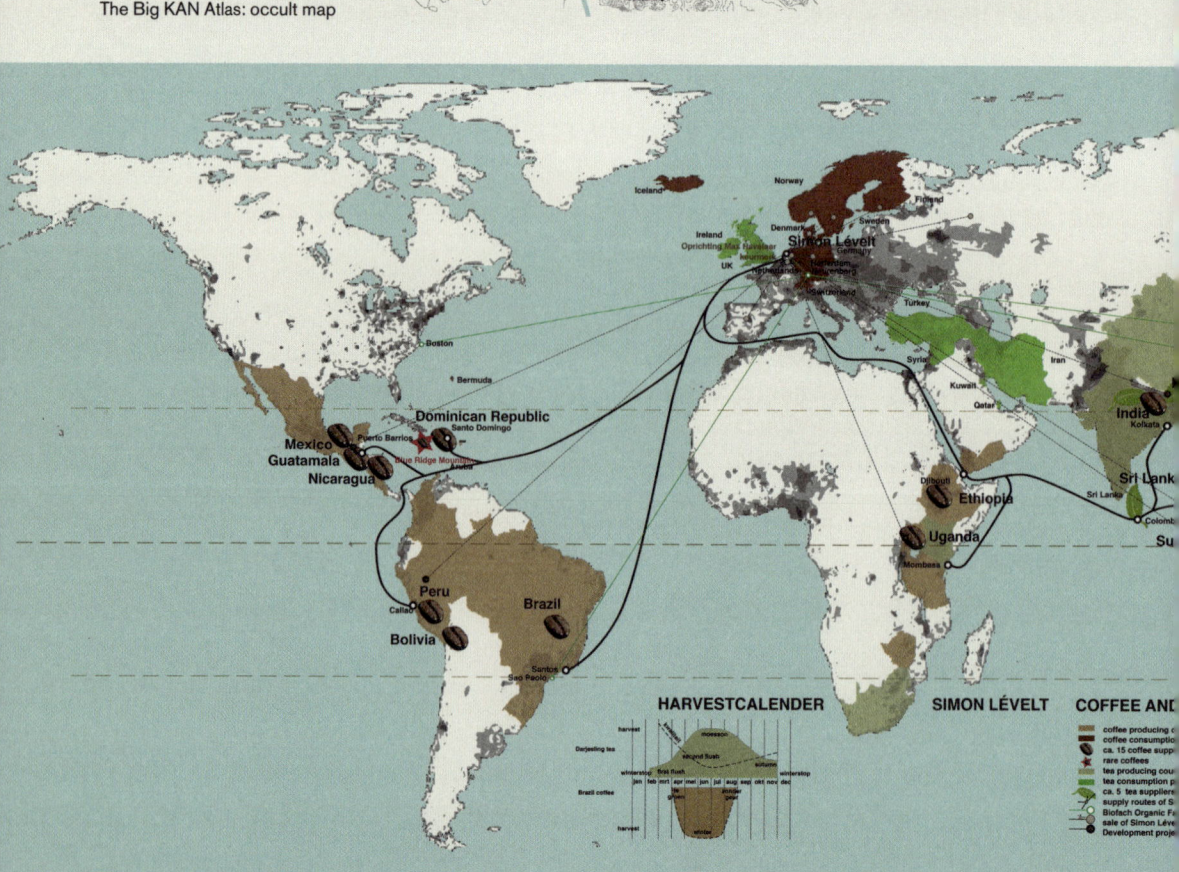

Legend:
- Giant
- Ghost
- Witch
- Werewolf
- Secret society
- Leycentre and leylines
- Cropcircles
- Radioconnection
- Main gaspipe
- Military terrain
- Ufosighting
- Hidden treasures

Wordwide production and distribution of Lévelt coffee

HARVESTCALENDER   SIMON LÉVELT   COFFEE AND

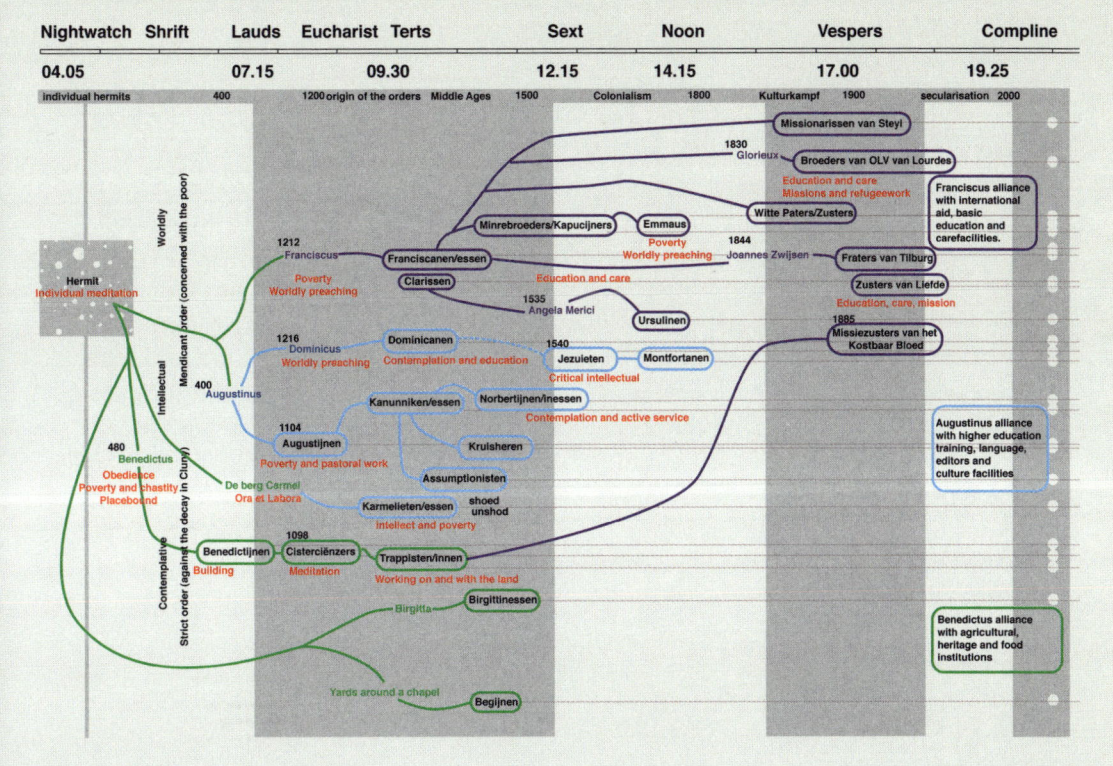

Nightwatch	Shrift	Lauds	Eucharist	Terts	Sext	Noon	Vespers	Compline
04.05		07.15	09.30		12.15	14.15	17.00	19.25

individual hermits | 400 | 1200 origin of the orders Middle Ages | 1500 | Colonialism | 1800 | Kulturkampf | 1900 | secularisation | 2000

Hermit — Individual meditation

Worldly
Mendicant order (concerned with the poor)
Intellectual
Contemplative
Strict order (against the decay in Cluny)

400 Augustinus

480 Benedictus
Obedience
Poverty and chastity
Placebound

De berg Carmel
Ora et Labora

Birgitta

Yards around a chapel

1098 Cisterciënzers — Meditation
1104 Augustijnen — Poverty and pastoral work
1212 Franciscus
1216 Dominicus — Worldly preaching

Benedictijnen — Building
Franciscanen/essen
Clarissen — Poverty / Worldly preaching
Dominicanen — Contemplation and education
Kanunniken/essen
Norbertijnen/inessen — Contemplation and active service
Kruisheren
Assumptionisten
Karmelieten/essen — shoed/unshod — Intellect and poverty
Trappisten/innen — Working on and with the land
Birgittinessen
Begijnen

Minrebroeders/Kapucijners
Emmaus — Poverty / Worldly preaching
1535 Angela Merici
Ursulinen — Education and care
1540 Jezuïeten — Critical intellectual
Montfortanen

1830 Glorieux
1844 Joannes Zwijsen
1885

Missionarissen van Steyl
Broeders van OLV van Lourdes — Education and care / Missions and refugeework
Witte Paters/Zusters
Fraters van Tilburg
Zusters van Liefde — Education, care, mission
Missiezusters van het Kostbaar Bloed

Franciscus alliance with international aid, basic education and carefacilities.

Augustinus alliance with higher education training, language, editors and culture facilities

Benedictus alliance with agricultural, heritage and food institutions

Descent of the Brabant monastic orders

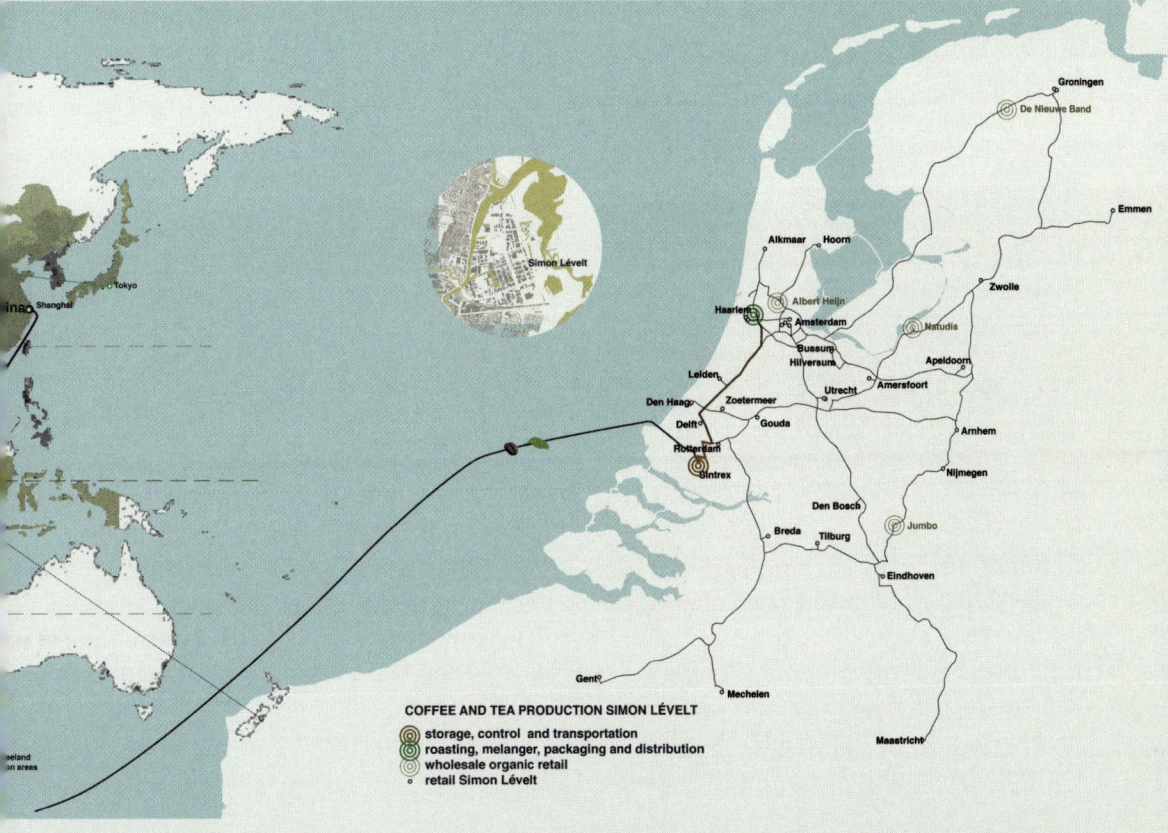

COFFEE AND TEA PRODUCTION SIMON LÉVELT
- storage, control and transportation
- roasting, melanger, packaging and distribution
- wholesale organic retail
- retail Simon Lévelt

173

things'. It is then also immediately apparent that all possible sources should and must be explored to find this out: from literature to interviews, from company reports to world records, from remote sensing to historical topography, etc. In contrast to cultural historical analyses, tracing also concerns time, whereby only things from the past that indicate they could have strategic potential in the present and the future are investigated. Moreover, tracing is also open on the scale level. It requires quite a lot of attention to find the appropriate scale for every unique characteristic, which could furthermore have a different role at several scale levels.

Mapping

Tracing includes only the qualities and potentials of an area, it does not offer a perspective on how these potentials can be utilized and become reality. This is what the process of – in Deleuzean terms – 'mapping or transformations' is for; here referred to as 'opportunity maps'. Opportunity maps are open maps, which are altering in the course of the planning process, but are always tracked in their transformation route and always retain *traced potentials*. They provoke a proper confrontation between the past and a new regime; the retrospective and prospective. A new regime is a new alliance of actors or new markets, which can refresh and measure themselves against that potential. For example, the potential of the Augustinian orders in Noord Brabant, mapped by *tracing*, was confronted with possible new markets in language training. *Mapping* thus comprises representing as temptingly as possible the manner in which this interaction could take place. *Mapping* is actually a type of *educated matchmaking between actor-networks and potentials*, where the secrets of the world could be revealed if the match works out. It is admittedly based on *tracing* – you cannot simply invent something – but the essence of *mapping* is in the creative and subjective addition of an image or vision. Every means of representation is then allowed to provoke the 'what if…'-enthusiasm as much as possible: maps, photo montages, films, diagrams, etc. Their strength must be in permitting a feasible temptation to realize a potential. The opportunity map must be open enough to be adapted to the specific interests of a new market or actor, but also precise enough to genuinely make a positive match, such that the potential or contemplated association comes to fruition.

Diagram

Ultimately, the world revolves around people and their dynamism. Initiative takers are needed to realize the potentials discovered via *tracing* and sketched via *mapping*. Finding partners and matching them is still often an underestimated component of the planning process. It is, in any case, still hardly conducted in an open and imitable manner. Possibly, this has something to do with the fact that it is primarily a personal and face-to-face process. However, in the global network society, meeting in time and space has become a considerable problem. Finding correct and new partners is a time-consuming and painstaking task that can be supported by the third navigation system of Deleuze and Guattari; in this case, the *diagram*. It serves particularly for charting the dynamic relationships between possible actors and actively seeking out what their joint interests could be. It is, so to speak, a more precise directory, well-founded and based on backgrounds, motives and ambitions – and in principle it is public. To get past the 'usual suspects' in a planning process, the diagram is also a possibility to approach and evaluate new actors.

Opportunity map Deep Forests in Brabant

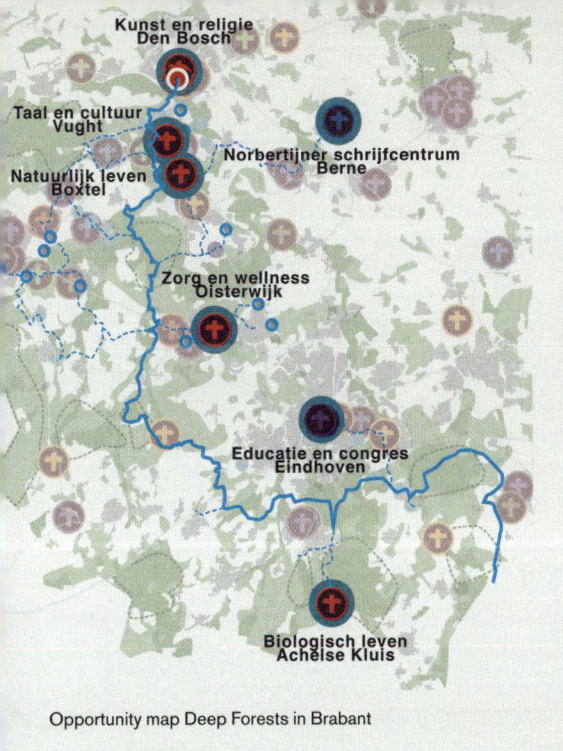

Continuing the values of Augustinus

Continuing the values of Franciscus

Continuing the values of Benedictus

Alliances in the Limburg region

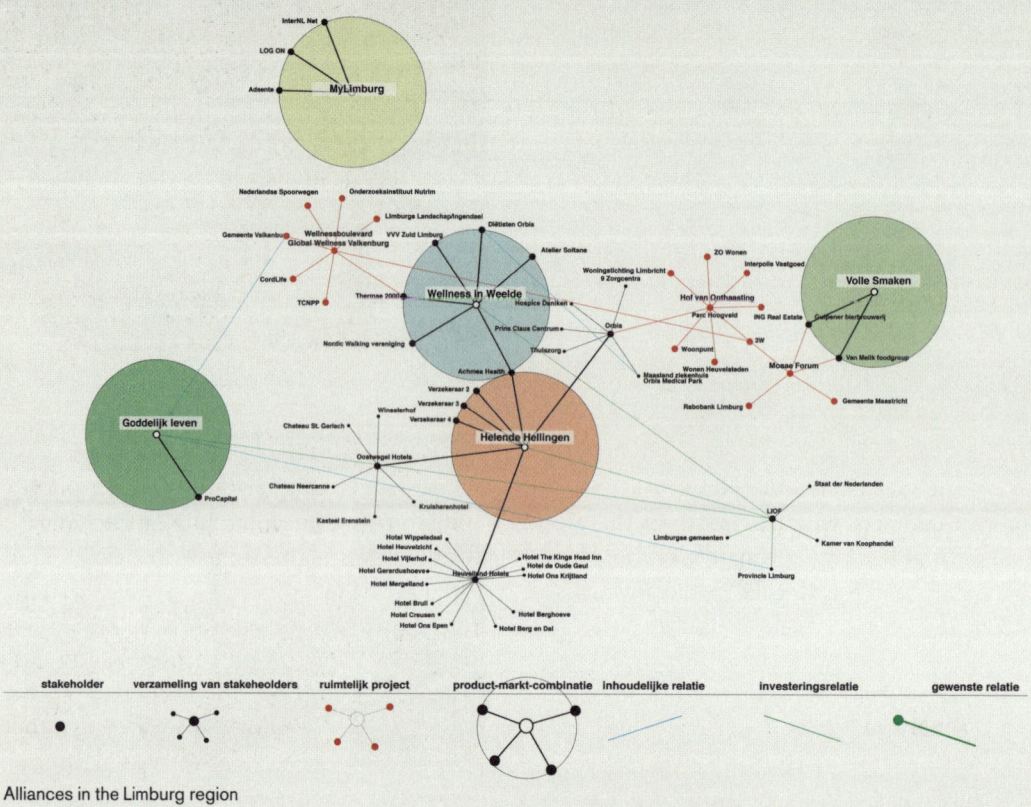

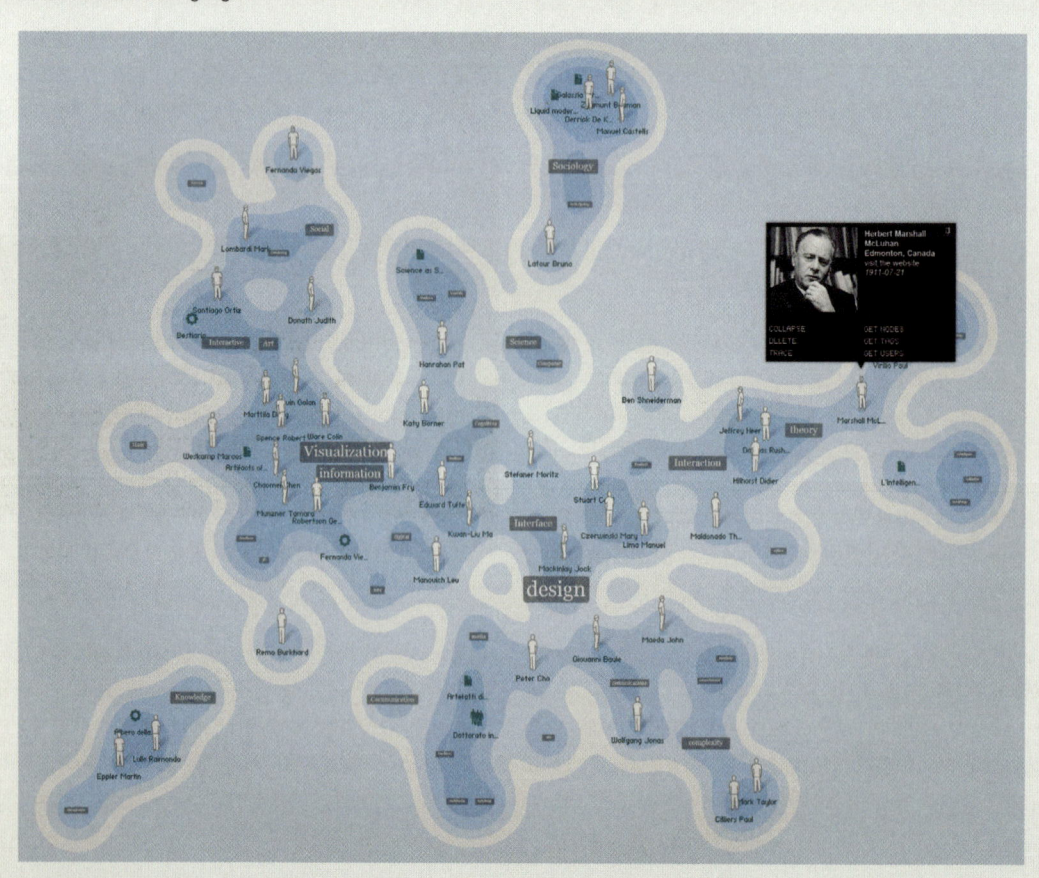

Connections in visual information (Marco Quaggiotto)

The diagram presents the necessary information about these actors, their relationships to others *and* their possible influence and position in the process. It is thereby also a more elaborated *LinkedIn*. However, in a networked society, several actors contribute to a project in different ways. A diagram can ensure a topical overview and display the historical progress of alliance formation, and so facilitate its continuity. For example, the interactive form, as is being developed in online social networks, along with face-to-face contacts, will turn out to be the most suitable form. Ultimately, it could even be a basis for a legal contract or formal alliance.

Agencements

Finally the *agencements*, according to Deleuze and Guattari are the agents or types of intermediate processes. They are, as remarked, the more passive elements that have a binding – or separating – effect on fields of influence, such as laws and regulations. In this context, one can think of the european *Habitat directive*, a building permit, or a concession granted, for example. In principle, a dynamic and open process is corroded with too many *agencements*. In nature, these are always strongly directed at the creation and retention of fixed agreements and predictable processes. It is also desirable, however, that a process of coagulation and positioning takes place, so that ideas and strategies can become anchored in regimes or institutions, projects and cultures. To be able to fulfil the role of *agencements* optimally, accessibility, transparency, completeness and topicality are of great importance. From time immemorial, this has been a role left to and appropriate for government agencies. Governments are so good at this, it has led to an unclear situation with generic rules and too much pressure from regulations. [see VROM: New Act on Spatial Planning 2008]
In an optimal process, data such as land registry, basic maps, photos, legal regulations and jurisprudences, permits, GIS files, zoning plans, etc. should be stored in a transparent, publicly accessible model. It forms, as it were, an area dossier that is accessible to every stakeholder and shareholder. In some countries, internet and Google Earth are used as such. In the Netherlands, a beginning is slowly being made with the digitization of spatial planning in DURP (meaning Digital Exchange Spatial Plans), but for the time being, rapid access to a totality of relevant spatial rules is reserved only for internal use by civil servants. Due to this, the *agencement* is too dominant and becomes an individual process. It therefore has a primarily separating rather than binding effect. Instead, a good *agencement* should be able to produce procedures to change itself and lead to a self-repairing, improved organ.

Towards an open planning future

The use of this Deleuzean cartography is to take the global information society seriously, use its technologies optimally, and make mapped images – instead of exclusively regulatory or representational – more imitable and thereby stronger in an actor-oriented, relational perspective. Up to now, most experience has been gained with the *Tracing* of qualities and *Mapping* of possible opportunities and regimes. However, tracing is usually dry cultural history (e.g., Belvedere) and/or sectorially deployed (e.g., MER's). The step towards the future can hardly be taken from here. Tracing is more detective work that also needs a curious, creative attitude to investigate potentials in different times and on several scale levels. It is the difficult task of designers, researchers and clients to see tracing from the very beginning

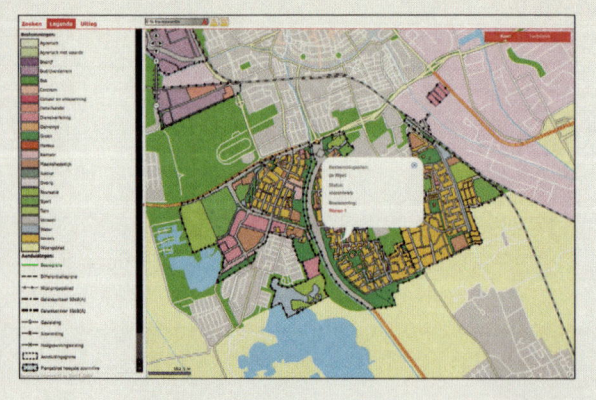

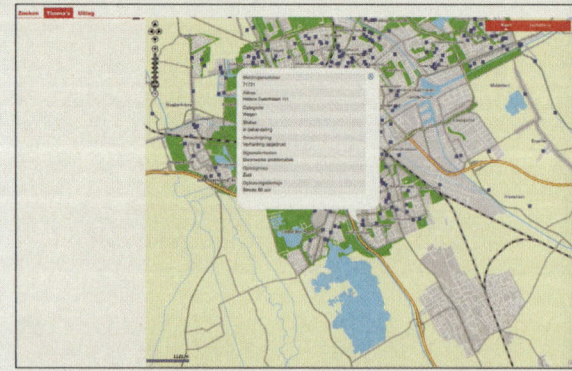

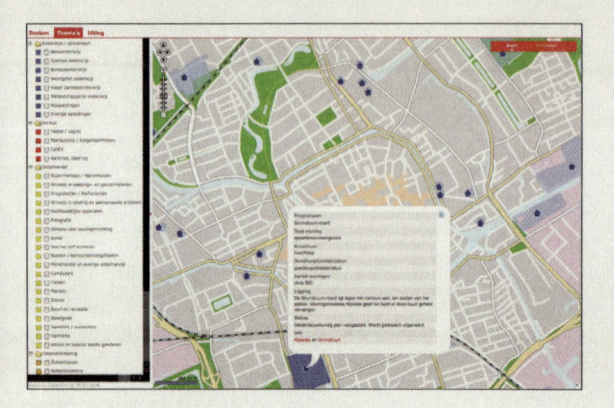

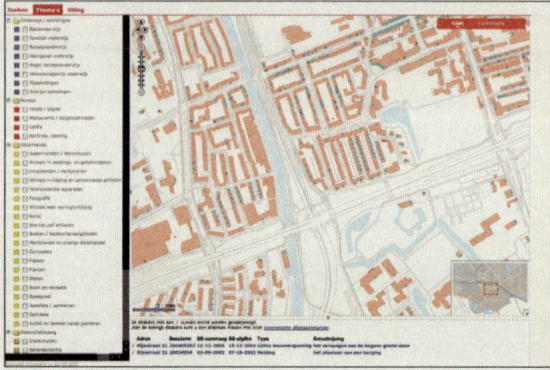

Building and zoning files of the city of Groningen (gemeente Groningen)

not as a neutral professional analysis, but the start of a planning process.

Mapping, in terms of representation, is often closest to the better known urban planning sketches, photo montages and the previously mentioned ideal planning images. It has now become primarily a domain for designers and planners, while in the context of Deleuze it may not actually become a separate domain. Mapping serves to transform the opportunities into regimes and this requires an open process, in which social and private actors are involved at an early stage so that they play a role in the formation of maps and futures. In any case, in the Netherlands, the reverse is often the case. Although lip-service is paid to public-private collaboration, much in the areas of functionality, zoning and appearance is established here, even before fundamentally crucial stakeholders have been consulted.[23] The difference with these 'visionary cultural productions' is that mapping should be used primarily as a process resource and must therefore have an inviting and not a recording effect. It should not become an objective in itself. In addition, it is seen as the start of a process of negotiation between private and public actors and does not represent the end of an either provisional and/or crystallized public planning process. With mapping, the spatial planners possibly also play a more active role in the match-making process. Gradually, the oppurtunity maps can be 'pragmatically adapted' [Hillier 2008] or thrown overboard because the potential has

23 See, for example, the review of the Zuid-As model in Amsterdam by Ton Kreukels. [in Salet/Majoor 2005, pp.150-66]

not (yet) been recognized or cannot be supported by those involved. Mapping is then in no way a closed final image that should be worked towards in phases, but a 'foreseen geography of the unknown' or a navigational map for a sea that has never been sailed. [Albrechts 2004] However, the large majority of current future images – certainly in a highly-developed planning country as the Netherlands – are often exclusively formed by the government, landowners/developers or cultural funds. This leads to a finally negotiated plan, a narrow plan, or an inoffensive plan, respectively, but in no case to the complex but also creative crossover maps intended by Deleuze and Guattari. Here lies a task for the visionaries to roll up their sleeves and take a position in the arena of planning processes. And there is a task for regular policy-makers not to purchase inspiration from visionaries, but first of all to seek it in the agency itself or in stakeholders.

Diagrams are actually not yet worthy of mentioning in ongoing planning processes. Approaching actors and abandoning ideas is often seen as an intimate process that must take place behind closed doors, for fear of the withdrawal or poaching of stakeholders and ideas by a competitor. Moreover, it is always important to do business face-to-face. Nevertheless, the whole success and the potential of informal and digital social networks has not remained unnoticed by professionals (see, e.g., *LinkedIn*, the role of professional blogs or *Google Books*) and it could well lead to workable diagrams that map knowledge about people and institutions, forces and influences that cannot be discussed around a table. There will have to be experiments with this in the coming years, where also the legal side of publicity, privacy and possibly contract formation should be investigated.

Agencements are particularly found in the areas of government nowadays, and they quickly become bogged down in bureaucratic processes (see, for example, the Digital Exchange in Spatial Processes, DURP project). There are remarkable innovation possibilities here with ICT developers who develop a technical application and subsequently bring it to the global market. Internet and Google Maps/Earth are the usual platforms. Its application by governments occurs in an *ad hoc* manner and furthermore only within a certain sector. This reticence is not expected to change soon in governments and commercial data banks, primarily because they are still too introverted. Possibly, a reverse outside-in orientation could give rise to new alliances. One could think, for example, of an Urban Google or Linux to access public data genuinely publicly, and close attractive deals with the information owners. It would in any case be scientifically, practically and technologically very attractive. In Boxes 5.1 and 5.2, an attempt is made to apply this concept.

[5]

Outlines for new planning futures
Towards an actor-relational-approach

Returning to the argument presented in chapter one; since the mid-1980s we have been facing a growing awareness of the need to embed spatial planning in the ambitions and controversies of key social and economic groups in everyday life. Spatial planning had become too bureaucratic, process-oriented, and single-focused on land-use regulation to deal with the growing (de-)fragmentation and ongoing multi-actor, multi-scaling of the network society. Next to that, the new political challenges to the apparent bankruptcy of the 'welfare-state' after the oil-crises of the 1970s also had a major effect on planning. Confronted with massive unemployment, governmental overspill and rising debts, neo-liberal administrations developed, focused on tax reductions for industry, the reduction of public deficits, cuts on public services, privatization of public enterprises, deregulation and decentralization. Planning itself was suddenly confronted not only with the traditional land-use regulation, but also with the task to improve the economic perspectives of a certain region, within the rising network society and massive environmental challenges. The social component of spatial planning shifted from social programming toward the way people and businesses experienced their surroundings and recognized themselves in them. [Boelens 1990] Regions and places were not just seen as passive spaces to be planned or designed by an authority, but as active milieus that influence, and are influenced, by the interactions of actors. [Giddens 1984] In Giddens [1998] view, this would not mean the death of the role of planning or institutions such as (national) governments, but the reorganization of the welfare state towards a kind of late-modern social investment state in which governments should focus on activating those critical, jammed parts of the civil and business society by cautiously introducing elements of market approaches, reforming civil services, and reorienting to a local and supranational level.

In the Netherlands, one of the first attempts to redirect planning in a more social embedded way was the intervention published by Ton Kreukels *Planning as mirror of western societies* or *Planning als spiegel van de westerse samenleving* (1985). Here he stressed – as did Clarence Stone recently [2005] – that planning was not a sole, not even the exclusive preserve of the government, but that many players and stakeholders play an equally substantial, if not greater role in spatial planning. To underpin his argument, he referred partly to the rising phenomenon of the urban regime approach at that time as a possible first step towards what he called 'a behavioural science-based response' to overcome the loss of direction in Dutch planning policy. Referring to the United States, he opted for a planning style which would again be directly linked with social movements and the various interests of the city in a kind of what he called an 'entrepreneurial style of planning'. This approach – also introduced by Susan and Norman Fainstein in their book *Regime Strategies* [1986] and subsequently described by Clarence Stone as 'the development of informal arrangements by which public and private interests function together in order to be able to make and carry out governing decisions' in *Regime Politics* [1989] – made its mark to some extent in a number of large-scale (public-private) city centre projects from the late

1980s onwards, as well as in the agreements approach of the *Fourth Report on Spatial Planning Extra* of the Dutch government, [VROM 1993] for instance.

Apart from that – as already stipulated in chapter four – following Jürgen Habermas's Theory of Communicative Action, others opted for a discursive, communicative or, later on, collaborative approach, in which planning was seen as an interactive and interpreting process, drawing on the multidimensionality of milieus rather than on a single formalized dimension. [Dryzek 1990, Inness 1995, Healey 1997] Characteristic for these kinds of interactive planning was the blurring of the fixed boundaries between public and private, the collective and the self-organization, while the plan became the means instead of the purpose of consensus building. As such, government also turned into more interactive governance [Pierre 2000, Teisman 1997, 2005, Cerfontaine 2006] and planning into a smart growth or integrated regional approach. [Wiegand 1997, Smutney 1998, Janssen-Jansen 2004, Healey 2007] It not only incorporated 'environment policy' (beyond the Nimby effect), but also put emphasis on *trade-offs* between spatial, economic, socio-cultural and ecological interests (instead of an emphasis on stated goals) and the quest for collaboration at *meso-governmental* level (instead of at local or national level). According to Hans van der Cammen [2006] and Riek Bakker, instead of setting land-use regulations, this so-called 'integrated developmental planning' or *integrale ontwikkelingsplanologie* is characterized by:
- an integrated approach to an area,
- on the basis of a shared quality vision, in which
- public, private and individual (i.e. public, business and civic society) supplement and reinforce one another in a co-production arrangement, with
- explicit attention to financing.

Reference is made to the need for all participants to sense the urgency of achieving development and for the equally great need for the partners to be able to build up a long-term relationship of trust.

The growing gap between planning practice and spatial-scientific dynamics

Whatever it may be, those ideas about a structurational, embedded, interactive or collaborative approach to geography and planning, acquired a more mature form in the relational approach of the pioneering 'post-structuralist' studies of Nigel Thrift, [1996, 2002] John Friedmann [1987, 2005] and Doreen Massey. [1995, 2005] Here, the object of planning – i.e., time and space, or better still, time-space [May/Thrift 2001] – is not seen as an independent and, as such, plan-comparable entity, but rather as a fundamentally relational entity, not only in interaction to other places and times, but also to a variety of heterogeneous practices that structure that space, and is itself structured by it in return. That being the case, the focus shifts from the spatial planning of the involved area and related processes in itself, towards the (f)actors, (institutional) settings and especially the exact networks behind them. Planning itself becomes embedded in a variety of socio-spatial practices, transforming and evolving along with the space-time dynamics while it plans. As such, it acquired also a broad impact in other, various approaches to space and geography.

In chapter two, I noted the important shifts that have occurred within, for example, spatial-economics: a classic, especially on-site features-oriented approach, via the behavioural and more structuralist approach, towards a kind of relational or evolutionary spatial economy. Regardless of how sophisticated and full of insight this might be; the existing planning practice is far from such developments. Spatial policy practice in the field of international competitiveness is still commonly (exclusively) focused on improving accessibility and the development of high-quality offices, industrial or residential areas. It is therefore still predominantly focused on the classical, particularly location-based approach, with a few small, but very little thoughtful planning trips to a behavioural (*Peaks in the Delta* report) or structuralist approach at best (land use policy, or tax incentive policy etc.). A more embedded interactive, relational or evolutionary approach is still a long way from here.

In chapter three, I noted the important and actually long-established conclusion within the social sciences that community-building, in addition to local-related criteria, is also increasingly structured around more thematic, functional and even cross-border criteria. One speaks not only of 'multi-focus households' with multiple bases and landmarks or 'networked communities' with strong and weak ties in the immediate environment and/or (if necessary) over ever-greater distances. But one also speaks about 'transnational' or even 'imaginative communities', which are no longer (only) vertically organized in geographic entities, but also increasingly horizontally organized in common interests, political, religious or other beliefs, specific grassroots interests, ethnicity or culture and multi-media organizations. Within planning policy practice, however – in regard to social integration and housing for example – it is currently still often exclusively focused on district and local bonds, mostly ignoring the growing importance of these relational, thematic or 'cross-geographical' ties.

In chapter four, I not only pointed out the leap in the study of governance in recent years within the (territorial) political, administrative and environmental sciences: at the same time, there is – under the influence of the recent financial crises, even among original die-hard neo-liberals [Fukuyama 2008] – a growing urge to advance beyond dominant forms of exclusive representative or neo-liberal democracy. They embed them within strict rules on social decency and/or the needs of a broad set of (f)actors of importance, i.e., various stake and shareholder groups. Here, new forms of discursive, or even radical participatory or associative plural democracy pass the review, each of which gives rise to customized public, private or private-public governance and additional forms of regulation, more embedded in everyday experiences of various citizens and businesses. But although Dutch government apparently embraces this new relational and decentralized management philosophy in the *White Paper on National Spatial Planning* [2006] and with the *New Law on Spatial Planning,* [2008] a closer look shows that the recent restructuring of tax, administration and legislation, concerning the water authorities, corporations or infrastructure planning, for example, point in the other direction. In this framework, one can discover a strong recovery of a vertical (state) control, or expansion of representative democracy, with all the bureaucracy and increasing distance to the daily life of citizens and enterprises, rather than relational, decentralized embedded governance.

So to conclude, in many geographic areas, there has been a disturbing gap between observed spatial (policy) practice and social and academic dynamics over the last twenty years. On the one hand, spatial (policy) practices tend – both in content and in procedure – toward a traditional lock-in. As observed in the Preface, the current *White Paper on National Spatial Planning* [2006] differs very little from the *Fourth Report on Spatial Planning,* [1988] as is the same with respect to the scenario explorations of Randstad 2040 in 2008 in comparison with those of *New Holland as a Design* or *Nieuw Nederland als Ontwerp* in 1987.[24]

But, on the other hand, social and academic insights of the last twenty years tend to a radical transition towards relational incitement and more horizontal associations, instead of vertical plan control. They have opted to restore a more direct link between planning and everyday practice of citizens and businesses in a networked society. So one can wonder: why is that gap here in the first place? In my practice as civil servant (1984-98) or as planning consultant (1998 until now), I have never observed that governors and politicians – although they were of course accountable to the representative democracy and its voting system – have been reluctant to renew, nor that they would refuse to restore a direct link with the daily affairs of the civic and business society. Therefore, looking more to our own planners' record, I think it has something to do with two main omissions.

On the one hand, we planners have failed to translate the more behavioural, collaborative or relational, post-structural planning theories into convincing, decisive and sustainable planning practices. The urban regime and entrepreneurial style of planning promoted in the mid-1980s were too hastily translated into development-oriented public-private partnerships, in which 'the public' still had to deal with the deficits, while 'the private' could go for the profits. Moreover they appeared to promote non-transparent, non-democratic decision-making in backrooms, to deliver selective distribution of material incentives and a fragmentary contextualism. [Sartori 1991, Imbroscio 1998, Davies 2002] There was a call for 'place entrepreneurs', [Logan/Molotch 1987] but these would inevitably be too locally focused, alienating planning from

---

24 This is not only the case in Dutch spatial policy practice. The new urbanism in the USA, for example, harks back to principles well into the 20th century. The structure plan for Antwerp 2008 is actually based on design principles that Oriol Bohigas conceived as far back as the eighties and that Bernardo Secchi at the same time has created in respectively Barcelona and Sienna. [Taverne 1989] And the principles of the European Spatial Planning in the field of (a) poly-centric spatial development, (b) 'parity' of access to infrastructure and knowledge, and (c) prudent management of the natural and cultural heritage, which were already drawn up by the Committee for Land Development (CRO) in 1991, are still prominent EU spatial policies etc. [Zonneveld/Evers 1995, Waterhout 2008]

the ongoing networked society. In addition, the interactive or discursive approaches – in Dutch: 'the polder model' – that were championed in the 1990s were over-focused on intermediary organizations (such as the employers' association, unions, and mobility, agricultural or environmental organizations, etc.) and hardly reached everyday practice or the ambitious members of civic and business society. [Porter 2000, Hoelen 2001] Even so, the collaborative, smart growth or integrated development planning were mostly only focused on a specific part of the business society (i.e., the project developers or the investment corporations), which often resulted in opportunistic trade-offs, temporarily zoning plans, or even a hit-and-run mentality on the part of private developers. [RPB 2004] There seemed to be hardly any robust 'long-term relationship of trust'. Thus the exemplary cases put forward by Van der Cammen and Bakker (such as *The Blue City of Groningen, Wieringerrandmeer, Transformationzone Rhine, Development Programme for West Brabant*, etc.), [Van der Cammen 2006] as well as those of Patsy Healey (*The South Axis of Amsterdam, The Milan Region and the East England Plan for Cambridgeshire*), [Healey 2007] as those of Mark Purcell (*The South Lake Union, Waterfront and The Duwanish River Cleanup in Seattle*, and the *Homeowner associations in Los Angeles*); [Purcell 2008] hardly prove to be convincing. Worse still, instead of demonstrating the lasting reinforcement of a long-term structure or the core values of the areas in question, it gives rise to the suspicion that it functions for the private sector more as an effective but mono-thematic trade-off to enforce lucrative developments on its own.

But on the other hand, I am convinced that it has also something to do with the fact that time and again the planning proposals were mostly still government-focused: inside-out. Take Fritz Scharpf, [1997] for instance; his actor-centred institutionalism remained mostly within governmental practices, explicitly focused on improving political research, deliberations and choice, and apparently tending towards associations with reference to collective purposes and collective control over action resources, in a somewhat hierarchical setting which would be able to support all varieties of modes of interaction. Patsy Healey, likewise, stressed that the importance of planning could no longer be in an explicitly formalized spatial strategy or legally required development plans, but also tended towards a governance of place, through all kinds of webs or intergovernmental relations that connect the organizations and procedures of formal government with informal governance arenas and networks, and the wider society. [Healey 2007, p.268] In similar terms and following John Friedmann, [1987] Louis Albrechts [2001, 2004, 2005] called in his valedictory speech for a transition towards a kind 'transformative planning practice', referring to 'framing activities of stake-holders to help achieve shared goals relating to spatial change'. To him, strategic spatial planning should evolve towards a transformative, integrative and *(preferably) public sector-led* socio-spatial process. Visions/frames of reference should be produced with a coherent justification for actions and means of implementation that shape and frame a place so that it might correspond to a multitude of relational networks of varying geographical reach. Although he pleaded for a transformative practice, in which planners, decision-makers and institutions needed to be taken out of their comfort zone, needed to challenge conventional wisdom and to look at the prospects of 'breaking out of the box', he also referred to his alternative as a strategic spatial planning process that was (preferably) public sector led. [Albrechts 2008] It is thus (preferably) government-oriented and therefore, in my view, inside-out. And precisely this is a major omission, because in this way the relational planning-proposals stay within the path dependences of the government, tending towards public-oriented problem-definitions of their own, focusing on internal time-consuming co-ordination processes, interaction overkill, and are ultimately exclusively oriented to vote-winning. They mostly result in less creative and innovative middle-of-the-road solutions, based on subsidiary and/or concession-driven principles.

Towards a behavioural actor-oriented view on planning

In this perspective, I advocate turning the focus radically around: outside-in instead of inside-out. Elsewhere I have provocatively called that approach 'planning without (a principal) government'. Governments should not be excluded in principle from all areas of planning, but it must be stated that it is high time for planners to focus primarily and in principle beyond the formal structures and 'ways of doing' of governments, and reoriented toward the goals and expectations of citizens and businesses; i.e., the civic and business society. Against this background, a number of modest attempts were developed in the niches and beyond the scientific and practitioners' establishment of Dutch planning to deal with the opposing approaches of planning practice and theory. Unlike the theoretical and/or primarily analytical views described earlier, these attempts were actually oriented towards an interchange between planning theory and planning practice. Therefore they were actually backed up by real, slightly remote planning projects in practice, rather than by case studies. It tried to reframe planning strategies in order to attract new markets in a sustainable, regional way, vice versa.

Basically, the starting-point here has been to get around the impasse between modernism and post-modernism, since there was no promising direction in neither a reversion to a supposed holism nor in a fragmented day-to-day project urbanism. [Boelens 1990] Others seem to be much too process-oriented, as is the case with, for instance, the resultant communicative, interactive and collaborative approaches, as well as discourse analysis and actor-centred institutionalism. [Boelens et al. 2000] Instead, the planners applied the approaches of the urban and regional regime methodology outlined earlier, those of smart growth and the behavioural approach and tried to deal with the critiques which have already been formulated elsewhere (see chapter one). An attempt has been made to bring these into line with one another so that they could become both effective in reality and justifiable in theory. [Mommaas/Boelens 2005]

The central theme of this kind of 'actor-relational-approach' is, first of all, an attempt to *develop beyond 'the plan'*. Instead of for instance present-day approaches, which have been focusing on 'a plan that works', [see for instance Faludi/v.d. Valk 1994, Geuze 2004, Hajer/Sijmons 2006 etc.] the actor-relational approach does not focus on a particular plan or a particular formal institution as the given central objective or subjective. A behavioural actor-relational view [Boelens, Spit, Wissink 2006] demands a prominent role for a more neutral moderator and an open medium to sketch opportunities. The focus is turned around: outside-in instead of inside-out. The point is not to formulate an objective, vision or plan, which then has to be implemented in trade-offs, whether or not in a public-private partnership, but to identify opportunities and connect them to possible actors who might want to associate with common opportunities, possibilities and/or themes from the ground up.

Second, the approach is not about actors as such, in the broad sense of interactive planning (all affected parties), but about *leading actors*. Here, the definition of *leading or focal actors* is in line with the evolutionary economic and urban sociological approach, 'those actors who have the capacity and incentive to invest in their local environment, doing so, moreover, for reasons of more or less self-interest'. [De Langen 2003, Yeung 2005, Boschma/Frenken 2006] In this context, we distinguish between leading actors within the *business society* (with a primary focus on profit-making), within the *public society* (with a primary focus on representational vote-winning) and within the *civic society* (with a primary focus on specific partnership interests). Although they thus have various focal points, we shall see that it is also possible to bring their interests together on specific planning items. The more they converge, the more durable the relationship will be. Moreover, it is acknowledged that the focus on *leading* actors also introduces a certain power connotation or subjectivity into this actor-relational approach. But in principle this is always the case, even with the seemingly more symmetrical communicative, collaborative and discursive approaches). Furthermore this evolutionary approach always departs from embedded actors in broad networks of economic, political and civic interconnectivity; and need therefore base their dominance on that interconnectivity.

Third, the concept of *sustainability* in particular is central to this actor-relational approach, but in a complex sense. It refers equally to sustainable economics (i.e., profit-generation), a sustainable social structure (i.e., broadly supported), a sustainable spatial solution (i.e., well embedded in an evolutionary, relational viewpoint), and sustainable environmental solutions, etc. [Mommaas 2006] The commonly discerned unique core values or unique selling points of a specific landscape, port design, social community, geographic constellation, etc. are included as meaningful, dominant (f)actors of mutual concern, that as such, constantly enjoy a central position in the actor-relational-approach. In fact, they become the central focal points, against which the planning associations are continually measured in terms of their objectives, development and results.

Fourth, the actor-relational-approach also has a primary focus *beyond the confines of government*. In line with the urban and regional regime approach, this arises from the conviction that the model of the welfare state or representative democracy does not work, or at least has seen its best days, [Stoker 1994, Pierre 2000, Purcell 2008] as well as from the conviction that the government is not the only actor within spatial planning, and often not even the dominant one. [Kreukels 1983] Moreover, the conclusion has been drawn that a lasting emphasis on central government negotiations leads to planning that lacks sustainability and is dependent on subsidies or volatile political commitment for example. [Mommaas/Boelens 2005] Accordingly, in actor-relational practice, a search is conducted right from the start for commissioning bodies in the private or semi-private/semi-public sphere, in order to circumvent these problems. It operates outside-in. Of course, the government always has a framework-setting or facilitating role. But the main process takes place in the focus on the specific embeddedness of actor-relational actions by and through stakeholders in the business and civic society.

Finally the actor-oriented approach is also *associative* through and through. This primarily consists of building effective actor-network associations around meaningful themes or issues as a starting-point, a working method and an objective. But it also ultimately ties in with the plea for an associative democracy made by Cohen, Rogers, Hirst and Bader, and others. [Cohen/Rogers 1992, Hirst 1994, Hirst/Bader 2001] This associative democracy sets out from the conviction 'that individual liberty and human welfare are both best served when as many of the affairs of society as possible are managed by voluntary and democratically self-governing associations'. [Hirst 1994, p.19] In their terms, associative democracy therefore has two distinguishing characteristics compared with all other possible forms of state:
- it bridges the gap between the state and civic and business society and transforms it into a situation that is actually more workable by 'pluralizing' the former and making the latter more *public and transparent* and
- it seeks to promote the democratic governance of collective entities in both public and private spheres by offering a bottom-up model of organizational self-efficiency. [Cohen/Rogers 1992, Hirst 1994]

Actor Network Theory and beyond

As such, and although it had been developed pragmatically within certain concrete planning practices, I introduce the Actor Relational Approach (ARA), which has evolved very closely to many features of the Actor Network Theory (ANT) with which Callon, Law and Latour have recently created a considerable furore. [Callon & Latour 1981, Latour 1993, Callon 1995, Law 2004, Latour 2005] ARA also starts off with actors and relations (or networks) – not only amongst each other but also between the human actors and the specific characteristics and entities of the locality – in order to reassemble them in such a way that they would become more innovative, enforceable and associative. On the other hand, it also has some deviant characteristics. I shall explain these later. Nevertheless ARA and ANT both agree on the proposition that technical, social or spatial artefacts are not outside or opposed to society, but are in fact the results of it. ANT argues that the world is made up of heterogeneous networks of actors. [Bos 2004] Or, as Latour puts it: 'sociology is best defined as the discipline where participants explicitly engage in reassembling the collective'. [Latour 2005, p.247] Not only is every (social) action thus fundamentally relational, it can also only occur as a consequence of the specific connection between people, entities and resources concerned. At the same time, those people, entities and resources only have a meaning in networks. [Law 1986] Or, in other words: 'What there is and how it is divided up should not be assumed beforehand. Instead it arises in the course of interactions between different actors. (…) Actors are entities, human or otherwise, that happen to act. They are not given, but they emerge in relations.' [Law 2004, p.102] Here – and this is possibly the most controversial assumption – ANT assumes that, in principal, there is symmetry between objects and subjects, nature and sociology, the human and the non-human. It is not as if ANT does not see a difference between humans and non-humans but, according to ANT, it cannot be presumed in advance who or what is most important for the action: a person, an entity or a resource. Thus in their description of the world and especially with regard to agency and actor-network associations they treat humans and non-humans symmetrically. For example, relevant people could reach an agreement about a plan, or all the elements to put a plan into practice could be present, but there may still be insufficient financial resources. In this case, no action or actor-network association will arise. However, ANT claims that it is possible for a specific actor subsequently to become more dominant than others, by seducing actors to behave according to his/its own prerogatives. In the given example, the people may involve other people with more money to enable the plan to be put into practice, or the limited financial resources may give rise to a less ambitious plan, with fewer elements involved, and hence to an adapted link between the people and entities. This is, in principle, what ANT calls 'the translation of the objectives, limitations and opportunities of other actors' so that these can start 'behaving' according to their own requirements, but in line with the wishes/characteristics of the dominant actor: 'the actant', in ANT terms. [Latour 1997] Thus as a result, for ANT, this actant – that dominates or organizes the association or network – may consist of either human or non-human entities. As such, the concept spans all rationally attributed differences between (conscious) subjects and (passive) objects, culture and nature, the technical and the social, the modern and the post-modern. It is not 'a sociology of the social, but a sociology of associations' [Latour 2005 p.9] in all kinds of assemblages between human, non-human and even lifeless entities.

Although the actor-network-theory may thus be characterized as a form of sociological epistemology, or perhaps even as a new 'a-modern monistic ontology', [Latour 1993] the actor-network theoreticians have also commented on space and the planning of space. Thus Jonathan Murdoch can refer to 'notions of space in a Latourian actor-network theory'. [Murdoch 2006 p.73] A crucial element of this type of notion is that there is no absolute time-space – just as there is neither absolute nature nor society – but only specific time-space configurations, which are conditioned by motives and relations in networks. [see also the notions of Lefebvre on 'space as a social construct', 1991] The attribution of any significance to scale or micro or macro-issues is in fact superseded. In principle, one should follow the actors, or better still the actor-networks, which condition specific time-space frames. The point here is not to analyse specific places within specific times. Instead, geography (and its future, planning) becomes the science or skill of the analysis (and/or planning) of heterogeneous associations or actor-networks in time and space. Spatial relations are reduced to network relations and spatial planning is understood as a process of network-building in which entities of various kinds are assembled in ways that allow networks to undertake certain functions. [Murdoch 1997] Even more strikingly, on the basis of his famous case-study looking at improvements in scallop cultivation methods on the Normandy coast, Michel Callon actually distinguishes four steps in the translation of actor-networks: [1986]

- *Problematization*

What is the issue that requires a solution? Who are the relevant actors? Can spokespeople be identified to represent specific groups?

- *Interest*

Can these relevant actors be interested in the solution to the issue? What 'terms of commitment' are there, and/or how can they be convinced that their own interests will be served?

- *Enrolment*

How can these common interests be converted into potential associations? Do the different actors also accept their role, or can they be geared to the available resources?

- *Mobilization of allies*

Is there broad support for the expected outcomes? Do the spokespeople actually represent their respective constituencies effectively, or how can the actor-network association be embedded in a wider setting?

Thus ANT appears at first sight to offer attractive prospects for contemporary spatial planning. The pitfalls of the (post-)modernity debate are elegantly circumvented, by refusing to assume the need for alternative thinking as a matter of principle, [Foucault 1968] the need for an emphasis on the small discourses, the so-called 'micrologies' [Lyotard, 1979] and an absolute desirability of a structure, holism or political interest imposed top-down or from the outside. [Frieling 1987 et al.] Instead, the focus is on the actors themselves, especially those that are capable, in networks, of developing meaningful spatial connections – albeit heterogeneous ones. At the same time, it sidesteps the stifling duality between macro and micro, because, the presumptions 'think global, but act local', its converse, or hybrid 'glocal' [McLuhan 1964, Drewe 1997, Swyngedouw 2004] do not really add anything new to our spatial knowledge. In principle, according to ANT, the actor-network associations in this network society cut right across different levels and layers. And finally, ANT offers a subtle extension to the discursive, entrepreneurial or growth management approaches, by also including things and entities as autonomous (not passive) forces or (f)actors of importance. The environment, the landscape, the cultural and historical heritage, the unique fauna and flora etc. can indeed assume a structuring or even dominant role of their own in actor-network oriented planning.

Even so, ANT comes in for fierce criticism from many theoreticians on the grounds that it incorrectly assumes a symmetrical *tabula rasa* between the relevant (human and non-human) actors, that there is always a certain (inherent) power discrepancy in evidence, that it confuses science as a research subject and as an authoritative source, and suchlike. [Bijker 1995, Hagendijk 1996 etc.] Law, Callon and Latour have reacted to these critiques in numerous polemics, and in this way improved and refined certain aspects of ANT. [Callon/Law 1997, Latour 2005] Nevertheless, I continue to maintain three serious objections with respect to the present subject of enquiry, planning.

At first sight ANT stands out – like so many post-structuralist and post-modern planning analyses, incidentally – mainly for its analytical power. In all analyses and case-studies, the main focus is on how things have turned out this way and how they work, not on how we can make them better and under which conditions. On the contrary, the actor-network theorists are very much reluctant and cautious to take any normative, proactive stance. [see the Interlude in Latour 2005, pp.141-56 for instance] Even Callon's multi-step scheme is based on a contemplative, albeit operational analysis of the phases in the cultivation of scallops, and finishes at step four (mobilization of allies), without providing further concrete detail in subsequent steps about the implementation. For a proactive skill and science such as planning, this is an insuperable shortcoming, because the point here is not just to survey and analyse plans, but also to facilitate or ensure improvements for the future, execute and implement them – a move which in turn, incidentally, changes the composition of affected actors and their networks. The actors, networks and their actions – i.e. the stake and shareholders, their specific (institutional) organizations, and the featured planning strategies – form an essential, indispensable triple classification for planning. [Wissink 2007]

Second – and partly related to the first point – it is difficult to assign a comparable proactive value within planning to non-human and/or non-living entities as is assigned to conscious, possibly negotiating human subjects. Of course, the climate or environment, the landscape and specific planning concepts are significant (f)actors of importance and so are housing, cars, stations, the available budget, materials, instruments etc. And it is proper that they should be involved in spatial actor-network associations at a far earlier stage. But in actual negotiations or the proactive formation of specific associations, they tend to be involved in a mediated form, via their representatives. The environment or the climate, the existing cultural heritage, and the available budget do not actually sit at the negotiating planning tables or on the planning forum itself. At best, the representatives and spokesmen of the environmental movement or those troubled by 'an inconvenient truth', by cultural deprivation, wasted money etc., propound their interests. In ANT terminology, these non-human entities can be proactively classified as intermediaries (who convey meaning without doing anything about it) or preferably as mediators (who convey meaning, but at the same time change, add or adjust something). [Latour 2005] Proactively, in an ARA however, they can scarcely be regarded as leading actors, only as mediated factors of importance.

Third, even in ANT, democratic legitimacy is still not a point of concern. It is true that Callon's fourth step is aimed at broadening support for the planned actor-network association, or for ensuring sufficient communication about the planned action with the public, but ANT does not answer the questions of how this ought to be guaranteed and how the specific actor-network associations can be embedded in a broader setting. Yet this, too, is crucial for planning because even the smallest, most marginal actions of planners often involve surprising and unexpected effects and interests. Likewise, planning should – in view of its long-term orientation – keep sight of the interests of those who are not yet born and those who cannot be addressed. Actor-networks 'in the blind', these are called, mainly consisting of what Latour characterises as 'the background plasma, namely that which is not yet formatted, not yet measured, not yet socialized and not yet engaged in metrological chains', [Latour 2005] as well as that which is still *in statu nascendi*. That is probably why Louis Albrechts, amongst others, calls for permanent 'performance monitoring and quality care'. [Albrechts 2003, cited in Hillier 2007 p.307]

New practical and theoretical impulses

In any case, partly in reference to these more or less theoretical reflections and partly in a somewhat incremental, learn-as-you-go manner, the following seven-step operational working scheme has been developed in the course of theorizing practice or practising theories. After the planning issue has been formulated or the problem has appeared (in ANT terms, the so-called perplexity or problematization phase) this seven-step scheme may receive its own interpretation and elaboration for each case (post-modern), but has nonetheless already demonstrated its effectiveness for a variety of themes and planning issues, with varying success (modern):

a *Interpreting the problem by determining the focal actors and unique core values*
The first step consists of (a) the identification of the primary problem-holder

or stakeholder(s), and (b) an analysis and joint determination of a region's, an issue's or an entity's unique core features. We can refer to the latter as the focal factors of importance. This step is fundamental, as planning issues are still sometimes formulated without clear focal (f)actors; not only in the public, but especially in business and civic society. Moreover, these unique core values and their incorporation by these actors – not least on the basis of self-interest – will have the effect of imparting meaning to the whole of the subsequent planning process. Should such unique core values or focal actor(s) not be present (not only in the public, but mainly in the business and civic society), then the controversy and the planning issue are non-existent in a relative sense and in ANT terms. However, I do not rule out the possibility that, in a specific case, with a view to possible future stakeholders, the government may still decide to approach the issue as exclusively a matter for government attention. But in view of the requirement for broad sustainability described earlier, it should only be considered in last instance, after other options have proved unworkable.

b *Actor identification and actor analysis*
After the unique core values and any controversies about them have been settled and (civic/business/public) focal actors have internalized them, the next step is the identification of other possible leading actors (actants) who feel connected or contented with these core values, or who see new chances and possibilities for themselves. They may be actants who live, spend time or work within the locality, and/or who seem to have some fundamental involvement with the issue in question. However, actants who view the planning issue from a distance may also be involved. The only criterion here is that those actants must be able and willing to act like a leading actor, in accordance with the definition given earlier. This is consistent with the view that actor-network associations and hence the actor-relational approach cut across the different scale levels, sectors and institutionalized fields of expertise. Innovation often emerges precisely from these crossovers. Moreover, identification occurs on the basis of a careful analysis of the internal motives, objectives and drives of the actants concerned. All kinds of resources may be used for this analysis, including ethnographical or anthropological studies, economic surveys based on annual reports and historic development, socio-cultural studies of past behaviour, etc., supplemented with bilateral talks where necessary.

c *Opportunity maps and developmental possibilities*
The third step consists of compiling opportunity maps and/or developmental possibilities on the basis of the analysed internal motives and drives of the identified focal and other actants, with a view to the conservation, reinforcement or harnessing of the unique core values of the issue or region concerned. In principle, we suggest that all available urban development and planning instruments should be used here: preliminary research and analysis, rough draft, elaboration of detail and plan proposals, cost/benefit analyses, appropriate

regulations and jurisprudence, attractive designs, 3-D models, photo manipulation, films, etc. The only criterion is that, instead of the tracing surveys in step one, these need to be proactive, future oriented proposals, enticing and convincing, to awake the commitment of the identified actants. It is here, then, that the professionalism of the urban development experts and planners will really need to come into play. As well as extending their expertise, which is often confined to a few sets of instruments, they will also need to become proficient in communication skills (especially with regard to negotiating in the case of conflicting interests). Often, these opportunity maps are therefore created in a team setting.

d *Bilateral talks and round tables*
The next step is then to discuss the opportunity maps compiled in this way in bilateral, trilateral and small round table discussions involving between 5 and 15 people. In principle, this is where the focal and other actants first come face to face. The objective is to see how far the compiled opportunity map, illustrating the course of development, meets expectations, and whether a willingness to invest (and to distribute roles in this respect) can be achieved. This is the first real test of the process, because the actual amount of interest is often revealed from this indication of willingness to invest. Investment is interpreted here in a broad sense: money, expertise, manpower, the promotion of commitment, etc. (with reference to the stakeholders in the business, civic and public society). However, extensive talks often bring to light a distinction between so-called 'pullers' and 'pushers'. Pullers take the initiative and are often more active and enthusiastic about elaborating an opportunity map further in accordance with their own and surrounding viewpoints (according to the identification of leading actors), whereas pushers, partly in view of their status and/or orientation, take a somewhat more passive, more facilitating and/ or more 'wait and see' approach. Even so, the actor-network association, which could be established over here, is the basis for the rest of the process. Where necessary, the opportunity map is adapted accordingly.

e *Business cases and pilots*
Step four is about a first possibility (a kind of tentative strategy) of developing new opportunities, which may be endorsed. But it still needs to be proven in reality. To this end, step five is the proof of the pudding. The associated opportunity map is put into concrete form in one or more business cases, respectively pilot project, for specific project components. This is the second real test of the process, as the ultimate division of roles is now determined far more concretely. Where necessary a contract sets out what each actant is prepared to invest and when, and/or where and to what extent the backing of representative constituencies is guaranteed. Each actant will undergo his/her own internal weighing-up and decision-making process in this regard. But it is precisely here that the project's make-or-break point lies. If there is failure at this point, it will be hard to come back to discuss the identified core values

again, but if there is success it often turns out that there are further implications and even spin-offs in other areas. This means that the project may have far broader effects and associations than originally expected.

f *Regime development and general plan outlines*
If the previous step has led to a range of successful and promising cases, the next question is whether or not it is possible to achieve project-transcending spatial added value that corresponds to the unique core values of the issue or region in question. We use the term 'regime' for this concept, referring to the broader and durable planning networks described in Fainstein's urban regime theories. Whether this is initiated by the original focal actor, or another dominant stakeholder, consideration is given to the reinforcing potentials of the separate cases, or the mutual inducement of some form of project-transcending planning strategy. This must primarily be done to enhance the value of the cases and projects as such and overcome the main obstacles given the harsh contradictions of (main) interests. It amounts to the old planners' holism, but not for its own sake or on the basis of an absolute concept of space, but on the basis of the cases and the related actor-network associations. If the focal actor or other public-private actants succeed here, the foundations are laid for a new, sustainable spatial regime, ready to adapt to changing circumstances. Expressed even more strongly, the spatial reality is redefined and the unique core values from the relevant region reconfirmed, reinforced or redeveloped.

g *Democratic anchoring in special districts*
As a final step, it is then necessary to see how far this new spatial development regime can be anchored in associative democracies. Partly in reference to an adaptive and improved model of the special district planning in the USA, the focus here is not on elaborating a generic representative democracy. According to Hirst, Cohen and others, this step focuses on parallel made-to-measure democratic organizations to which the affected households, businesses and institutions can affiliate of their own free will, because they will benefit from doing so. These organizations can also raise financial resources themselves and/or demand membership fees, set public rules, formulate a program for a specific project and appoint an authority, which could be held accountable for its achievements and revenues at periodic intervals. It is regarded not as an alternative but as a supplement to the current centrally organized institutions and representative democracy. From the political viewpoint, and with respect to those items which need to be centrally organized, it should fit more closely in the decentralization ambitions of governments and voluntary democratic organizations.

The key difference vis-à-vis a run-of-the-mill government taskforce or the co-operative public-private ventures examined earlier is that it focuses outside-in, right from the outset, instead of inside-out. It does not start from a governmental viewpoint about planning, or from the need for a periodic renewal of existing plans. On the contrary, it searches and starts from ventured stake and shareholders in the business and/or civic society themselves. Moreover, space (and its proactive facilitator: planning) is not considered here as a container, but as an assemblage, which emerges step by step in relation between actors and factors of importance. Apart from that – and instead of the discursive or pure actor-network approach – it starts with leading actors, although defined as those actors with the capacity and incentive to invest in their local environment, and therefore embedded in the interest of other networks and institutions out of pure self-interest. I shall explain this in more detail in Box 5.1. The most successful and/or durable planning interventions seem to be especially those that are able to facilitate an intensive convergence of the leading actor interests of the involved business, civic and public society in innovative crossovers, embedded in unique local features. These interventions could be the basis for democratic self-organizing associations in sustainable regimes (in broad economic, ecologic, spatial, social etc. terms) and special districts of self-organization around specific themes and proposals.

Recommendations for a practical actor-relational course

In the boxes presented parallel to this text, several practitioners' planning issues and project incitements have been described, which have been more or less proactively based on the efforts described above. They often concern relatively small bottom-up projects. However, because of their cross-over creativity, they also have a strong momentum and spin-off. At the same time, they show a great variety, from urban expansion projects to improving spatial-economic competitiveness, urban revitalization issues and transit-oriented development, preservation of rural areas, tourism, mapping, and embedded, associative decision-making. Although these examples are still highly experimental and fragile, and still have numerous imperfections, too, this first round of actor-relational-planning looks promising for the reinvention of spatial planning. They bypass in an up-to-date version the recurrent nostalgic call for more vision, regulations and straight governmental plans, given that those things are simply no longer possible in this age of ongoing globalization, individualization and borderless recollectivization in numerous specific social-economic interests. In addition, they also rest on a broad theoretical and scientific basis in the area of relational planning and actor-network associations, which has mainly been developed in Anglo-Saxon countries, in order to deal with the daily affairs of planning's heterogeneous subjects, too. Practising these theories and theorizing the forthcoming behavioural practices could give those relational views a new operational translation. Finally, they offer a sensible basis for a more locally and regionally embedded form of sustainable development, in the broad (and the political) sense of the word. The first cases show that it could be possible to arrange a sustainable economic, social, ecologic and cultural regime of various stakeholders in business, civic and public society. But what is needed now is to stimulate extensive evaluations, and to organize better institutional and associative frameworks in which the actor-network coalitions *in statu nascendi* could prosper. Associative democracies, parallel to an adaptive system of representational democracy, could be the focal course over here. And as such, we should refocus on the basic planning orientation and instruments: reassembling planning outside-in. Referring to actual planning practices, especially in the Netherlands but also elsewhere, some general basic recommendations could be formulated with respect to this type of more robust actor-relational spatial planning for tomorrow.

a *Find the planning problem first and foremost outside government*
Although there are always socially relevant issues and strategic planning projects that will continue not to be recognized as such by the citizenry and the business society at first sight (and thus need to be addressed by governments), the actor-relational approach always starts in principle beyond the government: outside-in. It is necessary to stress that. While even to this day, especially in developed planning systems such as that of the Netherlands – and although one stresses apparently the opposite – planning is too often considered an exclusive or at least first of all public affair; oriented inside-out at best. Too often the only legitimacy for new spatial planning projects is that they were requested by parliament, the government or democratically chosen representatives (see recently *Randstad 2040,* [2006-2008] the *Exploration of the Antwerp-Rotterdam Corridor,* [2008-2010] etc.) or that a revision of existing policy is seemingly periodically needed by governments (see for instance the recent revision of the *Regional Plans for South Holland* [2008-2009] or the *Structure Plan for Flanders,* [2006-2009] etc.). It is not always evident why that is desirable in view of the everyday real-life experiences of citizens or businesses alike. Thus exactly at this point, a growing gap is evolving between, on the one hand, an internal public lock-in, focusing mostly on negotiations between corporate actors and intermediaries of the several layers and departments of government and, on the other, real social and economic dynamics, which is also increasingly self-organized outside and beyond government (because of that and due to ongoing glocalization and reclustering). To respond to a more embedded planning, the actor-relational approach therefore and in principle always starts from jointly recognized issues, especially form leading actors in the business and civic society, in conjunction with those of public society remotely at hand. Large parts of the present development planning, but also those of the public management planning, could be dealt with in this way. Only those parts that require an explicit direction from above or in international co-ordination – such as the protection of exceptional (inter)national landscapes, main infrastructure and basic spatial features as preventing excessive pollution, etc. – could possibly be dealt with in the traditional vertical, representatively organized way.

b *No guidance, direction or management, but facilitation of spatial ambitions*
It has been said previously, [Kreukels 1985, Fainstein 1987, Stoker 1995, Amin/Thrift 2002, Murdoch 2006, etc.] but this kind of commitment requires a very cautious, and also the much wider

focus of spatial planners. Instead of, or at least in addition to, sharpening and ensuring the compliance of public or private rules, [Needham 2004, 2005] or developing a framework and/or granting concessions in which citizens and businesses could develop their own ambitions, [de Zeeuw 2006, 2008] or even directing c.q. managing desirable discourses between relevant stakeholders, [Hajer 2005, Hemel 2008] the actor-relational planning approach rather facilitates the needs and ambitions of leading players in civic and business society, within general (mostly already existing) public values, norms, ambitions, institutions, etc. That does not mean a passive, wait-and-see aspiration of spatial planners, but a very (pro-)active one, focusing on – given the outside-in problem definition and/or controversies at hand – a specific inventory and analysis of leading actors, bringing their changing aspirations and diverse backgrounds together, sketching possibly new cross-over associations to focus on the possible implications, identifying any bottlenecks in time and advancing proposals to overcome these, etc. Time and again, the aspirations and wishes of the leading players in the business and civic society are the central focus in this context. But it requires an intelligent use of planners not just to follow these, but to get them collectively on to a much higher (more desirable, sustainable, public) level, with all their available 'seductive' resources in terms of reporting, research, design, regulatory settlement, strategic expertise, etc. Existing education, training and research should be reconcentrated on that more horizontal, facilitating focus. It means at least an extension of the current, inside-out at best, 'vertical style specialization'.

c *Use an actor-associative definition of sustainability as a guiding criterion*
Not so much the definition of sustainability in 1987 given by the Brundtland Commission – 'Sustainable development is development that meets the needs of the present without compromising the ability of future generations to meet their own needs' [Brundtland 1987] – but the consequent exclusively government-directed environmental objectives in the long run, lead to a lock-in and, in fact, a kind of 'kidnapping of creativity'. Right from the start, the Brundtland Commission went for a concept of sustainability in which environmental, social and economic interests should come together (the so-called 'People-Planet-Profit' concept), for both current and future generations. Therefore Brundtland c.s. was actually much more project and actor-oriented than a general governmental objective of environmental norms and goals assumes. [Elkington 1998] In addition to the existing (inter)national public forums for documented sustainability reflection and structured debate on the various sustainable futures of society, it is therefore desirable to reintroduce that kind of actor-oriented sustainability as an associative, guiding principle in land-use (re)development. Instead of a holistic view on sustainability, it refocuses on more bottom-up robustness in broader terms, as well as being economically (profit), socially (people) as environmentally (planet) embedded. It implies that any robust planning proposal can only exist on the basis of an extensive association between (leading) actors from business, civic and public society, and thus must be based on both a profit-making, interest-provoking and vote-winning principle. It also

implies that this type of planning often goes beyond the usual public-private partnerships with developers and intermediate organizations from civic society (because business society is broader than these often hit-and-run parties may assume, while on their turn intermediary organizations hardly invest themselves, and only reactively respond from specific (sub)interests). Robust sustainability is therefore based on creativity beyond those opportunistic or mostly reactive circles.

d *Towards a real actor effect of decentralization and deregulation*
As previously stated, the adage 'Centralize what you must, decentralize whatever you can!' as released by the Dutch National Report on Spatial Planning, but also elsewhere within predominately neo-liberal democracies, has proven to be merely window-dressing. Chapter four concluded that even traditional self-organizing, associative organizations develop in the direction of increased centralization and bureaucratisation of government control, in accordance with the (in fact obsolete) principles of representative democracy. The same is actually the case with the adepts of the relational planning or transformative planning approach, which by the principle of '(preferably) public sector led' approach that still interact from a more or less traditional government-driven planning structuration. Therefore planning processes still remain viscous, the proposals inflexible, and capacity planning strongly dependent on a governmental inside-out style. To reflect in a better sense on social reality, or to be better embedded in it, it is necessary to take deeply seriously the fact that spatial planning is not exclusively governmental, but conditioned by a multitude of actors in civic and business society and that, as such, planning should be facilitated. In addition to a revaluation of private law, [Needham 2005a] it implies a much stronger anchoring of spatial planning in cross-sector or cross-border associations whether they be formalized or not; it will always be potential. If one takes these ambitions seriously, the actual organization of planning needs to change. Because – as mentioned previously – instead of, or at least in addition to, a vertical organization of planning, it rather opts to facilitate the planning of horizontal associations between different actors and therefore sectors of importance, right across different levels on any acting scales. As with representative and associative democracy, it is not about one or the other, but rather next to each other, and in two mutually complementing systems. The first one has already been in use for nearly one century, but the latter lacks still scientific and practitioners' sufficiency. Therefore my last recommendation will be that instead of the stubborn and exclusive focus on general government-controlled area planning with an appropriate public-private land-use policy, we need to revaluate our views more seriously on an actor-relational approach, refocusing on the emerging issues, themes and organizations in the actor-network society itself.

BOX [5.1]

Transit-Oriented Development in South-Holland

Since 2004, the evolving ideas about an actor-relational-approach have been in some ways constituted by, and formative for, a variety of specific planning puzzles in the Netherlands. Amongst others they have included:
- *Heerlijkheid Heuvelland* (Hillside Delights, South-Limburg 2004-06), a regional study towards the reframing of tourism and the landscape in the area, to generate a new more robust regime;
- *Stedenbaan* (South Wing Railtrack, Zuid-Holland 2006), a regional planning study towards Transit-Oriented Development in the South Wing of the Randstad according to an actor-oriented approach;
- *Nieuwe Vrije Tijd Amsterdam* (New Leisure, Amsterdam 2006-07), an urban study towards the possibilities for crossover leisure, from the perspectives of leading actors in the civic and business society of Amsterdam;
- *Nieuwe Markten voor het Brabants Land* (New Markets Brabant, Agro&Co 2007-08), a regional study for the sustainability and economic intensification of the agricultural landscape in Brabant;
- *Terug naar de kust* (Back to the Coast, Zeeland 2008), a general exploration of the future possibilities of the Delta of Rhine, Meuse and Scheldt for sectors as New Energy, Slow Sea Food, Relaxation and Water education;
- *Integrated Care Communities* (ICC, Orbis 2008-09), elaboration of business cases around integrated health care, cure and high-service living areas in a shrinking urban region;
- etc.

Each case has its own peculiarities, successes and failures. In this Box, I shall also go into the 'South Wing Railtrack' (*Stedenbaan*) case, which dealt with distinctive planning approaches to transit-oriented development and tried to implement ideas about Mapping, as explained in Box 4.1. Box 5.2 will cover the case of Hillside Delights, more or less the first case which also developed over the last five years.

Although it has played an important, probably even decisive role in spatial layout and development for centuries, [Filarski/Mom 2007] the mutual alignment of urbanization and public transport, under the term Transit-Oriented Development, is now receiving renewed attention due to the ongoing evolution of mobility. TOD refers to 'a mixed-use residential or commercial area designed to maximize access to public transport, incorporating features to entourage transit ridership, a pedestrian friendly environment, healthy economy and improved quality of life'. [Cervero 1998, Perl 2002 Dittmar/Ohland 2004] With increasing mobility, congestion and the consequential environmental burden, this approach is currently being underwritten more or less worldwide. This does not alter the fact that the exact manner, form and direction that this interaction assumes are also strongly dependent on the institutional setting, actors and socio-cultural development. In this context, one can distinguish between a European, Asian and American development model. And although it is self-evident that these are ideal-typical models, probably even abstract emblems, and that numerous diffuse models are manifesting themselves in the meantime, they can still

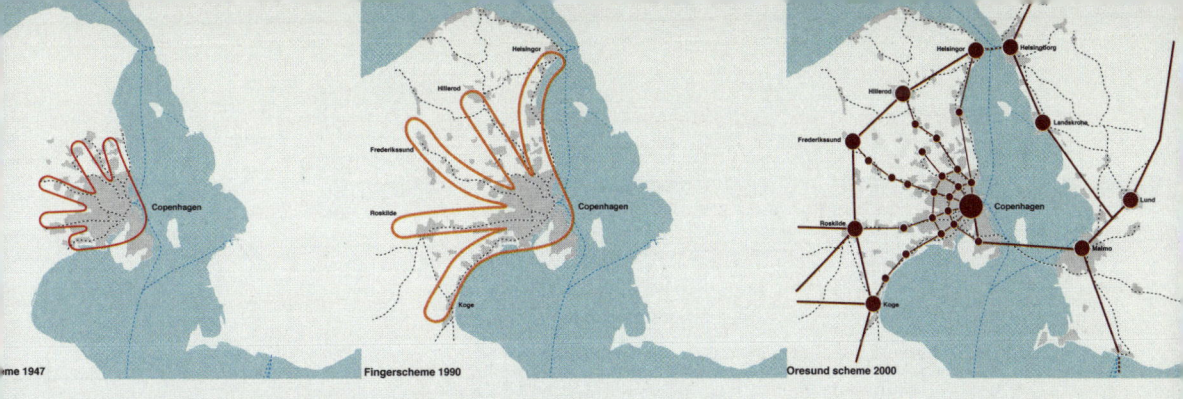

Integral city planning and rail expansion Copenhagen, 1947, 1990, 2000

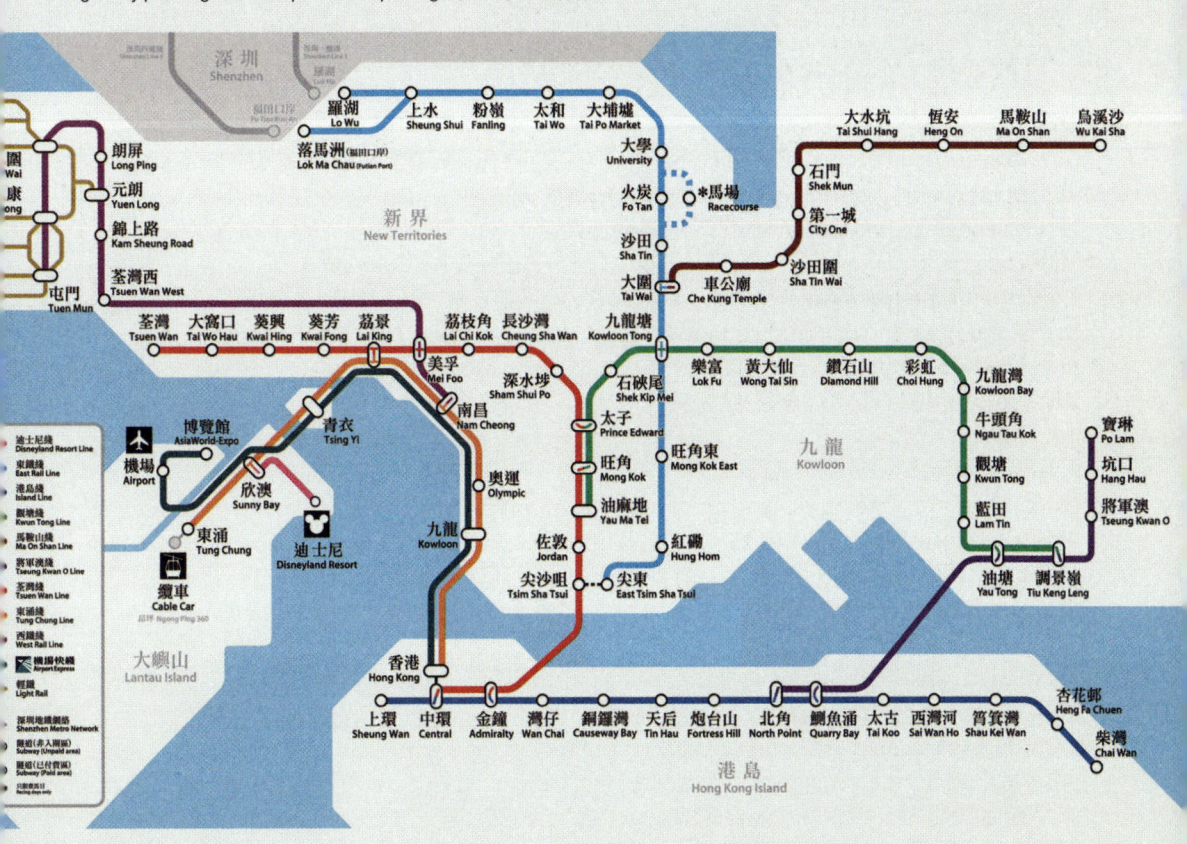

Hong Kong MRT (MRT)

203

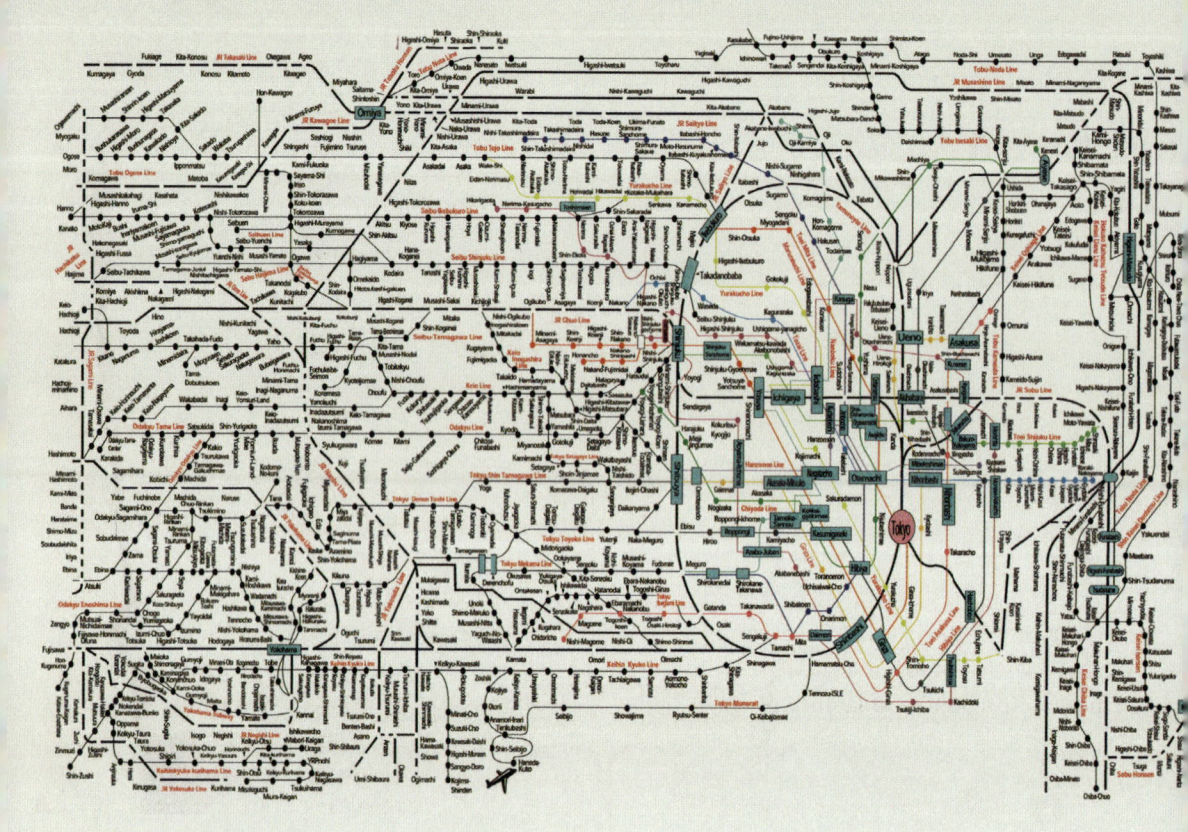

Yamanote loop as a public connection (Japan Rail)

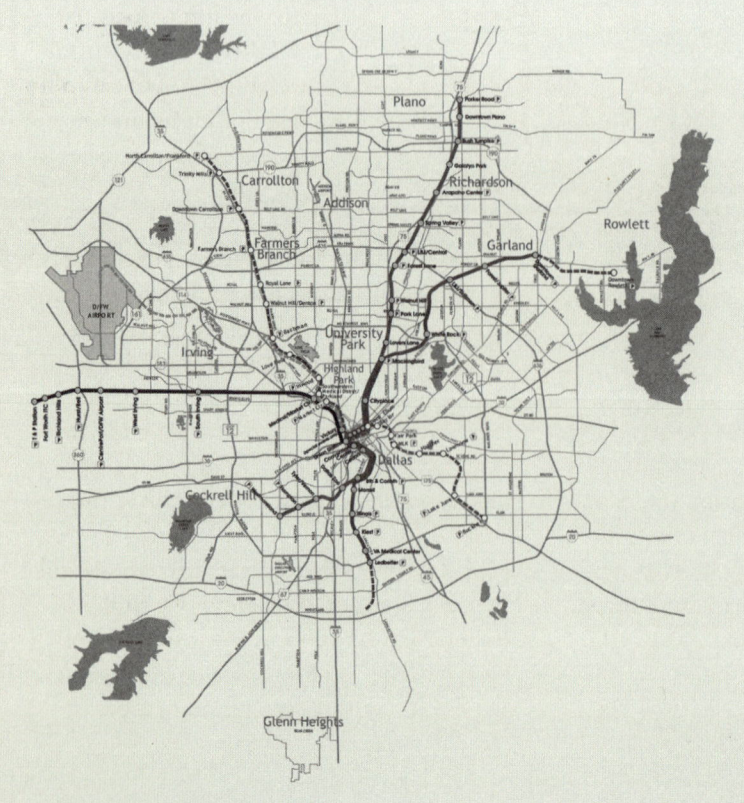

Dallas Rapid Transit network (DART)

give direction to the discussion on the relationship between spatial layout on the one hand and traffic and transport on the other. By approaching this interaction in this way, clarity regarding with whom, with what commitment and under which conditions an effective sustainable development of space and transport (in the broadest sense of the term) can be realized. For this purpose I shall first describe the relevant models, to subsequently return to a specific case that occurred in the Province of South Holland in 2004-06.

The public model – a European variant

When public transport first developed in France and England and later in other West European countries, there was more or less mention of exclusively private development. This was the case with the stage coaches, barge transport, and (steam) shipping, and also with the first forms of railway transport. Especially after the industrial revolutions of the 19th century and the beginning of the 20th century, the demand for the transport of goods and then people became so large that it became possible for private pioneers to invest in infrastructure, set up an inner-city and later even inter-local organization, and maintain transport services against a reasonable price and good profit margins.

Although state bodies also began to operate in these markets at a relatively early date, there was no mention of unashamed state support but rather of exploitation under an authentic capitalist regime. However, this changed in the course of the 20th century. First of all, as urbanization further expanded, the initial necessary investment increased enormously, especially in the inner city and particularly with the advent of electrification and the introduction of the underground metro system. This could hardly be (pre-)funded by private transport enterprises and the government was expected to assist in order to make this possible. At the same time, public transport – certainly in West Europe – was increasingly seen as a *common good*, not only as a consequence of the general contribution to the economic welfare of the city or urban region but also later due to the lower environmental burden in comparison to other modes of transport. And last but not least, it was privatization that had led to *heavy ridership* on the most profitable lines, while the less profitable lines were under-represented or even not exploited at all. This resulted in an uncoordinated provision of services and therefore to system deficiencies. [Vukich 2005] A greater role on the part of the government was deemed desirable in order to rectify this. Nevertheless, there was still mention of a sharp schism between the public and the private domain, where the former was mainly responsible for the infrastructure and/or operation, and the latter responsible for the adequate development of the adjoining property, although both were under the austere governance of the supra-local government.

Throughout the 20th century and certainly up to Reagan's and Thatcher's eighties, we encounter this model everywhere in West Europe: in Germany, Switzerland, Italy, Spain, France, the UK and the Low Countries. However, I wish to deal primarily with Scandinavia and especially the model of Copenhagen as an exemplary case in this context, in view of the fact that this is probably the most representative and is still in use to some extent right down to the present day. Since 1947, the general development scheme of the Greater Metropolitan Region of Copenhagen has been more or less determined by the renowned *Finger*

Plan or *Egnsplankontoret*, the Copenhagen Regional Planning Committee, set up after the relatively late approval of the Danish Planning Act of 1939. Based on Sir Patrick Abercrombie's *Greater London Plan 1944*, the aim of this *Finger Plan* was to concentrate housing for around 10,000 inhabitants along a rail infrastructure, partly existent and partly newly constructed or extended, in the shape of five fingers. The palm of the hand – the pre-war city centre of Copenhagen – would remain the primary regional centre, the large service and production centres were planned at the points of contact of the fingers and hand palm, in combination with a circular highway around the old centre, while the areas between the fingers were intended for nature, recreation and agrarian production. As such, an attempt was made not only to maintain a direct relationship with the surrounding countryside but also to guarantee a maximum commuting time from home to the most important working and facilities areas, and vice versa. [Hermansson 1999] The metaphor was simple and well chosen. And probably for this reason, it has managed to continue in force (practically) right down to the present day and it actually forms the norm for private property development in the next future– despite the fact that it has never been specified as such. Particularly the thumb (towards Køge) and the forefinger (towards Roskilde) were developed in this way up to the sixties, in combination with the forestation of the Westwood and a Beach Park, complete with dunes, a lagoon and marinas in a former swampy coastal area. Subsequently, in the seventies and eighties, the development of the other fingers took place, along *transportation corridors and junction centres* – in combination with the completion of the inner-city circular. As a consequence of the diminishing dynamics in the seventies, these developments took time to get under way. Confronted with the spirit of deregulation in the eighties, the Greater Copenhagen Council was disbanded and the regional planning responsibilities were decentralized to the local governments. Paradoxically, the time also witnessed a further evolution and processing of the *Finger Model*, this time with the wrist and underarm of the hand. Under the supervision of the state government, the south-east corridor toward Copenhagen international airport was developed in the nineties, along with a bridge/tunnel construction toward Malmö/Sweden as an extension of this. It was combined with an expansion of the international position of Copenhagen via investments in high-tech, research, education, tourism and large-scale congress facilities. [Jorgensen 2004] The dismantling of the Greater Copenhagen Council had also stimulated the formation of numerous new organizations and planning forums in the region. This required more co-ordination and coherence. As a result, a new Metropolitan Development Council was set up again in 2000 – the Hovedstadens Udviklingsrad (HUR) – which became responsible for the total traffic and transport planning and the co-ordination of spatial planning in the region.

Nevertheless – partly as a result of increasing car use – traffic and transport began to display more criss-cross patterns and was not so easy to regulate as it had been in the Finger Plan. In combination with the fact, and as a consequence of the rising ground and rental prices in the centre, the private sector tended increasingly toward peripheral locations. In addition, with the improved connections between Helsinger and Helsinborg, a transnational network city begins to arise around the Øresund, which is no longer wholly subordinate to

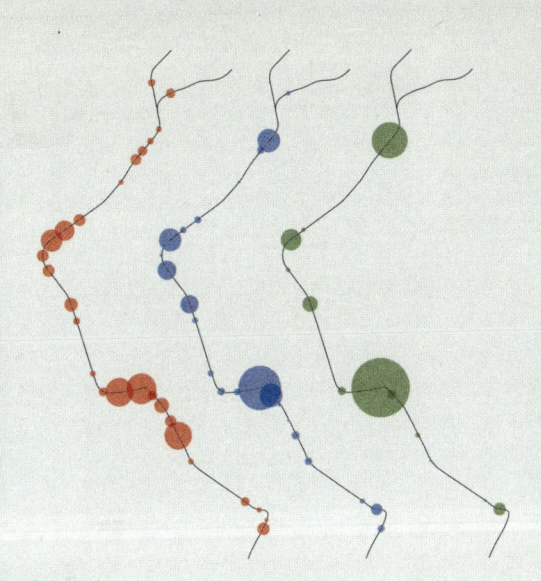

Inhabitants, employees and travellers in the station environment

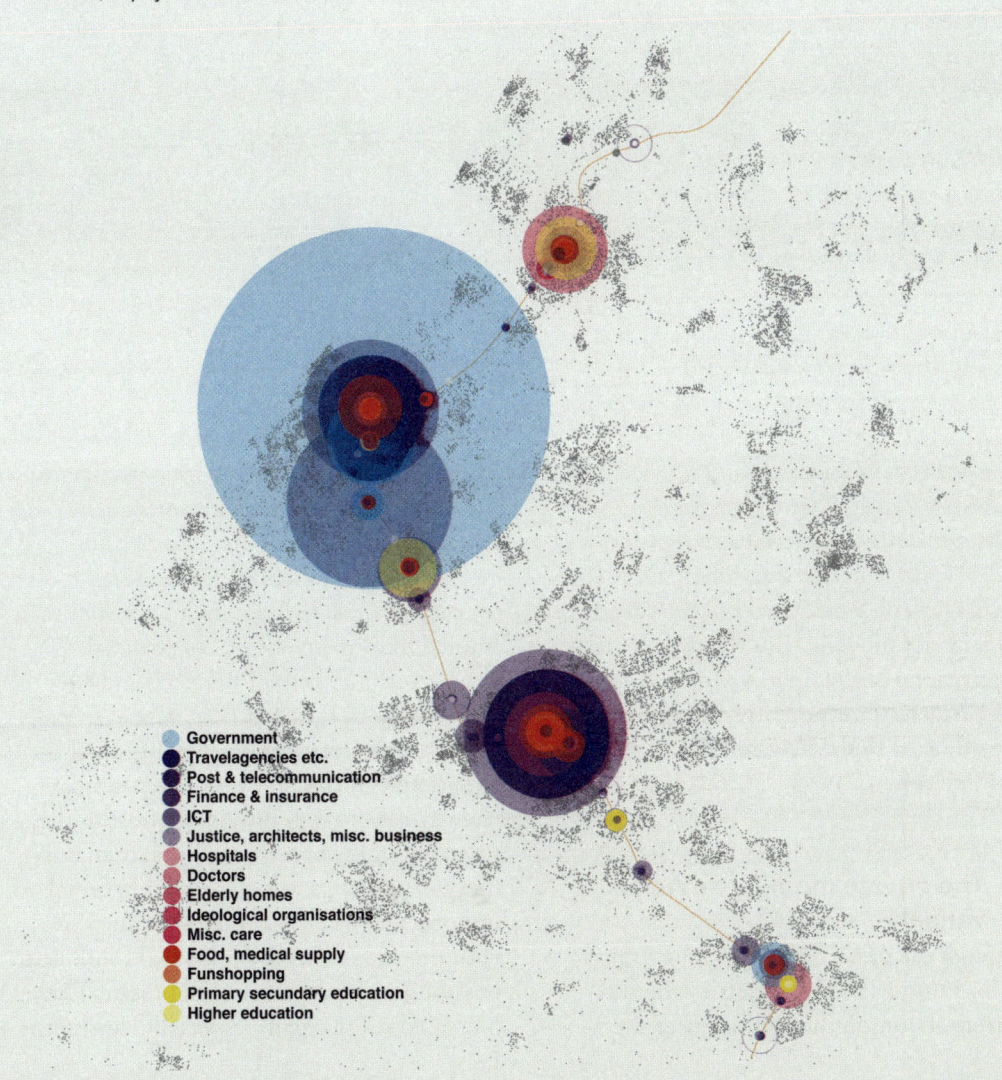

- Government
- Travelagencies etc.
- Post & telecommunication
- Finance & insurance
- ICT
- Justice, architects, misc. business
- Hospitals
- Doctors
- Elderly homes
- Ideological organisations
- Misc. care
- Food, medical supply
- Funshopping
- Primary secundary education
- Higher education

Unique selling point of the railway stations

Mobility styles

the Finger Plan and the HUR alone. Thus where Robert Cervero [1998] regards Copenhagen as one of the most 'carefully integrated rail transit and urban development examples', the more informed John Jorgensen [2004] typifies the current institutional developments with HUR rather as 'path dependent', and less capable of meeting the new, more network-oriented challenges of the future. The Fingerplan – and thus the overall steering principles of Denmarks and expecially Copenhagens governments – seem in need to be adjusted to the new conditions of space and time.

The private model – an Asian variant

Although the privatization of pubic transport in Europe (and especially in the UK) enjoyed a boom in the eighties after the wave of deregulation – albeit not always completely felicitous – this development had a longer and more successful tradition in Asia (particularly in Japan and Hong Kong). When a clear accent was placed on the modernization of the nation, and a more open attitude toward foreign countries arose with the restoration of the Meiji dynasty in 1868, the first mainly privately funded railway lines were constructed, largely with the help of British engineers. And, just as in Europe, these were eventually mostly nationalized in the beginning of the twentieth century for more or less similar reasons. [Aoki 1994a/1994b] But, in contrast to the situation in Europe, this took place mainly on the *trunk lines*, which were of national importance, whereas on the periphery or with the *feeder lines* there were still sufficient possibilities for private development. These increased substantially, especially during the industrial hey-days between the two World Wars (and the corresponding migration from the countryside to the town), in the outskirts of large cities such as Tokyo, Yokohama, Osaka, etc.

Ito and Chiba [2001] have described the project-driven development of garden cities – based on the English example – in an integrated (financial) combination with the realization of commuter transport between these peripheral towns and the downtown areas. In this way, the real estate profits could not only compensate the initial construction costs and operating losses of the rail transport, but a relatively high use of public transport (and, correspondingly, operating profits in the long run) was guaranteed. In order to stimulate this further, retail, recreation and entertainment facilities were realized at the ends of and along the railway lines, to ensure adequate use of public transport in the off-peak period and/or reversed commuter direction. In this way, the Minoo Tramway (and later the Kankyu Electric Railway, now Hankyu) Corporation in particular developed around 100 integrated railway-housing projects around the above-mentioned large cities in the period between the wars. Others – such as the Tokyu, Odakyu, Keio and Seibu Corporations – would soon follow this example after the Second World War. The spatial public transport structure of the Greater Metropolitan Region of Tokyo currently consists of a more or less public ring around the centre (the so-called 'Yamanote line') as a part of a larger national trunk network, while eight property-rail corporations run the lines between this Yamanote loop and the outskirts of Tokyo. In order to generate a better performance in the era of rising car use, the Japanese Railway (and thus also the Yamanote loop) was privatized in 1987 in six regional Railway Corporations in addition to a central Rail Freight Combination, a Management Stabilization fund and a Shinkansen Holding Company that is responsible for the lease and/or operation of the high-speed lines. [Imashiro 1997] This was combined with a strict governmental policy, introduced after the Second World War, to promote the development around public transport, its use, and the restriction of car use.[25] This has led to the situation that, even in times of stagnating economic growth, positive (financial and transport) results are being booked. Tokyo has at its disposal an extremely efficient transport network, with a high modal split and high-density development around the stations, although this is becoming more varied. [Paul Chorus 2008] In conjunction with the new setting, an increasing number of public-private co-operative alliances are also visible here. [Ito and Chiba 2001]

The Mass Transit Railway Corporation (MTRC) of Hong Kong was modelled on the private model of Japan from its beginnings in 1979. Although the MTRC was completely owned by the government for the first few decades and was fully privatized only in 2000 – after the reunion with China, in fact – there were profit aspirations right from the start via an integrated development of real estate and rail. Due to the enormous economic development that Hong Kong/the Pearl River Delta is still experiencing and the enormous urban density both on Hong Kong Island and on Kowloon and in the New Districts, the conditions for this appear to be favourable. [Van Hoogstraten et al. 2007] Effective and profit-making developments are enabled by the fact that the government has allocated the MTRC the exclusive development rights to the (occasionally newly raised) ground under and along the planned

25 For example, one may only have a car if one can demonstrate that one has a parking place at one's disposal.

railway lines. In exchange, it guarantees by contract an effective railway operation with high-frequency service and reasonable transport prices. In turn, in exchange for the issue of building rights on these grounds to property developers, it shares in the profits of these developers in the form of profit up-front, profit back-end or sharing in kind. With the revenues thus obtained from (participation in) property development and income from fares, the initial construction costs and the operational costs of the railway lines can be funded. Occasionally, completed projects are again taken over by the MTRC in order to guarantee adequate property management. In this way, a nett result of more than HK$ 6 billion was achieved in 2005, almost 900 million passengers were transported, on (currently) 91 kilometres of railway line, while 51 integrated stations were operated (often with offices, hotels, retail facilities or housing). To meet the current, boundary-bursting dynamism even more efficiently, a merger with the Kowloon-Canton Railway Corporation was realized in 2007, aimed at extending rail-property development and at upgrading the network to a regional (and perhaps eventually Pearl River Delta) project in the adjoining area of Shenzhen. [Chan 2007]

The private-public model – an American variant

The context in the USA is quite different again. Whereas in the Asian and in several European metropolises a public transport modal split of occasionally more than 50% is reached, this is 10% in American metropolises at the most (in New York), but often no more than 5%. [Van Susteren 2005] Since the fifties, when the motorization of America saw an unprecedented upsurge, public transport – and particularly inner-city public transport – has often been largely neglected. According to Julie Goodwill, [2002] the post-war period was primarily characterized by policy geared to 'post-war housing shortages, low gasoline prices, and major federal investment in the interstate highway system for national security and defence purposes'. With increasing car ownership and rising inner-city ground prices, urbanization and commercial property development followed the development of the infrastructure. Since the Second World War, this has manifested itself in three major suburban waves. Initially, it was mainly the middle and higher-income groups that settled in the suburbs. In an extension of this, the retail trade followed, settling on commercial motorway strips and in large shopping malls. Finally, a decentralization of employment to the suburban periphery also manifested itself in the 1970s and 1980s. In the meantime, the negative consequences of this are becoming unmistakably evident. Not only is there mention of a heavy burden on the environment and damage to the landscape here and there, but sometimes more than 20% of the family income is being spent on transport. [Goodwill 2002] In addition, Robert Cervero and Michael Duncan point to the increasing congestion in and around the large cities, the changing demographic developments, with much greater numbers of empty-nesters, DINKies and singles or single-parent families, who are increasingly preferring an urban environment, as well as the increasingly favourable attitude shown by planners, governments and Trade & Industry toward public transport. [Cervero/Duncan 2001] These forms of TOD dovetail with the Smart Growth approach discussed elsewhere and the proposals by Peter Calthorpe and others concerning New Urbanism. [1993] Since the eighties, TOD has undergone great progress in America. In 2002, the Federal Transit Administration could boast 30 realized

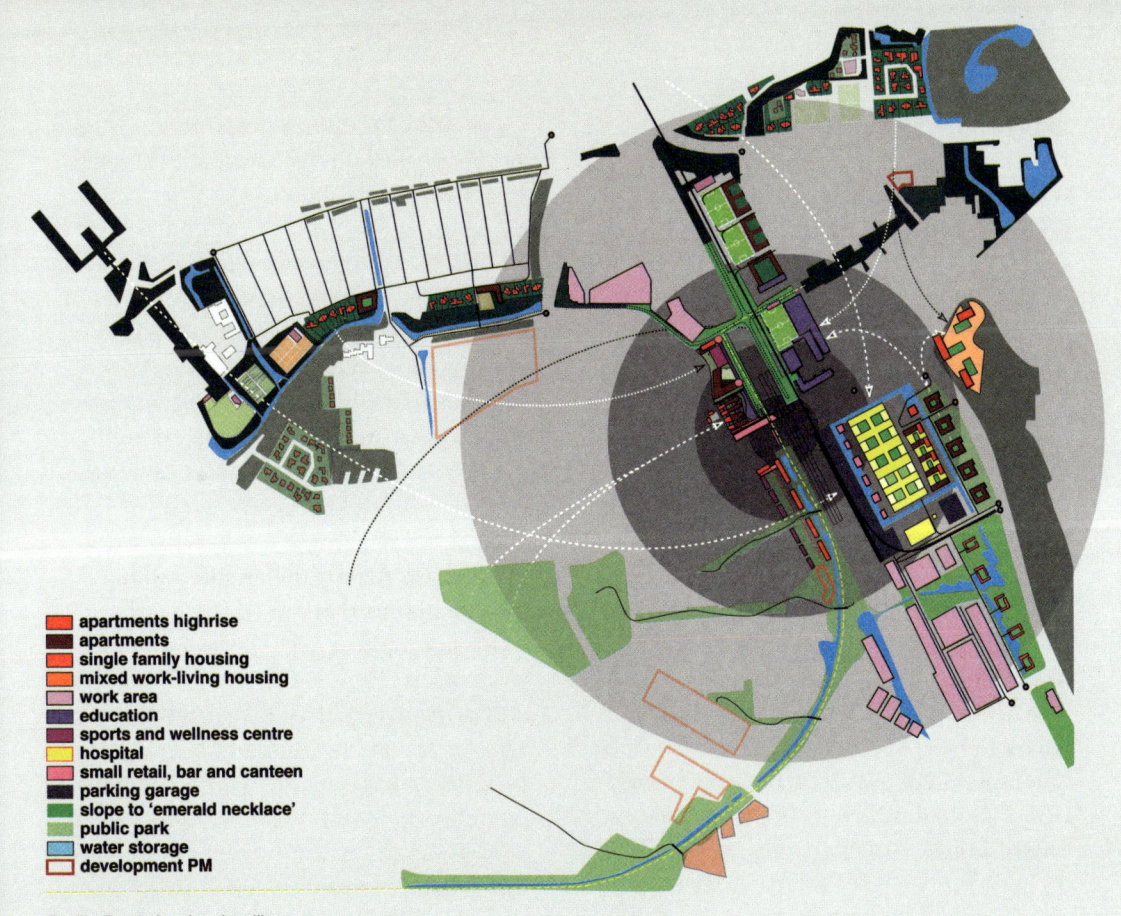

- apartments highrise
- apartments
- single family housing
- mixed work-living housing
- work area
- education
- sports and wellness centre
- hospital
- small retail, bar and canteen
- parking garage
- slope to 'emerald necklace'
- public park
- water storage
- development PM

Profile Rotterdam Lombardijen

projects and another seventy in preparation, planning or study in the beginning of the twenty-first century. [Dittmar et al. 2004, p.13]

One of these initiatives is that of the Dallas Area Rapid Transit (DART), for example. Both Gloria Ohland [2004] and Robert Cervero [2004] emphasize that the success of this initiative was largely due to the endeavours of a number of passionate and engaged developers and the suburban communities in the surroundings rather than to the active promotion and support of the central city of Dallas itself. And there were good reasons for this. For example, the suburb of Plano used the TOD concept to revitalize its entire downtown area. The same occurred in Richardson. In addition, sophisticated developers such as Ken Hughes, Robert Shaw and Pete Coughlin realized striking and imaginative projects in Mockingbird station, Addison Circle and South Side Lamar, respectively. Furthermore, when Boeing decided to move its head office to Chicago instead of Dallas in 2001, because the former had a 'more lively downtown and sophisticated urban culture', the central city council of Dallas also saw the need of, respectively became more enthusiastic about TOD. Since 1996, around 72 kilometres of light rail have been realized in combination with more than thirty stations and $7 billion worth of investment in the surroundings. In the coming ten years, this will be almost doubled. Moreover, there is a co-operative alliance with the Trinity Railway Express and more than 100 million passengers a year are currently served. [DART annual report 2007] The construction was mainly funded by the issue of obligations, while the light rail operation is largely funded via sales tax (85%) and income from fares (15%). [Hondelink et al. 2006] Nevertheless, in the meantime, for the construction of the new (green) line the suburb of Carrollton has been designated as a Transit Impact Zone and a Tax Increment Finance District has been set up for this purpose. This implies that possible future value appreciation in the vicinity (ground and property) will be capitalized and used for the funding of the construction on the basis of the principle of value capture. For other developments, either already in progress or intended, such as the Transit Village Victory Park, Info Market, Medical Centre. Medical District, Asian District etc., partial funding via property tax is currently being considered. Despite the fact that DART is in fact a delegated governmental body, this implies the genesis of an intensive reciprocal private-public funding model in which the parties are bound to mutual agreements via concessions and contracts in the field of property, lifestyle development and railway operation.

Zuid-Holland South Wing Railtrack – an actor-oriented variant

This exegesis and comparison formed an important basis for the chosen approach to the Zuid-Holland South Wing Railtrack or *Stedenbaan*. The actual impulse for that project was the construction of the new high-speed line between Amsterdam and Rotterdam on the flank of the south wing of the Randstad, the intended shift of existing national railway services to this new line and thus an underspending on the existing railway connections via the old Dutch cities of Haarlem, Leiden, The Hague and Delft. At the same time, the prognosis was that the use of public transport in the region would have to at least double in order to keep pace with the growth of car use. [Province of Zuid-Holland 2003] With this in mind, the proposal was advanced to use the subsequent free capacity for a phased introduction of a new intercity and regional transport within the south wing of the Randstad. In accordance with above-described European tradition, however, the starting point remained a kind of government-centred 'wishful thinking process' – inside-out – with intensive negotiation and design sessions primarily between the diverse policy sectors and administrative bodies at provincial and local level. As a result of this, the programme received little social and enterprise-oriented support, and advanced very laboriously. This being the case, developers, housing associations and enterprises were initially very hesitant about investing in the difficult locations at the stations in view of the fact that easier and more accessible (especially by car) building locations were available elsewhere. In turn, Dutch Rail delayed introducing a more extended service because more intensive use of transport was not (yet) guaranteed. It was a chicken and egg situation, with one party waiting for a move by the other. In order to break the impasse, the Asian variant seemed an attractive variant at first sight. But neither the density nor the economic growth in the south wing of the Randstad is comparable with those in the metropolises in South-east Asia, whereas the ground is certainly not always owned by the government. As a result, it is impossible to allocated development rights similar to those allocated by the authorities in Hong Kong, for example. This meant that, as a sequel to this situation, a public-private variant, more useful in this context, was proposed, partly comparable to that in the USA albeit with a separate adjustment to the mores, actors and institutional conditions present here.

This approach consisted of three components:

First of all, on the basis of an analysis of the specific socio-cultural, functional and spatio-economic area characteristics, the individual features – let us say the *unique selling points* – of each of the around 30 stations were defined in an Almanac. This occurred on the basis of the value of the place itself and the position that the station occupies in the network of various transport services, road infrastructures and slow traffic links. This actually produced a 'supply map' for the South Wing Railtrack: strings of beads of various values, possibilities and identities. [Urban Unlimited 2005a] We refer to this as 'Tracing' in Box 4.1.

Second, the 'supply map' was confronted by the possible demand side, the transport demand for the South Wing Railtrack. This not only concerned a quantitative analysis (covering the demographic development along the Railtrack in terms of size, household composition, income level and age), but also a qualitative one. It was assumed that, with the increased variation in lifestyles an increasing variation in mobility styles would also occur. On the basis of supplementary research at the University of Utrecht, in addition to the traditional commuters and students and school pupils, new forms of mobility styles were discovered. Instead of showing the usual departure-destination pattern, these mobility styles tended to flit from point to point, in chains, on a daily basis, involving people such as the (working) carer, the visitor to family/friends, the holiday-maker, working pleasure-seeker, or professional/representative making use of public transport. [Verburg et al. 2005] To facilitate these 'chain movers' better, various amenities, services, entertainment spots or meeting places that could better facilitate these new styles of mobility were envisaged.

This produced the opportunity maps of the South Wing Railtrack. In Box 4.1 we refer to this as *Mapping*.

Finally, for each station, these chances were bilaterally, trilaterally and/or at round-table sessions discussed with changing, potentially interested stakeholders. In Box 4.1 we refer to that as *Diagramming*. One example concerned the station of Lombardijen Rotterdam, which was typified on the basis of the supply and possible demand profile as a promising learning care station with a transferium function. With this as the underlying fundament, contact was sought with the local housing associations, a hospital and a care institution, secondary and special school communities, a project developer, a financier and sports and recreation retailer in order to generate a densification plan possible for and desirable to them, bottom-up and enterprise-oriented. They formulated the accompanying proposal. In total, it involved a densification of almost 2000 houses, 225,000 m^2 of school facilities, a new hospital annex medi-mall, a transferium with 2500 places, 20,000 m^2 of sports facilities, recreation and greenery. [Urban Unlimited 2005b] In view of the anticipated added value for each individual partner, as well as the possible joint alliance, the possibility of making extra investment or a contribution to the South Wing Railtrack was even discussed, in order to guarantee the desired continuing transport service.

After a first enthusiastic reception by the private parties involved, the municipal councillor and the district administrators, this proposal was more or less directly incorporated in the broader *Pact op Zuid*, which is a co-operative alliance between the five housing associations involved, the municipality and the three districts concerned – Charlois, IJsselmonde and

Feijenoord – to invest at least €1 billion in this district of Rotterdam between now and 2015. [Pact op Zuid 2006] At the same time, it formed a classic example of the South Wing Railtrack and has subsequently been concretized for other hubs in the Urban Region of Rotterdam. [Urban Unlimited 2007] Due to alterations to the political constellation, personnel changes, lock-ins within the existing civil service institutions as well as the corresponding fragmentation of the various components of the proposal concerning the various services and area units, the Private Alliantie Lombardijen IJsselmonde has also become fragmented. Parts of the original plan are currently being realized but the anticipated mutual added value and *value capturing* of the South Wing Railtrack programme has more or less vanished in that process. The elements of what we call *Agencements* in Box 4 – the more passive elements that have a binding or separating effect on the force field – appear to be decisive in determining whether or not the intended added value is achieved. Instead of steadfastly adhering to a government-centred approach, innovations seem desperately needed, especially here.

BOX [5.2]

The case of 'Hillside Delights' in South-Limburg[26]

Issue

South-Limburg is the only region in the southern parts of the Netherlands that has hills over 300 metres above sea level. As part of the Eiffel and the Ardennes, the range of hills from the German Aachen via Heerlen, Sittard/Geleen towards the Belgian Genk became one of the main sources of coal during the industrial period from the end of the 19th century onward. Next to that, from the early start of tourism in the post-war era, this region – and especially the Hillside and Maastricht part – also became a major vacation area for the Dutch. After the closure of the coal mines in this region in the early seventies, tourism even became one of the main economic sectors of South-Limburg. Its 20,000 employees constitute nearly 10% of the total regional employment nowadays and turn out almost 20% of the gross regional product. [Province of Limburg 2008] Moreover it has a major social impact, because the sector is embedded in the social structure through its human scale, hospitality and small-family structure. However, since the nineties, especially after the advent of low-cost carriers, the market of South-Limburg for domestic and foreign tourism has dropped dramatically.

At the same time, as a result of diminishing subsidies from the EU government, small-scale farming in the area has also

[26] See also: www.urbanunlimited.nl: Heerlijkheid Heuvelland.

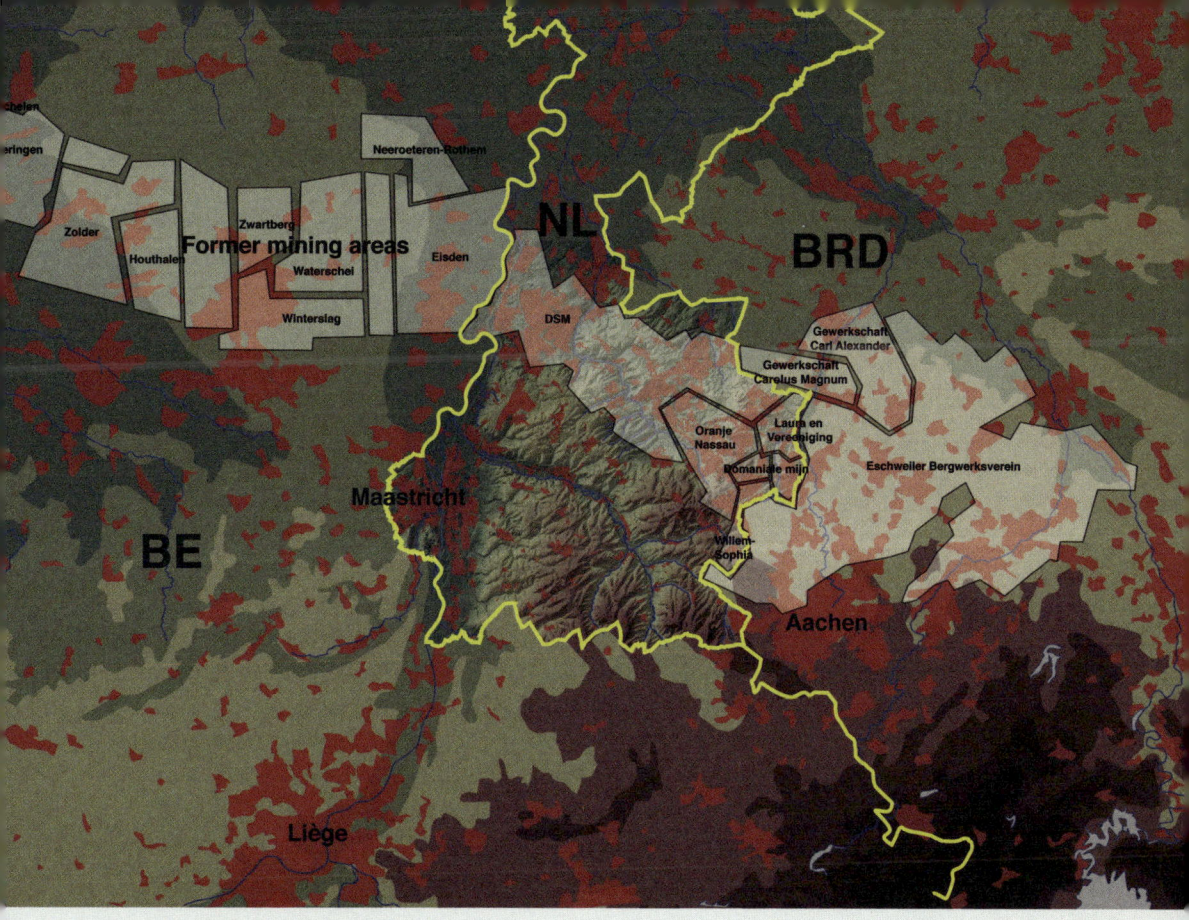

Context of present Heuvelland

experienced hard times. The cutbacks evoked a process of economies of scale in both the agricultural and the tourist sector, accompanied by a degradation of the rural and urban environment and the regional quality of leisure. In turn, this resulted in a further decline in tourist stays. An ongoing negative spiral was established. That was the reason for businesses, the government, and civic protectors of the environment and cultural heritage to act together to consider how this negative spiral could be redirected upwards again. It was facilitated by the Limburg Development and Investment Company (NV Industry LIOF), backed up by the EU program *TouriSME*, which granted the contract to a consortium of planners, leisure experts and two affiliated universities (the research group composed out of the leisure and spatial planners of the University of Tilburg and Utrecht) to develop a sustainable new market perspective, in order to give a fresh boost to economic development in the area, as well as to the preservation of the landscape and cultural heritage. This was managed according to the actor-relational approach described above.

Actants identification

In accordance with that programme, the consortium started its work in an effort to determine the unique selling points of the region. Various 'tracing surveys' were carried out (see Box 4.1). According to these and in comparison to its surroundings, the region turned out to have large concen-

Healing Hills

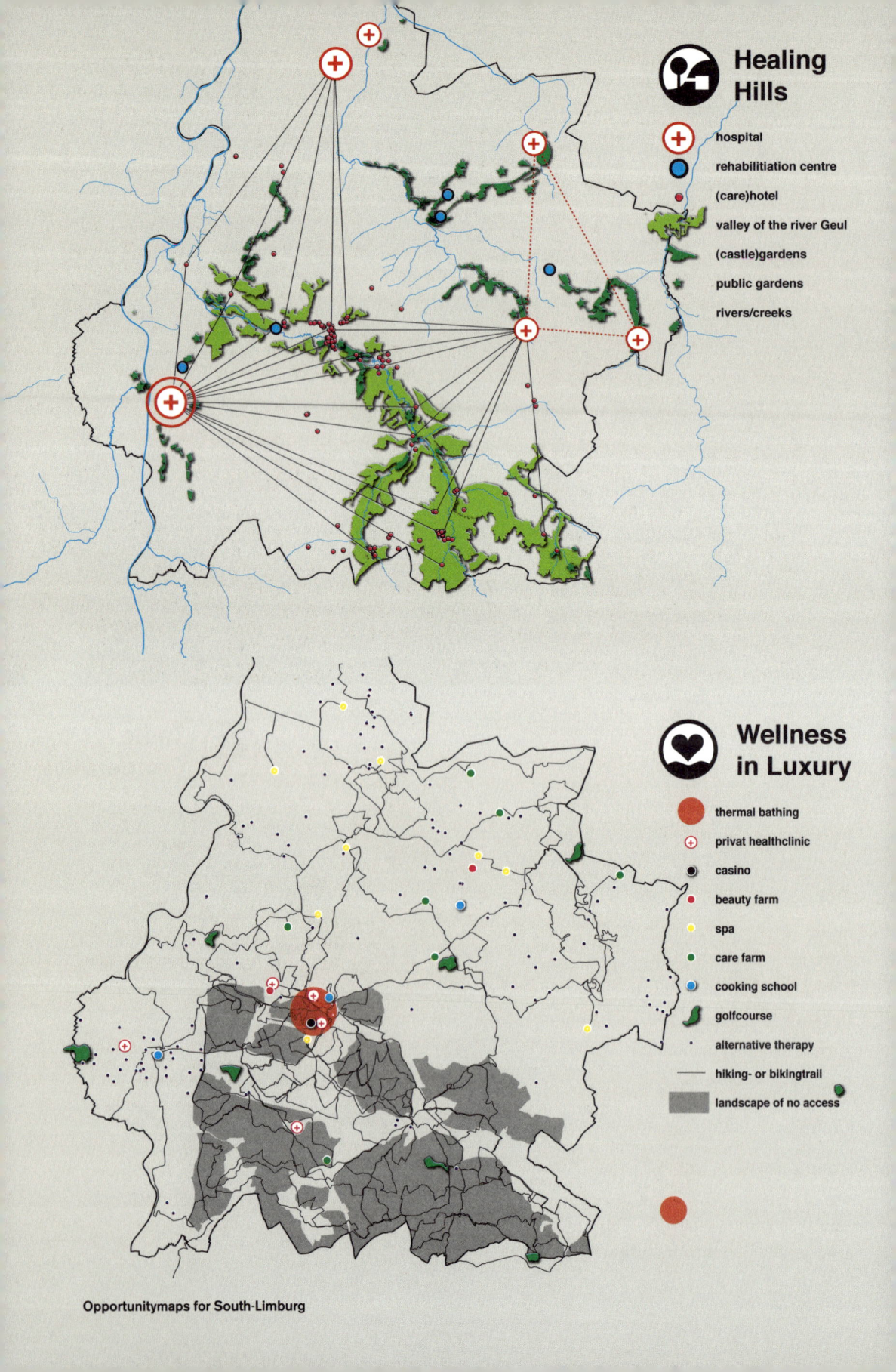

- ⊕ hospital
- ● rehabilitiation centre
- • (care)hotel
- valley of the river Geul
- (castle)gardens
- public gardens
- rivers/creeks

Wellness in Luxury

- ● thermal bathing
- ⊕ privat healthclinic
- ● casino
- ● beauty farm
- ● spa
- ● care farm
- ● cooking school
- golfcourse
- • alternative therapy
- — hiking- or bikingtrail
- landscape of no access

Opportunitymaps for South-Limburg

Glorious Life

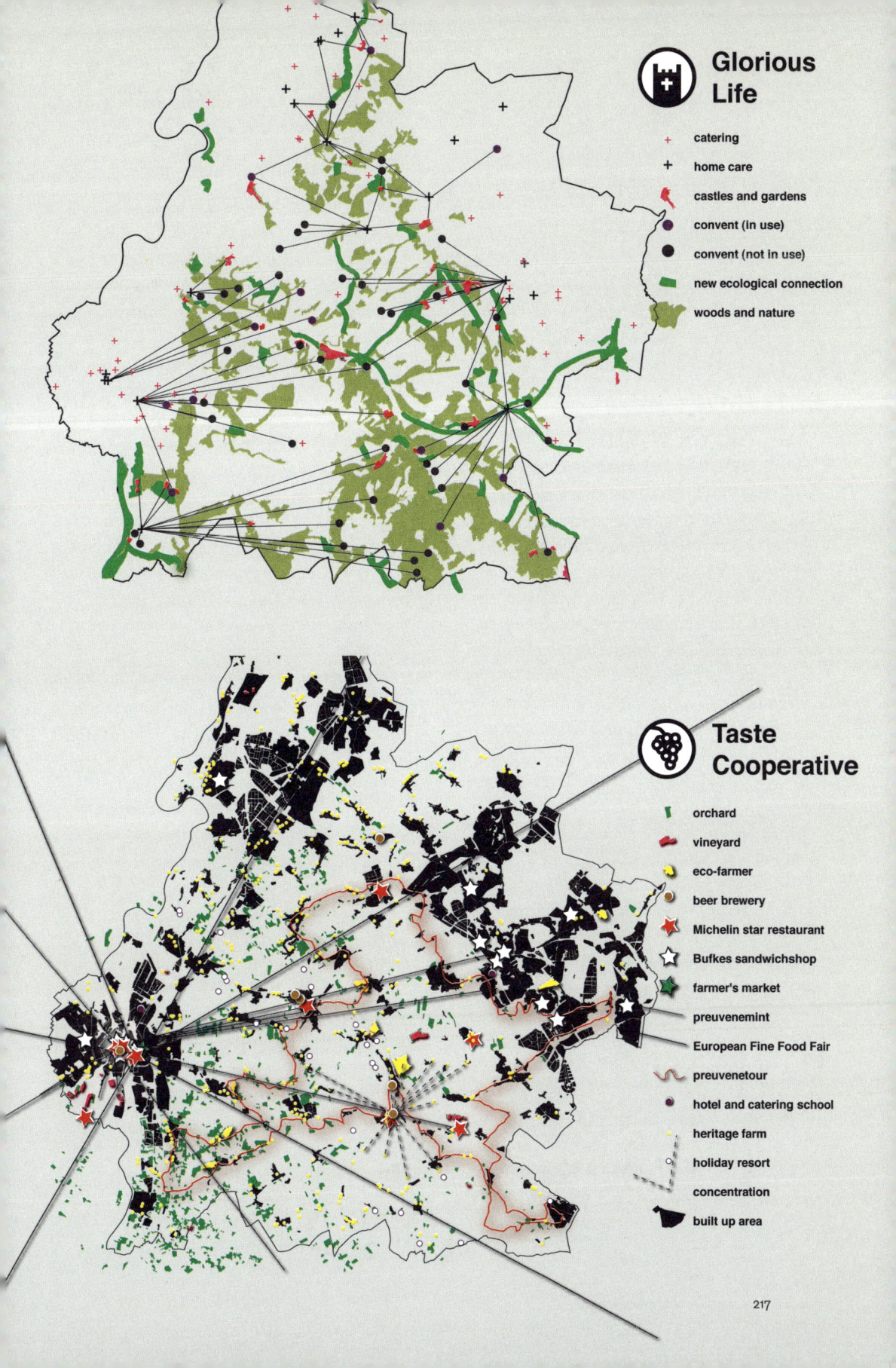

- catering
- home care
- castles and gardens
- convent (in use)
- convent (not in use)
- new ecological connection
- woods and nature

Taste Cooperative

- orchard
- vineyard
- eco-farmer
- beer brewery
- Michelin star restaurant
- Bufkes sandwichshop
- farmer's market
- preuvenemint
- European Fine Food Fair
- preuvenetour
- hotel and catering school
- heritage farm
- holiday resort
- concentration
- built up area

trations of therapists and wellness facilities, high-quality restaurants, beautiful square-farms and well situated castles, with an extensive Catholic religious heritage, residual watermills and extensive hike and bike trails and a fine tourist car network. These more or less urban and/or cultural highlights are marvellously flanked by hills and gentle glens, and also by beautiful wooded slopes, with fruit trees, gardens and 'hollow roads' in an imaginative small-scale setting. One of the researchers even claimed that 'if Walt Disney would have had to invent a landscape of his own, South-Limburg would have been it.' Next to that, an overall analysis and referential study was developed to discover potential new markets for the area in terms of applicability and momentum, to stimulate a combination of embedded market value and local qualities. This combination of different themes resulted in some preliminary sketches for possible opportunities: *Magnificent Gardens* (Retail with and around Castle Gardens), *Linked Fields* (informative WIFI facilitated by the extensive Catholic heritage network), *Healing Hills* (care & cure with leisure), *Elementary Heritage* (New energy with Industrial Heritage), *Taste co-operative* (Agri-leisure and Slow Food) and *Style Traffic* (New, sustainable leisure mobility). On this basis, potential leading actors were identified, according to an additional analysis of their annual reports, ambitions and motives. These concerned potential investors from both inside and outside the area, and – in line with previous definitions – actors from business and civic society who could be interested in investing in these local surroundings out of pure self-interest. By motivated reasons (to prevent traditional planning situations and dependencies) the regular urban and regional actors within the public society were temporarily passed by.

Bilateral talks, Opportunity Maps and Round Tables

Subsequently, various bilateral talks were organized with the potentially interested leading actors: investors, project developers, tourist entrepreneurs, other businessman, retailers, agrarians, representatives of interest groups etc. They resulted in the conclusion that some of the proposals lacked sufficient support (e.g., *Magnificent Gardens*, *Linked Fields*, *Elementary Heritage* and *Style Traffic*), others were embraced and expanded (e.g., *Healing Hills* and *Taste Co-operative*), while other issues were even added by the interviewees, enthusiastically stimulated by the initiative, such as *Wellness in Luxury* (wellness facilities extended with sport, multi-media and health food) and *Glorious Life* (integrated pension communities preserving cultural heritage and beautiful landscapes). Opportunity maps were created for each of these embraced themes, referring to both the distinct, unique selling points of the region, and the possible new and sustainable features of the future. They were discussed in five round tables with the identified and potentially leading actors on each of those themes. Especially the theme *Healing Hills* (a crossover between health care, leisure and landscape) and *Taste Co-operation* (a crossover between the agricultural sector, agri-leisure, gourmet restaurants and retail) came to the fore as key issues involving a large willingness to indulge in comprehensive and sustainable investment. At that time (spring 2005), the consortium presented its first report of the results and recommendations, before a full LIOF meeting of approximately 50 stakeholders in the business and civic society, including those of the public sector for the first time.

Business cases and pilots

The report and presentations received enthusiastic support, especially because the proposals were specific, (partly) derived from the ambitions of the leading actors themselves, and put in a new and creative setting of innovative crossovers, which promised mutual value adding in an economic, tourist, social, spatial and ecologic perspective. During the meeting, involved stakeholders had already agreed to elaborate the most promising opportunity charts in real business cases.

The first concerned a proposal for 'recovery' holidays as part of the theme *Healing Hills*. The intention was to move patients as soon as possible after surgery to one of the hotels in the local area to recover under the daily supervision of hospital nurses (and doctors at a distance). In this way, the hospital would profit, because it could decimate its waiting lists, as well as offer an attractive care & cure programme for patients from outside the region. That is cheaper for the health insurance companies, since a hotel bed is in principal less expensive than a hospital bed. And at last, it is lucrative for the innkeeper, because hotel occupancy is also guaranteed off-season. One agreed that part of the surplus profit should be used for improvements in the surrounding countryside. At present, several three-star packages (free for patient and partner) and one five-star package (free for patients, with an additional payment by partner) are offered by a coalition of Orbis Medical Service Provider, AZM (Academic Hospital Maastricht), Camille Oostwegel Chateau Hotels, Heuvelland Hotels and several health insurance companies. In the next future it could possibly be extended to more high tech programmes, such as cardiology and cancer research.

The second business case concerned the delivery of a highbrow daily fresh-food

Impressions of the opportunities Glorious Life

Wellness in Luxury

Taste Cooperative

Healing Hills

market in the inner city of Maastricht, with particular focus on the sale and promotion of regional agricultural production. The market should also give a boost to regulating more efficiently the entire chain from production via distribution and retail to the consumer. At the same time, the fresh-food market should also serve as a kind of front office for the related agrarians, who, in addition to their farming, want to offer new attractions with regard to regional cooking, dining and residence. This was combined with the periodic tasting event *Fine Food Fair* and *Preuvenemint Maastricht* with a presentation by the top (Michelin-star) cooks in and around the region. It offered a new (economic) perspective for the preservation of small-scale agricultural production in the region. It has boosted several affiliate slow food Limburg initiatives in the complete chain from producer to consumer networks.

Regional regime

The two pilots projects and especially the resulting boost to the area were so appealing that it also led to many new cases on issues such as *Wellness in Luxury* (including a Spa Boulevard Valkenburg), *Glorious Life* (including, for example, the development of integrated care communities in the western mining region of the area) and even a restoration of the initial ideas on a region-wide wireless network: *Linked Fields* (including the project *My Limburg*). All this resulted in a comprehensive network, whether or not interconnected, of projects and stakeholders. From here on, the leading actors themselves – linked in the so-called *Zwarte Ruiter* meeting (named after the cafe where they periodically met) – felt the need to develop and promote the various projects with a more collective profile. Upon request, this was partly facilitated by the above-mentioned consortium. Moreover, in order to gain greater support and a more sustainable regime alliance, the operation was directly connected to the more industrial, high-tech and educational innovations, facilitated by the provincial innovation agenda in the area, such as *Life Tech A2* (including R&D alliances between Philips, Medtronic, University Maastricht, et al.), *Chema-Energy Valley* (including new alliances between DSM, Solland, Sabic, et al.) and *Health Valley Campus* (including the co-operation of the cardiology departments of the University Medical Centres of Maastricht and Aachen). It resulted in a broad image of the region, with respect to:
a life-tech innovation and production,
b quality gastronomy and leisure,
c a caring and healing living environment,
d small-scale European character:
In sum, *High Life Hills*.

That commitment has by now been transformed into a broad regional private-public branding project, which currently includes approximately 40 stakeholders from business and civic society and 20 from the public sector, with actual participating investments (see www.maastrichtregion.com).

Associating in special districts

Last but not least, some elements of that regime are being anchored and institutionalized within Limburg society in a more innovative way. Here I refer to the impact of the integrated care project, which was recently being elaborated by the Orbis Medical Care Concern in co-operation with alternating partners. The original objective is to offer attractive alternatives to the current migration of Dutch elderly people to Mediterranean countries. Orbis opts for various markets: high income and middle-class health care or health-guaranteed

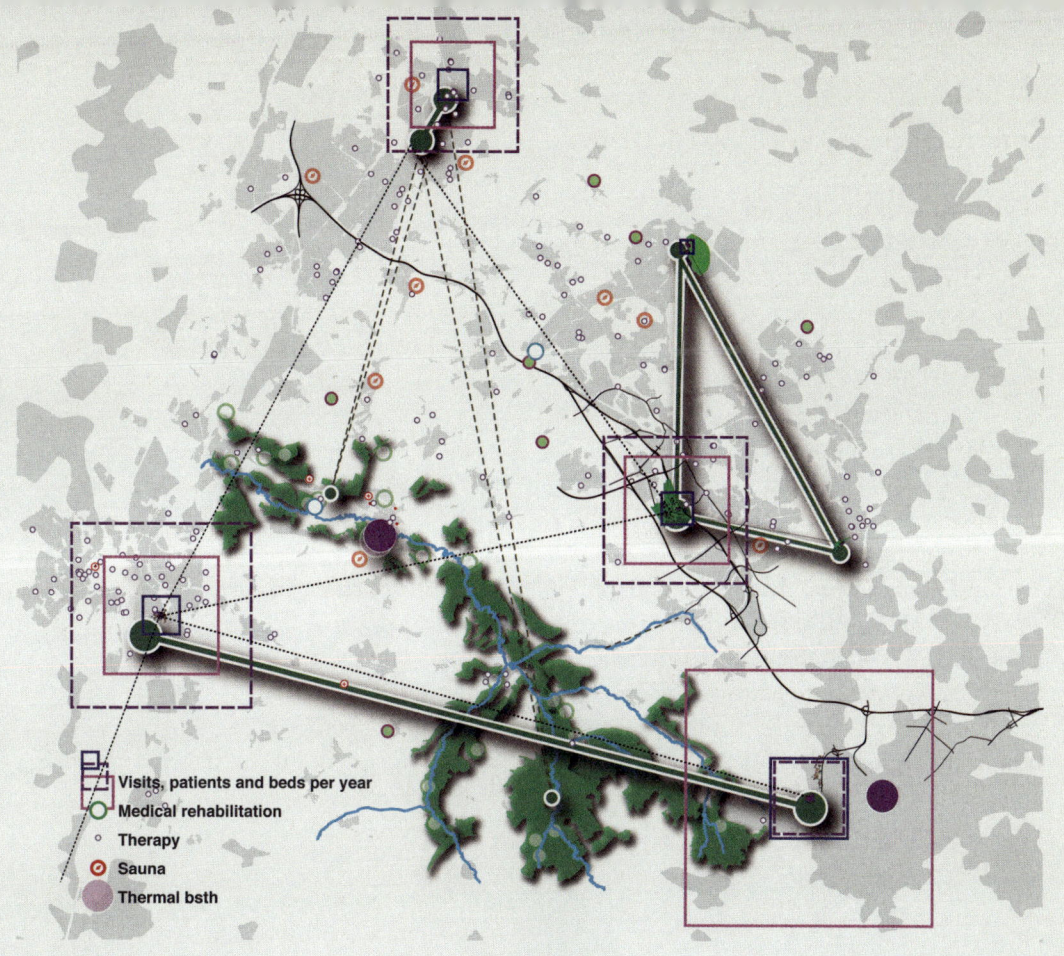

	Visits, patients and beds per year
○	Medical rehabilitation
·	Therapy
⊙	Sauna
●	Thermal bsth

International care environment

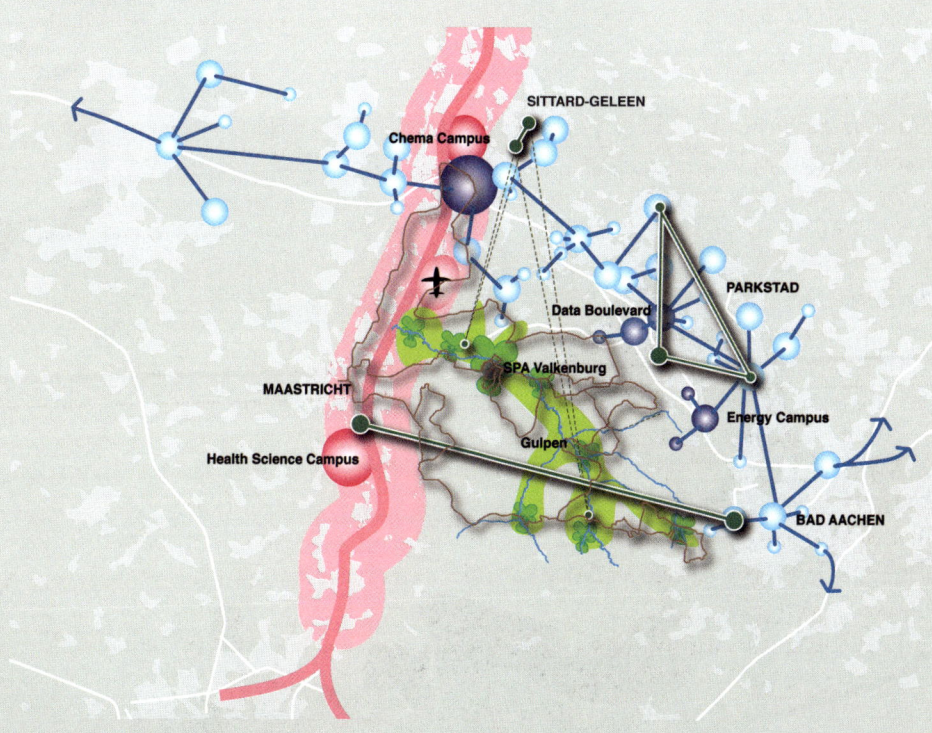

Profiling the larger region

221

Sittard

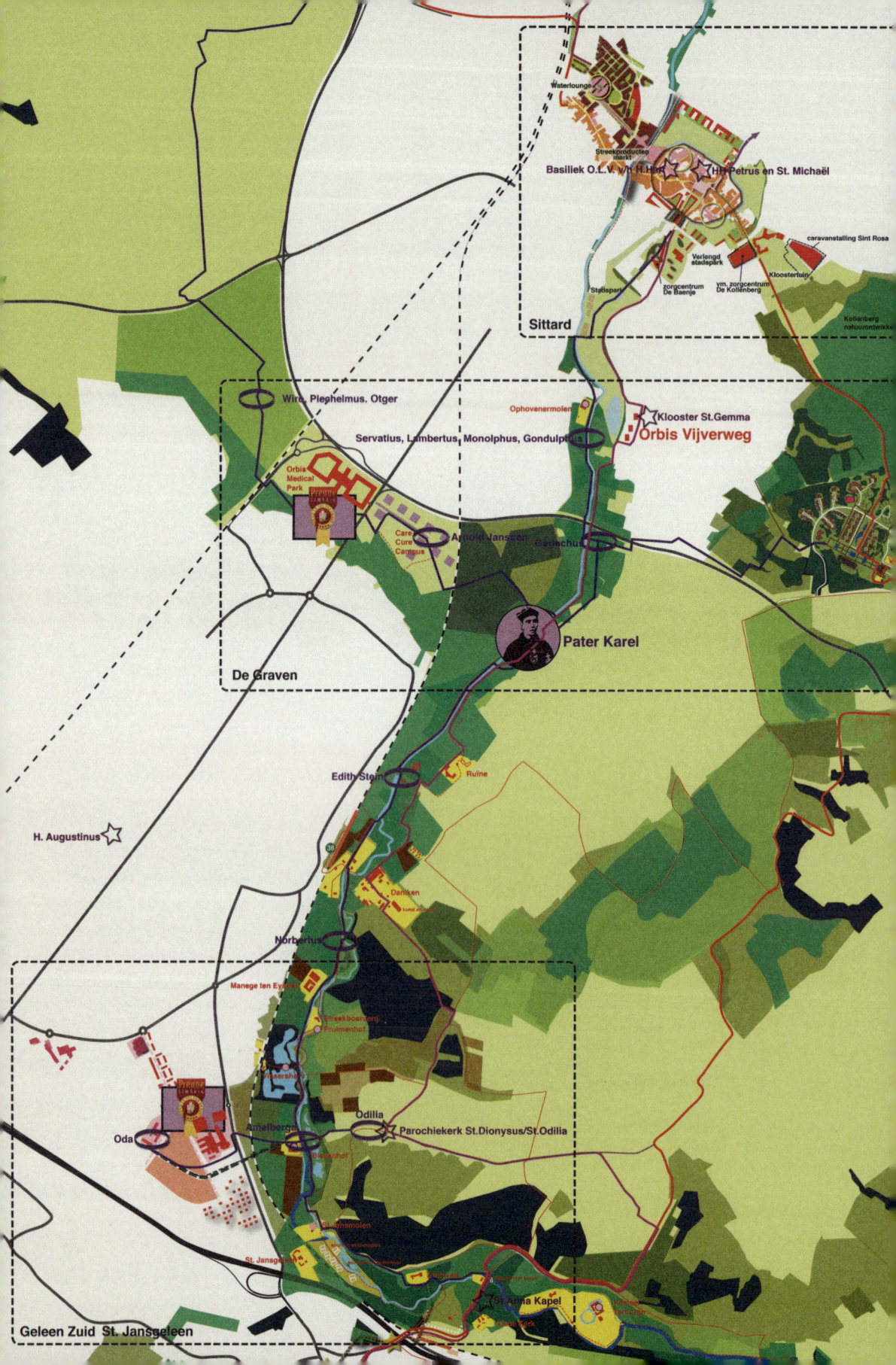

- Waterlounge
- Streekproducten markt
- Basiliek O.L.V. v/h H. Hart
- HH Petrus en St. Michaël
- Verlengd stadspark
- caravanstalling Sint Rosa
- Stadspark
- zorgcentrum De Baenje
- vm. zorgcentrum De Kollenberg
- Kloostertuin
- Kollenberg natuurontwikke...

De Graven

- Wiro, Plechelmus, Otger
- Ophovenermolen
- Klooster St. Gemma
- **Orbis Vijverweg**
- Servatius, Lambertus, Monolphus, Gondulphus
- Orbis Medical Park
- Care Cure Campus
- Arnold Janssen
- Gerlachus
- Pater Karel
- Edith Stein
- Ruïne

- H. Augustinus
- Daniken
- Norbertus

Geleen Zuid St. Jansgeleen

- Manege ten Eynder
- Streekboerderij
- Pruimenhof
- Visserhof
- Amelberga
- Oda
- Odilia
- Parochiekerk St. Dionysus/St. Odilia
- St. Jansmolen
- St. Jansgeleen
- St. Anna Kapel
- Klooster

settings, in a socially more open urban context or in a more rural, familiar social setting. To compensate the disadvantages of the cold climate in north-west Europe, extra attention is given to high-quality (care and other) services, integrated in a high-quality historical and cultural landscape setting. The aim is to actually invest in the development and/or preservation of that environment. To that end, adjacent to the new Orbis Medical Park, six integrated care projects for six corresponding markets are now being developed in an intensive coalition between Orbis, other (care) providers, investors, developers, housing corporations, leisure retailers, landscape and culture foundations. The goal is an Integrated Care Community (ICC), in which involved habitants no longer give their contribution to health insurance companies, but directly to Orbis and the related health care providers. In turn, these organizations provide adequate and specific care & cure. Avoiding too many overheads, some savings can be made, which are then used to realize extra services, such as gardening, repairing, nursery facilities, after-school services, food and mail delivery services, free taxi or car-sharing services, etc. Then the ICCs can also attract younger and double-income families, while they profit from a stress-free living environment. In this way gated or single-issue communities are avoided. On the other hand, with the direct premium payment of care services, one opts for a greater accountability of the health care providers to their customers and direct involvement of the residents with regard to the quality, size and type of the services delivered. As a result, it promotes not only a greater alignment of supply and demand, but also a better bonding of the residents, with ongoing voluntary work and self-organization to be expected in the long run. In fact, a new kind of special care district would then be institutionalized, according to the better USA examples, but also nicely reframed in a greater regional setting, as well as economically, socially, politically, and spatially.

Epilogue

Not pretending to have found the only or the right answer, we – the involved consortium of planners and experts – have taken a more facilitating role in the Limburg case rather than a steering/planning one. This facilitating role consists of supporting, promoting, or even inducing associations between stake and shareholders, from the outside in, with a sensible incorporation of the justified criticisms and resistance to pure modernistic (too much steering) and post-modernistic approaches (to less proactive alternatives). Despite numerous imperfections, this first round of actor-relational planning looks promising for the reinventions of spatial planning, and has done so, respectively is already doing so, with regard to other cases. Nevertheless the actor-relational proposals are still also highly fragile. While the other impulses mentioned before are only halfway, at best, the urban regime association in the Limburg case is still exclusively focused on region branding, not on preserving a holistic, interactive view on the various business cases. At the same time, the recent financial crises have also led to a more prudent attitude of the Orbis Medical Care Concern, with regard to the further development of the integrated care communities. Like its partners – and partly also pushed by the Dutch Ministry of Health, Welfare and Sport – it is tending to prioritize its actions around its apparent traditional core business. In addition, the actor-relational experiments still have to cope with the lock-ins of existing public spatial planning institutions, an ongoing evident mismatch between the different sectors and

Impression of new places for moments of meditation

Impression of a nature pool and renovation of the resort

departments of government and the reinstatement of numerous state regulations, or misplaced visionary actions from the old traditional view on spatial planning.[27] Nevertheless, the evaluation carried out at the moment of this writing, shows that several business cases are now being carried out and are receiving ongoing bottom-up support from the pioneers within civic, public and business society as well. Especially Healing Hills, Wellness in Luxury and Taste Co-operative are evolving well and will need to be given additional support from formal planning procedures. Additionally specific support is needed beyond those legislative, formal procedures. It will need a reorganisation within government towards governance to. Therefore Diagramming and Agencing, as explained in Box 4.1, are now in the making.

The reworking of Dutch planning beyond the planning paradise will therefore be continued.

[27] See for instance the process of the regional vision on Middle Limburg, carried out by the traditional planner Riek Bakker (www.goml.nl).

The referential argument

A relational tale of metropolises
Travelogues in the form of a matrix

Several demographists at the North Carolina State University and the University of Georgia have referred to 23 May 2007 as being the most important turning point in the demographic history of the world. On the basis of trend reports and population prognoses of the United Nations, [2007] that moment would mark, for the first time in the history of mankind, the moment at which there would be more city dwellers than country dwellers in the world. Since the summer of 2007, our world can thus be regarded as being mainly urban, and even more than half of those city dwellers live in agglomerations of more than 500,000 residents, interconnected by corridors of airports, railway lines, motorways and electronic highways. In fact, there is mention of one large all-embracing urban field in the world. As far back as several decades ago, some people had already predicted a 'Global village', [McLuhan 1964] others analysed 'Global Cities' [Sassen 1991] or a tight and interactive 'Global Urban Network'. [Taylor 2004] Nevertheless Amin & Thrift [2002] still adhere to the idea of cities as specific places, which can be mutually distinguished, each with its own specific (economic, political, social and spatial) signature. This opinion is allied to their relational vision of space, which reaches back to Henri Lefebvre's [1991] notion of space as a 'social product' where it is no longer understood as 'practio-inert container of action' but is rather conceptualized as a 'socially produced set of manifolds'. [Thrift & Crang 2000] Space is relational through and through, not only due to the fact that developments at one location can no longer be seen as separate from those at other locations, but also because of the fact that the specific properties of that place are actually inextricably linked to the longings, ambitions, expressions and singularities of the (leading) actors involved, as well as the institutional settings which, in turn, arise from heterogeneous relationships between the specific space and the actors in question.[28]

28 In line with ANT, in this case, Latour et al., with regard to both the human and the non-human. [Latour 2006]

In the form of reference research for the theoretical and practical argument presented in this book, six metropolitan locations have been visited under the auspices of the Ministry of VROM and the University of Utrecht in the past five years: Denver and Dallas/Fort Worth (in December 2005), the Pearl River Delta (PRD) and Tokyo (in March 2007), and Buenos Aires and São Paulo (in March 2008). On each occasion, one of the themes discussed previously in this work filled the study agenda:
- the administrative-political theme (chapter four) in Denver and Dallas/Fort Worth,
- the spatial-economic theme (chapter two) in the PRD and Tokyo, and
- the transnational community theme (chapter three) in Buenos Aires and São Paulo.

For the purpose of approaching the relevant areas in all their heterogeneity, there was consistent mention of an appropriate heterogeneous research team, composed of five students, five civil servants and five practitioners (the Triple Helix of Education, Government and Enterprise), based on various expertises and backgrounds: sociologists, environmental specialists, historians, social administrators, architects, civil engineers, artists, planners etc. This being the case, we were able, in each of the above-mentioned themes and areas, to uncover the dynamic place-network relationships that are partly connected to specific relational concepts, structures and patterns, path-dependent factors that partly determine current educational comparisons, and the position that these locations currently occupy in a global setting.

But rather than present three research reports of these three study trips,[29] I prefer, at the end of this contribution, to undertake an attempt to define more specifically the path-dependent factors that jointly determine the possible 'historical-geographical DNA profile' of the previously mentioned metropolitan (sub)areas. With an approach similar to the one I developed with Ed Taverne for the delta of the Rhine, Maas and Scheldt (hereafter EuroDelta), [Boelens/Taverne 2009] I regard this as a provisional impulse for a more substantial research programme that requires further in-depth study and probably further application to other metropolises and urban areas. On the basis of an actor-oriented, relational vision on urbanized delta, I define this impulse as an interaction strongly varying in time and space, between:
a institutional *environment* of which urban appearances form a component;
b overriding and decisive *actors* and their associative, network-oriented economic, political, socio-cultural relations etc., and
c *spatial strategies* steered by the preferences of people, institutions and enterprises, and structured by regulations, laws, norms, and perhaps (in)formal organization.

In other words, I wish here, on the basis of the studies performed in the fields of administration-management, spatio-economic development and transnational communities,[30] to develop a preliminary attempt to advance towards an initiative to determine the specific DNA profile of metropolises – in this case Dallas, Denver, PRD, Tokyo, Buenos Aires and São Paulo –. This DNA is set in a global/local (i.c. glocal) urban context and derived from the interaction of physical-geographical circumstances, institutional conditions and alliances or conflicts between entrepreneurs, administrators and citizens, as well as the position that urban units occupy with respect to one another. I wish to attempt (provisionally and as a promising thesis requiring further research) to show that this is consistently different for each location, city and metropolitan region, and is specific, dependent on time and place, openness to the surroundings, capacity for innovation, development procedures, accessibility, and the position it occupies in a global network economy. But at the same time, I wish to demonstrate that (robust) common denominators can be discovered that reach back to geographical-physical and socio-cultural backgrounds, over a long duration, resulting in an individual 'style of (political, economic and spatial) action'. For this purpose I make use of a matrix, in which I cross cultural-geographical backgrounds with the positioning, function and (probably still simple) model ranking of specific metropolitan areas with

---

[29] These can be requested from the Faculty of Geosciences, Spatial Planning Department of the University of Utrecht.

[30] See the previous chapters two to four.

regard to one another. This already produces interesting insights that align with the specific research that is being carried out on administrative-political governance, spatial-economic processes, and transnational communities in the above-mentioned metropolises. On the horizontal axis, I currently distinguish an Asian, European and American metropolitan cultural background,[31] and on the vertical axis I currently recognize Capital, Colonial and Delta metropolises. In the meantime, I restrict myself to the truly large metropolitan regions of more than 5 million inhabitants, which, although they may not always be equally clear and sharply demarcated, do fulfil a specific significance for a larger surrounding area and now accommodate around 1/6 of the total world population. In global terms, the *Capitals* can here best be typified as *mono-centric metropolises* – at the same time the (original) capital cities of a certain country or region – despite the fact that they may also embrace many specialized (sub)centres and concentrations of housing, employment and entertainment, while often simultaneously accommodating headquarters and service centres in the domains of finance, management, and administration of the world economy. Occasionally, this is also the case with the *Colonials*, although these have frequently functioned as (one-time) outposts of the *Capitals*. In the meantime, their inhabitants have often fought independence and, due to their size and global significance, now go their own way. As such, their institutional setting, actor networks and the relational significance for a wider environment are often different to those of the Capitals. In turn, the metropolitan Delta Regions can be characterized as compound *polycentric archipelagos* along the estuaries and branches of large delta rivers, none of which – with the exception of the Chinese deltas – accommodate more than 5 million inhabitants, but jointly form a mutually strongly linked urban field and density. They often possess strong concentrations of manufacturing industries, refineries, trade, transport & distribution, and occasionally also Research & Development. Although more diffuse patterns are currently demonstrable, this division is a reason to assume that – disregarding environmental and water management issues for the moment – these metropolises require their own political-economic and sociocultural conditions and therefore also a specific individual approach and planning structure. In this final contribution I first wish to give a brief elucidation of this provisional division into a geographical-cultural background and model typology, and then return to its impact on the themes we studied in Dallas, Denver, PRD, Tokyo, Buenos Aires and São Paulo. Provisional conclusions that could be significant for reference research elsewhere are implicitly processed in this summary.

31 This division is in line with the division that was made in the behavioural economic approach of Trans National Corporations discussion in chapter two, [Yeung 2002] as well as the divisions made in the fields of cultural history and anthropology.

Asian model – the paradox of strict regulation and local freedom

The Asian urbanization model (at least that of China and Japan) has traditionally been characterized by the paradoxical combination of intensive economic and social-cultural developments, with strongly limited political autonomy on the one hand and scope for local self-organization on the other. [Eisenstadt 1996, p.187] Although some change appears to be occurring periodically (under Western pressure), the situation remains rather robust, since it reaches back to institutional frameworks and the ideology of Confucianism from the Qing dynasty of the 2nd century BC. It acquired political-administrative shape especially in the Chinese Tang and Sung empires of the 7th to the 13th centuries AD. That was the period in which a powerful administrative system was set up, where the emperors ruled thanks to a 'divine mandate' with three departments under them: the imperial secretariat, the imperial chancellery and the department for state affairs, which supervised state governance, finances, religion, justice and public works from the central capital (Xian and later Hangzhou). The empire was further divided into 15 administrative districts, each with 1 to 6 seats of military governors – depending on the size, external threats and possible internal disquiet – such as Guangzhou (or Canton), Hang (later Nanchang) and You Jojun (later Beijing). In fact, these early urban seats – often with several hundred thousand inhabitants – were outposts of the empire and an expression of imperial power. Order and essential facilities – such as firefighting services, defence forces and a variety of welfare amenities – were guaranteed by the representatives of the imperial power, sometimes in a coalition with the local merchants and (lower) nobility. It was also common for the governmental outposts to be physically based on a walled grid structure, erected around a residency for the military governors also sectioned off by a wall. In addition, there was mention of a hierarchical division of separate urban envelopes for administration, religion and housing, categorized according to perceived classes of importance. Whereas in the imperial capital it was primarily the presentation of divine power on earth that was emphasized, the administrative outposts were in themselves complementary articulations of absolute power, according to Spiro Kostoff: 'places of enforced residence under political control'. [Kostoff 1991, p.99] This was particularly expressed in the urban grid, public space and the urban facilities. Trade and production – even in Suzhou, the traditional trading city *pur sang* – were subordinate to this 'political grid' and had to dovetail with this imperial urban scheme. This is where the so-called 'danwei' developed, separate working units around an inward-looking collective space, separated from the public street and public spaces. [Friedmann 2005]

Although Chinese empires alternated, governors and provinces rebelled, and the Ming dynasty was exchanged for that of Manchu after the Mongolian invasions, with the republican Kwo Min Tang and the Chinese People's Republic later taking over, this system of an archipelago of regions, under strictly hierarchical urban state system, has determined not only the social and political but also the spatial and urban order right down to the present day. Even at the end of the 20th century, the Chinese cities with more than a million inhabitants were still divided by the central authority in Beijing according to the strict regime of south-eastern coastal cities that were allowed to apply the so-called 'secrets of Western capitalism', the metropolises in the centre of the country

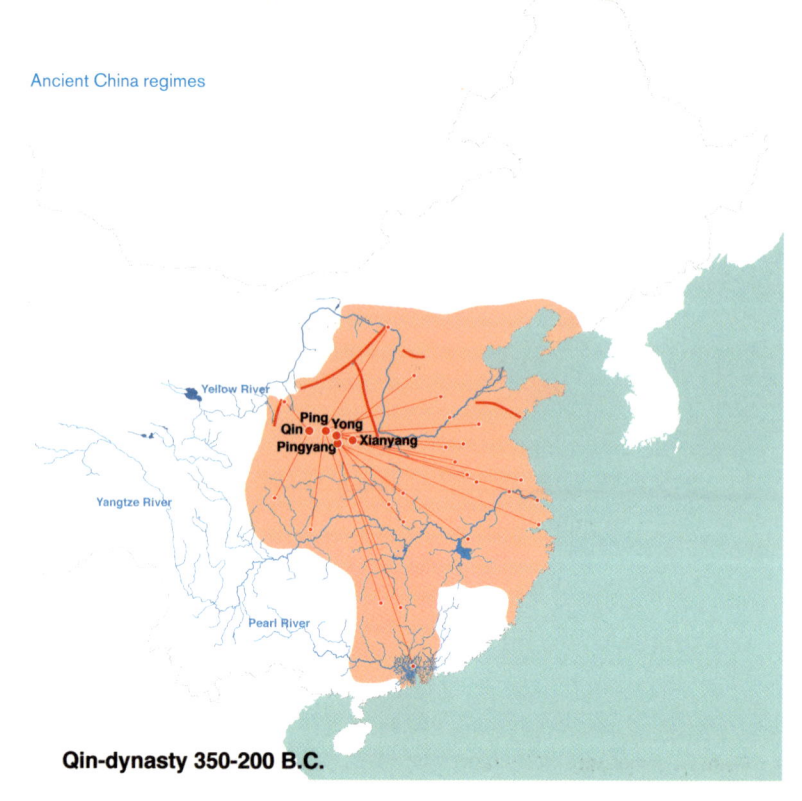

Ancient China regimes

Qin-dynasty 350-200 B.C.

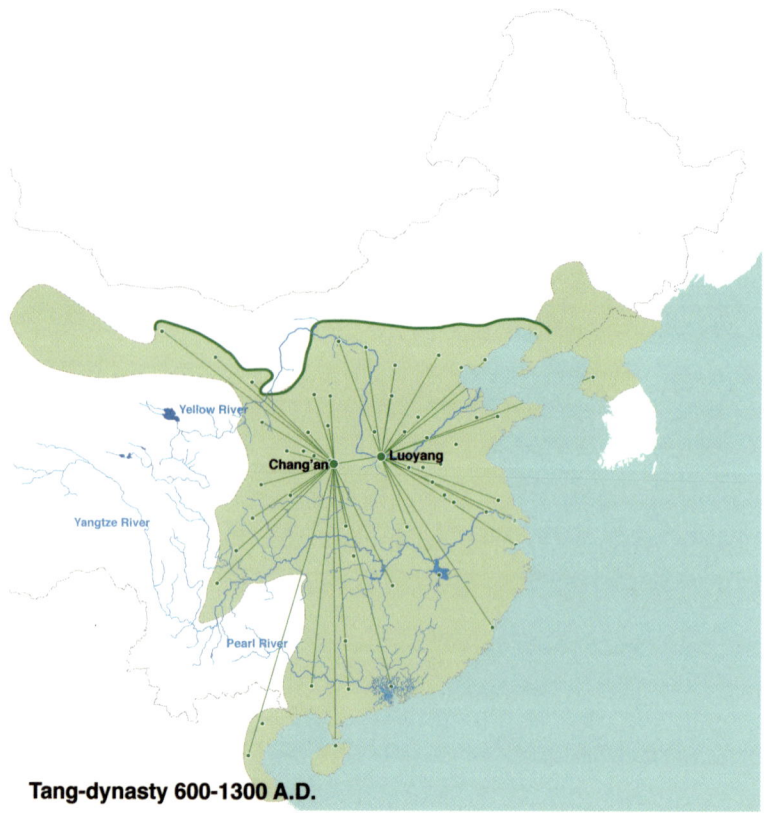

Tang-dynasty 600-1300 A.D.

232 A relational tale of metropolises

Mantsjoe-dynasty 1600-1800 A.D.

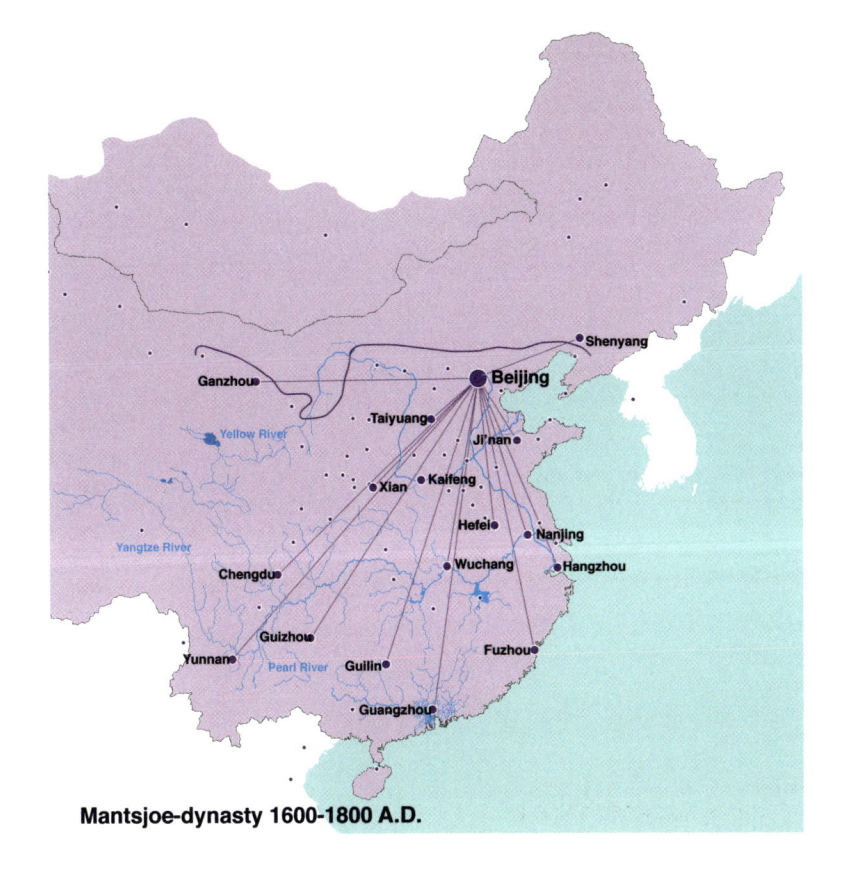

Ladder step regime of China

with the emphasis on the production of energy and (the supply of) raw materials, and the areas in the west that were primarily oriented to agrarian production and possible future expansion. It was self-evident that Beijing was regarded as the central Capital of the state that had been united for more than 20 centuries. [Yang 1997] Only cities in the large deltas of the Pearl River and the Yangtze (such as Macau, Hong Kong, Shanghai, and more or less Suzhou and Gaungzhou) have been able to follow a more individual (commercial) course since the middle of the nineteenth century, in line with the Nanjing treaties.

However, this had further consequences, as the Chinese imperial urban model determined also the national economy and urban structure of Japan from the 7th and 8th centuries onward. At that time, the Yamoto monarchs, who originated from the mainland, controlled almost the whole of Japan and, following China's footsteps, adopted a constitution that confirmed the 'divine mandate' of the Japanese emperors, and thus their absolute power over the nobility and their complete disposal over all earthly grounds and the population. Just as was the case with the Chinese emperors, this also implied the virtue of the emperors, in line with Confucianism, and the provision of a good example to the people. This was mainly translated in the development of a high-principled culture at Court, which was seated in Heian (the later Kyoto) from the eighth century onward. In addition, they gave (trained) favourites and aristocratic representatives the right to found reinforced country estates, so-called 'shoens', in order to maintain imperial order in the provinces. However, these strengthened themselves with an ever-increasing number of vassals in the course of time, and began to act more and more independently. In around 1500, in addition to the Imperial Court, there were almost 400 hundred mini-empires, ruled by warlords who harassed one another to the limits. [Haywood 1999] At the beginning of the 17th century, one of these warlords – Tokugawa Ieyasu – was successful in putting an end to the 'civil war' and in uniting Japan under his rule. Although the divine Imperial Court was still seated in Kyoto, real power lay with the Tokugawa shoguns, who had their main seat in Edo (the later Tokyo). [Sorensen 2002] Having learned from the first experiences of the (Yamoto) emperors, the Tokugawas also set up urban outposts in the region, but concentrated the families of the dispatched feudal governors (the *daimyo*) more or less as hostages in/around the castle of Edo. At the same time, Japanese society – besides the monks and the nobility – were divided into four hereditary classes: the *samurai* with a specific professional code of honour and lifestyle, the *farmers* as the morally superior class but without the right to leave their land, the *artists* or *craftsmen* whose primary function was to support the samurai, and the *traders* who, although they were regarded as the lowest class, profited most from this system. At the same time – with the exception of a small Dutch trading post in Nagasaki – it was forbidden to have any contact with non-Japanese, in order to maintain this social structure and to prevent the incursion of external influence. In exchange for this, besides this strictly feudal hierarchy, the actual management of everyday activities was left to the inhabitants of the various towns and villages. They were assigned the (self-)responsibility for the collection of local taxes, for the firefighting services, community facilities, festivals and the maintenance of essential infrastructure such as roads, dikes, water supply, etc. Everyone was responsible for everyone else in the community. This even went as far as a situation where, if one member of the community could not pay his/her (local) taxes, the others in the community would have to ensure that these were paid, or if a member of the community committed a crime, the others ought to call him/her to account or share the (inevitable) punishment, etc. As such, a strong tradition of local self-organization and participation in neighbourhood organizations developed, under the auspices of paternalistic large-scale land owners or detached shogun-governors, who feverishly ensured that, whatever happened, they would at least retain control over the central political areas and institutions. [Sato 1990, Wakita 1999]

When, in the mid-nineteenth century, the Meiji emperors – partly with the assistance of the West – restored their power over the shoguns, they not only inherited an effective social and stratified cultural system of respect for central authority and collective self-responsibility for their own local community or neighbourhood, but also a well-equipped urban infrastructure, governed from a single central capital which was one of the largest in the world at that time: Edo. The restored Meiji emperor immediately moved his seat from Heian to Edo, and renamed these places Kyoto and Tokyo, respectively. In addition, to prevent the threatening colonization by Western superpowers, the Meiji dynasty committed itself fully to a stronger nationalization of Japanese consciousness and powerful industrialization following Western example. Besides the support and extension of the railway infrastructure (see Box 5.2), there was a (more or less compulsory) general openness to foreign trade, as well as effective support for innovative Japanese entrepreneurs. To this end, the co-operation with the regional shoguns at the reinforced Tokugawa outposts was exchanged for collaboration with the *zaibatsu* or *keiretsu*, respectively large industrial conglomerates or promising entrepreneurial families in production and trade. On the basis of the development of Toshiba (Mitsui keiretsu), NEC (Sumito keiretsu) and Fujitsu (Dai-Ichi Kangyo keiretsu), Peter Hall, [1998] among others, shows how this mutual interaction between the (imperial) government and trade & industry, in the areas of technology, R&D and banking, led to prosperity for both in the twentieth century. And although the Second World War and the subsequent push toward democracy of the American victors brought about great changes in (democratic) governance, the same administrative, urban and economic principles as in bygone days still apply. Each of the *keiretsu* is not only strongly stratified and structured in a strictly top-down hierarchy, with self-management on the workfloor, but also has direct links with the (imperial) government via the Ministry of International Trade and Industry (MTI) and restricted funding by the Japanese Central Bank. Similarly, the urban planning system also has a powerful hierarchy between the cities as well as a strict zoning based on functions, densities and construction heights. However, it

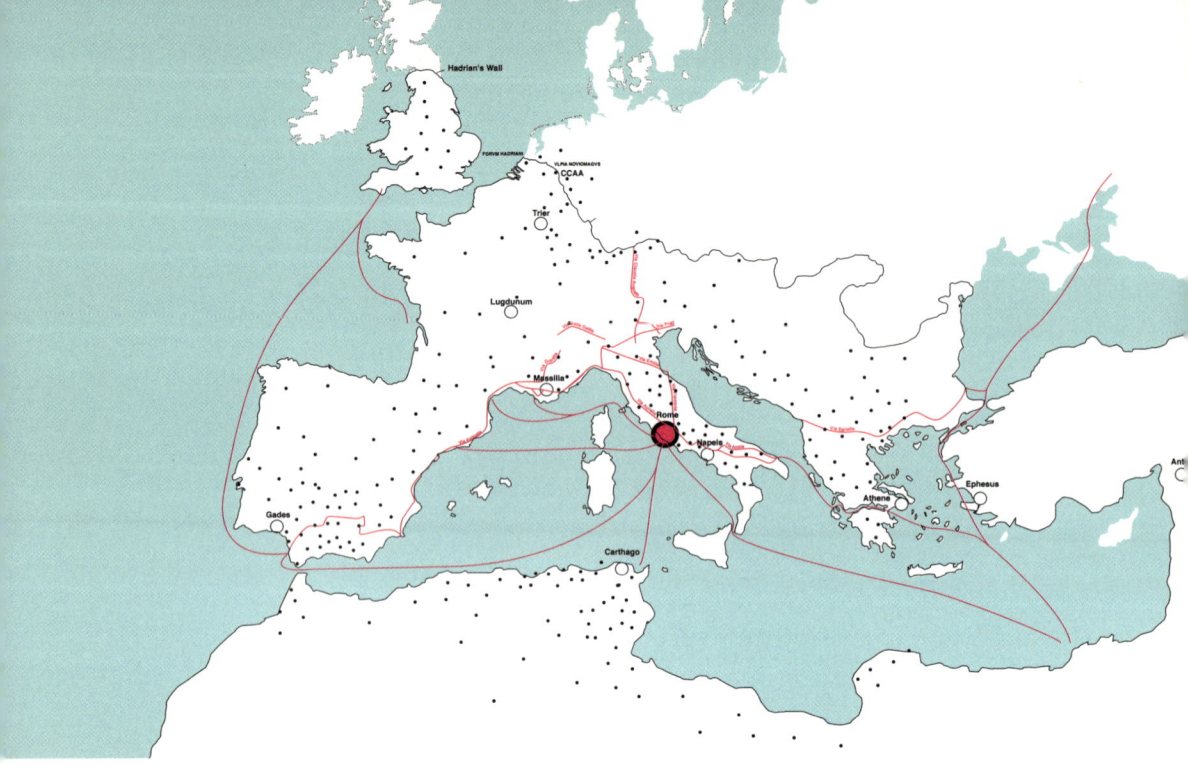

The roman empire

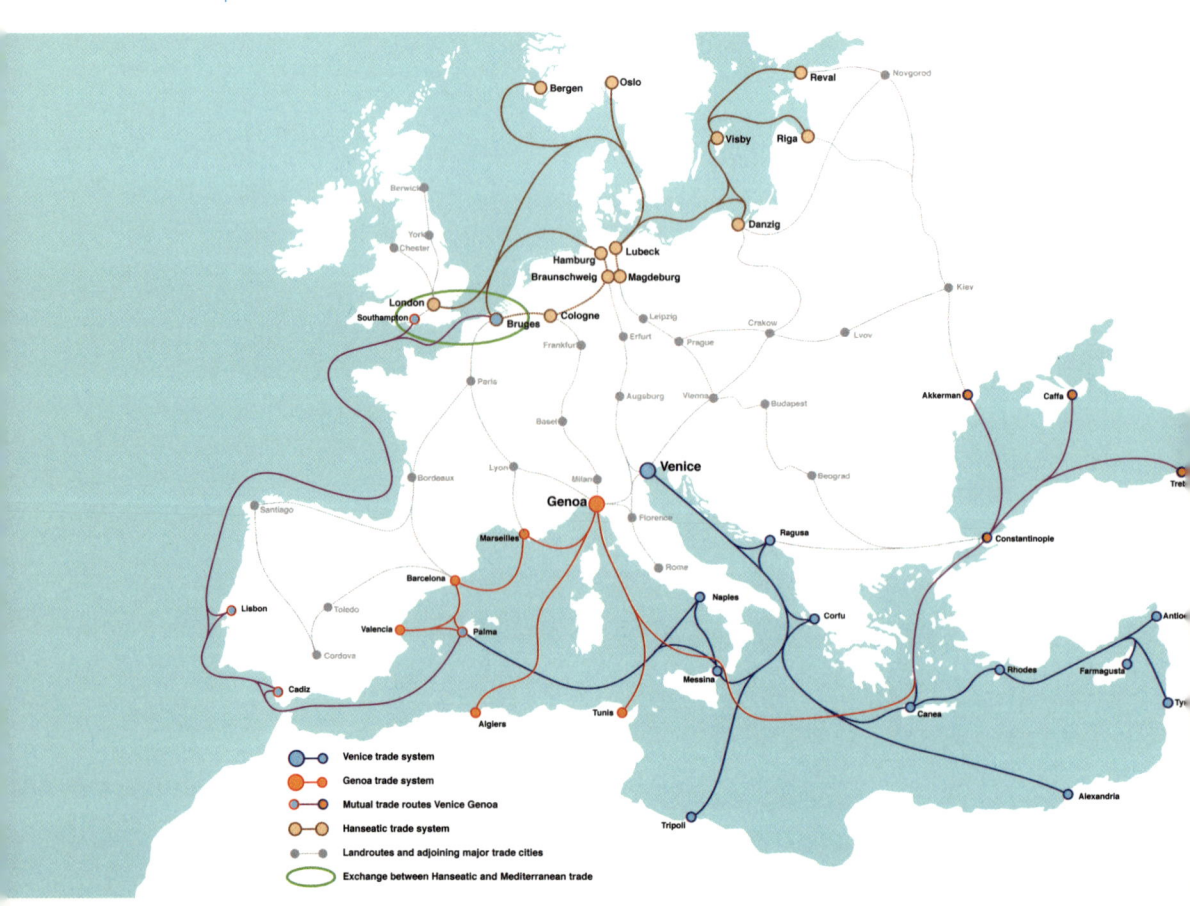

Major trade routes Middle Ages

also offers possibilities to act creatively within these frameworks and to exchange (zoning) rights among one another, as well as possessing plenty of leeway for self-organization at neighbourhood level. This urban institutional 'Asian DNA' seems to be still pretty robust in the young, advanced and, to a certain extent, liberated Japan.

European model – the story of the public trading space

The European cities (at least those of the so-called 'Latin West') arose on the ruins of the Roman Empire. Actually, the Roman Empire, despite consular authorization rather than the divine mandate of the principal, was strongly modelled on a system that was comparable to that of the Chinese empire. According to Le Goff, [1984] the history of Rome, in all its grandeur, can best be typified as the history of a camp of a conquering army. The city of Rome expanded its surrounding space further and further until an ideal size was reached that could supposedly be defended and managed economically. This area was finally screened off by Hadrian's Wall, the Limes and other natural barriers. In this structure, cities were first and foremost administrative-military centres and then economic cores. After the partition of the Roman Empire, this model would determine the Byzantine Empire until well into the 15th century, and also the Umayyad and the Abassid Caliphates as well as that of the Ottoman Empire. [Bosker et al. 2008] In contrast, the West-Roman Empire disintegrated in the 5th century, and the cities founded by the Romans shrivelled up to form only a small block within an oversized circumvallation. Their function as a political and administrative centre had definitively lapsed. Although the later Carolingian and other feudal monarchs were periodically successful in restoring peace to Europe or parts of it, their power was largely based on 'being continually on tour' as well as on their possessions in estates. It was only the episcopal seats that upheld any form of urbanity. At the end of the first millennium, Europe was thus primarily an agrarian continent with a degree of urbanization that barely reached 5%, much less than in the Arabian, Asian and even North African (sub)continents.

Thus, Pirenne [1959] regards (West) European urbanization as first and foremost a creation of traders and merchants, in contrast to what was the case in Asia and the Middle East, for example. Nevertheless, the feudal lords did play an important role in this, since the funding and protection necessary for urban development had to come mainly from them, allied to the fact that the first cities were still strongly dependent on the raw materials and products from the surroundings controlled by the feudal lords. But under the auspices of those lords, the hawkers, the parvenus who had escaped serfdom or the *monastic familiae*, and the functionaries who had fulfilled a high function with the *ministerials* of the feudal monarchs began to settle at the hubs of the large-scale trading routes: as in northern Italy at the intersection of the great routes across the Alps and those over the Mediterranean Sea, in northern Germany and Denmark at the transition of the Baltic and the North Seas, and in the Low Countries on the turntable of the Mediterranean and North European urban system. In addition, these cities gave a boost to the development of the surrounding agrarian countryside, just as that development determined the prosperity of the city to a major extent. There was thus mention of a tight mutual city-countryside relationship, as well as mutual benefits for prominent citizens from the urban citizenry and the feudal ruler.

Le Goff [1984] demonstrates convincingly that these cities soon became the guide, melting pot and mainspring of social development in Europe. This development first manifested itself in the domain of trade. As a consequence of the above-mentioned geographical position of the first (trading) cities, the most important trade vehicle was not the camel, dromedary, elephant or even the donkey or domesticated horse, but primarily the ship. Trade, which had been limited to luxury products up until then, could consistently expand thanks to (technological and logistical) improvements in shipping and could eventually deal in mass products. [Bernstein 2008] This development assumed two different institutional forms. In northern Italy, city states such as Genoa, Venice etc. received the privilege of setting up settlements and outposts along the coasts of Asia Minor, the Adriatic Sea, Crete and the Ionic islands thanks to a treaty with the Byzantine emperors. In northern Europe, however, the more open and flexible Hanseatic League, which nevertheless protected the trading interests of its members, eventually stretched in various combinations of cities from Riga and Novgorod on the Baltic, Lübeck and Hamburg in Northern Germany, to Bruges and London on the North Sea. When even greater distances became feasible after the voyages of discovery at the end of the 15th and beginning of the 16th centuries, delta cities arose on the Rhine, Maas and Scheldt, and this development even went hand in hand with the forming of geographic city relationships (or perhaps relationships with nation states) to protect shipping over longer distances.

Second, urban development was also crucial for the development of industrial production. Although the urban workplace was originally set up for trading, in the course of time the craft industries began to dominate trading. A crucial element in this development was the forming of trade guilds. They were initially a kind of cartels aimed at eliminating competition, but due to their specialization and specific craft development they became essential in the improvement of the product, the production and research & development. [Gunnar Mickwitz 1936] Due to specialization among not only the guilds but also the cities, however, trade itself ultimately benefited.

Third, according to Le Goff, European urban development was crucial to the development of the monetary economy. Although Charlemagne had attempted to introduce a rudimentary form of a monetary system, with the increasing importance of cities as centres of production, trade and consumption there was a growing need to finalize transactions in money rather than in traditional bartered goods. This being the case, the Florentine florin dates from 1252, the Shield of Louis IX from 1263, the Venetian ducat from 1284 etc., and, parallel to the real economy, there also developed a separate monetary economy with its own places of storage (banks), trading places (stock centres), and financial centres, where even the feudal monarchs went borrowing money to finance their wars, expeditions and crusades, thus becoming dependent on the citizenry. [Le Goff 1984, p.106]

And last but not least, the cities in Europe left their mark on artistic and cultural life. Whereas those aspects of life had been primarily reserved for esoteric monasteries and cloisters until that time, the cities picked up the torch of culture from the 12th century onward, thus increasingly extracting it from the devotional and erudite aura that surrounded it. This turned out to be the case not only in architecture, painting, literature etc., but especially in education. The first universities did issue from the cathedral, dome and monastic schools, but distanced themselves from their scholasticism by recruiting schoolmasters from the guilds and by orienting their educational programmes and methods to general social aims: *universitates magistrorum et scolarum*. In this way, the first universities of Europe arose, such as those in Bologna (1158), Paris (1170) and Oxford (1219), which was initially a dependence of Paris university. Others soon followed, such as those in Padua (1222), Orléans (1229), Angers (1231), Siena (1246) etc. [Duroselle 1990 pp.149-50] Each time there were local differences and nuances, but in general it was here that the Book of Idols by Kalibi became a tool. And just as with every tool, there was the need to manufacture, produce and trade this book in series, in the service of general knowledge development and open innovation. The other side of the coin, that citizens became increasingly self-opinionated and self-reliant, was accepted as part of the process.

This development of the West European city thus more or less corresponded to the parallel development of a new self-opinionated social class, the petty bourgeoisie. This class not only developed a new economy – bourgeois or mercantile – which, in the view of Heide Berndt, was not exclusively focused upon production for its own needs, but especially for exchange and trade. [Berndt 1978, p.99] Moreover, particularly after the English and French revolutions, a political system arose along with a tendency toward democratization on the basis of the Enlightenment, which would dominate the nobility and the clergy. The relative freedom, openness and concentrated opportunities for exchange that these cities offered implied enormous development possibilities for citizens who could seize the opportunities. Where the city represented progress, country areas were often typified by epithets such as 'backward' and 'stagnant', until deep in the past century. [Weber 1922] The city was regarded as the place where nature was dominated by mankind, with a new clock time and network society, while the surrounding rural area was still controlled by geographical laws of nature and the rhythm of the sun, moon and seasons. [Urry 2000] Whereas in the countryside it was difficult to escape the oppressive social institutions of paternalism, community and church, the West European city was actually the picture of modern advancement and all the economic, political and cultural opportunities that it provided. This model would have an important power of attraction upon many people, even far beyond the boundaries of Europe. This is amply illustrated in Louis Wirth's [1938] *Urbanism as a Way of Life*, in which he emphasizes in particular the positive effects of modern urban life as 'a civilization which is without question the best civilization that human beings have ever devised', and as 'the centre of freedom and toleration, the home of progress, of invention, of science, of rationality'. It is an exaltation of the versatile, unlimited possibilities and the unexpected aspects of the city and especially of the urban setting, which we later also discover in the work of Jane Jacobs and many others.

American model – liberal colonization by means of real estate

The American metropolitan model, however, is of a different alloy. In addition, it is the youngest and is actually no older than 500 years. Although there were highly developed civilizations featuring the Mayas, Toltecs, Aztecs and Incas in Central and South America from 1000 BC onward, the conquests from the beginning of the 16th century AD onward by the Spanish and Portuguese and later the French, British and Dutch meant that little remained of the original urban-institutional structure. Only as ruins, tourist attractions or in some details can the influences of the original Incas, Aztecs and Indian peoples be rediscovered. In their place, the model of the so-called Spanish Laws was introduced: 'Leyes de Indias' (1512 and subsequent amendments). Although these laws attempted to regulate the interaction with the natives and the rights and responsibilities of the new pioneers, the *'Ordenanzas de descubrimiento, nueva población y pacificación de las Indias'* (1573) – the decrees later specified by King Philip II – also comprised orders with regard to the place, the design, the construction and the use of new settlements. These decrees were not only borrowed from Marcus Vitrivius's *De Architectura* (c. 50 BC) and Leone Alberti's *De re aedificatoria* (1443-52), but also from the specific context of the erstwhile urbanization in Spain. In contrast to elsewhere in Europe, this consisted mainly of *presidios* (military camps) or *ciudads* that had grown to become reinforced towns, as the first line of defence against Moorish invasions. Thus, with the establishment of these towns, the motive was not primarily an urban-economic one but rather a military and agrarian one, with classic agrarian activities being implemented in the surrounding countryside. [Kinsbruner 2005] In addition, the first Spanish outposts realized in South America, such as Santo Domingo (1496), Vera Cruz (1519), Buenos Aires (1536), Guatemala (1542) etc., were not exactly a success and had to be regularly relocated and/or rebuilt as a consequence of hurricanes, volcanic eruptions, flooding, an unhealthy climate or even a poor position with regard to the supply routes or the fertility of the surrounding countryside. There was every reason to tackle the mainly urban-agrarian cultivation of the new land in a more plan-oriented, almost military

City of Lawrence [Reps 1998]

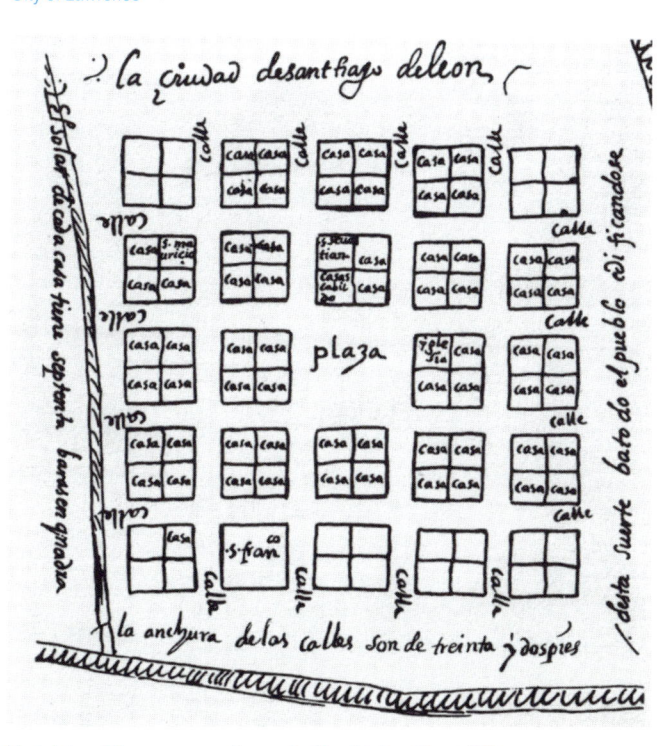

Model city of Caracas according to the Spanish laws [Benevolo 1975]

241

manner (following the example in Spain). For this purpose, Philip's *Ordenanzas* contained rules for the choice of settlement location, the structure and phasing of the built expansion, the orientation with respect to the prevailing winds, sun and river or coast, the size of the central square and the (eight) main routes from this square, the location of the most important buildings such as the prefecture, church, monasteries, perhaps a hospital, shops and/or other facilities, the situation of any production areas and waste-processing industries, such as abattoirs and tanneries, the distribution of the often-fixed living parcels according to a system of status, annuity etc., and an open mind to any future expansion. [Mundigo/Crouch 1977] The cultivation of the Americas was thus primarily urban, according to the decrees of Philip II, and was implemented rigorously by the conquistadores in an often regular chess-board pattern, scarcely walled but with cannons and bastions facing the sea because there was more to fear from pirates than from the native population. In this way, more than 900 towns arose up until the beginning of the 19th century, under the central governance of the Spanish Viceroys mainly in Central and South-east America but also in the USA and Argentina. [Verdejo et al. 2007]

This did not apply to the Portuguese, however, the other early colonists. Initially they did not wish to stay, but simply take what they could get and/or trade with the local population. [Bartelt 2008] In line with their more 'fluid empire concept' based on profit-making flows of goods instead of dominance, they restricted themselves initially to setting up a few supporting points along the coastal strip: after Sao Vicente (1530), mainly São Paulo (1532), Olinda (1537), Bahia (1549), Recife 1563, Rio de Janeiro (1565), Natal (1597) etc.[32] Something similar was also occurring with the first colonization expeditions of the English, French and Dutch in North America. Although new settlements were founded here from the beginning of the 17th century onward, including Jamestown, Virginia (1608), Quebec, Canada (1608), Plymouth, MA (1620), New Amsterdam (1622), Boston, MA (1630), Portsmouth, New Hampshire (1630), New Haven, Connecticut (1638), Annapolis, Maryland (1649), Philadelphia, Pennsylvania (1681) etc., these were generally only regarded as mere 'entry points' for the mainly agrarian population that settled in the hinterland. Only the French set up a lucrative fur trade with trading posts along the Hudson and later at other interesting locations on the Mississippi, even as far as New Orleans. After the war of independence and the acknowledgement of independence of the first United States by the British, and the withdrawal of Napoleon Bonaparte from 'the American Adventure', this definitively changed with the acceptance of the *Land Ordinance* by the *Confederation Congress* in 1785. With the aim of obtaining income to pay the debts incurred in the war of independence against the UK and to prevent the threatening unbridled occupation, Congress formulated a plan to research, sell and cultivate land for urbanization, in a structured manner. This referred by then especially to the land in the concession areas

32 This was even determined several decades previously in the so-called 'Tordesillias Treaty' with Spain, concerning the division of the South Americas, where Portugal was allocated the small eastern part and Spain the large western part of the 45° of longitude (1494). Nevertheless, these supporting points represented the supply routes for the slaves transported from Africa, who were set to work on the sugar and later cocoa and coffee plantations beyond the 45° of longitude boundary. At the same time, these supporting points were also the home bases for expeditions into the hinterland of Portuguese freebooters (often) and also of Jesuit missionaries looking for precious metals or to bring Christianity to the natives. Although until deep in the 18th century the Portuguese (coast) governor tried to limit their expeditions, to avoid war with Spain, these first supporting points began to undergo their own modest, often unplanned and organic development due to the influx of traders, missionaries, and others. This continued until well into the 19th century, when the first urban plans for Rio de Janeiro and São Paulo were drawn up in the New Republic of Brazil in the 1880s.

east of the Mississippi and north of the Ohio River, which the US had just acquired from France. To do so, it reached back to the above-described pattern of Spanish colonization, albeit in its own adapted way. The basis was formed by a fictive township measuring 36 square miles and consisting of 36 equal planes of 1 sq. mile. One field in the middle was reserved for the public school or other community facilities, and four were reserved for future functions or (if required) to compensate veterans from the war of independence. But in principle, the area was further divided in this way and offered for public sale. [Barr et al. 2006] Because, people believed they had developed a righteous system of land distribution, corresponding to the principles of modern democracy: 'Besides offering simplicity in land surveying, recording and subsequent ownership transfer, this grid system should also favor a fundamental democracy in property market participation'. [Conzen, quoted in Kostoff 1991, p.100] However, real-life practice turned out to be more recalcitrant than it appeared on paper. It seemed to work well in the initial stages. But as soon as a strong concentration of pioneers arrived and a certain area was recognized as being an urban area, it turned out to be increasingly difficult to obtain open plots, even on the edge of a town, in a more or less democratic way. Underhand dealings and capital from elsewhere turned out to be necessary in order to realize this. Moreover, the integrated urban-agrarian model that had applied to the Spanish model was abandoned and replaced by that of the US real estate managers. On the basis of its democratic liberal train of thought, the Federal government felt neither the need nor had the power to resist such developments. On the contrary, when the railway era took off in the mid-19th century, increasingly reliance was placed upon the colonization model along the main routes of private railway companies, which received the concession from the Federal government to issue hundreds of urban plots around the station. By purposeful acquisitions by France, Spain, later Mexico and even Russia, as well as an effective suppression of the native Indian peoples, the grid model could not only be rolled out across the entire country, but the expansion of the existing first colonial settlements (such as New York and Philadelphia) could also be organized in this way. According to Peter Marcuse, [1987] the closed grid was definitively replaced by the open grid as a fundamental basis of the modern capitalist economy. In this context, land became a commodity – unlimited and unbounded – that could be traded, densified, thinned out, or put to altered use in an assumingly 'democratic and open-market process'. This resulted in the share of the urban population in settlements of more than 8000 people growing from less than 5% to a little more than 30% of the total US population in the course of the 19th century. By around 1900, almost 500 of such settlements had been added, of which almost 30 had more than 100,000 inhabitants and 11 more than 250,000. [Reps 1998, p.12] It formed a suitable context for the enormous industrial and economic development that the US would make in the 20th century. On the other hand, it also formed a reason for harsh criticism of the monotony of the grid and the lack of genuinely physical openness and public space from to the 'City Beautiful Movement' and the late 20th-century revival of 'New Urbanism'. With the exception of a few stutterings and detailed elaborations even in established industrial or services metropolises (see Olmstedt in New York or Burnham in Chicago, for example) it scarcely had any impact. The model of a Central Business District with surrounding housing neighbourhoods, alternating with shopping malls, sports arenas, recreation centres and probably a few 'edge cities' has become the standard model of the North American city. Only the capital, Washington DC, has a fundamentally deviating pattern. Here, under the influence of Pierre Charles L'Enfant, an urban structure arose in the so-called 'grand manner', with long sightlines, boulevards and majestic squares, appropriate to the capital of a great nation. [Kostoff 1991, pp.209-11]

The Capital, Colonial and Delta metropolises

Recapitulating, whereas the Asian metropolis in the interplay of actor-networks can briefly be summarized as a top-down structure with scope for self-activation on the workfloor, [Sorensen 2002, Friedmann 2005] and the European urban model can be seen as a mainly bottom-up trading system with (inter)national agreements and conventions with reference to the securing of major (trading) routes, [see also Zacher/Sutton 1996] the American model is primarily characterized by far-reaching (neo-)liberalism within universal and generic basic rules of (an assumed democratic) land issue and zoning policy. [Hackworth 2007] Nevertheless, it will be self-evident that there are exceptions and/or more detailed immunities to 'the rule' which can also be traced back to the position of those metropolises with regard to one another. [see also Taylor 2004] As mentioned, I distinguish (at least provisionally) Capital, Colonial and Delta metropolises. This is preliminary based on or related to the distinction that Max Weber [1922, 1958] previously made between 'production' and 'consumption cities'. Although Weber was particularly referring to the difference between European medieval cities and those of Ancient Europe in this context, this distinction is also useful for this analytical framework in adapted form. [see also Bosker et al. 2008]

The Capitals

The classical 'consumption city', as described by Weber, was primarily the centre of government and administration, whose most important responsibility was to provide services to protect and provide structure for the inhabitants/subjects. This was done in exchange for taxes and ground rent (thus not direct but derived market transactions) for the land in the city, the surroundings, and eventually far beyond. Ultimately, the consumption city is also the city of the sovereign. His/her (power) development eventually shone upon the welfare and development of the metropolis itself. As such, it is a capital that was not necessarily situated on the major transport routes, but owed its effectiveness mainly to its more or less central position in the area that it wished to have 'under control'. As a result, it was itself the cause of the expansion of the infrastructural network instead of vice versa, in order to be able to exercise this control and display of power effectively. Baghdad, Delhi,

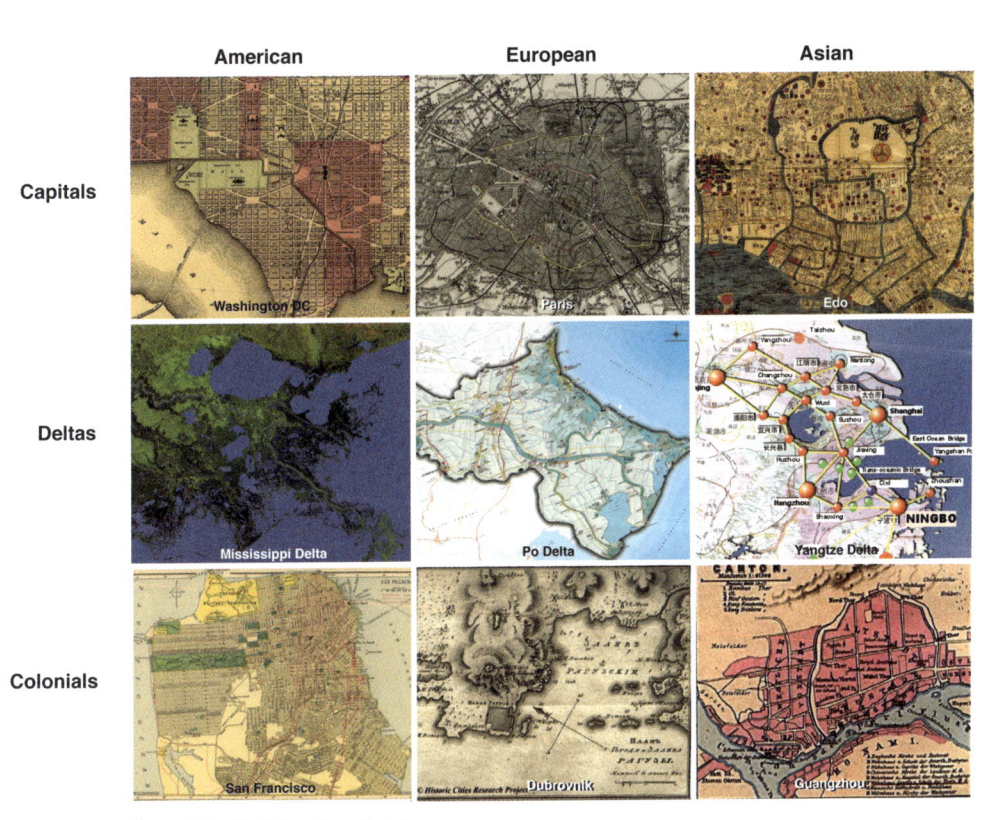

	American	European	Asian
Capitals	Washington DC	Paris	Edo
Deltas	Mississippi Delta	Po Delta	Yangtze Delta
Colonials	San Francisco	Dubrovnik	Guangzhou

The capitals, the deltas, the colonials

Moscow, Xian, Heian etc. are good examples of this kind of capital. This does not alter the fact that this central position can make it an economic and socio-cultural factor of significance. After all, a capital metropolis such as the Seoul National Capital Area is much more than a political capital. It is the financial, cultural, commercial and industrial heart of South Korea, of which Seoul, with more than ten million inhabitants, is the major city. Paris and Berlin are European, and Washington DC and Tenochtitlan (c.q. Mexico City) are American examples of such 'capital areas'. Many capitals have also become economic governing centres, with numerous national and (later) international offices, such as Moscow, Madrid, Beijing etc. Dependent on their position and actor-network history, some capitals also have a trading and/or production function, such as Tokyo or London.[33] However, they are generally enormous, centrally situated and/or accessible capitals of (inter)national political and economic governance, and therefore cities with a completely individual DNA profile in geographical-relational terms, which determines their power and the position they occupy in relation to other, perhaps much larger, metropolitan regions.

The Deltas The production city, or the city oriented to the market, was founded on the production and trade of goods, originally for the

[33] An interesting element here is the example of London, which actually has a dual profile, with primarily the dominance of the sovereign in the West End (also often focused upon landed property), and trade (c.q., original manufacture) in the East End. After the English King Edward III decided to make London his capital in around the 11th century, and especially with the UK developing as the *primus inter pares* of the Commonwealth of Nations, London developed not only as the capital of the country but also of the entire intergovernmental Commonwealth. It is also interesting to compare the migration waves to Amsterdam and London, which began to be in favour of the latter from 1650 onward. [Van Lottum 2007]

immediate surroundings but later also for the other production and trading cities at greater distances. Ades and Glaeser [1995] point out that the links with the sovereign are much less direct here, and occasionally develop in a manner more or less detached from, or autonomous of, the political entity. They are actually more oriented to their own economic regime, which is guaranteed by the sovereign in transnational contacts, but nevertheless has its own order and course of development. Whereas these 'production cities' could originally be found at the sources of raw materials and precious metals, we now find the largest production and trading metropolises near the sea, due to the importance of accessibility in a world-embracing economic system, and preferably with good hinterland connections and water, road, air and telecommunications transport hubs, if possible. At present, the largest and most rapidly growing of these cities are located in the deltas of the large rivers, such as the Yangtze Delta, Pearl River Delta, Mekong Delta, Rhine-Maas-Scheldt Delta etc. As a result of this geographical background and the more open and fluid character of trade and goods flows, there is less mention of the dominance and monopoly-forming in a single large metropolis – as that would only push up the transaction costs – but rather of a polycentric network of separate archipelagos that compete with one another to the limit. At the same time, their mercantile and industrial elites are alert to such mutual cohesion and co-operation, in order to be able to match the competitive position and the challenge from the whole in larger economic networks, and to uphold the rapid mutual exchange of goods and the market relationships (see also Box 2.1). The specific DNA profile of Metropolitan Delta Regions are mainly typified by a (competitor-colleague, i.c.) 'comcoll' attitude, which can assume forms and dominant features depending strongly on the time and place.

The Colonials The so-called 'post-colonial' or 'ex-colonial' metropolises are actually a combination of the production and consumption city discerned by Weber. Originally, the colonial settlements were mainly seen as regional outposts of the sovereign, with the aim of guaranteeing his or her power into the furthest corners of the regime. The first reinforced army camps of the Romans, the *shoens* of the Japanese empire, the reinforced outposts of the Arabic caliphates, the trading posts of the city-states of Venice and Genoa and/or the colonial settlements in the newly discovered Americas, and the coastal regions of Asia, are all excellent examples of such colonial settlements. The regime of the sovereign not only extended outward to these outposts in political and institutional terms but also, as we have seen, with regard to spatial form and representation. At the same time, Robert Home shows that the colonial settlements were thoroughly capitalist in their nature. The Dutch East India Company or the English East India Company etc. was not only oriented to the organization of trade abroad, but also to the reinforcement of agrarian production and industry on the spot. This was originally to reduce the costs of the colony or to supply the ships with provisions at the right time, and later it was purely to make profit. 'Thus colonialism was from the beginning a mixed venture, combining private enterprise with state or crown control'. [Home 1997, p.4] When the influence of the sovereign on the outposts began to wane in the course of time – perhaps as the result of a (bloody) war of liberation – or when the outposts began to adopt a more independent attitude, the second part – market orientation – increased in importance. In this, the colonial settlements turned out to be particularly successful with the passage of time, especially because of the more or less innovative pioneering mentality, unimpeded by the lock-ins that had evolved over time in the old country, and because of the (idealistic) wish to experiment with new forms of social-cultural, economic and political institutions. As such, they could effectively implement the conditions and changes demanded by 'the new era'. The DNA profile of post-colonial or ex-colonial metropolitan regions is thus often based on the traditional, classical hardware of the sovereign (the grid), but nevertheless displays a completely individual, modern, more or less liberal substantiation, organization and use (the software and orgware of the Colonial Metropolis).

References as suggestion for further research

The previously described cultural-historical actor-network characterization of typical Asian, European and American metropolises, coupled to the relational urban-typological approach described here, produced the 'DNA categorization' of present-day large metropolitan regions. And although exceptions or numerous changing combinations are possible,[34] as is the case with every classification, it is also useful to elucidate the reference research on the metropolises mentioned in this study. The often obligatory statement that research results at one place are not straightforwardly applicable in another can be further qualified here as well as intensified. At the same time, this actor-relational division can promote recommendations with regard to establishing whether or not the institutional conditions that enable successful planning strategies elsewhere could possibly have an effect here. For this purpose, the arguments presented in this work (particularly chapters two, three and four) have given an initial impulse on the basis of the metropolises visited, in comparison to the those of the EuroDelta. The arguments given can be regarded as a partial underpinning, an oversize endnote, as well as an appeal for further study and in-depth examination.

[34] For example, the profile of London with its West End and East End can be typified as a Capital and as a Delta, and Buenos Aires is both a Colonial and (nowadays) Capital metropolis.

Denver and Dallas – the metropolises of regimes, TIFs, PIDs and special districts

In line with the co-ordinates given here, Denver and Dallas-Fort Worth can be regarded as pioneer metropolises (post-colonials) of pure North American alloy. Denver arose after rumours about gold discoveries near the confluence of the Cherry Creek and the South Platte River. It was the impulse for a gold rush in the 1860s and 1870s, that lured ten of thousands across the Great Plains in search of instant wealth. Although little gold was ever found in Denver itself, the new city flourished as the main supply centre for mining operations in the Rocky Mountains. [Reps 1998, p.85] After the advent of the railways, the city developed as 'the cow city of the west' with the important Denver Livestock Exchange and the National Western Stock Show as the last point of assembly for transport over the Rockies toward the cities on the West Coast. At the end of the 20th century, that central position in the USA was again relevant for the positioning of the primary hub of United Airlines, which is now a part of the Star Alliance. Partly in combination with this, Denver now has a wide range of companies in the field of space travel and defence technology, telecommunications, biotechnology, geographical information and satellite navigation systems.

Although Dallas arose as a trading post at a fork in the Trinity River in 1846, it appeared on the international Utopian-socialist agenda in 1855 when Victor Considerant founded a *phalanstére* here, in line with the theories of Charles Fourier: *La Reunion*. [Boelens 1983] The community was granted only a short life. It did mean that many of the Utopians subsequently continue to stay in Dallas, and they have given the city an idealist image right down to this very day.

Dallas and Denver

Mobility in Dallas and Denver

Dallas Rapid Transit

Dallas Katy Trail

Denver River Platte

However, especially since the 1870s when Dallas became the junction of the railway lines from Chicago to Mexico and New York to Los Angeles, the city has enjoyed enormous growth as a trading city. In combination with the cotton industry and the discovery of the East Texas Oil Fields, it even became one of the largest financial centres of USA. In 1950, Texas Instruments also started up its activities here and this was where the first integrated circuit computer chip, microprocessor and electronic hand-held calculator first saw the light of day. Partly due to the prime-time television soap opera of the same name, Dallas became primarily known as the city of oil tycoons, where wealth, sex, intrigue and power struggles vied for primacy.

On the basis of further research into the 'relative valorization and devalorization of the housing stock' during the last three decades of that century, Waddell and others typify Dallas-Fort Worth in a well-grounded study as one of the most dispersed metropolises in the United States: 'it may be not polycentric, but rather truly fragmented'. [Waddell 1994, quoted by Hackworth 2007, p.93] In their opinion, Dallas-Fort Worth displays an 'almost kaleidoscopic pattern of housing values' and therefore also strong differentiation of various social groups. Nevertheless, bottom-up focused co-operations have arisen around specific themes and planning issues, between and among those social groups, and in conjunction with business and public society in special districts and concrete, project-oriented urban regimes. Inspiring examples in this context include the Rail-to-Trail programme – where green corridors and a sports/leisure network have been laid out on former railway beddings throughout the entire city and region – and the civic-private community building and housing/business associations around specific stopping places of the Dallas Area Rapid Transit (see also Box 5.1). Compared to West European norms, these are flexible, direct forms of thematic governance, where citizens, trade & industry and the government collaborate around so-called Common Interest Developments (CID), funded by Tax Increment Finance (TIF) in Public Improvement Districts (PID), and in Transit Oriented Developments (TOD) where possible. Similar inspiring forms of implementation-oriented tripartite co-operation can be found in Denver around the Denver Regional Transportation District (the T-REX), the Business Improvement District (BID) around the 16th ST Mall, the E 470 Public Highway Authority (funded by Tax Increment Bonds (TIB), covered by tolls and housing associations), as well as, and above all, the South Platte River Corridor, with the REI Outdoor Flagship Store and the adjoining leisure facilities to test the REI products directly. And although these forms of co-operation and funding are not without risk and therefore criticism, the important advantage of this kind of 'occasional organization' is that the more direct relationships between planning and execution also promote stronger involvement among all the participants. Next to that one can arrive at more rapid and more effective decision-making via forms of associative democracy. Here, co-operation is generated on the basis of genuinely shared interests and responsibilities. It is in exactly the increasingly fragmented and 'de-idealized' societies that such direct associations around specific, shared themes can occur, especially in new towns, new-construction areas and renovation zones. If applied prudently (see chapter four), a pioneering attitude and innovativeness can be coupled to the existing self-organizing capacity and thus to 'creative community building'.

The Pearl River- and EuroDelta – competing where possible, co-operating where necessary

Of the Metropolitan regions visited, the Pearl River Delta (PRD) and the EuroDelta are the most similar. If we do not restrict the latter to merely the estuary of the Maas and Scheldt, but include the entire area from around the Rheingebiet in the east to the Reie/Zenne tributaries in the south and to the IJssel/Vecht in the north, then this Delta region on the North Sea accommodates almost 35 million inhabitants on a surface area of 52,500 km^2. The PRD houses around 47.5 million inhabitants on approximately 48,000 km^2 (figures 2005). It contributes around 20 to 25% of the Gross National Product of China, while the EuroDelta, depending on the area, contributes between 15% (Germany), 45% (the Netherlands) and 65% (Belgium). Originally, this EuroDelta functioned mainly as a turntable for the Mediterranean and Hanseatic merchant cities, but in the course of time it has acquired a primarily east-west trade and economic orientation (see also Box 2.1). With regard to the PRD, Guangzhou (or Canton) was traditionally the most important place, first of all as the Capital of the Nanyue Kingdom, later as governmental outpost of the Han, Qing, Tang and Manchu dynasties, as well as being the most important harbour in China for foreign trade. From the mid-nineteenth century onward, this prominent position in the Delta was increasingly assumed by the (former) British colonial outpost of Hong Kong, and by that of Portugal, Macau, to a certain extent.

The EuroDelta is also a European variant, and the PRD a purely Asian actor-network variant of this type of Metropolitan Region. In fact, in the case of the PRD, one might expect powerful (plan-oriented) governance from above, certainly after the transfer of Hong Kong (1997) and Macau (1999) to China by the UK and Portugal respectively. And this is also the case to a certain degree, as is shown by the economic plan politics and the construction of major works such as the High-Speed Line from Beijing to Ghuangzhou, with a branch toward Hong Kong. But at the same time, the Pearl River Delta will have a 'one country, two system' context in administrative and institutional terms until the middle of the 21st century, and the PRD consists of 11 relatively independently operating provinces of which two were designated by Deng Xiaoping at the time as Special Economic Zones – Shenzhen and Zhuhai – with more liberal rules in the field of foreign investment, international trade and capitalist means of production. Nevertheless, a kind of uncriticized and generally accepted 'Front Shops-Back Factories Model (FSBF)' was accepted here until recently, in which Hong Kong primarily developed as a window on the world in the

Hong Kong and Tokyo

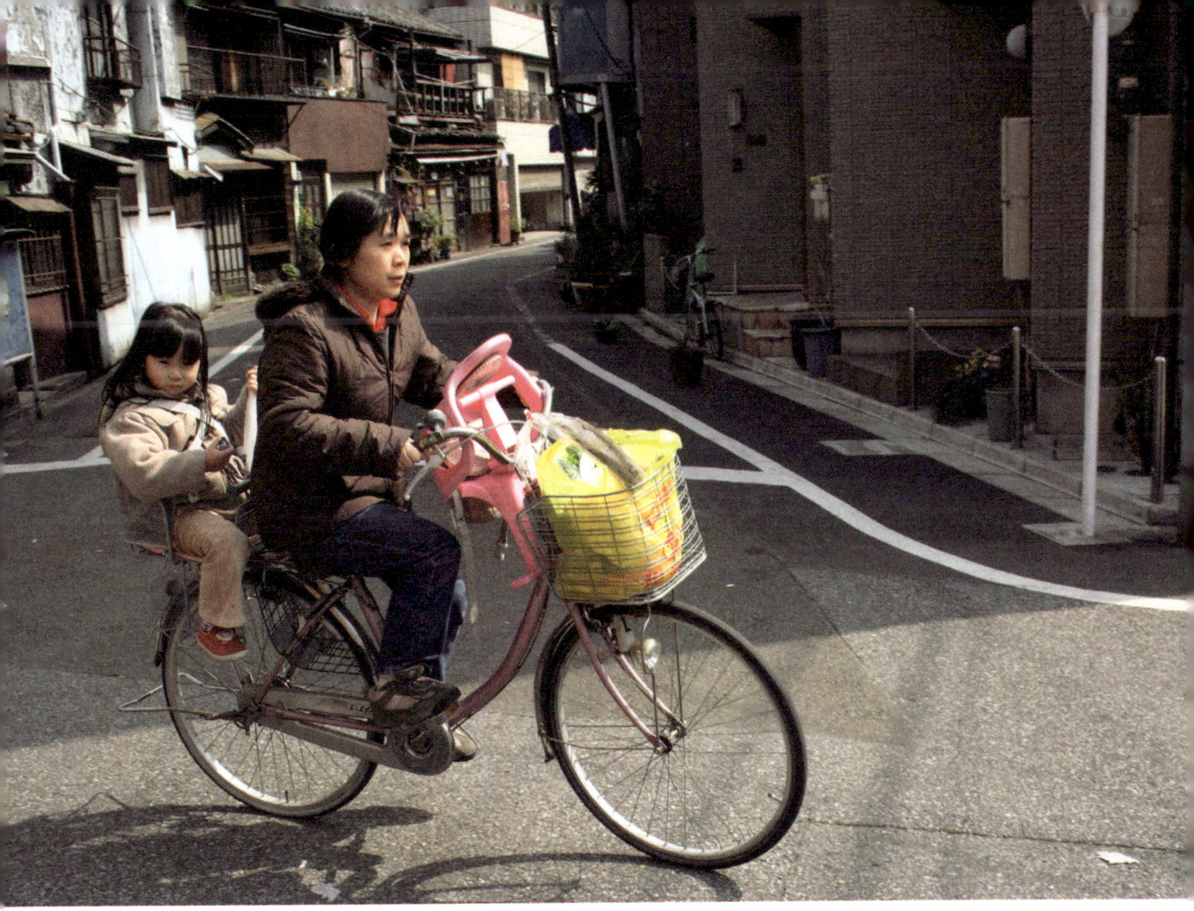

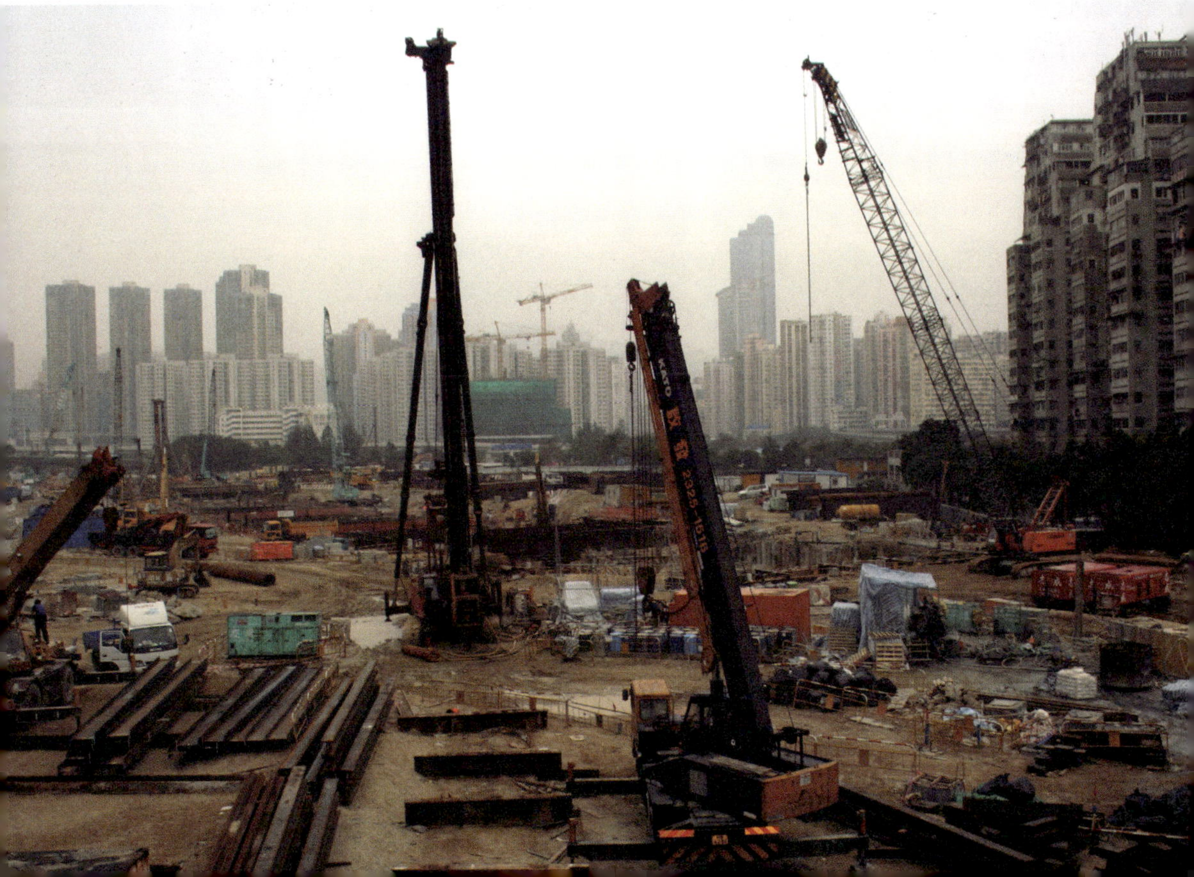

Airport of Hong Kong

Brainports in Guangzhou and Tokyo

Seaport of Tokyo

field of International Head Offices, Designing, Marketing and Financial Control, while the rest of the PRD mainly specialized in the area of production, raw materials, and the corresponding T&D facilities. In turn, Macau developed in this same period into the largest gambling city in the world, easily displacing Las Vegas from its position at the top of the list. [Sit et al. 2006, p.18] In line with this FSBF model, the inner-city airport of Hong Kong was also renovated and relocated to Lantau Island, being simultaneously incorporated into a kind of Multi-Airport System in which Lantau International Airport should orient its activities increasingly to international hub functions and low-fare flights, Zhuhai to be concentrated more on freight, Shenzhen on the low-cost carriers, and Macau on inland destinations. As a component of this plan, there was not only mention of the development of an extensive water transport between these specialized airports but also of the construction of a new tunnel/bridge between Hong Kong – Lantau Island and Macau annex Zhuhai, in this case, the western shore of the PRD. [Van Hoogstraten et al. 2007]

However, the Delta hinterland – and particularly Guangzhou – is beginning to orient itself increasingly to management functions, as well as facilitating high-tech and the knowledge industry. This is manifest not only in the International Congress Centre and the University Town of 10 top universities with possibly 300,000 students in the long term, but also in the nearby bio-island directed toward companies and research facilities in the field of Life Sciences. [Van den Bosch et al. 2007] At the same time, the central authorities in Beijing have assigned it privileges similar to those allocated to Shenzhen and Zhuhai. Accordingly, increasing competition is arising between the separate urban centres of the Pearl River Delta, although this is still within standard Asian relationships. It is particularly expressed in the alternatives proposed by the urban archipelagos in the north – Guangzhou, Dongguan, Heimen, Nansha, Foshnan, etc. – which plead for the above-mentioned Hong Kong-Lantau-Macau-Zhuhai connection with more northerly landings, as well as the expansion of, or even completely new, deep-water harbours further inland. [Li & Wang quoted in Sit et al. 2006, pp.402-23, 435-46] At the same time, the people and cities in the PRD are wary of the enormous development that the Yangtze Delta (Shanghai-Nanjing-Suzhou-Hangzhou etc.) is currently going through. [Zhang, quoted in Sit et al. pp.551-67] There too, the urban setting and the DNA of the Pearl River Delta is increasingly beginning to resemble the 'comcoll mentality' of the EuroDelta, [see also Boelens/Taverne 2009] although an overarching Delta bond seems to be very distant in the latter, much more so than in the PRD, despite or perhaps because of the EU and the Benelux.

Buenos Aires and São Paulo – trans-colonial communities in a Spanish and Portuguese variant

Finally, we come to Buenos Aires and São Paulo. These former colonial settlements of Spain and Portugal respectively were compared with one another and with the EuroDelta, particularly with regard to the theme of *transnational communities* discussed in chapter three. The reason for this was that in both metropolitan regions, there are hardly any inhabitants issuing from the original native or colonial population. Especially from the end of the 19th century onward, these metropolises were populated by mainly immigrants of European origin in less than 150 years (three to four generations). For example between 1857 and 1940, around 3 million Italians and 2 million Spaniards, almost 250,000 French, almost 200,000 Poles, Russians and Turks, as well as 150,000 Germans and around 100,000 Austrians, British and even Portuguese (a total of more than 6.5 million people) immigrated to the greater Buenos Aires region.[35] [Census Argentina 2005] The reason was not only the economic and political malaise in which Europe found itself in 1900, but particularly the enormous economic potential of Buenos Aires, thanks to the opening up of the relatively fertile hinterland with the railways and the extraction of the raw materials that were available there. Thanks to the Spanish Laws, the city offered a more or less appropriate settlement structure and new development potential for (especially Mediterranean) Europeans. After all, there was a certain order and urban infrastructure present, without the restrictions of the old country, which provided opportunities for a strong but also innovative and modern business development.

[35] The central city grew in this period from less than 50,000 to around 3 million inhabitants, to remain stable at that level.

The situation in São Paulo was different. As mentioned, the Portuguese did not originally come to Brazil to stay but only to seize what they could get. Until deep into the 19th century, São Paulo was therefore not much more than a point of support for Jesuit missionaries, or otherwise a home base for *bandeirantes*, who, in contrast to what had been specified in the *Tordesillas Treaty* between Portugal and Spain (1494) concerning the division of South America, spread out across the hinterlands in an attempt to get their hands on gold, silver and slaves. It was only after the declaration of the independent Republic of Brazil and the formal abolition of slavery in 1888 that São Paulo began to grow substantially, from a little more than 50,000 to almost 1.5 million inhabitants in 1940. It was the period of Brazilian coffee expansion, which attracted mainly Italian, Portuguese, Spanish, Syrian, Lebanese, as well as Jewish and Japanese migrants. After the Second World War, when the economy of São Paulo underwent a transition toward the American car and production industries, that the migrant flows altered. These then came from the inland areas of Brazil itself, especially Minas Gerais, rather than from European countries. In this way, São Paulo grew further so that it now has a population of around 11 million (almost 20 million in the whole Grande São Paulo region).

In contrast to the case in Buenos Aires, this did not happen in São Paulo in accordance with the Spanish Laws or on a fixed grid, but initially in an organic way and as it more or less suited the elite in geographical and institutional terms. It was only in the last decade of the 19th century that the first spatial planning policies arose. But these concerned mainly the inner city and the neighbourhoods of the coffee barons. These plans were primarily aimed at defending these zones against 'pollution', (hygienic) neglect, and further densification. Accordingly, the majestic Avenida de Paulista was inaugurated in 1891, as a classical example of high-quality urban living. [Rolnik 2008] The rest, in other words, mostly the neighbourhoods of the labourers and migrants, was abandoned to individual initiatives and speculation. Nevertheless, in 1930, the architect and later Mayor Prestes Maia produced a more extensive *Avenida plan*, based on the ideas of Baron Haussmann in Paris, and after the Second World War (when the change had been effected from trams to cars and diesel buses), the American Robert Moses came up with a concentric *Expressway plan* that stretched far into the region. However, the above-mentioned urban centre-periphery organization continued to be the guideline, in the sense that a sharp distinction remained between the various classes and an almost schizophrenic planning system in which 'the wealthier central parts of the city continued to be hyper-supervised, while the urbanization of the *pereferia* was left to private owners with little or no respect for building codes or planning norms. [Caldiera and Maricato, quoted in Sá 2007, p.14] However, home ownership was pursued as a more or less liberal principle by both the wealthier and the poorer classes, so that there was scarcely mention of public housing (initiated by the state of the private sector). The migrant groups thus generally had to rely on their own resourcefulness. Here, there is a high degree of self-organization and sense of collective responsibility on the part of like-minded migrants or migrants with similar backgrounds. They survived right down to the present day, across generations and even after people have moved up in society and away to another neighbourhood (see the example of Liberdade in chapter three). The same applies to favelas such as Paraisópolis and Heliopolis in São Paulo. In this framework, too, there is a high degree of social (self-)organization and there is a fertile breeding ground for 'participatory democracy experiments'. [Bos et al. 2008] Nevertheless, even the wealthier population groups are beginning to settle in the (former) periphery and a vacuum is forming in the centre. Rolnik [2008] indicates that there was a registered demand for 200,000 houses in 2005, whereas around 400,000 in the centre were empty. As a consequence of this, the traditional sharp segregation is beginning to blur and puissant wealth – albeit enclosed in gated communities – directly adjoins manifest poverty now and again. This is completely different in Buenos Aires, where, on the basis of the grid, a sharper division yet a more supple transition between the wealthier and poorer neighbourhoods exists, and the migrant groups – apart from a few exceptions (such as Villa 31) – are less tightly organized. Whereas in Buenos Aires the liberal, self-reliant urban society has formed on the austere grid of the former sovereign, this (institutional and spatial) basis appears to be completely absent in São Paulo. It is exactly here that flagrant excesses arise, of which not only the planning system, the direct spatial confrontation of great wealth and poverty, but also the helicopter density are expressions. This last feature is not only to avoid hour-long tailbacks but also for reasons of pure security (robbery, kidnapping).

Conclusion in the form of an assignment

Recapitulating, Denver and Dallas prove to be typical American post-colonial metropolises, in which physically a massive open and flexible grid-structure prevails, as a fertile basis for leading actors in the field of real estate and project-development. On *soft- and orgware* level however, also creative and effective associations occur between main stake- and shareholders in the public, business and civic society with respect to various themes and items. It is flanked by an open and effective set of instruments on a financial, legal as socio-cultural and spatial level as well.

The Pearl River Delta in turn, although it was and is strictly zoned and structured by the central government in the Capital of Xian, Hangzhou, and later Beijing, it also proves to be a genuine Delta Metropolises consisting of competing regions and nodes. Leading actors are here not only the political elites of the local and regional governments, but also the CEO's and entrepreneurs of logistic services, harbour industries, aviation, high tech and the like, which organise their 'comcoll networks' themselves. They compete and coordinate their strategies, in order to evolve their global markets to a maximum effect and minimalise transaction costs at the same time.

And last but not least Buenos Aires and São Paulo have proven and still prove to be post-colonial settings in which self-organisation is not only flourishing, but in fact also demanded to survive in a global, networked world. Here the main actors are still the individual businessmen, civic agents and migrants, which are able to organize mutual interest around specific items, options or challenges on an ever increasing and more complex scale. The main difference between Buenos Aires and São Paulo is that the first is a more strict Spanish and the latter a more open Portuguese kind of metropolis, in which the latter seems to get the biggest social challenge in regulating the ever increasing and direct conflicts between the *haves* and *have-nots*.

The relational co-ordinates presented here appear therefore to be not only useful to clarify metropolitan regions, reveal glocal DNA and trace possible background issues, but may also provide further insight in lessons to be learned from this type of actor-relational research. In the arguments presented above, several components have been mentioned, such as the conditions under which a multi-airport system can function, the way in which a cultural identity of underprivileged areas can be guaranteed despite improvements in the social position of their original inhabitants, under which conditions people in deltas can pursue metropolis-forming, in which context associative democracy has a real chance of survival, etc. The translation of those inspirational conditions, as well as the precision with which this ought to occur requires further and more accurate institutional and actor-oriented deepening. I regard the provisional impulses and referential results given here therefore first and foremost as an inspiration, challenge and possible invitation for further research. Actor-relational research could deliver new analytical glocal insights and help to improve planning in an increasing urbanizing world.

São Paulo

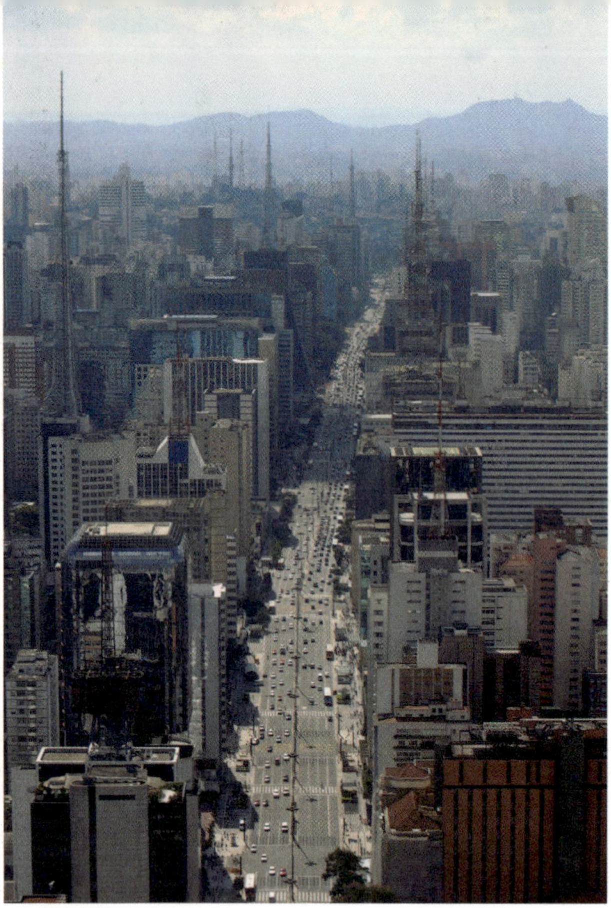

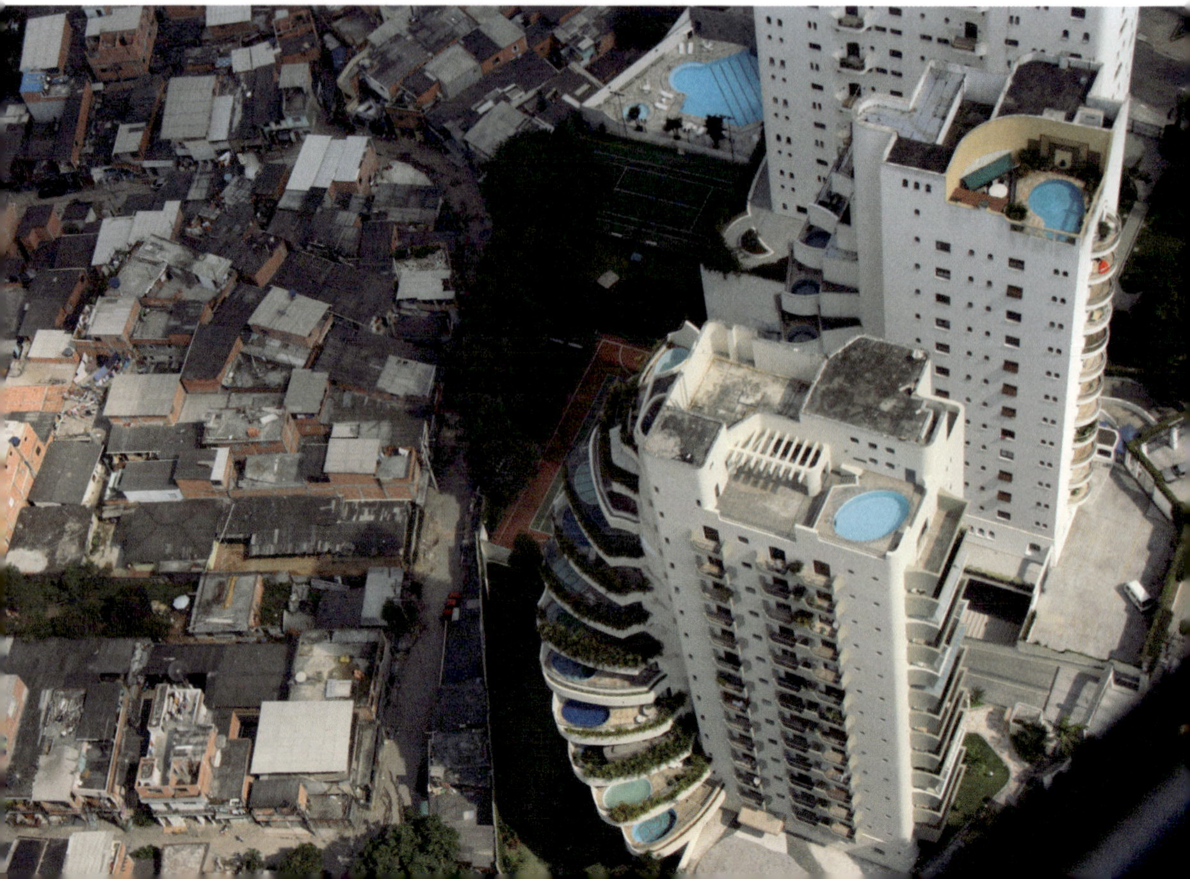

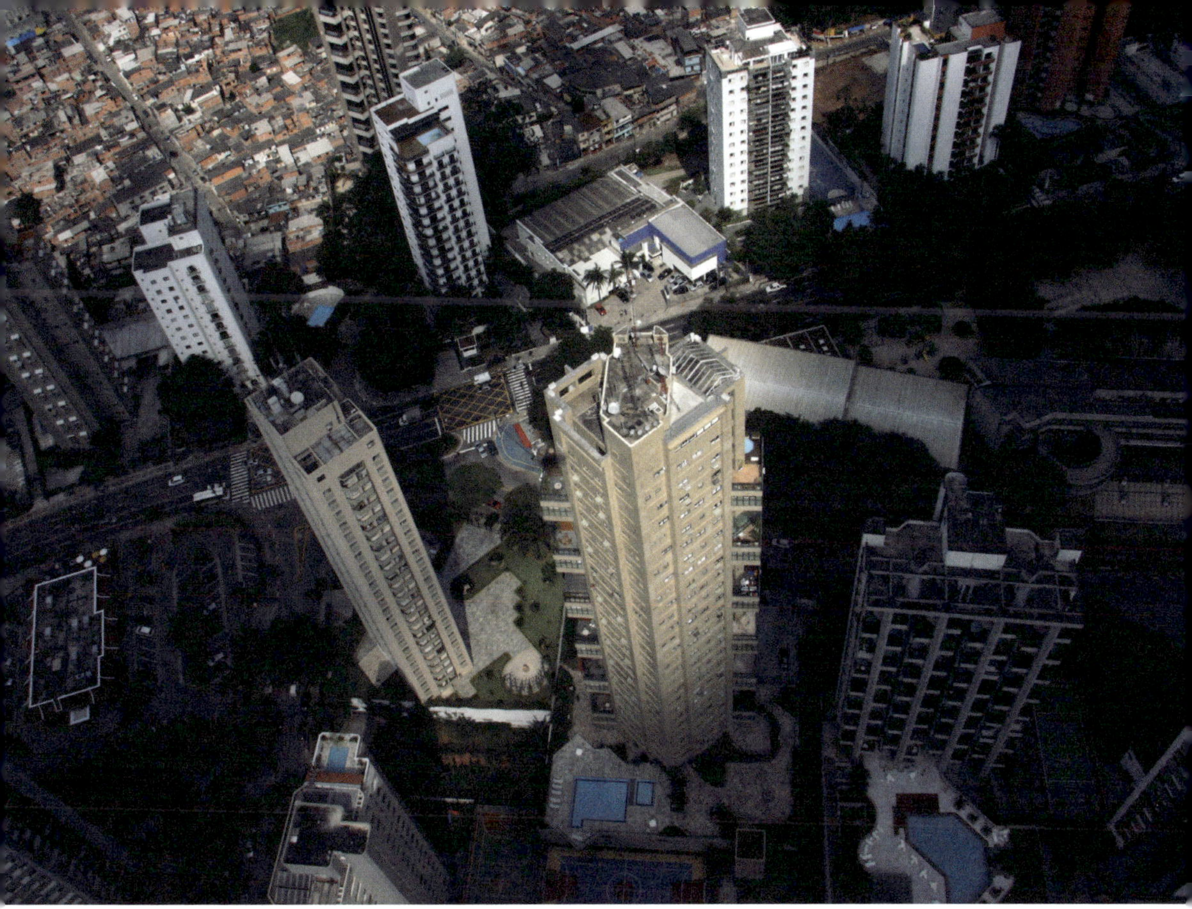

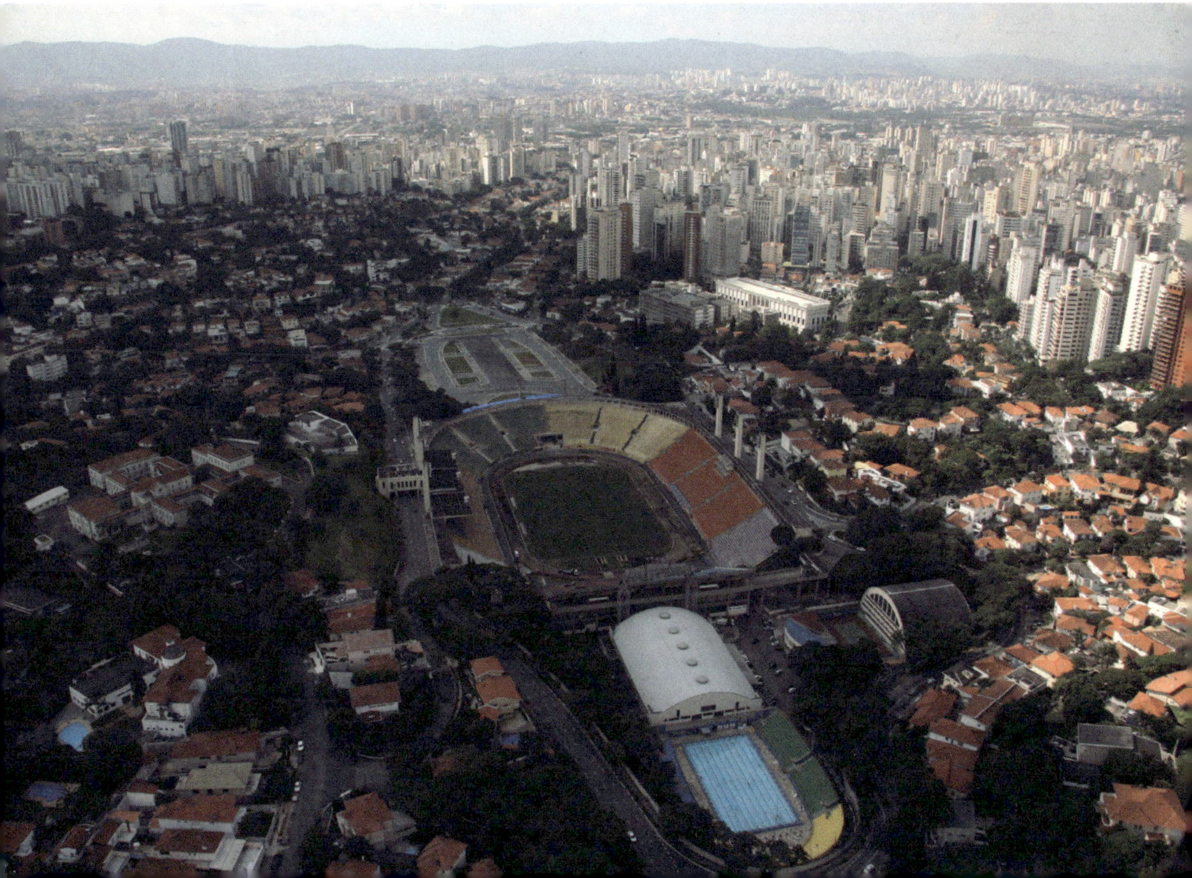

Liberdade, Japanese in São Paulo

Sem Tieto and Heliopolis

Expats environment

Expats environment

Indexes

Annexes

PhD projects during 2004-2009

Title Glocal alliances at major airports – the case Schiphol
Supervisors prof.dr.ir. L. Boelens, prof.dr. O. Atzema, prof.drs. G. Cerfontaine, Dr. Bart Wissink
PhD drs. Bart de Jong
Financing BSIK 8.1 + Schiphol Group
Term 2006-2009
Planning PhD expected in 2009

Title Rotterdam harbour – European logistic core region
Supervisors prof.dr. O. Atzema, prof.dr.ir. L. Boelens
PhD drs. Amanda Mackloet
Financing BSIK 8.2 + Rotterdam Port Authority
Term 2005-2007
Result preliminary closure

Title Landing of an airport – the case Charles de Gaulle
Supervisors prof.dr. O. Atzema, prof.dr.ir. L. Boelens
PhD drs. Mariëlle Prins
Financing private funding
Term 2008-2011
Planning PhD expected 2011

Title Self-organization in urban development
Supervisors prof.dr.ir. L. Boelens, prof.dr. W. Hafkamp
PhD ir. Beitske Boonstra
Financing TNO, NICIS, third parties
Term 2008-2011
Planning PhD expected 2011

Master theses during 2004-2009

Title Ruimtelijk-economische impact low-cost luchthavens
Candidate Wouter van Leeuwen
Planning April-December 2004

Title Planning kwaliteit Stedenbaan Zuid-Holland
Candidate Robert Jan Arts
Planning September 2004-March 2005 (incl. fieldwork)

Title De keuze van de reiziger
Candidate Teije Goris
Planning November 2004-May 2005

Title Multi-Airport-Systemen; Een toekomst voor Schiphol?
Candidate Niels Herber
Planning November 2004-July 2005 (incl. fieldwork)

Title Concurrentie tussen modaliteiten in een multi-airport systeem
Candidate Erik Brave
Planning November 2004-July 2005

Title The only way is up
Candidate Rob v.d. Sande
Planning September 2005-October 2006 (incl. fieldwork)

Title Kennismaken met netwerken in Twente
Candidate Marjan v.d. Bosch
Planning February 2007-July 2007

Title Airfreight at Schiphol
Candidate Tom van Es
Planning February 2007-October 2007 (incl. fieldwork)

Title Stadshavens Rotterdam
Candidate Arjen Koene
Planning February 2007-January 2008 (incl. fieldwork)

Title Co-siting in het Rotterdams haven en industrieel complex
Candidate Gijsbert Damen
Planning February 2007-June 2008 (incl. fieldwork)

Title Classic diaspora
Candidate Maaike Besemer
Planning February 2008-July 2008

Title Mondialisering en transnationalisme
Candidate Ilse Meier
Planning February 2008-July 2008

Title Transnationale gemeenschappen in de Aandachtswijken
Candidate Jan Breukelman
Planning February 2008-November 2008

Title Transnational communities en Krachtwijken
Candidate ir. Carolien Bos
Planning February 2008-end 2009

Research journeys during 2005-2008

Title Mobile Assets I
Object Field research on the pro's and con's of district-planning in the USA
Subjects Aiport planning
Transit oriented development planning
Leisure/greenpark planning
Cities Denver, Dallas-Fort Worth
Added master Maurits Schaafsma
Period 10th-20th of December 2005 + second period Masterprogramme
Research members
Christiaan Blonk (University of Utrecht)
Maartje Dros (Design Academy)
Björn Hondelink (Ministry of VROM)
Willemieke Hornis (Spatial Planbureau of the Netherlands)
Wim Heiko Houtsma (Ministry of VROM)
Maarten Jenniskens (Ministry of VROM)
Arjen Koekoek (University of Utrecht)
Philline Krosse (Technical University of Delft)
Eva Stegmeijer (University of Amsterdam)
Jan Terwecoren (University of Gent)
Loes van der Vegt (University of Utrecht)
Mark Verbeet (University of Utrecht)
Christiaan Wallet (Ministry of VROM)
Sebastiaan de Wilde (Holland Railconsult)
Jan van der Zwan (University of Utrecht)
Budget €40,000
Financed partly by VROM, Holland Railconsult & private funding
Planning 6 weeks preparation
2 weeks research journey
5 weeks reworking and reporting results
Results
Report 'Airports Reviewed', University of Utrecht 2006
Report 'TOD&D', University of Utrecht 2006
Report 'PMC Dallas-Denver', University of Utrecht 2006
Seminar on April 24 2006 at Ministry of VROM
Exhibition in April 2006 at Ministry of VROM and in May 2006 at the University of Utrecht
Newspaper Mobile Assets I

Title Mobile Assets II
Object Field research on spatial economic planning in Asia
Subjects Mainport planning
Gateway planning
Brainport planning
Cities Hong Kong (PRD), Tokyo
Added Master Michiel van Wijk
Period 10th-20th of March 2007 + third period Masterprogramme
Research members
Frank van den Beuken (Municipality of Rotterdam)
Marjan van den Bosch (University of Utrecht)
Gijs Broos (Development Agency Rotterdam)
Sytske de Crocq (Ministry of VROM)
Gijsbert Damen (University of Utrecht)
Tom van Es (University of Utrecht)
Christiane van Gent (Municipality of Amsterdam)
Erik van Hoogstraten (Ministry of VROM)
Caroline van Kampen (University of Amsterdam)
Arjen Koene (University of Utrecht)
Tim van Moer (University of Amsterdam)
Saskia Newrly (Ministry of VROM)
Susanne Teunissen (University of Utrecht)
Susanne Vleeshouwers (Ministry of VROM)
Budget €50,000
Financed partly by Ministry of VROM, municipalities of Amsterdam and Rotterdam & private funds
Planning 6 weeks preparation
2 weeks research journey
5 weeks reworking and reporting results
Results
Report 'Mainportplanning' Utrecht University 2007
Report 'Gatewayplanning' Utrecht University 2007
Report 'Brainportplanning' Utrecht University 2007
Seminar on April 27 2007 at Ministry of VROM
Four Masterthesises (see above)

Title Mobile Assets III
Object Field research on transnational communities in South America
Subjects Classic diaspora
Modern diaspora
Post-Modern diaspora
Cities Buenos Aires, São Paulo
Added Masters Francisco Colombo
Roberto Rocco de Campos Pereira
Period 8th-24th of March 2008 + third period Master-programme
Research members
Wander van Beek (University of Utrecht)
Maaike Besemer (University of Utrecht)
Bart van Bleek (Ministry of VROM)
Caroline Bos (University of Utrecht)
Nicole Bosch (Municipality of Amsterdam)
Jan Breukelman (University of Utrecht)
Ton Dassen (Netherlands Environment Assesment Agency)
Judith van El (HaagWonen)
Rob Folkert (Netherlands Environment Assesment Agency)
Bregit Jansen (HaagWonen)
Ilse Kessels (Com.Wonen)
Juanita Mattemaker (Province of South Holland)
Ilse Meier (University of Utrecht)
Hanna Lára Pálsdóttir (Ministry of VROM)
Rachèl van Rooijen (Het Oosten)
Budget €52,000
Financed partly by VROM, HaagWonen, Het Oosten, Com.Wonen,
Municipality of Amsterdam & Province of South Holland
Planning 6 weeks preparation
2 weeks research journey
5 weeks reworking and reporting results
Results
Report 'Classic diaspora – Jews and Japanese' University of Utrecht 2008
Report 'Modern diaspora & power districts' University of Utrecht 2008
Report 'Exit Expats' University of Utrecht 2008
Seminar on April 24 2008 in Ministry of VROM
Five Masterthesises (see above)

Index of names

Abbe, H.J. van 86
Abercrombie, Patrick 18, 168, 206
Aboutaleb, Ahmed 126
Ades, Alberto F. 245
Adorno, Theodor 20
Alberti, Leone 240
Albrechts, Louis 186, 193
Alterman, R. 19
Amin, Ash 228
Anderson, Benedict 25, 102, 159
Appadurai, Arjun 25, 103
Aristotle 148
Asscher, Lodewijk 81
Atzema, Oedzge 12, 57, 67, 90

Bader, Veit 151, 189
Bakker, Ineke 11
Bakker, Riek 183, 186
Bakker-Schut, F. 19
Beck, Ulrich 25
Bennett, Edward 18
Berlage, Hendrik Pieter 18
Berndt, Heide 239
Beuningen, Daniël G. van 61-63, 74
Blijdendijk, Frank 12
Boggs, Jeffrey 41
Bolan, Richard 19
Bollens, John 158, 159
Boonstra, Cor 91
Boot, Tom 12
Boschma, Ron 67
Bosma, Koos 18
Boyle, Paul 105
Brenner, Neil 26, 27
Brenner, Thomas 45
Brook, Daniel 147
Brückenhaus, Gustav 86
Bruijn, Henk de 12
Burnham, Daniel 18
Burnham, James 66

Callon, Michael 185, 189, 191-193
Calthorpe, Peter 210

Cammen, Han van der 7, 8, 183, 186
Casseres, Joël Meier De 18, 19, 86, 87
Castells, Manuel 102, 105, 115, 132
Cerfontaine, Gerlach 12, 84
Cervero, Robert 208, 210, 211
Chabot, Abraham Sebastiaan 61
Chabot, Jean Joseph 61
Charlemagne 238
Charles V 155
Chesbrough, Henry 91
Chiba 209
Christaller, Walter 44, 95, 101
Cohen, Joshua 151, 164, 189, 196
Colombo, Francisco 12
Connolly, William 149
Considerant, Victor 250
Coughlin, Pete 211
Cramer, Jacqueline 5, 11

De Gaulle, Charles (president of France) 50
Dekker, Wisse 91
Dekker, Sybille 11
Deleuze, Gilles 170, 171, 174, 177-179
Dellaert, Jan 75
Dicken, Peter 36, 47
Disney, Walt 218
Doevendans, Kees 101
Doorn J.A.A. van 101
Douglas, Donald 74
Draaisma, Jaap 128
Duncan, Michael 210

L'Enfant, Pierre Charles 244
Engbersen, Godfried 118, 122, 126
Engels, Friedrich 149
Engelsdorp-Gastelaars, Rob 92
Etzkowitz, Henry 92

Fainstein, Norman 182
Fainstein, Susan 12, 182, 196
Faludi, Andreas 20, 31
Farnese, Alexander 118
Fentener van Vlissingen, F.G. 74
Flap, Henk 25

Florida, Richard 36, 39
Fokker, Anthony 74-78
Fourier, Charles 250
Fraser, Nancy 149
Frederiks, K.J. 19
Friedmann, John 44
Fukuyama, Francis 147

Gans, Herbert 101
Geddes, Patrick 18, 168
Giddens, Anthony 40, 182
Glaeser, Edward L. 245
Goodwill, Julie 210
Goudriaan, Albert 61
Granpré Molière, Marinus Jan 87, 101
Guattari, Félix 170, 171, 174, 177, 179

Habermas, Jürgen 20, 148, 183
Hägerstrand, Torsten 27
Hall, Peter 19, 49, 50, 235
Hall, Peter A. 58
Hardt, Michael 149
Harvey, David 27, 147, 149
Hassani Idrisi, Abderrahman 130
Haussmann, Georges-Eugène 128, 265
Healey, Patsy 148, 186
Heerma, Enneüs 162
Hemel, Zef 12
Hillier, Jean 170
Hirst, Paul 151, 152, 154, 164, 189, 196
Home, Robert 246
Hooimeijer, Pieter 12
Hoornstra, Annius 12
Horkheimer, Max 20
Hughes, Ken 211

Innes, Judith 148
Ito 209

Jacobs, Jane 240
Janelle, Don 28

Kempen, Ronald van 162
Kleisterlee, Gerard 91

Klerk, Len de 64
Klink, Arjen van 66
Klugt, Cornelis van der 91
Kock, Elize de 11
Kohr, Martin 147
Kröller, Anthony 74
Kreukels, Ton 9, 12, 186
Krol, Marloes 91
Krul, Joop 12
Kuijpers, Chris 11

Laan, Eberhard van der 32
Laar, Paul van der 63
Laclau, Ernesto 149-151
Langen, Gustav 18
Latour, Bruno 189-193
Law, John 189, 192
Leerkes, Arjen 126
Lefebvre, Henri 150, 228
Lefort, Claude 149
Le Goff, Jacques 237, 238
Lemstra, Derk 146
Leyasu, Tokugawa 226, 234
Leydesdorff, Loet 92
Lohuizen, Theo van 168, 170
Lopion, prof. 112
Lottum, Jelle van 118
Luxembourg, Rosa 149
Lyotard, Jean-Francois 11

Mandele, Karel Paul van der 61, 62
Marcuse, Peter 243
Markussen, Ann 44
Marx, Karl 149
Massey, Doreen 27, 31, 183
Meer, Myrke van der 91
Mees, Marten 61, 62
Merton, Robert 122, 139
Meyer, Han 63
Mitterrand, François (president of France) 50
Monchy, Engel P. de 61
Monmonier, Mark 168
Mommaas, Hans 12
Moses, Robert 265

Morand, Paul 29
Mouffe, Chantal 149-151
Mori, Hiroshi 19
Mujica, Padre 112, 115
Murdoch, Jonathan 191
Murray, Charles 101

Napoleon Bonaparte 50, 242
Negri, Antonio 149
Nieuwpoort, Nick 12
Nycolaas, Jacques 160

Ohland, Gloria 211
Olmstedt, Frederick Law 244
Oostwegel, Camille 219
Oranje-Nassau, Wilhelmina H.P.M. (Queen of the Netherlands) 74
Oranje-Nassau, Willem I (King of the Netherlands) 85
Oranje-Nassau-Zorreguieta, Maxima (Princess of the Netherlands) 101
Osinga, Johan 11
Ostrom, Elinor 151
Ovink, Henk 11
Oyen, H.J.H. van 19

Pálsdóttir, Hanna Lára 12
Pateman, Carole 149
Perrenod, Virginia 159
Perry, Clarence 101
Philip II (King of Spain) 240, 242
Philips, Anton 84-86
Philips, Gerard 84-86
Pincoffs, Lodewijk 61, 62
Pirenne, Henri 237
Plate, Antoine 63
Plesman, Albert 75
Poincaré, Raymond (president of France) 50
Polin, Robert 147
Pompidou, Georges (president of France) 50
Porter, Michael 44
Purcell, Mark 148-151, 186

Quay, Jan de 87

Raadschelders, J.C.N. 154, 157
Rantisi, Norma 41
Reagan, Ronald (president of the USA) 205
Richmond, Anthony 105
Reijndorp, Arnold 101
Rocco de Campos Pereira, Roberto 12
Rogers, Joel 164, 189
Rolnik, Raquel 266
Rijckevorsel, Huibert van 63
Ruys, Willem 61, 63

Said, Edward 101
Salhi, Abdel 130
Sally, Razeen 48
Sanders, Wies 12, 166-179
Sarkozy, Nicolas (president of France) 50
Sassen, Saskia 48
Schaafsma, Maurits 12
Schama, Simon 50
Scharpf, Fritz 186
Shaw, Robert 211
Smith, Peter Michael 102, 103
Snel, Erik 126, 131
Soskice, David 49, 58
Spit, Tejo 12
Stolk, Adriaan Pieter van 63
Stone, Clarence 182
Strijbis, Klaas 12
Sutton, Brent 27
Swyngedouw, Erik 149

Taylor, Peter 25, 44, 101
Taverne, Ed 12, 50
Thatcher, Margaret (premier of the UK) 50, 205
Thrift, Nigel 12, 27, 30, 183, 228
Timmer, Jan 91
Toonen, Th.A.J. 154, 157

Unwin, Raymond 18
Urry, John 29

Valenzuela, José 115
Velzen, Nico van 162
Verhaagen, Piet 87
Vink, Jasper 19
Visser, Evert-Jan 57, 67
Vogelaar, Ellen 31, 32, 98, 101, 123
Vorm, Willem van der 61, 63
Vuuren, Louis van 18
Valk, Arnold van der 20
Vitrivius, Marcus 240

Waddell, Jenifer 256
Wagt, Marijn van der 11
Weber, Max 244, 246
Weinrich, Harald 148
Wellman, Barry 101
Wever, Egbert 91
Whitley, Richard 48
Wilkinson, Richard 147
Wijk, Michel van 12
Wirth, Louis 240
Woodworth, Nancy 159

Xiaoping, Deng (president of China) 257

Yeung, Henri 41, 47, 49
Yücesoy, Eda 126

Zacher, Mark 27
Zwaan, Bert van der 12
Zwan, Arie van der 52

Index of places

Aalsmeer 57
Aken 85
Almere 131
Amstelveen 134
Angers 232
Antwerp 12, 25, 63, 85, 102, 107, 118, 198
Amstelveen 134
Amsterdam 7, 12, 25, 26, 36, 37, 44, 47, 57, 62, 63, 74, 75, 80-82, 84-86, 91, 98, 102, 117, 128, 133, 134, 152, 160, 168, 170, 186, 202, 212
Annapolis 242
Arnhem 160

Baghdad 244
Bahia 242
Beijing 44, 47, 231, 234, 245, 257, 263, 266
Bergen op Zoom 62
Berlin 44, 245
Bloemendaal 134
Bologna 239
Borne 92
Boston 242
Bruges 44, 107, 118, 238
Braunschweig 85
Brussels 25, 92, 107, 118
Buenos Aires 11, 104, 107-109, 112, 114-117, 121, 122, 229, 230, 240, 263, 264, 265, 266

Canton 44, 210, 231, 257
Capelle a/d IJssel 134
Charlotte 47
Chicago 18, 211, 244, 256
Copenhagen 205, 206, 208

Dallas-Fort Worth 11, 211, 228-230, 250, 256, 266
Darlington 28
Delft 127, 134, 212
Den Bosch 98
Den Haag/The Hague 134, 160, 162, 212

Delhi 238
Denver 11, 228-230, 250, 256, 266
Dongguan 263
Dordrecht 62

Ede 98
Edo 234, 235
Eindhoven 18, 52, 53, 55, 56, 58, 84, 85
Enschede 5, 131
EuroDelta (Rhine, Maas Scheldt Delta) 50, 51, 61, 202, 223, 229, 238, 244, 246, 254, 257, 263, 264

Foshnan 263
Frankfurt 26, 47

Genk 214
Genoa 44, 238, 246
Gent 107
Gouda 98
Groningen 186
Guangzhou 231, 257, 263

Haarlem 118, 134, 212
Haarlemmermeer 57, 81, 84
The Hague 134, 160, 162, 212
Hamburg 238
Hang 231
Hangzhou 231, 263, 266
Hasselt 92
Heemstede 134
Heerlen 214
Heian 234, 235, 244
Heimen 263
Helmond 92, 93
Helsingborg 206
Helsinger 206
Helsinki 85
Hong Kong 208, 209, 212, 234, 257, 263
Hoofddorp 82

Île de France 50

Jamestown 242

Køge 206
Kyoto 234, 235

Las Vegas 263
Leiden 118, 134, 161, 212
Leuven (Louvain) 82, 92
Lommel 92
London 26, 44, 47, 50, 118, 168, 206,
	238, 245
Los Angeles 256
Lübeck 238

Maastricht 214, 219, 220
Macau 234, 257, 263
Madrid 44, 245
Malmö 206
Mechelen 118
Mexico City 245
Milan 186
Moscow 244
Munich 85

Nagasaki 234
Nanchang 231
Nanjing 263
Nansha 263
Natal 242
New Amsterdam 242
New Haven 242
New Orleans 242
New York 25, 47, 74, 80, 98, 210, 243,
	244, 256
Novgorod 238

Olinda 242
Orléans 239
Osaka 209
Oxford 239

Padua 239
Paris 47, 50, 76, 98, 128, 239, 245, 265
Pearl River Delta 11, 209, 210, 228, 234,
	246, 257, 263, 266
Philadelphia 242, 243
Portsmouth (NH) 242

Quebec 242

Randstad 7, 20, 21, 38, 104, 107, 132, 134,
	136, 146, 152, 168, 185, 198, 202, 212
Recife 257
Riga 238
Rio de Janeiro 242
Rome 237
Roskilde 206
Rotterdam 12, 26, 37, 38, 52-56, 60-66,
	72, 74, 76, 80, 85, 98, 127, 128, 132,
	134, 136, 138, 161, 168, 198, 212-214
Rovere (NJ) 139
Ruhrarea 85

Santo Domingo 240
São Paulo 11, 104, 107, 108, 110, 111, 114-117,
	122, 124, 228-230, 245, 263-266
São Vicente 242
Seattle 186
Seoul 245
Shanghai 138, 234, 263
Shenzhen 210, 257, 263
Singapore 46
Siena 239
Sittard-Geleen 214
Soesterberg 74
Southampton 127
Stockholm 85
Stockton 28
Stuttgart 85
Suzhou 231, 234, 263

Tel Aviv 25
Tonga 106
Tokyo 11, 47
Turnhout 85, 92

Utrecht 5, 9, 12, 18, 26, 45, 61, 85, 98

Västerig 85
Veere 74
Venice 166, 238, 246
Venlo 85
Vera Cruz 240

Vlissingen 62

Washington DC 245
Wassenaar 134, 136

Xian 231, 244, 266

Yamoto 234
Yokohama 209
You Jojun 231

Zhuhai 257, 263
Zürich 47

Index of subjects and actors

A2 53
AAIE-accredited international schools 115
ABN-AMRO Bank 83
Academic hospital of Aken 92
Academic hospital of Maastricht (AZM) 92, 219
ACC 26
Actant 190, 194-196
Action Plan for Power Districts 103
actor (leading, focal) 74, 78, 83, 95, 99, 103, 104, 120, 139, 146, 189, 196, 197, 200, 218
actor centered institutionalism 180, 181
actor (network) approach of planning 24, 32, 74, 75, 130, 187, 190, 193-198, 200
actor relational approach of planning (ARA) 33, 188-200, 202, 218, 223
actor network theory (ANT) 10, 189, 191-200
AEG 87
Aerotropolis 38
African slavery 109
agencements 170-179
AGIT Mbh. 82
Airey dwellings 87
Air France 77
Airline Deregulation Act 77
Airport City 38, 55, 80, 83
Airport Corridor 38, 53, 55, 82
Airport Region 87
Airport Rotterdam 136
allochtonen 98
Albeda College 54, 70
Alcatel 82
Alliance Francaise 132
Alto de Boa Vista 115
AMBX 91
American community 120-121, 126, 133-139
Amerindians 108

Amish 107
Amnesty International 27, 154
AMU 26
Anaxis 92
ANCOM 26
Angkasa Purra Jakarta Airport 78
Anglo-Saxon Church 116-117, 122, 136
Anglo-Saxon model 147
Anteryon 91
Antillean community 120-121, 126-127
APEC 26
Apple 29
Arabian migrants 109
architectural planning 186
Aruba Airport 76
Asia House 132-139
ASEAN 26, 44, 47
ASML 91
Association Cultural Assistential da Liberdade (ACAL) 111
associative democracies/planning 151, 152, 154, 160, 163, 164, 196, 198
associationalism 153, 154
Augustinian order 171
Austrian migrants 108
automotive cluster 92
Avenida plan 265

Balkenende administration 100
behavioural economic approach/ planning theory 39, 184-186
Barcelona standard EC 85
Barrio Norte 115
Bar Kokhba Revolt 107
Basic Planning Act 1941 19
Batavian Republic 60
Bayer 66
Belgian migrants 133
Belvedere 177
Betuwe raillink 37
Binnenhaven Rotterdam 62
Biz Botuluyuz Rotterdam 128-132
Blauwhoed Eurowoningen 133, 138
Blijdorp Zoo 63
Boeing 211

Bolivian migrants 108, 112-115
Book of Idols 239
Bos-Group 101
Bospolder-Tussendijken 127
Boston Corridor 36
Bourbons 50
Brabantia Nostra 87, 90
Brainport 32, 52-57, 83-95
Brainport Eindhoven Spatial Programme 93
Brisbane Airport 80
British expats 115
Brundtland Commission 199, 200
business society 148, 186, 188, 189, 194, 195, 197-200, 218
Byzantine Empire 237

Capetians 50
Cape Verdans 127
Capital City 230
Capsular Society 29
CARICOM 26
Carter Administration 76
CCC 26
Chateau Hotels 219
Chema-Energy Valley 92
Chinese communities 107-112, 124, 133-139
Chinese European Centre Rotterdam 132
Chipshol 80
Christian Occident 120
Cisco 83
City Beautiful Movement 18, 244
civic society 148, 188, 189, 194, 195, 197-200, 218
Civil Aircraft Authority 139
classic form of diasporic communities 107, 109-112
cluster processes 70
Collaborative planning (theory, apprach) 148, 185-188
Colonial City 230
Common Interest Development (CID) 256

Communicaciones Autopista 112
Communicative action, theory of 148, 183, 187-188
communism 87
Company of Merchant Adventurers 51
competitor-colleague (comcoll) 246
Com.Wonen 12, 128, 130
Confederation Congress 243
Confucianism 231, 234
Copenhagen Regional Planning Committee 206
corporation, housing 162-164
Cosco 65
cosourcing 2, 46
cosmopolitan liberalism 90
Criollo 108

Dallas Area Rapid Transit (DART) 210-212, 256
Danish Planning Act of 1939 206
danwei 231
daimyo 234
DCMR 54
De Architectura 240
De re aedificatoria 240
Delphi Social Welfare 128
Delfshaven 126-132
Delft University of Technology 54, 134
Delta City 230
Deltalinqs 54
Denver Livestock Exchange 250
Denver Regional Transportation (T-Rex) 256
de-territorialization 23, 29
Development Diamond Policy Rotterdam 128
Development Oriented Planning (*Ontwikkelingsplanologie*) 21
Development Plan Brabant (sixties) 90
diagramming 171-179
diaspora 107
Dichterlijke Vrijheid 128

Digital Exchange Spatial Plans (DURP) 177, 179
Digital Signal Processing Valley (DISP) 92
Directors Forum Schiphol (BSF) 80, 83
discursive approach 186, 188, 192
district bond 184
Drenthe village 90
Doctors without Borders 154
DSM 92, 220
Duijvenstein Parliamentary Working Group 9, 10
Dutch expats 115
Dutch-Indonesians 118
Dutch Design Cluster 92
Dutch National Policy Document on Spatial Planning 9, 10, 21, 32, 200
Dutch Scientific Council for Government Policy (WRR) 21, 101, 103, 104, 146
Dutch Surinamese 118, 127
Dutch Water Management Law 157

E 470 Public Highway Authority 256
East India Company (EIC) 51, 247
East Texas Oil Fields 256
Eastland Companies 51, 60
Ebben, Damens, Aukes & Ettema (EDAH) 87
Eindhoven-Leuven-Aken triangle (ELAt) 85, 92
Eindhoven canal 85
EFTA 26
emotional identification 104, 121-122
English community 127, 133
English East India Company 247
entrepreneurial approach, style of planning 185, 192
Environment Effect Reports (MER) 169, 177
EON-Benelux 66
Eonic Systems 92
ERA-Bouw 130
Estacion Retiro 112

Erasmus University 54, 63, 134
ethnoscapes 103
European China Centre (ECC) 138
Euro House 132-139
Euromast 138
European Union (EU) 44, 47, 76
Evoluon 90-91
evolutionary economy 38
Exegese on Nationalism 102
expatriate diasporic community 107, 115-117, 132-139
Expressway Plan 265

Fabric 11
factionalism 153
familism 48
Federal Transit Administration 210
FEI Company 91
Feijenoord 62
financescapes 103
Fine Food Fair 220
Finger Plan (Egnsplankontoret) 206-208
First Airline Exhibition Amsterdam 75
First Report on Spatial Planning 9
Flanders Multimedia Valley 92
Flemish community 107, 127
flexible familism 87
Fourth Report on Spatial Planning (VINO) 9, 38, 185
Fourth Report on Spatial Planning Extra (VINEX) 9, 183
Fourth Report on Spatial Planning Actualisation (VINAC) 9
fragmentation 23
French migrants 108, 133
Free University of Brussels (VUB) 92
Frontier Design 92
Front Shops-Back Factories Model (FSBF) 257
Fujitsu 235
functional identification 104, 121-122

G8 26, 149

Gateway 32, 37, 38, 53-57
Genius Landscape 92
German migrants 108, 118, 132
Global Cities 228
Global Fortune 500 43
Global Urban Network 228
Global Village 228
globalization 23
Global network cosmopolitanism 25
Goethe Institute 132
Google Books 179
Google Earth 177, 179
governance 164, 184, 186
Graphic Valley 92
Great Jewish Revolt 107
Greater Copenhagen Council 206
Greater London Authority 50
Greater London Plan 1944 206
Green Heart 20, 36
Greenpeace 27
Greenwich Mean Time 28
guest worker diasporic communities 107, 112-115

HaagWonen 12
Hadrian's Wall 237
Han dynasty 257
Handshake Solutions 91
Hanseatic network 44
Hankyu Corporation 209
Hanseatic League 238
Happy Shrimp Farm 66
Havenziekenhuis Hospital 63
health care district 160
Heiplaat 138
Heliopolis 122-124
Het Oosten 12
High Speed Train 136
High Tech Campus 58, 70, 91
Hillside Delights (*Heerlijkheid Heuvelland*) 214-225
holism 187, 192, 196, 223
Holland International Distribution Council (NDL) 38, 53
Housing association 154

Housing Bill (*Woningwet 1901*) 19, 161
Housing district 160
House of the Neighbours 132
Humanitas 131
Huntsman 65
Hutchinson 66
hypermobility 30

Identification with the Netherlands (WRR Report) 101
ideoscapes 103
imaginative community 184
IMEC 92
Imperial Court 234
Inconvenient truth 186
Indian migrants 133
ING 83
Inmigrantes Güemes YPF 113
Innovation Programme Urban Renewal (IPSV) 130
insourcing 24, 46
Integrated Care Community (ICC) 214, 223
Integrated Development planning (*integrale ontwikkelingsplanologie*) 183, 186
Interactive approach 186-187
International Congress Centre 263
International Governmental Organizations (IGO's) 26
International Monetary Fund (IMF) 147, 149
International Non-Governmental Organizations (INGO's) 27
Interprovinciale Verstedelijkingsvisie Randstad (IPVR) 21, 38
Iraqis community 120-121, 126
IREX 91
Irish community 107
Islamic cultures 118
Itaim Bibi 115
Italian community 107-109

Japanese community 108-112, 120-122, 126, 133

Japanese Central Bank 237
Japanese Immigration Museum 111
Japanese Railway (JR) 209
Jewish community 107-108, 121
JFK International New York 80

Kankyu Electric Railway Corporation 209
Kasbah 128
Katendrecht/Rijnhaven 138
keiretsu 235
Keio Corporation 209
kluswoning 128
Korean migrants 108-109, 111-112, 124
Kop van Zuid Rotterdam 21
Kostoff, Spiro 231
Kowloon-Canton Railway Corporation 210
Kruisplein 134
Ksar 130-131
Kuip (Feijenoord footbal stadium) 63, 168

Land Ordinance 242
Lantau International Airport 263
Leefbaar Rotterdam Party 126, 132
Le Havre-Hamburg range 37
leading firms 24, 52, 57, 58
Le Medi Rotterdam 128
Le Riad Rotterdam 131
Leuven Inc. 85
Levant Companies 51
Leyes de Indias 240
Liberation Theology 112
Liberdade 109-112, 124
Life Tec A2 92
Lifetec Aken Jülich 85
Limburg Development and Investment Company (LIOF) 215-220
Limes 237
Linkedin 174, 179
Lisbon agenda 85
Liquavista 91
Little Hoover Commission 159
local bond 184

location-based approach 184
low-cost carrier/low-fair carrier/
   no frills airlines 77, 215, 263
Lyondell 65, 66

Maasvlakte 60
Maersk 65
Mainport 32, 36, 37, 52-57, 60-83
Malaccan community 111
Manchu dynasty 263
mapping 177-185
Maroccan community 107, 120-121,
   126-133
Mass Transit Railway Corporation
   (MTRC) 209
Mayflower 127
mediascapes 103
Medtronic 92, 220
Meiji dynasty 208, 235
MERCOSUR 26, 112
meso-governmental level 183
Mestizo 108
Metropolitan City Agreement of
   Bologna 26
Metropolitan Development Council
   (Hovedstadens Udviklingsrad/
   HUR) 206
Michelin 220
Micro electronics 92
micrologies 186
Microsoft 83
migrant communities 105
Milan Malpensa Airport 80
Ministry of Economic Affairs 99
Ministry of Education and
   Culture 99
Ministry of Health, Welfare and
   Sport 223
Ministry of Internal Affairs 99
Ministry of International Trade
   and Industry (MTI, Japan) 237
Ministry of Justice and Laws 99
Ministry of Spatial Planning,
   Housing and the Environment
   (VROM) 9, 10, 115, 228

Ministry of Transport and Water
   Management (V&W) 74, 138, 156
Minoo Tramway 209
Mittal 136
modern(ism) 164, 187, 190, 223
Movares 12
multi actor society/governance
   146, 182
multi airport system 263, 266
multi focus households 184
multi layered organisation 154
multi level governance 146, 151
multi scaling 182
Muscovy Companies 51
MVDRV Skycar City 188

Nadere Uitwerking Groene Hart 21
NAFTA 26, 44, 47
Nanjing treaties 234
National Housing Council 161
National Plan 19
National Spatial Framework 146
National Western Stock Show 250
Natlab 70, 87, 92
NATO 26
Nazi german propaganda maps 186
Nazi-occupation 65
NEC 235
neighbourhood association 155
neo-classical economic approach 39
neo-liberal society/democracy 22,
   147, 150, 163, 164, 184, 200
neo-Marxist economic approach 40
networked communities 184
network society 22, 23, 25, 192
New Law on Spatial Planning
   (NWRO) 32, 146, 185
New Netherlands Project 9, 185
New Urbanism 210, 244
Nieuwe Westen (Rotterdam) 127
Nimby 183
NIROV 18
No-frills airlines/low-cost carrier/
   low-fair carrier 77, 215-218, 263
Nordestinos 108

normative identification 104, 121-122
North Carolina State University 228
North West Airlines 77
Norwegian migrants 118
Not In My Backyard (NIMBY) 32
NXP 91

object approach of planning 24
Odakyu Corporation 209
OECD-countries 105, 115
Office for the National Plan 19
Olympic Games 1928 75
Oneworld 77
OPEC 26
open innovaion business model 56
opportunity maps 195, 218
Orbis (Medical Care Concern) 218,
   220, 223
Orbis Medical Park 223
Ordenanzas 242
Ottoman Empire 237
outsourcing 24, 46

Pact op Zuid 214
Paleremo 115
Paraguayan migrants 108, 112-115
Paraisopolis 122-124
Paris Convention 77
Parkhaven 138
Parkstad van Hof tot Haven 21
participatory democracy 151, 164
particularism 153
paulistas 109, 110
Peaks in the Delta Report 10, 31, 45,
   56, 184
people-planet-profit (PPP) 199
Peruvian migrants 108, 112-115
Phalanstère 250
Philips 53, 55-57, 85, 87-95, 220
Philips estate 90
Pilgrim fathers 127
place entrepeneurs 186
Plan 2000+ 65
Plan Ooievaar 21
planologie 18

287

Plaza San Martin 112
polder 154-156
Poldermodel 186
Polish migrants 108
Polymer Vision 91
Polynorm dwellings 90
portenos 108, 114
Port of Rotterdam Authority 12, 54, 60-70
Portuguese migrants 108-109
post-capitalist society 22
post-modern society 22, 187, 191, 194, 223
post-structural planning theory 185
Power Districts Policy (*Vogelaar wijken*) 10, 31, 32, 98-124
Power of Identity 102, 115
Presidio 240
Preuvenemint 220
private domain 205
private-public governance 185
project urbanism 187
Province of South Holland 205
Prussia 60
public investment fund for pleasant districts 100
public society 148, 188, 195, 197, 198
Puerto Madero 114
puller 195
pusher 195
PVV (Party For Freedom) 126

Qing dynasty 231, 257

radical pluralism 151-152
Rail-to-Trail program 256
Randstad 2040 146, 185, 198
Raumplanung 18
regime (development) 196, 198, 205, 214
Regional Economic Outlook for Schiphol (REVS) 82
regional plans of South Holland 198
Regioplan 115, 134
REI Outdoor Flagship Store 256

relational economic geography approach 30-31, 33, 40, 43, 59
remittances 104-106
representative democracy 152, 160, 164-165
research, design & manufacturing initiative 54, 72
research & development 85
re-territorialization 23
Rijnhaven Rotterdam 62
Romans/Roman Empire 107, 237
Rotterdam Climate Initiative 54
Rotterdamse Droogdok Maatschappij (RDM) 54
Rotterdam University of Applied Sciences (Rotterdam Academy) 54, 70
Royal Begeman Group 87
Royal Dutch Airline for the Netherlands and Colonies (KLM) 75-78
Ruhrarea 61
Russian migrants 108, 133
RUVEIN 37
RVS 65
RWTH Aken 85

Sabic 220
San Telmo 112, 115
Seaport Rotterdam 52
Schiphol 38, 52, 53, 54, 74-83
Schiphol Area Development Corporation (SADC) 81-82
Schiphol Group Inc. 12, 76, 80-83, 138
Schiphol Real Estate 80-82
school district 158
SDAP 18
Second Report on Spatial Planning 9
Second White Paper on Traffic and Transport 38
Seibu Corporation 209
self-governing associations/ organisation 153, 154
self-organizing democracy 164
Shanghai Construction Group 138

shareholder 155, 162, 223
Shell 65, 133, 136
Shinkansen Holding Company 209
shoen 234, 246
Silicon Hive 91
Silicon Valley 36
single function distric 158
Skyteam 77
smart growth 186-187, 210
Social Democratic Workers' Party (SDAP) 161
Sociedade Brasiliera de Cultura Japonesa (RUNKYO) 111
Solland 220
South African migrants 133
South Axis of Amsterdam 80, 82, 188
South Wing Railtrack (Stedenbaan) 212-214
Spanish community 107-108, 127
Spanish laws 240, 264
spatial development policy (*Ruimtelijke Ontwikkelingspolitiek*) 21
spatial planning 18
spatial program Brainport 56
special care district 223
special district (planning) 154, 158, 160, 163-164, 196-197
special economic zones 257
Spoorhaven Rotterdam 62
Squint Opera's Restoration of Jeddah 188
stadsregio 26
stakeholder 146, 148, 155, 157, 162-163, 186, 195, 196, 198, 223
Staralliance 77, 250
Stockholm Airport 80
state planning 164
stratified planning approach (*lagenbenadering*) 21
Stratagem 11
Strijp S 91
structuralist economic approach 40, 184
Structure Group for Experimental Housing 128

structure plan for Flanders 198
Sung empire 231
Supervillage concept 93
supranational level/association 154, 182
sustainability 188, 194, 200, 214

Taiwanese migrants 108, 134
Tang dynasty/empire 231, 257
tax increment bond (TIB) 256
tax increment finance (TIF) 212, 250, 256
technonationalism 48
technoscapes 103
Technical University Eindhoven (TUE) 85, 90, 92
Telos 11
Terminal de Omnibus 112
Texas Instruments 256
The City and the Grassroots 115
The Greater Copenhagen Authority 26
The Greater London Authority 26
The Hannover Regional County 26
The Metropolitan Region Frankfurt/Rhein Main 26
The Stuttgart Regional Agency 26
third, fourth and fifth party logistics 85
Third Report on Spatial Planning 9
time-space 183, 191
Tokyu Corporation 209
Tom Tom 83
Trots op Nederland (TON, Proud of the Netherlands) 126
Tordesillas Treaty 264
Toshiba 235
TourisME program 215
town and country planning 18
tracing 171-179
tradeport Hong Kong 78
transformative planning practice 186
transit impact zone 211
transit oriented development (TOD) 165, 197, 202, 211, 214, 256

transmigrant 126
transnational activities 131
transnational communities 104-126, 184, 264
TransNational Corporations (TNC's) 10, 36, 41, 47, 58, 83, 115, 132
transnationalism 102-103
Trinity Railway Express 211
Triple Helix 55, 92, 95
Turkish community 107-108, 127-133
tweede Maasvlakte 53

Unilever 136
United Airlines 250
United Nations (UN) 105, 228
University of Amsterdam 9
University of Gent 92
University of Georgia 228
University of Leuven 85, 92
University of Maastricht 92, 220
University of Tilburg 215
University of Utrecht 10, 12, 18, 213, 215, 228
Universitytown 263
Urban Affairs 11
urban planning 186
urban regime approach/urban regime theory 182, 185, 196, 223
Urban Unlimited 11, 171
USA House 132-139

value added logistics (VAL) 85
Vienna International Airport 78
Villa 31 112-115, 122-124
Villa Nova Conciecáo 115
Volker Wessels 138
Vopak 65
VROM-council 95
VVD (Dutch Liberals) 126

Waalhaven Rotterdam 62
Walloon coal basin 61
Wal Mart 46
water board (waterschap/watering) 154, 156, 157, 163

Welfare Balance Brabant 90
welfare state 182, 189
West India Company (WIC) 51, 60, 127
Westphalian State model 26, 147
White paper on Spatial Perspectives 36
White paper on Dutch Economy without Borders 38
Witte dame 91
Woensel West 90
Woonbron Housing Association 54, 130
World Bank 147
World Trade Organisation (WTO) 147, 149
World Wildlife Fund (WWF) 27

Yamanote line/loop 209
Yugoslavian community 120-121, 126

zaibatsu 235
Zapatistas 115
ZKA consultancy 11
zoning plan, temporary 186
Zwarte Ruiter Meeting 220

References

Abercrombie, Patrick (1933) *Town & country planning*. London: T. Buttersworth.

Abrams, Janet & Hall, Peter (ed.) (2006) *Else/Where: Mapping new cartography of networks and territories*. University of Minnesota Design Institute.

Abu-Lughod, J.L. (1999) *Before European Hegemony: The World System AD 1250-1350*. New York: Oxford University Press.

Ades, Alberto and Glaeser, Edward (1995) 'Trade and Circuses: Explaining Urban Giants'. In: *Quarterly Journal of Economics* 110 (February), pp.195-258.

Adorno, Theodor & Horkheimer, Max (1947) *Die Dialektiek der Aufklärung*. Amsterdam: Querido Verlag.

Agro&Co (2008) *Nieuwe Markten in het Brabantse Land: Waardecreatie, Ondernemersschap en Regionale Ontwikkeling*. Tilburg: Agro&Co.

Alberti, Leon Battista (1998) *De re aedificatoria: On the art of building in ten books*. (translated by Joseph Rykwert, Neil Leach, and Robert Tavernor). Cambridge, MA: MIT Press.

Albrechts, Louis (2001) 'In Pursuit of new Approaches to Strategic Spatial Planning'. In: *International Planning Studies*. Vol.6(3), pp.293-301.

Albrechts, Louis (2004) 'Strategic (spatial) planning reexamined'. In: *Environment and Planning B: Planning and Design* 31(5), pp.743-758.

Albrechts, Louis & Mandelbaum, Seymour (2005) *The network society: a new context for planning?* New York/London: Routledge.

Albrechts, Louis (2008) 'Spatial planning as transformative practice'. In: *Ruimte en planning* 2008-3, pp.10-18.

Almandoz, Arturo (ed.) (2002) *Planning Latin America's capital cities 1850-1950*. London: Routledge.

Alterman, R. (1997) 'The Challenge of Farmland Preservation: Lessons from a Six Nation Comparison'. In: *Journal of the American Planning Association* 63, 220-243.

Althusser, Louis et al. (1968) *Lire le Capital*. Paris: Éditions Maspero.

Amemiya K. K. (1998) 'Being "Japanese" in Brazil and Okinawa'. In: *JPRI Occasional Paper*, no.13: May 1998.

Amin, Ash & Thrift, Nigel (2002) *Cities: Reimagining the Urban*. Cambridge: Polity.

Anderson, Benedict (1983): *Imagined Communities: Reflections on the origin and spread of nationalism*. London/New York: Verso.

Aoki, Eiichi (1994a) 'Dawn of Japanese Railways'. In: *Japan Railway & Transport Review*, March 1994, pp.28-30.

Aoki, Eiichi (1994b) 'Expansion of Railway Network'. In: *Japan Railway & Transport Review*, June 1994, pp.34-37.

Appadurai, Arjun (1991) 'Global Etnoscapes – Notes and queries for a transnational anthropology'. In: Fox, R.G. (1991) *Recapturing anthropology*. Santa Fe: School of American Research Press.

Appadurai, Arjun (1996) *Modernity at Large: Cultural Dimensions of Globalization*. University of Minnesota: The Public Worlds.

Architectuur Centrum Eindhoven (2005) *Eindhoven Supervillage; plan de campagne*. Eindhoven: ACE.

ARCUSplus (2007) *Ontwikkeling Fysiek Expat Loket*. Amsterdam: Topstad Amsterdam.

Asaert, Gustaaf (2004) *De val van Antwerpen en de uittocht van Vlamingen en Brabanders*. Tiel: Uitgeverij Lannoo.

Atzema, Oedzge & Lambooy, Jan & Van Rietbergen, Ton & Wever, Egbert (2002) *Ruimtelijk-economische dynamiek*. Bussum: Coutinho.

Atzema, Oedzge & Visser, Evert-Jan (2005) 'Innovatie vanuit bedrijfsperspectief'. In: VNO-NCW Midden, Kamer van Koophandel Utrecht, Kamer van Koophandel Gooi en Eemland (2005) *De unieke innovatiekracht van de regio Utrecht, Gooi & Eemland: Een bedrijfsgerichte benadering*. Utrecht: Provincie Utrecht, pp.14-21.

Atzema, Oedzge & Wever, Egbert & Krol, Marloes (2008) 'Philips: a global electronic firm restructuring its home base'. In: Pellenbarg, Piet & Wever, Egbert ed. (2008) *International Business Geography – Case studies of corporate firms*. London/New York: Routledge.

Bader, Veit (2001) 'Introduction'. In: Hirst, Paul & Bader, Veit (ed.) (2001) *Associative Democracy: The Real Third Way*. Abington: Frank Cass & Co, pp.1-14.

Bakker-Schut, F. (1937) 'Een nationaal plan voor Nederland'. In: *Tijdschrift voor Volkshuisvesting en Stedebouw*, p.72.

Barber, Benjamin R. (1995) *Jihad versus McWorld: How Globalism and Tribalism are reshaping the World*. New York: First Ballantine Books.

Barnum, J. (1998) *What Prompted Airline Deregulation 20 Years Ago?* Presentation to the Aeronautical Law Committee of the Business Law Section of the International

Bar Association, September 15.

Barr, Daniel (ed) (2006) *The Boundaries Between Us: Natives and Newcomers Along the Frontiers of the Old Northwest Territory, 1750-1850*. Kent, OH: Kent State University Press.

Bartelt, Dawis (2008) 'Hinterland ist überall: Das Verhältniss von Küste und Sertao als Konstituens der Brasilianischen Gesellschaft'. In: *Arch+* 190, Dezember 2008, pp.6-11.

Bathelt, Harald & Glückler, Johannes (2002) *Wirtschaftsgeographie: Ökonomische Beziehungen in räumlicher Perspektive*. 2., korrigierte Auflage. Stuttgart: Verlag Eugen Ulmer.

Beck, Ulrich (1986) *Risikogesellschaft: Auf dem Weg in eine andere Moderne*. Frankfurt am Main: Suhrkamp Verlag.

Benz, Arthur & Fürst, Dietrich (2002) 'Policy learning in regional networks'. In: *European Urban and Regional Studies* 9(1).

Berlage, Hendrik Pieter (1904) 'Stedenbouw'. In: *De Beweging*, deel 2.

Berndt, Heide (1978) *Die Natur der Stadt*. Frankfurt: Verlag Neue Kritik.

Berryman, Phillip (1987) *Liberation Theology: Essential Facts About the Revolutionary Movement in Latin America and Beyond*. New York: Pantheon Books.

Bernstein, William (2008) *A Splendid Exchange: How Trade Shaped the World*. New York: Atlantic Monthly Press.

Besemer, Maaike et al. (2008) *Classic Diaspora in Buenos Aires and São Paulo: A quick scan at the success factors of the Argentinean Jews and Brazilian Japanese*. Utrecht: University of Utrecht.

Bijker, Wiebe (1995) *Of bicycles, bakelites and bulbs: Towards a Theory of Sociotechnical Change*. Cambridge, MA: MIT press.

Blauwhoed-Eurowoningen (2008) *Bewust Blauwhoed: Initiatieven voor stedelijke vernieuwing*. Rotterdam: Blauwhoed-Eurowoningen.

Blokland-Potters, Talja (1998) *Wat stadsbewoners bindt: Sociale relaties in een achterstandswijk*. Kampen: KOK Agora.

Bock, Manfred (1983) *Anfänge einer neuen Architektur: Berlages Beitrag zur Architektonischen Kultur der Niederlande im ausgehenden 19. Jahrhundert*. Den Haag/Wiesbaden: Staatsuitgeverij/Franz Steiner Verlag.

Boelens, Luuk (1990) *Stedebouw en planologie – een onvoltooid project: naar een communicatieve benadering van de ruimtelijke planning en ontwerppraktijk*. Delft: Delft University Press.

Boelens, Luuk (1993) 'De patroonloosheid van de Randstad: Het probleem van de gespleten werelden'. In: Agricola, E. (ed.) et al.: *Archipolis – over de grenzen van de architectuur*. Delft: Eburon.

Boelens, Luuk (ed.) (2000) *Nederland Netwerkenland: Een inventarisatie van de nieuwe condities van planologie en stedebouw*. Rotterdam: NAi publishers.

Boelens, Luuk (2003) 'La citta muovere'. In: Meurs, Paul & Verheijen, Marc (2003) *In Transit*. Rotterdam: NAi Publishers.

Boelens, Luuk (2005) *Fluviology: a new aproach of spatial planning*. Inaugural lecture. Utrecht: University of Utrecht January 13th 2005.

Boelens, Luuk (2005b) 'Streaming spatial planning – Technological changes and their impact on space'. In Hulsbergen, Edward et al. (ed.): *Shifting Sense in Spatial Planning*. Amsterdam: Techne Press.

Boelens, Luuk (2006) 'Beyond the plan; towards a new kind of planning'. In: *disP* ETH-Zürich 4-2006, pp.25-40.

Boelens, Luuk (2008) 'Review Recapturing Democracy-Neoliberalization and the Struggle for Alternative Urban Futures, by Mark Purcell. New York and London: Routledge, 2008'. In: *Journal of Planning Education and Research* 2008 28: pp.268-269.

Boelens, Luuk (2009) 'Networking Mainports: An alternative for location based approaches'. In: *Mainports Revisited* (forthcoming)

Boelens, Luuk & Sanders, Wies (2003) *De grote KAN-Atlas: Mentale atlas van het stedelijk netwerk Arnhem-Nijmegen*. Rotterdam: 010 Publishers.

Boelens, Luuk & Atzema, Oedzge (2006) 'Connecting Randstad Holland – A network approach of competition between clusters'. In: Koekoek, A.F. (ed.) et al, *Cities and globalisation*. Utrecht: Nederlandse Geografische Studies 339: pp.61-72.

Boelens, Luuk & Spit, Tejo & Wissink, Bart (Eds.) (2006) *Planning zonder overheid*. Rotterdam: 010 Publishers.

Boelens, Luuk & Taverne, Ed (2009 forthcoming) 'Waarom steden als delta's floreren: De geografische/planologische dimensie'. In: Lucassen, Leo & Willems, Wim (2009) *Waarom mensen in de stad willen wonen: Steden, instituties en migratie in de Nederlanden 1200-2000* (forthcoming).

Boggs, Jeffrey & Rantisi, Norma (2003) 'The "Relational Turn". In Economic Geography'. In: *The Journal of Economic Geography*, 3 (2), pp.109-116.

Bohigas, Oriol et al. (1991) *Barcelona – City and Architecture 1980-1992*. New York: Rizzoli.

Bolan, Richard (1999) *The Dutch Retreat of the Welfare State and its implications for metropolitan planning*. Amsterdam: AME.

Bollens, John (1961) *Special District Governments in the United States*. Berkeley/Los Angeles: University of California Press.

Bolte, Wouter & Meijer, Johan (1981) *Van Berlage tot Bijlmer: Architectuur en stedelijke politiek*. Nijmegen: SUN.

Bomhoff, Eduard (1999) *Van Wonen naar Samenleven: de rol van corporaties*. Utrecht: Nyfer.

Boomkens, René (2006) *De Nieuwe Wanorde: Globalisering en het einde van de maakbare samenleving*. Amsterdam: Van Gennep.

Bos, A. (1946) *De stad der toekomst, de toekomst der stad*. Rotterdam: Voorhoeve.

Bos, Caroline et al. (2008) *Moderne diaspora en krachtwijken: referenties uit São Paulo en Buenos Aires*. Utrecht: University of Utrecht.

Bos, Bram (2004) *Een kwestie van beheersing: over de rol van planten, dieren en mensen in technologische systemen*. Amsterdam: VU Amsterdam. PhD thesis.

Bosch, Marjan van den (2007) *Kennismaken met netwerken in Twente*. Utrecht: Universiteit van Utrecht. Masterthesis.

Boschma, Ron (2005a) 'Proximity and innovation: A critical assessment'. In: *Regional Studies*, vol.39, no.1, pp.61-74.

Boschma, Ron (2005b) 'Competitiveness of regions from an evolutionary perspective'. In: *The Association of Regional Observatories*, pp.10-13.

Boschma, Ron & Frenken, Koen & Lambooy, Jan (2002) *Evolutionaire economie*. Bussum: Coutinho.

Boschma, Ron & Frenken, Koen (2006) 'Why is Economic Geography not an Evolutionary Science'. In: *Journal of Economic Geography*, vol.6, no.3, 273-302.

Bosker, Maarten et al. (2007) *From Baghdad to London: The dynamics of urban development in Europe and the Arab world, 800-1800*. Utrecht: University of Utrecht.

Bosma, Koos (2003) *J.M. de Casseres: De eerste planoloog*. Rotterdam: 010 Publishers.

Bouwens, A. & Dierikx, M. (1997) *Tachtig jaar Schiphol: op de drempel van de lucht*. 's-Gravenhage: SDU Uitgevers.

Boyer, Christine M. (1996) *Cybercities: Visual perception in the Age of Electronic Communication*. New York: Princeton Architectural Press.

Boyle, Paul et al. (1998) *Exploring Contemporary Migration*. Harlow: Pearson.

Brand, H. & Müller, L. (ed.) (2007) *The Dynamics of Economic Culture in the North Sea- and Baltic Region in the Late Middle Ages and Early Modern Period*. Hilversum: Verloren.

Braudel, Fernand (1984) *The perspectives of the World*. London: Collins.

Braziel, Jana Evans et al. (2003) *Theorizing diaspora*. Malden: Blackwell.

Brenner, Neil (1999) 'Globalisation as Reterritorialization: The Re-Scaling of Urban Governance in the European Union'. In: *Urban Studies* 36(3), pp.431-451.

Brenner, Neil (2004) *New State Spaces: Urban Governance and the rescaling of Statehood*. Oxford/New York: Oxford University Press.

Brenner, Thomas (2004) *Local Industrial Cluster: Existence, Emergence and Evolution*. London/New York: Routledge.

Briels, J. (1976) 'De emigratie uit de Zuidelijke Nederlanden omstreeks 1540-1621-1630'. In: *Opstand en Pacificatie in de Lage Landen*. Bijdrage tot de studie van Gent. Gent.

Bröcker, Johannes et al (ed.) (2003) *Innovation clusters and interregional Competition*. Berlin/Heidelberg/New York: Springer-Verlag.

Brook, Daniel (2007) *The Trap: Selling Out to Stay Afloat in Winner-Take-All America*. New York: Times Books.

Brundtland cie (1987) *Our Common Future:* Report of the World Commission on Environment and Development. Oxford: Oxford University Press.

Burghouwt, Guillaume (2005) *Airline network development in Europe and its implications for airport planning*. Utrecht: Faculty of Geosciences.

Burghouwt, Guillaume & Huys, Marcel (2003) 'Deregulation and the consequences for airport planning in Europe'. In: *disP*, 154, pp.37-45.

Burnham, James (1941) *Managerial Revolution*. New York: Pelican Books.

Burnham, Daniel H. & Bennet, Edward H. (1993) *Plan of Chicago* (with a new introduction by Kirsten Schaffer). New York: Princeton Architectural Press.

Cabannes, Yves (2004) 'Children and young people build participatory democracy in Latin American Cities'. In: *Environment & Urbanization*, vol.18(1): pp.195-218.

Cairncross, Francis (1997) *The death of distance*. Massachusetts: Harvard Business School Press.

Callahan, Maureen (1981) *The Harbour barons: Political and commercial elites and the development of the port of Rotterdam*. New York: Princeton.

Callon, Michel (1986) 'Some elements of a sociology of translation: domestication of the scallops and the fishermen of St Brieuc Bay'. In: Law, J. (ed.) *Power, Action and Belief, a new sociology of knowledge?* pp.196-229, London: Routledge & Kegan Paul.

Callon, Michel (1995) 'Agency and the hybrid collective'. In: *The South Atlantic Quarterly* 94/2, 481-507.

Callon, Michel & Latour, Bruno (1981) 'Unscrewing the big Leviathan'. In: Knorr, K & Cicourel, A.: *Advantages in Social Theory*. New York: Routledge pp.277-303.

Callon, Michel & Law, John (1997) 'After the individual in society'. In: *Canadian Journal of Sociology* 22, pp.505-522.

Calthorpe, Peter (1993) *The Next American Metropolis: Ecology, Community, and the American Dream*. New York: Princeton Architectural Press.

Cammen, Hans van der (1986) 'De moderne ruimtelijke planning: een situatieschets'. In: *Stedebouw en Volkshuisvesting* 12.

Cammen, Hans van der, et al. (ed.) (1987) *Nieuw Nederland: Onderwerp van Ontwerp*. Achtergronden en Beeldverhalen. 's-Gravenhage: SDU.

Cammen, Hans van der (2008) *Ruimtelijke Ordening en de Broze Regels*. Uittreerede gehouden op 20 november 2008. Amsterdam: UVA.

Cammen, Hans van der & Klerk, Len de (2003) *Ruimtelijke Ordening: Van grachtengordel tot VINEX-wijk*. Utrecht: Het Spectrum.

Cammen, Hans van der, Bakker, Riek (2006) *Gebiedsontwikkeling: kansen en condities voor maatschappelijke meerwaarde*. Den Haag: NIROV.

Cardoso, R. C. L. (1998) *Estrutura familiar e mobilidade social: estudo dos japoneses no Estado de São Paulo*. São Paulo: Organizacao Masaot Ninomiya.

Casciato, Maristella (1980) 'De Woningwet: 1901-1912'. In: Casciato, Maristella et al. (ed.) (1980) *Architectuur en Volkshuisvesting: Nederland 1870-1940*. Nijmegen: SUN. pp.24-29.

Casseres De, Joël (1929) 'Grondslagen der planologie'. In: *De Gids*, April.

Cassese, A. (1986) *International Law in a divided world*. Oxford: Clarendon.

Castells, Manuel (1996) *The Rise of the Network Society: Volume I of The Information Age: Economy, Society and Culture*. Cambridge/Oxford: Blackwell.

Castells, Manuel (1997) *The Power of Identity: Volume II of The Information Age: Economy, Society and Culture*. Cambridge/Oxford: Blackwell.

Castells, Manuel (1998) *End of the Millennium: Volume III of The Information Age: Economy, Society and Culture*. Cambridge/Oxford: Blackwell.

Cauter, Lieven de (2000) 'The rise of the mobile society'. In: *Archis 2-2000*, Amsterdam.

Central Office for Statistics of the Netherlands (2008) *Statline*. The Hague: CBS.

Cerfontaine, Gerlach (2006) *Governance in de Randstad*. Oratie. Utrecht: University of Utrecht.

Cervero, Robert (1998) *The Transit Metropolis: A Global Inquiry*. Washington: Island Press

Cervero, Robert & Duncan, Michael (2001) *Rail Transit's Value*. University of California: Institute of Urban and Regional Development, June 2001, p.1.

Cervero, Robert et al. (2004) *Transit Oriented Development in the United States: experiences, Challanges and Prospects*. TRCP-report 102.

Chan, Victor (2007) *Presentation to Delegates from the Dutch Ministry of Housing, Spatial Planning and the Environment*. MTRC Limited. March 7th 2007.

Chesbrough, Henry (2003) *Open Innovation: the new imperative for creating and profiting from technology*. Harvard Business School Press.

Christaller, Walter (1933) *Die zentralen Orte in Süddeutschland*. Jena: Gustav Fischer.

Coe, Neil M., Kelly, Philip F. & Yeung, Henry W. (2007) *Economic Geography: A Contemporary Introduction*. Malden/Oxford/Victoria: Blackwell Publishing.

Cohen, Joshua & Rogers, Joel (1992) 'Secondary associations and democratic governance'. In: *Politics and Society* 20/4, pp.391-472.

Cohen, Robin (1997) *Global Diasporas: An introduction*. Seattle: University of Washington Press.

Coleman, James S. (1990) *Foundations of Social Theory*. Berkeley: Harvard University.

Commissie Sistermans (2005) *Brainport Navigator 2013: Lissabon voorbij*. Eindhoven: BE.

Cosgrove, Denis (2005) 'Mapping/Cartography'. In: Atkinson, David & Jackson, Peter & Sibley, David & Washbourne, Neil (ed.) *Cultural Geography: A critical dictionary of key concepts*. London: I.B. Tauris, pp.27-33.

Cowling, Keith & Sugden, Roger (1998) 'The Essence of the Modern Corporation: Markets, Strategic Decision-Making and The Theory of the Firm'. In: *The Manchester School*, vol.66, no.1, pp.59-86.

Crampton J. W., & Elden, S. (ed.) (2007). *Space, knowledge, power. Foucault and Geography*. Hampshire: England and Burlington, Ashgate.

Culot, Maurice et al (2000) *Dynamic City*. Brussel: Fondation pour l'Architecture/Skira.

Cushman & Wakefield/Healy & Baker (2005) *European Cities Monitor: Best Cities in Europe to lace a business*. London: Cushman & Wakefield.

Cymbalista, R. & Nakano, K. (2005) 'São Paulo, Brazil: A need for stronger policy advocacy'. In: Balbo, Marcello (ed.) (2005) *International Migrants and the City*. Venezia: IUAV.

Dahrendorf, Ralph (1987) *Fragmente Eines Neuen Liberalismus*. Stuttgart: Deutsche Verlags-Anstalt.

Dam, Petra (2004) 'De nieuwe waterstaatsgeschiedenis. De interactie tussen mens en natuur in Holland'. In: *Holland. Regionaal-historisch tijdschrift*. Themanummer 'De nieuwe waterstaatsgeschiedenis' 36 (2004) 3, pp.128-142.

Damen, Gijs (2008) *Co-siting in de Rotterdamse Haven: Een innovatief concept voor de Kwaliteitshaven*. Utrecht: University of Utrecht.

Daskalis, Geogia & Waldheim, Charles & Young, Jason (ed.) (2001) *Stalking Detroit*. Barcelona: Actar.

Davis, Mike (1990) *City of Quartz: Excavating the Future in Los Angeles*. London: Verso.

Davies, J.S. (2002) 'Urban regime theory: a normative empirical critique'. In: *Journal of Urban Affairs* 24, pp.1-17.

Dekker, Paul (2005) 'Civil society and the non-profit sector in the Netherlands'. In: Li, Yuwen (ed.) (2005) *Freedom of association in China and Europe: Comparative perspectives in law and practice*. Leiden/Boston: Martinus Nijhoff, pp.251-282.

Deleuze, Gilles & Guattari, Félix (1980) *Mille plateaux.*

Capitalisme et schizophrénie. Paris: Editions de Minuit.

Dicken, Peter (2002) *'Placing' firms – 'Firming' places – Grounding the debate on the 'global' corporation* Paper presented at the Conference on 'Responding to Globalization: Societies, Groups and Individuals'. Boulder: University of Colorado.

Dicken, Peter (2003) *Global Shift: Reshaping the global economic map in the 21st Century* (fourth edition). London/New Delhi: Thousand Oaks, Sage Publications.

Dicken, Peter & Thrift, Nigel (1992) 'The organization of production and the production of organization: why business enterprises matter in the study of geographical industrialization'. In: *Transaction of the Institute of British Geographers*, 17: pp.279-291.

Dieleman, F.M. & Priemus, H. & D. Clapham (1999) 'Current Developments in Social Housing Management, Introduction to Special Issue'. In: *Netherlands Journal of Housing and the Built Environment*, vol.15, pp.211-223.

Dierikx, M. & Werff, C. & Mom, G., & Bogaard, A. van den (1999) *Schiphol:* haven, station, knooppunt, sinds 1916. Zutphen: Walburg Pers.

Dijkink et al. (2002): *De Zuidvleugel van de Randstad: Instituties en discoursen*. Amsterdam: AME.

Dijst, Martin, et al (2005) *Leef- en mobiliteitstijlen Stedenbaan*. Utrecht: Universiteit van Utrecht.

Ditmar, Hank & Ohland, Gloria (ed.) (2004) *The New Transit Town: Best Practices in Transit-Oriented Development*. Washington/Covelo/London: Island Press.

Doevendans, K. & Stolzenburg, R. (1988) *De wijkgedachte in Nederland: gemeenschapsstreven in een stedenbouwkundige context*. Eindhoven: Technische Universiteit Eindhoven.

Dolfing B. (1993) 'Vroegste ontwikkeling in het waterschap'. In: Raadschelders, J.C.N. & Toonen, Th. A.J. (ed.) (1993) *Waterschappen in Nederland: Een bestuurskundige verkenning van de institutionele ontwikkeling*. Hilversum: Verloren, pp.61-80.

Dollinger, P. (1970) *The German Hansa*. London: Macmillan.

Doorn. J.A.A. van (1955) 'Wijk en stad reële integratiekaders'. In: *Prea-adviezen voor het congres over sociale samenhangen in Nieuwe stadswijken*. Amsterdam.

Doorn-Jansen, M.J. van (1966) *Groei en gestalte van een nieuwe stadswijk: Verslag van een sociologische verkenning in Rotterdam-Zuidwijk anno 1955*. Utrecht: Rijks-

universiteit van Utrecht.
Drewe, Paul (1997) *In search of new spatial concept inspired by information technology*. Delft: Delft University Press.
Drucker, Peter (1993) *Post-Capitalist Society*. Oxford: Butterworth-Heinemann.
Dryzek, John (1990) *Discursive Democracy*. Cambridge: Cambridge University Press.
Dryzek, John (1996) *Democracy in Capitalist Times: Ideals, Limits, and Struggles*. New York: Oxford University Press.
Duijn, Dick van (2007) 'Biz Botuluyuz in Rotterdam, de bewoner als opdrachtgever'. In: *Vitale Stad*, jaargang 10 oktober/november, pp.4-5.
Duijvenstein, Adri cie. (2000) *Notie van ruimte. Op weg naar de Vijfde Nota ruimtelijke ordening*. Tweede Kamer der Staten-Generaal. Vergaderjaar 1999-2000. 27 210 nrs, 1-2/'s-Gravenhage. Sdu. 2000. 4°. Pap. 9012091780.
Duroselle, Jean Baptiste (1990) *Europa: Geschiedenis van zijn bewoners*. Utrecht/Antwerpen: Uitgeverij Kosmos

Einstein, Albert (1919) *Was ist Relativitäts-Theorie*. In: Mein Weltbild, vol.7, Doc.25, 28 November.
ELAt (2008) *Engineering the future: Expanding innovation ecosystem*. Eindhoven: Brainport Operations BV.
Eisenstadt, Shmuel Noah (1996) *Japanese Civilization: A Comparative View*. Chicago: University of Chicago Press
Elkington, John (1998) *Cannibal with Forks: The triple bottom Line of 21st Century Business*. Oxford: New Society Publishers Ltd.
Engbersen, Godfried (2006) *Publieke Bijstandsgeheimen: Het ontstaan van een onderklasse in Nederland*. Amsterdam: Amsterdam University Press.
Engbersen, Godfried & Rusinovic, Katja & Meeteren, Masja van (2007) *Transnational Capital and integration*. Paper presented at the Compas Annual Conference 5th and 6th July 2007. Oxford.
Engelen, Ewald (2001) 'Globalisation and Multilevel Governance in Europe'. In: Hirst, Paul & Bader, Veit (ed.) (2001) *Associative Democracy: The Real Third Way*. Abington: Frank Cass & Co, pp.131-156.
Engelsdorp-Gastelaars, Rob (2007) *De nieuwe stad: Stedelijke centra als brandpunten van interactie*. Ruimtelijk Planbureau, Den Haag.
Enright, Michael J. (2000) 'Regional Clusters and Multinational Enterprises: Independence, Dependence, or Interdependence?'. In: *International Studies of Management & Organization*, 30 (2), pp.114-138.
Eurostat (2005): Eurostat European Statistics – Structural indicators.

Fainstein, Susan S. & Fainstein, Norman I. (1986) 'Regime Strategies Communal Resistance, and Economic Forces'. In: Fainstein S. et al. (ed.) (1986) *Restructuring the City: The political economy of Urban Redevelopment*, pp.245-282.
Faludi, Andreas (1973) *Planningtheory*. Oxford: Pergamon Press.
Faludi, Andreas (1986) *Critical Rationalism and Planningtheory*. London: Pion.
Faludi, Andreas & Valk, Arnold van der (1994) *Rule and Order: Dutch Planning Doctrine in the Twentieth Century*. Dordrecht: Kluwer Academic Publications.
Feyerabend, Paul (1975) *Against Method: Outline of an anarchistic theory of knowledge*. London: Humanities Press.
Figgis, John N. (1913) *Churches in the Modern State*. London: Longmans Green and Co.
Filarski, Ruud & Mom, Gijs (2007) *Van Transport naar Mobiliteit 1800-2000* (twee delen). Zwolle: Walburg Pers.
Fischer, Claude S. (1992) *America Calling: A social history of the telephone to 1940*. Berkeley/Los Angeles/Oxford: University of California Press.
Flap, Henk et al. (2005) 'Gemeenschap, informele controle en collectieve kwaden'. In: Völker, Beate (2005) *Gemeenschap der burgers: Sociaal kapitaal in buurt, school en verenigingen*. Amsterdam University Press, pp.25-52.
Florida, Richard (2002) *The Rise of the Creative Class: And how it's transforming Work, Leisure, Community and everyday Life*. New York: Basic Books.
Flusser, Vilém (1992) *Bodenlos*. Köln: Bollmann Verlag.
Fogelson, Robert (1993) *The Fragmented Metropolis: Los Angeles 1850-1930*. Berkeley/Los Angeles/London: University of California Press.
Flusty, Steven (2004) *De-Coca-Colonization: Making the Globe from the inside out*. New York/London: Routledge.
Fogelson, Robert M. (1993) *The fragmented metropolis: Los Angeles 1850-1930*. Berkeley/Los Angeles/Londen: University of California Press.
Foucault, Michel (2003) *Society Must Be Defended*. Lectures at the Collège De France, 1975-76. New York: Picador.
Friedman, Thomas L. (2005) *The World is flat: A brief history of the Twenty-first Century*. New York: Farrar,

Straus & Giroux.
Friedmann, John (1986) 'The World City Hypothesis'. In: *Development and Change*, 17: pp.69-93.
Friedmann, John (1987) *Planning in the public domain: From knowledge to Action*. Princeton: Princeton University Press.
Friedmann, John (2005) *China's Urban Transition*. Minneapolis: University of Minnesota Press.
Frieling, D.H. et al. (ed.) (1987) *Nederland Nu als Ontwerp*. Den Haag: SDU.
Foucault, Michel (1968) *L'archeologie du savoir*. Paris: Editions de Minuit.
Foucault, Michel (1975) *Surveiller et punir: Naissance de la Prison*. Paris: Gallimard.
Fukuyama, Francis (1989) 'The End of History'. In: *The National Interest 16*.
Fukuyama, Francis (2008) 'They Can Only Go So Far: The world's bullies are throwing their weight around, but history isn't on their side'. In: *The Washington Post* August 24 2008.

Gaastra, Femme S. (2002) *De geschiedenis van de VOC*. Zutphen: Walburg Pers.
Gans, Herbert (1962) *The Urban Villagers: Group and class in the life of Italian-Americans*. New York/London: The Free Press.
Gans, Herbert (2003) *Democracy and the News*. Oxford/New York: Oxford University Press.
Gellner, Ernest (1983) *Nations and Nationalism*. Ithaca: Cornell University Press.
Gemeente Amsterdam (2008) *Plan Amsterdam: Metropool in ontwikkeling*. Amsterdam: DRO.
Gemeente Rotterdam (2004) *Havenplan 2020: Ruimte voor kwaliteit*. Vastgesteld door de gemeenteraad op 16 september 2004. Rotterdam.
Gemeente Rotterdam (2007) *Stadsvisie Rotterdam: Ruimtelijke Ontwikkelingsstrategie 2030*. Rotterdam: dS+V.
Gemeente Rotterdam (2008) *Stadshavens Rotterdam: Uitvoeringsprogramma 2007-2015*. Rotterdam Stadshavens.
Geuze, Adriaan et al. (2003) 'Crisis, richtingloze planologie'. In: *Stedebouw en Ruimtelijke Ordening 2*.
Ghent Urban Studies Team (1999) *The Urban Condition: Space, Community and the Self in the contemporary metropolis*. Rotterdam: 010 Publishers.
Giddens, Anthony (1984) *The Constitution of Society: Outline of the Theory of Structuration*. Cambridge: Polity Press.
Giddens, Anthony (1995) *Politics, sociology and social theory: Encounters with classical and contemporary social thought*. Stanford: Stanford University Press.
Giddens, Anthony (1998) *The Third Way: The Renewal of Social Democracy*. Cambridge: Polity Press.
Giessen, Peter (2008) 'Deze tijd vraagt om linkse daden'. In: *de Volkskrant* 18-10-2008, Het Betoog 1.
Glick-Schiller, N., L. Basch & Szanton-Blanc, C. (1992) *Towards a transnational perspective on migration: race, class, ethnicity, and nationalism reconsidered*. New York: New York Academy of Sciences.
Goey, Ferry de (1990) *Ruimte voor industrie. Rotterdam en de vestiging van industrie in de haven 1945-1975*. Rotterdam.
Gordon, D. (1988) 'The global economy; New edifice or crumbling foundations?'. In: *New Left Review* 16, pp.24-64.
Graham, Stephen & Marvin, Simon (1996) *Telecommunications and the City: Electronic Spaces, Urban Places*. London/New York: Routledge.
Graham, Stephen & Healey, Patsy (1999) 'Relational concepts of space and place: issues for planning theory and practice'. In: *European Planning Studies*, 7/5 pp.623-646.
Granovetter, Mark (1985) 'Economic Action and social structure: the problem of embeddedness'. In: *American Journal of Sociology* 91, pp.481-510.
Gualini, E. (2001) *Planning and the intelligence of institutions*. Aldershot: Ashgate.

Habermas, Jürgen (1984) *Theorie des kommunikativen Handelns*. Zwei Bände. Frankfurt: Suhrkamp Verlag.
Habermas, Jürgen (2001): *The Postnational Constellation. Political Essays*. Cambridge: MIT Press.
Habermas, Jürgen (2008): 'Die Dialektik der Säkularisierung'. In: *Blätter für deutsche und internationale Politik*, April.
Hackworth, Jason (2007) *The Neoliberal City: governance, ideology and development in American urbanism*. Ithaca and London: Cornell University Press.
Hagendijk, Rob (1996) *Wetenschap, constructivisme en cultuur*. Amsterdam: Luna Negra.
Hägerstrand, Torsten (1970) 'What about people in regional science?'. In: *Papers of the Regional Science Association*, vol.24, pp.7-21.

Hajer, Maarten (2000): *Politiek als Vormgeving*. Oratie. Amsterdam: Universiteit van Amsterdam.

Hajer, Maarten & Sijmons, Dirk & Feddes, Fred (ed.) (2006) *Een plan dat werkt*. Rotterdam: NAi Publishers.

Hakfoort, Jacco & Schaafsma, Maurits (2000) 'Planning AirportCity Schiphol: een heroriëntatie op de toekomst van de luchthaven'. In: Boelens, Luuk (ed.) *Nederland Netwerkenland*, pp.79-97, Rotterdam: NAi Publishers.

Hall, Peter (1997) 'The Future of the Metropolis and its Forms'. In: *Regional Studies* 31, 211-220.

Hall, Peter (1998) *Cities in Civilizaton*. New York: Pantheon Books.

Hall, Peter A. & Soskice, David (ed.) (2002) *Varieties of Capitalism: The institutional Foundations of Comparative Advantage*. Oxford: Oxford University Press.

Hamilton, David K. (2004) 'Developing regional regimes: A comparison of two metropolitan areas'. In: *Journal of Urban Affairs*, Volume 26, number 4, 455-477.

Harms, Lucas (2003) *Mobiel in de tijd: Op weg naar een auto-afhankelijke maatschappij. 1975-2000*. Den Haag: SCP.

Harley, Brian (2001) *The New Nature of Maps: Essays in the History of Cartography*. Baltimore/London: The Johns Hopkins University Press.

Harvey, David (1985) *The Urbanization of Capital: Studies in the History and Theory of Capitalist Urbanization*. Baltimore: John Hopkins University Press.

Harvey, David (1989) *The Condition of Postmodernity: An Enquiry into the Origins of Cultural Change*. Malden, MA: Blackwell.

Harvey, David (2000) *Spaces of Hope*. Berkeley/Los Angeles: University of California Press.

Harvey, David (2001) *Spaces of Capital: Towards a Critical Geography*. New York: Routledge.

Harvey, David (2005) *A Brief History of Neoliberalism*. New York: Oxford University Press.

Hastings, Adrian (1997) *The Construction of Nationhood: Ethnicity, Religion and Nationalism*. Cambridge: Cambridge University Press.

Hauben, Theo & Vermeulen, Marco & Boer, Florian (2007) *Ruimtelijke scenario's voor de Brainport*. Rotterdam: Urban Affairs & VHP.

Havenbedrijf Roterdam NV (2008) *Jaarverslag 2007*. Rotterdam: Havenbedrijf.

Haywood, John (1999) *World Atlas of the past*. Oxford: Andromeda.

Healey, Patsy (1997) *Collaborative Planning: Shaping Places in Fragmented Societies*. Basingstoke/New York: Palgrave Macmillan.

Healey, Patsy (2001) 'Towards a more place focused planning system in Britain'. In: Madanipour, A. & Hul, A. & Healey, P. (2001) *The Governance of Place: Space and planning processes*. Burlington: Ashgate.

Healey, Patsy (2007) *Urban Complexity and Spatial Strategies: Towards a Relational Planning for our Times*. London/New York: Routledge.

Hear, Nicholas van (1998): *New Diasporas: The mass exodus, dispersal and regrouping of migrant communities*. Seattle: University of Washington Press.

Hemel, Zef (2004) *Creatieve steden/Creative Cities*. Den Haag: Forum/Ministerie van VROM.

Hemel, Zef (2007) 'Happyland'. In: *Stedebouw en Ruimtelijke Ordening* 4.

Held, David et al. (1999) *Global Transformations: Politics, Economics and Culture*. Cambridge MA/Oxford: Blackwell.

Hermansson, Johan (1999) *Greater Kopenhagen: The Finger Plan*. Copenhagen: Transland.

Heynen, Hilde et al (ed.) (2001) *Dat is Architectuur: Sleutelteksten uit de twintigste eeuw*. Rotterdam: 010 Publishers.

Hillier, Jean (2007) *Stretching beyond the horizon: A multiplanar Theory of Spatial Planning and Governance*. Aldershot: Ashgate.

Hillier, Jean (2009) 'Poststructural complexity: strategic navigation in an ocean of theory and practice'. In: Cerreta, M. &Concilio, G. & Monno, V. (ed.) *Knowledges and Values in Strategic Spatial Planning*. Amsterdam: Kluwer.

Hirst, Paul (1994) *Associative Democracy: New Forms of Economic and Social Governance*. Cambridge: Polity Press.

Hirst, Paul (2001) 'Democracy and Governance'. In: Pierre, Jon (ed.) (2000) *Debating Governance: Authority, Steering and Democracy*. Oxford/New York: Oxford University Press.

Hirst, Paul & Thompson, Grahame (1996) *Globalization in question: The international economy and the possibilites of governance*. Cambridge: Polity Press.

Hirst, Paul & Bader, Veit (ed.) (2001) *Associative Democracy: The real third way*. London, Frank Cass.

H+N+S (1998) =*Landschap*. Amsterdam: Architectura &

Natura Pers.

Hoekema, André (2001) 'Reflexive Governance and Indigeneous Self-Rule'. In: Hirst, Paul & Bader, Veit (ed.) (2001) *Associative Democracy: The Real Third Way*. Abington: Frank Cass & Co, pp.157-186.

Hoelen, Herman (2001) *Beschouwingen over het poldermodel*. Assen: Van Gorcum.

Home, Robert (1997) *Of planting and planning. The making of British colonial cities*. London: Chapman & Hall.

Hondelink, Bjorn et al. (2006) *TOD&D: Transit Oriented Development in Denver and Dallas*. Utrecht: University of Utrecht

Hoogstraten, Eric van et al (2007) *In de lijn van de Luchthaven: Ruimtelijk-economische ontwikkelingen in de omgeving van de luchthavens in Tokio en Hong Kong*. Utrecht: University of Utrecht.

Hoover, E.M. (1948) *The location of economic activity*. New York: Wiley.

Houben, Francien (2002) *A room with a view*. Oratie TU Delft, afdeling Bouwkunde op 9 oktober 2008, Delft: TUD.

Hubbard, Phil et al (ed.) (2004) *Key Thinkers on Space and Place*. London/Thousand Oaks/New Delhi: Sage.

IJff, J. (1993) 'Omwenteling in het waterschapsbestel 1968-1993'. In: Raadschelders, J.C.N. & Toonen, Th. A.J. (ed.) (1993) *Waterschappen in Nederland: Een bestuurskundige verkenning van de institutionele ontwikkeling*. Hilversum: Verloren, pp.13-30.

Imashiro, Mitsuhide (1997) 'Changes in Japan's Transport Market and JNR Privatization'. In: *Japan Railway & Transport Review*, september 1997, pp.50-53.

Imbroscio, David (1998) Reformulating Urban Regime Theory; in: *Journal of Urban Affairs* 20, 233-248.

Innes, Judith (1995) 'Planning Theory's Emerging Pardigm: Communicative action and interactive practice'. In: *Journal of Planning Education & Research* 14, pp.140-143.

Instituto Brasileiro de Geografia e Estatística (2007) *Contagem da População 2007*.

International Alliance of Inhabitants (2007) *Villa 31-Retiro Buenos Aires Argentina*. On: http://www.habitants.org/article/articleview/1653/1/459.

Jacobs, Jane (1961) *The Death and Life of Great American Cities*. New York: Random House.

Janelle, Don (1968) 'Central place development in a time space framework'. In: *Professional Geographer* 20; pp.5-10.

Janssen, Joks (2006) *Vooruit Denken en Verwijlen: De reconstructie van het plattelandschap in Zuidoost Brabant 1920-2000*. Tilburg: Stichting Zuidelijk Historisch Contact.

Janssen-Jansen, Leonie (2004) *Regio's uitgedaagd: Growth management ter inspiratie voor nieuwe paden van pro-actieve ruimtelijke planning*. Utrecht: University of Utrecht. PhD thesis.

Jong, Arie de (1985) 'Planologie: Een toekomst met minder pretenties'. In: *Stedebouw en Volkshuisvesting* 4.

Jong, Bart de (2009) *Reconsidering Amsterdam Airport Schiphol: Using Actor-Network theory to reappraise spatial planning and governance in the airport region of Amsterdam*. Utrecht: University of Utrecht. PhD. (forthcoming).

Jorgensen, John (2004) 'Evolution of the Finger Structure'. In: Dubois-Taine, Geneviève (ed.) (2004) *European Cities: Insights on Outskirts*. METL/PUCA.

Kasarda, John D. (2000) 'Aerotropolis: Airport-Driven Urban Development'. In Washington DC, *ULI on the Future: Cities in the 21st Century*, Urban Land Institute, pp.12-19.

Katz, James E. & Aakhus, Mark (2002) *Perpetual Contact: Mobile Communication, Private Talk, Public Performance*. Cambridge UK: Cambridge University Press.

Kearney, A.T. & Knight Wendling (1993) *Visie op Nederland als distributieland: Value Added Logistics door logistieke en industriële dienstverlening*.

Keeling, David J. (1996) *Buenos Aires: Global dreams, local crises*. West Sussex: John Wiley & Sons Ltd.

Kempen, B.G.A. & Velzen, N. van (1998) *Werken aan Wonen: 75 jaar Nationale Woningraad*. Almere: Nationale Woningraad.

Kempen, Ronald van & Pinkster, Fenne (2002): *Leefstijlen & Woonmilieuvoorkeuren*. Utrecht: URU.

Kerski, Joseph J. (2003) 'The revenge of geography'. In: *The economist*, March 13 2003.

Kinsbruner, Jay (2005) *The Colonial Spanish-American City: Urban Life in the Age of Atlantic Capitalism*. Austin TX: University of Texas Press.

Klerk, Len de (1998) *Particuliere plannen*. Rotterdam:

NAi Publishers.

Klerk, Len de (2008) *De modernisering van de stad 1820-1914: De opkomst van de planmatige stadsontwikkeling in Nederland.* Rotterdam: NAi Publishers.

Klerk, Len de & Laar, Paul van de & Moscoviter, Herman (2008) *G.J. De Jongh: Havenbouwer en stadsontwikkelaar in Rotterdam.* Bussum: Uitgeverij Thoth.

Klink, Arjen van (1995) *Towards the borderless mainport Rotterdam: An analysis of functional, special and administrative dynamics in port systems.* PhD thesis. Rotterdam: Thela Thesis.

Kloos, W.B. (1939) *Het national plan: proeve ener beschrijving der planologische ontwikkelingsmogelijkheden voor Nederland.* Alphen a.d. Rijn: Samsom.

Kloosterman, Robert (2001) *Ruimte voor reflectie.* Oratie UvA op 7 november 2001, Amsterdam: Vossiuspers UvA.

Kloosterman, W.L. (1993) 'Het waterschapsbeheer in de Bataafse-Franse tijd: 1795-1813'. In: Raadschelders, J.C.N. & Toonen, Th. A.J. (ed.) (1993) *Waterschappen in Nederland: Een bestuurskundige verkenning van de institutionele ontwikkeling.* Hilversum: Verloren, pp.93-106.

Klijn, E.H. (1995) 'De stille revolutie in de Volkshuisvesting'. In: *Bestuurskunde*, jaargang 4, nr.2, pp.53-61.

Koolhaas, Rem & Mau, Bruce (1995) *S,M,L,XL.* Office for Metropolitan Architecture. Rotterdam: 010 Publishers.

Kostof, Spiro (1991) *The City Shaped: Urban Patterns and meanings through history.* London: Thames and Hudson.

Kreukels, Ton (1985) 'Planning als spiegel van de westerse samenleving'. In: *Beleid en Maatschappij* 12.

Kreukels, Ton & Wever, Egbert (ed.) (1998) *North Sea Ports in transition: Changing Tides.* Assen: Van Gorcum.

Kreukels, Ton & Vliet M. van (2001) *Een verruimd perspectief.* Gouda: Habiforum.

Kuenzli, Peter & Lengkeek, Arie (2004) *Urban Jazz: Pleidooi voor de zelfgebouwde stad.* Rotterdam: 010 Publishers.

Kuiper, J.A. (1991) *Visueel en dynamisch: De stedebouw van Granpré Molière en Verhagen 1915-1950.* Delft: Publicatieburo Bouwkunde.

Kuijpers, Chris (2007) 'Een volle agenda voor de ruimtelijke ontwikkeling van Nederland'. In: *Stedebouw en Ruimtelijke Ordening* 5.

Kyle, D. (2001) *Transnational peasants.* Baltimore, MD: Johns Hopkins University Press.

Laar, Paul van de (2004) 'Een Eeuw ondernemend Rotterdam'. In: *Rotterdamse Ondernemers 1850-1950.* Rotterdam: Plantijn Casparie.

Laar, Paul van de & Jaarsveld, Mies (2004) *Historische atlas van Rotterdam.* Nijmegen: SUN.

Laclau, Ernesto & Mouffe, Chantal (1985) *Hegemony & Socialist Strategy: Towards a Radical Democratic Politics.* London/New York: Verso.

Langen, P.W. de & Nijdam, M.H. (2003) *Leader firms in de Nederlandse Maritieme cluster: Theorie en praktijk.* Delft: Delft University Press.

Larosse, Jan et al. (2001) *ICT clusters in Flanders: Co-operation in the New Network Economy.* Brussels: IWT-studies.

Laski, Harold (1925) *A Grammar of Politics.* London: Allen and Unwin.

Latour, Bruno (1993) *We have never been modern.* Cambridge MA: Harvard University Press.

Latour, Bruno (1997) *On actor network theory.* Paper to the actor network and after conference. Keele, Staffordshire: Keele University.

Latour, Bruno (2005) *Reassembling the Social: An Introduction to Actor-Network-Theory.* Oxford: Oxford University Press.

Latour, Bruno et al. (ed.) (2006) *Making Things Public.* Cambridge MA: MIT Press.

Lauria, Mickey et al. (ed.) (1997) *Reconstructing Urban Regime Theory: Regulating urban politics in a global economy.* London: Sage.

Law, John (1986) 'On power and its tactics'. In: *Sociological review* 34, pp.1-34.

Law, John (2004) *After Method: Mess in social science research.* London/New York: Routledge.

Lefebvre, Henri (1991) *The Production of Space.* Oxford: Basil Blackwell. Originally published 1974.

Le Goff, Jacques (1984) *La Civilisation de l'Occident Médiéval.* Paris: Les Éditions Arthaud.

Leydesdorff, Loet & Etzkowitz, Henry (2000) 'The Dynamics of Innovation: From National Systems and Mode 2 to a Triple Helix of University-Industry-Government Relations, Introduction to the special Triple Helix'. In: *Research Policy* 29(2) pp.109-123.

Lin, Jan & Mele, Christopher (2005) *The Urban Sociology Reader.* New York/London: Routledge.

Little Hoover Commission (2000) *Special Districts: Relics of the Past or Resources for the Future?* Sacramento:

State of California.

Logan, John & Molotch, Harvey (1987) *Urban Fortunes – The Political Economy of Place*. Berkeley: University of California Press.

Lottum, Jelle van (2007) *Across the North Sea: The impact of the Dutch Republic on international labour migration, 1550-1850*. Amsterdam: Aksant.

Lucas, Robert E. B. (2004): *International Migration Regimes and Economic Development*, Paper prepared for the Expert Group Meeting on Development Issues, Stockholm, 13 May 2004.

Lucassen, Jan (1987) *Migrant labour in Europe, 1600-1900: The Drift to the North Sea*. London.

Lucassen, Jan (1993) *Dutch Long distance migration: A concise history 1600-1900*. Amsterdam: HSH Research paper 3.

Lucassen, Jan (2002) *Immigranten in Holland, 1600-1800: Een kwantitatieve benadering*. Amsterdam: CGM Working paper 3.

Lynch, Kevin (1975) *Das Bild der Stadt*. Braunschweig: Vieweg.

Lyotard, Jean-Francois (1979): *La Condition Post-moderne: Rapport sur le savoir*. Paris: Editions de Minuit.

Madison, James (1987) *The Federalist Papers*. New York: Penguin.

Maguid, A (2004) 'Immigration and the Labour Market in Metropolitan Buenos Aires'. In: *International Migration*, March 2004, pp.104-120.

Malenstein, A.C. van (1993) 'Theorie, casus en perspectief in onderzoek'. In: Raadschelders, J.C.N. & Toonen, Th. A.J. (eds.) (1993) *Waterschappen in Nederland: Een bestuurskundige verkenning van de institutionele ontwikkeling*. Hilversum: Verloren, pp.171-178.

Mandeville. P. (2001) *Transnational Muslim Politics: Reimagining the Umma*. London: Routledge.

Marcuse, Peter (1987) 'The Grid as City Plan: New York City and Laisser Faire Planning in the Nineteenth Century'. In: *Planning Perspectives* 2, 1987, pp.287-310.

Markusen, Ann (1996) 'Sticky Places in Slippery Space: A Typology of Industrial Districts'. In: *Economic Geography*, pp.293-313.

Martin, Ron (1999) 'The New Geographical Turn, in: Economics: Some Critical Reflections *Cambridge Journal of Economics*, 23, pp.63-91.

Marx, Karl (1858) Das Kapital: Buch I – Der Produktionsprozess des Kapitals. Berlin: Dietz Verlag.

Massey, Doreen (1993) Power-geometry and a progressive sense of place; in: Bird, J. et al (1993) *Mapping the Futures: Local Cultures, Global Changes*; London/New York: Routledge.

Massey, Doreen (1995) *Spatial Division of Labour: Social Structures and the Geography of Production*, 2nd edition. Basingstoke: Mcmillan.

Massey, Doreen et al. (eds.) (1999) *Human Geography today*, Cambridge: Polity Press.

Massey, Doreen (2005) *For Space*. London: Sage Publications.

Massumi, Brian (2002) *A Shock to Thought: Expressions after Deleuze and Guattari*. London: Routledge.

May, John & Thrift, Nigel (2001) *Timespace: Geographies of temporality*. London/New York: Routledge.

Mayntz, R. & Scharpf, F.W. (1995) 'Der Ansatz des akteurzentrierten Institutionalismus'. In Mayntz, R. et al (ed.) (1995) *Gesellschaftliche Selbststeuerung und politische Steuerung*. Frankfurt/New York: Campus.

McGrath, Brian (2008) *Digital modelling for urban design*. New York: John Wiley & Sons.

McKenzie, Evan (1994) *Privatopia: Homeowner Associations and the Rise of Residential Private Government*. New Haven/London: Yale University.

McLuhan, Marshall (1964) *Understanding the media: The extensions of man*. Cambridge, MA: The MIT Press.

Mitchell, William J. (1996) *City of Bits: Space, Place and the Infobahn*. Cambridge, MA/London: The MIT Press.

Meer, F.M. van de & Raadschelders, J.C.N. (1993) 'Waterschapspersoneel en waterschapsorganisatie: 1900-heden'. In: Raadschelders, J.C.N. & Toonen, Th. A.J. (ed.) (1993) *Waterschappen in Nederland: Een bestuurskundige verkenning van de institutionele ontwikkeling*. Hilversum: Verloren, pp.31-46.

Meer, Myrke van der (2008) *Spin-offs van Philips R&D: Een economisch geografische blik vanuit het moederbedrijf*. Utrecht: Universiteit van Utrecht. Masterthesis.

Meier, Ilse et al. (2008) *Expats – Excellent or exit?: Post-modern diaspora in Buenos Aires and São Paulo*. Utrecht: University of Utrecht.

Merton, Robert (1949) *Social Theory and Social Structure*. New York: The Free Press.

Meyer, Han (1996) *De Stad en De Haven: Stedebouw als Culturele Opgave in Londen, Barcelona, New York en*

Rotterdam. Utrecht: Jan van Arkel.

Meyer, Han, Jong, Josselin de & Hoekstra, Maarten Jan (2006) *Het ontwerp van de openbare ruimte: De kern van de stedebouw in het perspectief van de eenentwintigste eeuw. Deel 2*. Amsterdam: Uitgeverij SUN.

Mickwitz, Gunnar (1936) *Die Kartelfunktionen der Zünfte und ihre Bedeutung bei der Entstehung des Zunftwesens*. Helsinki.

Ministerie Economische Zaken (1990) *Economie met open grenzen*. The Hague: Ministry Economic Affairs.

Ministerie Economische Zaken (2004): *Netwerken in cijfers*. The Hague: Ministry Economic Affairs.

Ministerie Economische Zaken (2006) *Pieken in de Delta*. The Hague: Ministry Economic Affairs.

Ministerie van Volkshuisvesting, Ruimtelijke Ordening en Milieubeleid (1986) *Nota Ruimtelijke Perspectieven*. The Hague: Ministry of VROM.

Ministerie van Volkshuisvesting, Ruimtelijke Ordening en Milieubeleid (1988) *Vierde Nota over de Ruimtelijke Ordening: Op weg naar 2015, deel d regeringsbeslissing*. 88-89 20 490. The Hague: Ministry of VROM.

Ministerie van Volkshuisvesting, Ruimtelijke Ordening en Milieubeleid (1991) *Vierde Nota over de Ruimtelijke Ordening Extra: deel 4 regeringsbeslissing*. The Hague: Ministry of VROM.

Ministerie van Volkshuisvesting, Ruimtelijke Ordening en Milieubeleid (1995) *Actualisering Vierde Nota over de Ruimtelijke Ordening Extra: deel 4 regeringsbeslissing*. The Hague: Ministry of VROM.

Ministerie van Volkshuisvesting, Ruimtelijke Ordening en Milieubeleid (200-2001) *Vijfde Nota over de Ruimtelijke Ordening*. The Hague: Ministry of VROM.

Ministerie van Volkshuisvesting, Ruimtelijke Ordening en Milieubeleid (2005) *Nota Ruimte: Ruimte voor Ontwikkeling*. The Hague: Ministry of VROM.

Ministerie van Volkshuisvesting, Ruimtelijke Ordening en Milieubeleid (2007) *Actieplan Krachtwijken*. The Hague: Ministry of VROM.

Ministerie van Volkshuisvesting, Ruimtelijke Ordening en Milieubeleid (2008a): *De kracht van samenwerking*. The Hague: Ministry of VROM.

Ministerie Volkshuisvesting, Ruimtelijke Ordening en Milieubeheer (2008b) *Structuurvisie Randstad 2040: Naar een duurzame en concurrerende Europese Topregio*. The Hague: Ministry of VROM.

Ministerie Verkeer en Waterstaat (1986) *Tweede Structuurschema Verkeer en Vervoer: Deel a Beleidsvoornemen*. The Hague: Ministry of V&W.

Ministerie Verkeer en Waterstaat (1990) *Tweede Structuurschema Verkeer en Vervoer: Deel d Regeringsbeslissing*. The Hague: Ministry of V&W.

Ministerie Verkeer en Waterstaat (2005) *Living in a fast lane*. The Hague: Ministry of V&W.

Ministerie van Verkeer & Waterstaat (2008) *De Nieuwe Waterschapswet*. The Hague: Ministry of V&W.

Mommaas, Hans (2005) *Steering for opportunities: Towards an actor-based approach in sustainable regional development*. Positioning paper for the BSIK programme 'Transitions to sustainable Agriculture'. Transforum Agro & Groen.

Mommaas, Hans & Boelens, Luuk (2005) 'De nieuwe markten benadering in het Heuvelland'. In: Aarts, Noelle & During, Roel & Van der Jagt, Pat (ed.) (2005) *Land te Koop*. Wageningen: Universiteit en Researchcentrum.

Mommaas, Hans (2006) *Duurzaamheid biedt Brabant nieuwe kansen*. Tilburg: TELOS.

Monmonier, Mark (1991) *How to lie with maps*. Chicago: University of Chicago Press.

Mossberger Karin & Stoker, Garry (2001) 'The Evolution of Urban Regime Theory: The challenge of conceptualization'. In: *Urban Affairs Review* 36, pp.810-835.

Morand, Paul (2000) 'Le Retour' quoted in: Lambrichs, Anne: 'De gevleugelde eeuw'. In: *Dynamic City*. Brussel: Foundation pour l'Architecture, p.135.

Mori, H. (1998) 'Land, Conversion at the Urban Fringe'. In: *Urban Studies* 9 1541-1558.

Mouffe, Chantal (2005) *On the Political*. New York: Routledge.

Mundigo, Axel & Crouch, Dora (1977) 'The City Planning Ordiances of the Laws of the Indies revisited'. In: *Town Planning Review*, vol.48 July 1977, pp.247-268.

Murdoch, Jonathan (1997) 'Towards a geography of heterogeneous associations'. In: *Progress in Human Geography* 21, pp.321-337.

Murdoch, Jonathan (2006) *Post-structuralist geography*. London: Sage.

Murray, Charles (1984) *Losing Ground: American Social Policy 1950-1980*. New York: Basic Books.

Nadvi, K & Schmitz, H. 1(994) 'Industrial clusters in less developed countries: Review of experiences and research agenda'. In *Discussion Paper No.339*, Brighton, Institute of Development Studies, University of Sussex.

Needham, Barrie (2005a) *Planning, Laws and Economics: The rules we make for using land*. New York: Routledge.

Needham, Barrie (2005b): *Een andere marktwerking: Een verkenning van de mogelijkheden bij het Nederlandse ruimtelijk beleid*. Ruimtelijk Planbureau, Rotterdam: NAi Publishers.

Norberg-Schultz, Christian (1980) *Genius Loci: Towards a phenomenology of architecture*. London: Academy Editions.

Nycolaas, Jacques (1980) 'Woningbouw in Nederland: Een historische benadering'. In: Casciato, Maristella et al. (ed.) (1980) *Architectuur en Volkshuisvesting: Nederland 1870-1940*. Nijmegen: SUN. pp.6-12.

OECD (2003) *Territorial review*. Paris: OECD-Publications.

OECD (2007) *International Migration Outlook*. Paris: OECD-Publications.

Ohland, Gloria (2004) 'The Dallas Case Study: Mockingbird Station and Addison Circle'. In: Ditmar, Hank & Ohland, Gloria (ed.) (2004) *The New Transit Town: Best Practices in Transit-Oriented Development*. Washington/ Covelo/London: Island Press, pp.156-174.

Ohmae, Kenichi (1995) *The End of the Nation State: The Rise of Regional Economics*. New York: Free Press.

Ormeling, Ferjan & M.J. Kraak (2003). *Cartography: Visualization of Spatial Data*. 2nd Edition. Harlow: Pearson.

Oswald, Franz & Baccini, Peter (2003) *Netzstadt: Designing the Urban*. Basel/Boston/Berlin: Birkhaüser.

Oswalt, Philipp et al. (2004) *Schrumpfende Städte: Band I; Internationale Untersuchung*. Leipzig/Dessau.

Oudheusden, J.L.G. van (1990) *Brabantia Nostra: Een gewestelijke beweging voor fierheid en 'schoner' leven 1935-1951*. Stichting Zuidelijk Historisch Contact Tilburg.

Pact op Zuid (2006) *Intentieovereenkomst van de partners binnen het Pact op Zuid*. Rotterdam.

Pascoe, David (2001) *Airspaces*. London: Reaktion Books.

Pateman, Carole (1985) *The Problem of Political Obligation: A Critique of Liberal Theory*. Berkeley/Los Angeles: University of California Press.

Pellenbarg, Piet & Wever, Egbert (ed.) (2008) *International Business Geography: Case studies of corporate firms*. London/New York: Routledge.

Perl, Anthony (2002) *New Departures: Rethinking Rail Passenger Policy in the Twenty-first Century*. Lexington: The University Press of Kentucky.

Perrenod, Virginia Marion (1984) *Special Districts, Special Purposes: Fringe Governments and Urban Problems in the Houston Area*. Texas A&M University Press.

Perry, Clarence A. (1929) 'The Neighbourhood Unit'. In: *Neighbourhood and Community Planning. New York: Regional Plan of New York and the Environs, volume VII*.

Peters, Ralph (2006) 'Blood Borders: How a better Middle East would look'. In: *Armed Forces Journal*, June 2006.

Pierre, Jon et al. (ed.) (2000) *Debating Governance*. Oxford: Oxford University Press.

Pirenne, Henri (1959) *Geschiedenis van Europa van de invallen van de Germanen tot de zestiende eeuw*. Amsterdam: Aula.

Plate, Antoine (1934) *Mémoires 90*. Private edition.

Provincie Noord-Holland (2007) *Vestigingslocaties Schiphol: een globale verkenning voor de lange termijn*. Haarlem: Provincie Noord-Holland.

Provincie Zuid Holland (2003) *Provinciaal Verkeer en Vervoer Plan (PVVP): Deel A*. Den Haag: Provincie Zuid-Holland.

Pollin, Robert (2003) *Contours of Descent: U.S. Economic Fractures and the Landscape of Global Austerity*. New York: Verso.

Polyani, K. (1944) *The great transformation*, New York: Beacon Press.

Pool, M.S. & DeSanctis, G. (1990) 'Understanding the use of group decision support systems – the theory of adaptive structuration'. In: Fulk, J. and Steinfield, C.W. (ed.) (1990) *Organizations and communication Technology*. Newbury: Sage.

Porter, Michael E. (1990) *The Competitive advantage of nations*. New York: The Free Press.

Porter, Michael E. (1998) 'Clusters and the New Economics of Competition'. In: *Harvard Business Review* (November December 1998): pp.77-90.

Porter, Michael E. (2001) *Innovation and Competitiveness: Findings on the Netherlands*. Innovation lecture given at the Ministry of Economic Affairs. The Hague December 3, 2001.

Pred, A. (1967) *Behaviour and location*. Lund: Lund Studies in Geography.

Prince, Gé (2006) 'De commerciële revolutie en het wereldsysteem'. In: Frijthof/Wessels (ed.) (2006) *Veelvormige dynamiek: Europa in het ancien regime 1450-1800*. Amsterdam: SUN.

Province of South Holland (1986) *PEB-nota: Provinciaal Economische Beleid*. Den Haag.

Province of Limburg (2008) *Toeristische Trendrapportage Limburg 2007-2008*. Maastricht: Kenniscentrum Toerisme & Recreatie.

Purcell, Mark (2008) *Recapturing Democracy: Neoliberalization and the Struggle for Alternative Urban Futures*. New York: Routledge.

Raadschelders, J.C.N. & Toonen, Th. A.J. (1993) 'Theorie, casus en perspectief voor onderzoek'. In: Raadschelders, J.C.N. & Toonen, Th. A.J. (ed.) (1993) *Waterschappen in Nederland: Een bestuurskundige verkenning van de institutionele ontwikkeling*. Hilversum: Verloren, pp.179-192.

Randstadprovincies (1990) *De Randstad maakt zich op: Interprovinciale Verstedelijkingsvisie op de Randstad 1990-2015*. Den Haag/Haarlem/Utrecht/Lelystad.

Rast, Joel (2001) 'Manufacturing industrial decline – the politics of economic change in Chicago 1955-1998'. In: *Journal of Urban Affairs* 23, pp.175-190.

Ratha, D. (2003): 'Workers' Remittances: An Important and Stable Source of External Development Finance'. In: *Global Development Finance*, p.158.

Ravesteyn van, Nico et al (2004) *Unseen Europe: A survey of EU politics and its impact on spatial development in the Netherlands*. Ruimtelijk Planbureau, Rotterdam: NAi Publishers.

Rawls, John (1993) *Political Liberalism*. New York: Columbia University Press.

Regioplan (2005) *Spannend Wonen. Woonwensen van expats in Randstad Holland*. Haarlem/Amsterdam.

Reijndorp, Arnold et al (1998): *Buitenwijk – Stedelijkheid op Afstand*. Rotterdam: NAi Publishers.

Reps, John (1998) *Bird's Eyes Views: Historic Lithographs of North American Cities*. New York: Princeton Architectural Press.

Richardson, Helen (2005) 'What are you willing to give up?'. In: *Logistics Today*. Penton Media, Inc. 22-01-2008.

Richmond, Anthony H. (1988) 'Sociological Theories of International Migration: The Case of Refugees'. In: *Current Sociology* 1988 36: pp.7-25.

Rifkin, Jeremy (2000) *The Age of access: How the shift from ownership to access is transforming capitalism*. London: Penguin Group.

Rijks Planologische Dienst (1986): *RUVEIN; Ruimtelijke Verkenningen hoofdinfrastructuur*. Studierapporten 33, 's-Gravenhage: RPD.

Ritzer, George (2004) *The Globalization of nothing*. Michigan: Thousand Oaks/Pine Forge Press.

Rojek, Chris & Urry, John (Ed. 1997) *Touring Cultures: Transformations of Travel and Theory*. London/ New York: Routledge.

Rolnik, Raquel (2008) 'São Paulo: Eine chronologische Stadgeschichte'. In: *Arch+* 190 (Dezember), pp.12-15.

Rotterdam Stadshavens (2008) *Creating on the edge: Vijf strategieën voor duurzame gebiedsontwikkeling*. Rotterdam: Projectbureau Stadshavens.

Rotterdam Climate Initiative (2008) *Rotterdam Climate Campus: Businessplan*. Rotterdam: RCI.

Ruimtelijk Planbureau (RPB) (2004) *Ontwikkelingsplanologie: Lessen uit de praktijk*. Rotterdam: NAi Publishers.

Ruimtelijk Planbureau (RPB) (2005) *Nieuwbouw in beweging*. Den Haag: SDU.

Sá, Lúcia (2007) *Life in the Megalopolis: Mexico City and São Paulo*. New York: Routledge.

Salet, Willem et al (ed.) (2003) *Metropolitan Governance and Spatial Planning: Comparative Case Studies of European City Regions*. London/New York: Spon.

Salet, Willem (1994) *Om recht en staat: Een sociologische verkenning van sociale, politieke en rechtsbetrekkingen*. Den Haag: WRR.

Salet, Willem & Molenaar, Joost (2003) *Oefeningen in de regio Amsterdam*. Amsterdam: AME.

Salet, Willem & Majoor, Stan (ed.) (2005) *Amsterdam Zuidas: European Space*. Rotterdam: 010 Publishers.

Salet, Willem & Thornley, Andy & Kreukels, Ton (2003) *Metropolitan Governance and Spatial Planning: Comparative Case Studies of European City Regions*. London/New York: Spon Press.

Sally, Razeen (1994) 'Multinational enterprises, political economy and institutional theory: Domestic embeddedness in the context of internationalization'. In: *Review of International Political Economy*, vol.1, issue 1 Spring 1994, pp.161-192.

Samenwerkingsverband Regio Eindhoven (2008) *Ruimtelijk Programma Brainport.* Eindhoven: SRE.

Sanders, Wies & Boelens, Luuk (2003) 'Cartografie als onderzoeksmiddel: het onzichtbare zichtbaar maken', in *S&RO* 5.

Sartori, Giovanni (1991) *Social science concept: Systematic analyses.* Beverly Hills: Sage Publications.

Sassen, Saskia (1991) *The Global City: New York, London, Tokyo.* Princeton: Princeton University Press.

Sassen, Saskia (2006) *Territory-Authority-Rights: From Medieval to Global Assemblages.* Princeton/Oxford: Princeton University Press.

Sato, T. (1990) 'Tokugawa Villages and Agriculture'. In: Nakane, C. & Oishii S. (ed.) (1990) *Tokugawa Japan: Social and Economic Antecedents of Modern Japan.* Tokyo: University of Tokyo Press, pp.37-80.

Sato, Cristiane A. (2007) *Japop: O poder da Cultura Japonesa.* São Paulo: NSP

Saussure, Ferdinand de (1916). *Le Cours de linguistique générale.* Lectures at the University of Geneva. Paris: Galimard.

Schaafsma, Maurits & Amkreuz, Joop & Güller, Mathis (2008) *Airport and City: Airport Corridors, drivers of economic development.* Schiphol: Schiphol Real Estate.

Schama, Simon (1988) *Overvloed en onbehagen: De Nederlandse Cultuur in de Gouden Eeuw.* Amsterdam: Contact.

Scharpf, Fritz W. (1997) *Games Real Actors Play: Actor Centered Institutionalism in Policy Research.* Boulder: Westview Press.

Schiphol Group (2007) *Lange termijn visie 2030: een betrouwbare mainport voor een concurrerende regio.* Schiphol: Schiphol Group.

Schmidt-Eichstaedt, G. (1999) 'Baulandbereitstellung nach dem Niederländischen Modell'. In: *Grundstückmarkt und Grundstückswert* 2.

Schnabel, Paul (ed.) (2004) *Individualisering en sociale integratie.* Den Haag: SCP.

Secchi, Bernardo (1984) *Il racconto urbanistico: La politica della casa e del territorio in Italia.* Torino: Einaudi.

Secchi, Bernardo & Viganò, Paola (2007) *Antwerpen Ontwerpen: Strategisch Ruimtelijk Structuurplan.* Antwerpen: Dienst Stadsontwikkeling.

Sellers, Jeffrey (2002) 'The Nation State and urban regime building'. In: *Urban Affairs Review* 37, pp.611-642.

Sharpe, L.J. (1973) 'American Democracy Reconsidered'. In: *British Journal of Political Science* 3 1/28, pp.129-167.

Schivelbusch, Wolfgang (1986) *The Railway Journey: The Industrialization of Time and Space in the 19th Century.* Berkeley: University of California Press.

Sieverts, Thomas (1999) *Zwischenstadt: Zwischen Ort und Welt, Raum und Zeit, Stadt und Land,* 3., verbesserte und um ein Nachwort ergänzte Auflage. Berlin/Basel/Boston/Berlin: Bertelsmann/Birkhäuser.

Simon, H. (1960) *The new science of management decision.* New York: Harper & Row.

Sit, Victor Fung-Shuen et al. (2006) *Developing a competitive Pearl River Delta in South China under one Country-Two Systems.* Hong Kong: Hong Kong University Press.

Sklair, L. (2000): *The Transnational Capitalist Class,* London: Blackwell Publishers.

Sloterdijk, Peter (2004): *Im Weltinnenraum des Kapitals: Für eine philosophische Theorie der Globalisierung.* Frankfurt am Main: Suhrkamp Verlag.

Smith, Adam (1776) *An Inquiry into the Nature and Causes of the Wealth of Nations,* London: Strahan & Cadell.

Smith, Anthony D. (1986): *The Ethnic Origins of Nations.* Oxford: Blackwell.

Smith, Christian (1991) *The Emergence of Liberation Theology: Radical Religion and Social Movement Theory.* Chicago: University of Chicago Press.

Smith, D.M. (1971) *Industrial location: An economic geographical analysis.* New York: Wiley & Sons.

Smith, Michael Peter (2001) *Transnational Urbanism.* Malden/Oxford/Victoria: Blackwell.

Smutney, G. (1998) 'Legislative support for growth management in the Rocky Mountains'. In: *Journal of the American Associations* 64/3-, pp.311-323.

Snel, Erik & Engbersen, Godfried & Leerkes, Arjen. 'Voorbij Landsgrenzen: Transnationale betrokkenheid als belemmering voor integratie?'. In: *Sociologische Gids,* jaargang 51, 2004-2; pp.75-98.

Soja, Edward W. (1996) *Thirdspace: Journeys to Los Angeles and Other Real-and-Imagined Places.* Malden MA/Oxford: Blackwell.

Sorensen, André (2002) *The Making of Urban Japan: Cities and planning from Edo to the twenty-first century.* London: Routledge.

Spit, Tejo J.M. (1995) 'De ambities van het ruimtelijk

planningstelsel'. In: *Bestuurswetenschappen* 5, pp.314-324.

Squires, Grecory D. (2002) *Urban sprawl: Causes, consequences & policy responses.* Washington DC: Urban Institute Press.

Staring, R. (2001) *Reizen onder regie: het migratieproces van illegale Turken in Nederland.* Amsterdam: Het Spinhuis.

Stark, Oded (1991) 'Migrant Remittances and Development'. In: *International Migration* 30(3-4): pp.267-87.

Steenbergen, Clemens (2008) *Ontwerpen met landschap: De tekening als vorm van onderzoek.* Bussum: Thoth.

Stein, Jay (1993) *Growth management: The planning challenge of the nineties.* London: Age.

Stichting Brainport (2008) *Brainport en route.* Eindhoven: BE.

Stone, Clarence (1989) *Regime politics: Governing Atlanta 1946-1988.* Lawrence: The University press of Kansas.

Stone, Clarence (2005) 'Rethinking the policy-politics connection'. In: Policy Studies, 26, pp.241-260.

Stoker, Garry & Orr, M. (1994) 'Urban regimes and leadership in Detroit'. In: *Urban Affairs Quarterly* 1, pp.48-73.

Storper, Michael & Salais, Robert (1997) *World of production: The Action Framework of the Economy.* Cambridge/ London: Harvard University Press.

Strijland, René (2006) 'Tweede privatiseringsronde corporaties noodzakelijk'. In: *Cobouw,* September 2006.

Sunyoung Yoon & Kyungran Choi (2002) *Comparative Study on Korean and Chinese housing bases on cultural patterns: from the 15th century to the present.* Paper presented at the 6th Asian Design International Conference. October 14-17 2003.

Swyngedouw, Erik et al. (ed.) (2003) *The Globalized City: Economic Restructuring and Social Polarization in European Cities.* Oxford: University Press.

Swyngedouw, Erik (2004) *Glocalisations.* Philadelphia: Temple University Press.

Taverne, Ed (1989) 'Sleutelen aan een draaiende motor: Bernardo Secchi's plan voor Siena. Een vraaggesprek met Bernardo Secchi'. In *Archis* 12, pp.15-27.

Taverne, Ed (2008) *Bij de gratie van het conflict: Wonen, organiseren en besturen in het tijdperk van de stuifzand-samenleving.* Amsterdam: SUN.

Taylor, Peter J., & Knox, Paul L. (ed.) (1995) *World Cities: In a World-System* New York: Cambridge University Press.

Taylor, Peter J. (2004) *World City Network: A Global Urban Analysis.* London/New York: Routledge.

Taylor, M. & Asheim, B. (2001) 'The concept of the firm in economic geography'. In *Economic geography* 77, pp.315-328.

Teisman, Geert (1997) *Sturen via creatieve concurrentie: Een innovatie-planologisch perspectief op ruimtelijke investeringsprojecten.* Nijmegen.

Teisman, Geert (2005) *Publiek Management tussen chaos en orde.* Den Haag: Academic Service.

Thrift, Nigel (1981) 'Owners time and own time: The making of a capitalist time consciousness 1300-1880'. In: Pred, A. (ed.) *Space and Time in Geography:* Essays dedicated to Torsten Hägerstrand. Lund: Lund Studies in Geography Series B., no.48.

Thrift, Nigel (1996) 'New Urban Eras and old Technological Fears; Reconfiguring the Goodwill of Electronic Age'. In: *Urban Studies,* vol.33, no.8.

Thrift, Nigel & Crang, Mike (ed.) (2000) *Thinking Space.* London: Routledge.

Thünen, J.H. von (1826) *Der isolierte Staat in Beziehung auf Landwirtschaft und Nationalökonomie.* Jena: Gustav Fischer Verlag.

Tilly, Charles (2002) *Stories, Identities and Political Change.* Lanham, MD: Rowman & Littlefield Publishers.

Toffler, Alvin (1981) *De derde golf.* Utrecht/Antwerpen: Veen Uitgevers.

UN-Habitat (2004) *State of the World's Cities 2004/2005: Globalization and Urban Culture.* United Nations.

UNDP (1999) *Human development report 1999: Globalization with a human face.* United Nations.

United Nations (2005) *World Migration Stock: The 2005 revision population database.* New York.

Unwin, Raymond (1994) *Town Planning in Practice: An Introduction to the Art of Designing Cities and Suburbs.* New York: Princeton Architectural Press.

Urban Unlimited (2004) *Milieudifferentiatie langs de Stedenbaan.* Rotterdam/Den Haag: Provincie Zuid-Holland.

Urban Unlimited (2005a) *Almanak Stedenbaan.* Rotterdam/Den Haag: Provincie Zuid-Holland.

Urban Unlimited (2005b) *Station Lombardijen: Sporen Op Zuid. Private Alliantie Lombardijen IJsselmonde (PALIJS).* Rotterdam/Den Haag: Provincie Zuid-Holland.

Urban Unlimited (2007a) *Wonen Rond Knooppunten.*

Rotterdam: Stadsregio Rotterdam.

Urban Unlimited (2007b), *Analyse Bospolder-Tussendijken*. Rotterdam: Com.Wonen.

Urry, John (2000) *Sociology beyond Societies: Mobilities for the twenty-first century*. London/New York: Routledge.

Urry, John (2003) *Global Complexity*. Malden MA/Oxford: Blackwell.

Valk, Arnold van der (1990) *Het levenswerk van Th. K. Van Lohuizen 1890-1956: De eenheid van het stedebouwkundig werk*. Delft: Delftse Universitaire Pers.

Ve, G.P. van de (1993) *Man-Made Lowlands: History of watermanagement and land reclamation in the Netherlands*. Utrecht: Matrijs.

Veen, Cie. van (1973) *Rapport van de Commissie Interdepartmentale Taakverdeling en Coördinatie*. Den Haag: SDU.

Verburg, Thijs et al. (2005) *Leef- en mobiliteitsstijlen Stedenbaan: Een onderzoek in opdracht van Urban Unlimited*. Utrecht: University of Utrecht.

Verdejo, Ramon et al (2007) 'Considerations Concerning Measurements Relating to the Urban Design of the Spanish-American City. In: *Journal of Asian Architecture and Building Engineering* May 2007/16, pp.9-16.

Vitruvius, Pollio (transl. Morris Hicky Morgan, 1960) *The Ten Books on Architecture*. Courier Dover Publications.

Vogelaar, Ella (2008): *Voortgang wijkenaanpak. Brief aan de Tweede Kamer*. Den Haag, April.

Völker, Beate (2005): *Gemeenschap der burgers – Sociaal kapitaal in buurt, school en verenigingen*. Amsterdam: Amsterdam University Press.

Vrande, Vareska van de (2007) *Wat en hoe inzake open innovatie*. Rotterdam: RSM Erasmus Universiteit.

Vreeze, Noud de (1993) *Woningbouw, Inspiratie & Ambities: Kwalitatieve grondslagen van de sociale woningbouw in Nederland*. Amsterdam: Nationale Woningraad.

VROM-raad (2004) *Nederlandse steden in internationaal perspectief: profileren en verbinden*. Den Haag: VROM-raad.

Vuchic, Vukan R. (2005) *Urban Transit: Operations, Planning and Economics*. Hoboken: John Wiley & Sons.

Wakita, O. (1999) 'The Distinguishing Characteristics of Osaka's early Modern Urbanism'. In: McClain, J. & Wakita, O. (ed.) (1999) *Osaka: The Merchant's Capital of Early Modern Japan*. New York: Cornell University Press, pp.261-272.

Weber, A. (1909) *Über den Standort der Industrien: Rheine Theorie des Standorts*. Tübingen: Mohr Verlag.

Weber, Eugene (1976) *Peasants Into Frenchmen: The Modernization of Rural France, 1880-1914*. Paris.

Weber, Max (1922/1978), 'The city (non-legitimate domination)'. In: *Economy and Society: An Outline of Interpretive Sociology*. Berkeley: University of California Press, 2, vols., vol.2, ch. XVI: 1212-372.

Weber, Max (1958) *The City*. Translation and edited by Don Martindale and Gertrud Neuwirth. New York, The Free Press.

Weeber, Carel et al. (2007) *Bouwmeesters: Het podium aan een generatie*. Rotterdam: NAi Publishers.

Wellman, Barry (2001) 'Computer Networks as Social Networks'. In: *Science 293* (September 14), 2031-34.

Welters, H.W.H. & Langen, P.W. de (ed.) (2003) *Het onzekere voor het zekere nemen: een visie vanuit de wetenschap op de ontwikkeling van het haven- en industriecomplex Rotterdam op de lange termijn*. Rotterdam: Elsevier.

Wennekes, Wim (1993) *Aartsvaders: De grondleggers van het Nederlandse Bedrijfsleven*. Uitgeverij Contact.

Wetenschappelijke Raad voor het Regeringsbeleid (WRR) (1998) *Ruimtelijke Ontwikkelingspolitiek*. The Hague: SDU.

Wetenschappelijke Raad voor het Regeringsbeleid (WRR) (2007) *Identificatie met Nederland*. Amsterdam: Amsterdam University Press.

Weinrich, Harald (1987) 'System, Diskurs und die Diktatur des Sitzfleisches'. In: *Merkur* 8.

Whatmore, C. (2002) *Hybrid Geographies*. London: Sage.

Wheeler, James O. et al (ed.) (2000) *Cities in the Telecommunication Age: The fracturing of geographies*. New York/London: Routledge.

Whitley, Richard (1999) *Divergent Capitalisms: The Social Structuring and Change of Business Systems*. Oxford: Oxford University Press.

Wiegand, J.C. (1997) 'Highlights of the 1999 Land Use Institute'. In: *Environmental and Urban Issues* 24/3, pp.9-34.

Wijk, Michiel van (2006) *Airports as cityports in the City-region: spatial-economic and institutional positions and institutional learning in Randstad-Schiphol (AMS), Frankfurt Rhein-Main (FRA), Tokyo Haneda (HND) and Narita (NRT)*. Utrecht: NGS.

Wilkinson, Richard (2005) *The Impact of Inequality: How to Make Sick Societies Healthier*. New York: Routledge.

Wigmans, Gerrit (1982) *Het stedelijk plan; Staat, stad en stedelijke planning.* Delft: Delft University Press.

Wirth, J.D. & Jones, R.L. (1978) *Manchester and São Paulo. Problems of rapid urban growth.* Stanford: Stanford University Press.

Wirth, Louis (1938) 'Urbanism as a way of life'. In *American Journal of Sociology* 44, pp.1-24.

Wissink, Bart (2007) *Decentring the Planner: The Institutional Basis of Planning Success in Hong Kong and the Netherlands.* Paper presented at the 9th AESOP Conference, Naples, Italy, July 11-14 2007.

World Bank (2007) *Economic Implications of Remittances and Migration.* Washington.

Yeung, Henry (2002) *Entrepreneurship and the Internationalisation of Asian Firms: An Institutional Perspective, New Horizons.* International Business Series. Cheltenham: Edward Elgar.

Yeung, Henry (2005) 'Rethinking relational economic geography'. In: *Transactions of the Institute of British Geographers,* New Series, vol.30(1) pp.37-51.

Zacher, Mark & Sutton, Brent (1996) *Governing global networks: International regimes for transportation and communications.* Cambridge: University Press.

Zischka, Anton (1951) *Het wereldverkeer door alle eeuwen: Geschiedenis, invloed en techniek van schrijven, seinen, drukken, rijden, varen en vliegen.* Tilburg: Nederlands Boekhuis.

Zonneveld, Wil (1991) *Conceptvorming in de ruimtelijke ordening: Encyclopedie van planconcepten.* Amsterdam: PDI-UVA.

Zorreguieta, Máxima (2007) Toespraak van prinses Maxima op 24 september 2007 bij de presentatie van het WRR rapport *Identificatie met Nederland.* Geciteerd op 6 januari 2008.

Zwan van der, Arie (Cie.) (1985) *Schiphol op weg naar 2000.* Den Haag.

Credits

This book reports on a five-year study conducted by
the faculty of Geosciences at the University of Utrecht,
Department of Human Geography and Urban and
Regional Planning in co-operation with the Dutch
Ministry of Housing, Spatial Planning and the Environment and other Dutch public/private planning institutions.
The publication has been made possible by financial
contributions from that ministry and from the Dutch
consultancy firm Urban Unlimited.

Text editing and translation by George Hall, Groningen
Book design by Piet Gerards Ontwerpers, Amsterdam
(Piet Gerards & Monique Hegeman)
Printed by DeckersSnoeck, Antwerp

© 2009 Luuk Boelens, Urban Unlimited,
010 Publishers, Rotterdam
www.010.nl

ISBN 978 90 6450 706 9

Tokyo

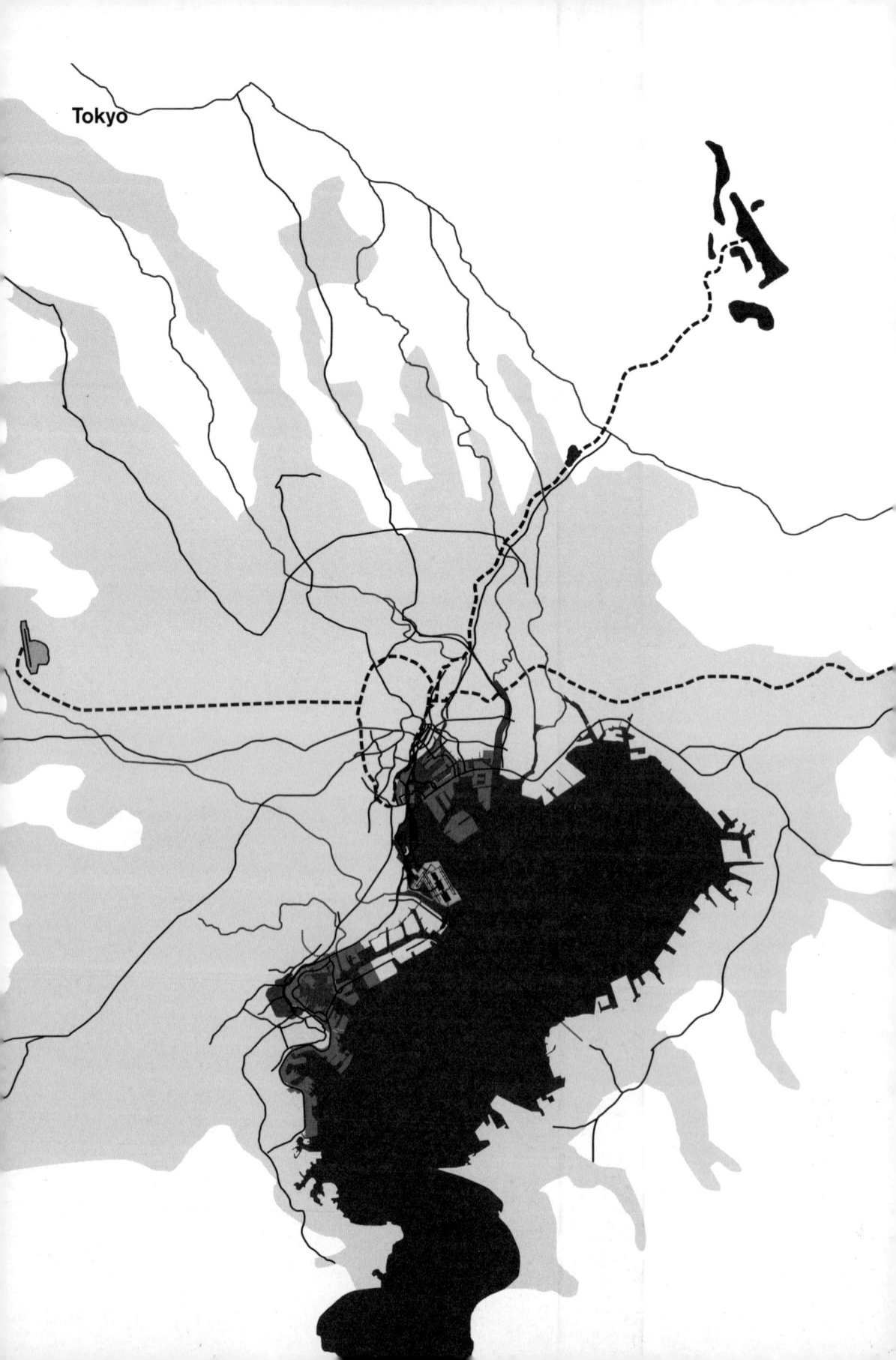